Black Theater,
City Life

Black Theater, City Life

African American Art Institutions and Urban Cultural Ecologies

✦

Macelle Mahala

NORTHWESTERN UNIVERSITY PRESS
EVANSTON, ILLINOIS

Northwestern University Press
www.nupress.northwestern.edu

Printed in the United States of America

10   9   8   7   6   5   4   3   2   1

Library of Congress Cataloging-in-Publication Data

Names: Mahala, Macelle, author.
Title: Black theater, city life : African American art institutions and urban cultural
    ecologies / Macelle Mahala.
Description: Evanston : Northwestern University Press, 2022. | Includes
    bibliographical references and index
Identifiers: LCCN 2022015951 | ISBN 9780810145146 (paperback) | ISBN
    9780810145153 (cloth) | ISBN 9780810145160 (ebook)
Subjects: LCSH: African American theater—History. | American drama—African
    American authors—History and criticism. | American drama—20th century—
    History and criticism. | American drama—21st century—History and criticism. |
    Urban geography—United States.
Classification: LCC PN2270.A35 M34 2022 | DDC 792.08996073—dc23/
    eng/20220404
LC record available at https://lccn.loc.gov/2022015951

To all those who work to sustain and support black theater
and to my aunt, Sandra Gums, for sharing our
family's history, strength, and resilience

CONTENTS

ACKNOWLEDGMENTS

I am forever grateful to the people who shared their experiences and history with me so they could be included in this book. To all the artists, activists, administrators, and educators I interviewed: Chandra Stephens-Albright, Elva Branson, LaTeshia Ellerson, Laurence Glasco, André Kimo Stone Guess, Toni Simmons Henson, Steven Anthony Jones, Thomas W. Jones II, Jamil Jude, Ernest McCarty, Sardia Robinson, Joy Roller, Curtiss Porter, Tony Sias, Mark Clayton Southers, Terrence Spivey, Sala Udin, and Sherri Young, thank you! Nothing could substitute for the lived history and wisdom you all so generously shared.

Thank you to William Daw, curator of the University of Pittsburgh's Curtis Theatre Collection for your research assistance. I would also like to thank Freda Scott Giles, the founding and managing editor of *Continuum: The Journal of African Diaspora Drama, Theatre, and Performance*. Chapter 3 was derived, in part, from work that was presented at the 2015 Black Theatre Network's annual conference and subsequently published as "Neoliberalism, Gentrification, and Black Theatre in San Francisco and St. Paul," in *Continuum: The Journal of African Diaspora Drama, Theatre, and Performance* 3, no. 1 in May 2016, available online at http://continuumjournal.org. Thank you to Faith Wilson Stein, Maia Rigas, Sharon Brinkman, Gianna Francesca Mosser, Trevor Perri, Parneshia Jones, and Patrick Samuel at Northwestern University Press for shepherding this book to publication. Thanks to my colleagues at the University of the Pacific and to my family, especially Andreas Franz, Maceo Johnson, and Robin Mahala, who enabled and supported the work and travel that were necessary to bring this book to fruition.

INTRODUCTION

> The nation's African American theatres are as various as the experiences and regions they represent, though they share some common goals and hurdles.
>
> —Kelundra Smith, "Black Theatres in the U.S.:
> Building, Surviving, Thriving"

When I stepped outside of Fulton County's Southwest Arts Center on a summer evening in 2018, a hypnotic and pulsating sound surrounded me, making it seem as if the air itself were alive. I asked the woman next to me what it was. "You must not be from around here," she laughed. "Those are crickets." The cumulative effect of hundreds of these tiny creatures making the air sing was as awe-inspiring as the excellent theater production I had just witnessed: Colman Domingo's *Dot*, produced by Kenny Leon's True Colors Theatre Company. As I drove back to Atlanta, I thought about the joy of witnessing black theater in the South. I had never before seen theater performed in a space built and maintained by a cadre of wealthy and influential African American county commissioners and patronized almost entirely by an enthusiastic and well-heeled black audience. Experiencing the atmosphere of this production reinforced my belief that all theater is site specific. The location and community in which a play takes place are as important to the meaning making and overall theatergoing experience as the material being produced. Watching *Dot* in the suburbs of Atlanta confirmed my belief that to truly understand the cultural importance of theater, one must examine all of the material conditions that go into production, including and perhaps especially the arts ecology in which a particular work circulates.

Black theater institutions are vital parts of pluralist arts ecologies. Just as symphonies, orchestras, and opera companies primarily celebrate the European patrimony of America, publicly supported black theaters, dance companies, and arts institutions celebrate America's African cultural patrimony. The significance of a well-supported black theater in a multiethnic urban area is an assertion that the city as a whole values and celebrates its African heritage. Black theaters thus *play a role in the performance of the social and cultural identity of the city*. In their essay "Reflections on Publics and Cultures," Gary Bridge and Sophie Watson state that "performative bodies and rational discourse are interleaved as forms of communication in a continuum of human intelligent response to the environment."[1] Bridge and

Watson focus primarily on public spaces such as parks and squares and the corporeal ways that people culturally assert themselves and influence each other in these spaces. Their theory is also quite applicable to the practice of black theater. One way a city recognizes the importance of African American culture is by providing explicit funding and support to the intellectual labor and bodily performances of African American artists. Census projections tell us that in the next half century, "the U.S. will become a plurality nation, where the non-Hispanic white population remains the largest single group, but no group is in the majority."[2] In terms of urban arts funding, planning, and programming, it is no longer controversial to assert that arts programming in American cities should reflect the cultural backgrounds, histories, and identities of a particular city's constituents. While accepted in theory, in practice arts funding continues to exhibit racial and ethnic inequalities in the portions of funding directed to arts organizations focused on nonwhite cultural production.[3] Black theaters are thus an important, yet underfunded, component of many cities' "mosaic" approach to arts administration and support.

For the past decade I have focused my scholarship on articulating the important cultural, artistic, and civic work done by African American theater institutions. Like historically black colleges and universities, the contributions of black theater institutions are underappreciated both in terms of financial support and in terms of widespread recognition of the critical purpose they serve in their field. By chronicling the history of black theater institutions in several American cities, the aim of this book is to call attention to their artistic and civic import and to articulate how they shape as well as reflect the culture and history of the cities in which they reside.

As the organization and makeup of American cities have changed, so has the place of African American theaters in contemporary urban arts ecologies. As institutions that engage a diverse range of artists and patrons at the intersection of racial politics, city planning, and aesthetic production, these organizations both reflect and contribute to notions of civic engagement within a multiethnic public sphere at the same time as they articulate the cultural specificities, sociopolitical realities, and histories of African Americans. Today's black theaters continue the important civic work of previous generations and contribute to the enactment of cultural pluralism within the public sphere. They also reflect and have had to adjust to three decades of neoliberal social and economic forces that have challenged the very existence of many urban black communities. In the essay "Neoliberal Urbanism: Cities and the Rule of Markets," Nik Theodore, Jamie Peck, and Neil Brenner describe the process of American urban neoliberalization as the "destruction of the 'liberal city' in which all inhabitants are entitled to basic civil liberties, social services, and political rights," and the "'rolling forward' of new networked forms of local governance based upon public-private partnerships and the 'new public management.'"[4] For black Americans, these rights and services have never been secure. The shift from previous decades of discriminatory housing restrictions and urban neglect to contemporary development and displacement has altered the way arts organizations, particularly arts organizations of color, operate. Today, many cities operate within a neoliberal framework that sees art as part of "the creative economy" and a tool for urban renewal and gentrification.[5] While many African American arts institutions have participated in these "renewal" efforts, they also continue to be deeply invested in the concept of the liberal city as a place for civic action and social responsibility. Each of the institutions I study in this book does unique work and has responded to the social challenges and histories of the cities of which they are a part in different ways. Each has faced substantial challenges over the past several decades, and each offers a different strategy for survival, social activism, and community engagement within what are often aggressively neoliberal environments.

In this book, I focus on four specific urban arts ecologies. Looking closely at African American theater institutions in these cities is critical to a holistic understanding of American theater history and the cultural history of urban areas as places of civic and artistic engagement. Very few black theater companies have been the primary subjects of academic scholarship, although this is now, thankfully, starting to change.[6] Some of the questions this book seeks to answer include the following: How do the histories of these specific institutions intersect with the cultural histories of the cities in which they operate? How do specific institutions contribute to local and national practices of African American theater, and how do these practices overlap? How are the management and production choices of these companies representative of recent changes in the field?

My effort to chronicle the contributions of specific black theater institutions builds upon the work of my first book, *Penumbra: The Premier Stage for African American Drama*. I see *Black Theater, City Life* as an extension of the scope of my previous study. I have therefore used a similarly methodology, drawing from oral interviews, traditional archival research, and production site visits to engage with and write about the achievements of these important institutions. My case studies include black theaters that offer unique models for artistic production that have not yet been the subject of book-length academic inquiries. I have also chosen theaters in arts ecologies that have not received extensive critical examination. By focusing on Cleveland, Pittsburgh, San Francisco, and Atlanta, my study articulates a vibrant practice of nonprofit black theater in areas away from New York and Chicago (the cities often thought of as the centers of theater's cultural power). These four cities, nonetheless, have been able to impact the practice and theorization of black theater on a national as well as local level.

While I focus primarily on professional and semiprofessional organizations (that is, organizations that pay all of their contributing artists), I agree with Hillary Miller when she writes, "Sharp delineations between 'community theater' and 'professional theater' are regressive as well as constraining to a theatrical public sphere."[7] In all four of the cities I cover, the professional practice of black theater is a direct result of decades of work on the part of unpaid African American theater practitioners that laid the groundwork for professional organizations to develop. Therefore, I have included an analysis of preprofessional Karamu alongside the professional Karamu House theater in Cleveland; I trace how the community theaters Black Horizons and Kuntu Repertory Theatre helped to support and launch Pittsburgh Playwrights Theatre and the professional career of August Wilson; I list Atlanta University Center theater endeavors alongside Jomandi Productions and Kenny Leon's True Colors Theatre in Atlanta; and I note the artistic exchange and crossover in artistic personnel in the community-based Black Repertory Group, the professional Lorraine Hansberry Theatre, and the African-American Shakespeare Company in the San Francisco Bay Area. The successful establishment of professional companies in each of these cities was made possible only by the fertile ground nourished by their unpaid forbearers.

I also want to acknowledge that increasingly black theater is being produced by different kinds of arts organizations. There are multidisciplinary arts organizations dedicated to African American culture such as Pittsburgh's August Wilson African American Cultural Center and San Francisco's African American Art and Culture Complex that produce and present black theater in addition to visual art, dance, and music. There are also local black theater festivals such as the Atlanta Black Theatre Festival, which boasts, "40 plays in 4 days," that contribute robustly to the national practice of black theater.[8] I include these diverse production models in my analyses of black theater in urban areas.

Chapter 1 examines the history and influence of Karamu House in Cleveland, Ohio. The oldest institution in my study, Karamu House was founded during the settlement house movement in 1915. It has attracted many prominent African American artists in its more than one hundred–year history, the best-known being Langston Hughes, who was Karamu's resident playwright for several years during the 1930s. Karamu House has continued the tradition of community-based neighborhood theater common to many African American theater institutions and has also experienced waves of economic challenges that have threatened to close its doors on several occasions. This chapter looks at Karamu House's national importance as well as its place within the theater ecology of Cleveland, a city with a plethora of professional and semiprofessional theatrical institutions and a unique history of racial tension amidst the economic booms and busts typical of many Rust Belt cities. Because of Karamu's longevity and import, this chapter is longer than any of the subsequent ones and is organized by decade instead of by institution. Looking at Karamu's theatrical activity decade by decade reveals that it has indeed shaped the cultural practices of its city, often pushing against normative discriminatory civic practices and enacting a progressively more inclusive and just form of art making.

The second chapter focuses on Pittsburgh and some of the many theater-producing African American arts organizations there that were supported by the internationally renowned playwright August Wilson. I include theater companies that were started in the 1960s and 1970s that Wilson participated in, such as Black Horizons and Kuntu Repertory Theatre. I then look at theaters started in the 1990s and 2000s that were nurtured and encouraged by Wilson, specifically, Pittsburgh Playwrights Theatre Company. Finally, I examine the August Wilson African American Cultural Center, a $40 million facility located in the downtown arts district that was created by city planners and several private foundations to honor Wilson's memory and legacy. The diversity of these institutions and their achievements and struggles serve as a rich and varied example of black theater production tied to one of the most influential American dramatists of the twentieth century.

Chapter 3 looks at black theater production in the San Francisco Bay Area. In this chapter, I analyze the history and mission of the Black Repertory Group, the Lorraine Hansberry Theatre, and the African-American Shakespeare Company in light of the rapid gentrification of San Francisco. The strategies these companies have employed to obtain performance space, tell the stories and histories of African American Bay Area residents, and engage with a rapidly decreasing black population in America's most expensive city demonstrates a resilient and innovative approach to arts management that may be useful to other arts organizations that face similar challenges. In this chapter I also examine the nuances of nontraditional casting in the African-American Shakespeare Company's productions and articulate how Bay Area black theater companies have effectively broadened the conceptualization and practice of black theater in the twenty-first century.

Chapter 4 examines Atlanta, a city with an African American majority that has had forty years of progressive black leadership. I look at Atlanta as one of the most important hubs of black cultural production in America. I link the success of African American artistic production there to the support and patronage of Atlanta's black leadership and political power. I trace the activities of Atlanta's first wave of black political leadership as they are interwoven with the patronage of black theaters like Jomandi Productions and the later establishment of Kenny Leon's True Colors Theatre Company and the Atlanta Black Theatre Festival. I offer Atlanta as a unique example of black theater production that has benefited from critical mass, black power, and recent successive waves of "reverse migration" of African American artists and entrepreneurs.

My concluding chapter offers a brief comparative analysis of the strategies, influences, and practices common to the institutions I cover. I examine the commonalities found among the black theater institutions in these four cities and why certain approaches to art making have worked better in some regions than in others. Finally, I articulate how the founding and continued practice of African American theater institutions are resistive to the normative practices of white supremacy that are deeply entrenched in the production of American theater. Black theater institutions are perhaps most essentially enactments of racial justice. This chapter will be of particular interest to arts administration professionals and students. The book as a whole will appeal to those interested in African American theater history, urban geography, performance studies, ethnic studies, and cultural studies.

A note on language and terminology. What is black? What is black theater? When I use the phrase "black theater" I mean theater created by African Americans in leadership positions. I mean plays written by African Americans and work done at institutions run by African Americans with a specific mission, either explicitly stated or implicitly observed, to explore and communicate the nuances of African American life and cultures. Thus, black theater in my conception is theater that not only depicts black people and black culture but that is shaped at the highest levels of production by those of African heritage. Because my focus is on American work, I use the words "black" and "African American" interchangeably while acknowledging that, of course, blackness goes beyond American contexts. When international black theater practice or practitioners come into my analysis, I identify them as such.

My treatment of each of the institutions and cities in this book is not meant to be exhaustive. For example, in each of the four cities I focus on, there are several other arts organizations that could have been included in my analysis that I hope other scholars will examine in the future. Nor did I try to cover the full production history of any single company. I selected the specific organizations and productions I examine in this book as examples of innovative ways of producing black theater that have reflected and shaped the cultural histories of the cities in which these institutions operate. I hope my efforts reveal the indomitable spirit of black theater practitioners and the strength and diversity of the institutions they have created—institutions that have not only created great art but that have actively contributed to a more equitable practice of artistic production and to a better understanding of the histories and cultures of their cities and their cities' black residents.

Chapter 1

Karamu

A Hundred Years of Joyful Gathering in Cleveland

You cannot separate African American history from Karamu.
—Woodie King Jr.

As the oldest continuously operating African American theater in the country, Karamu is the result of the efforts of several generations of artists and community members. Karamu's history intersects with Progressive Era politics and the settlement house movement, the Works Progress Administration (WPA) and efforts to build a national state-sponsored theater practice, the civil rights movement and integration efforts of the 1940s and 1950s, the Black Power and black arts movements of the 1960s and 1970s, the push to establish and support professional black theater companies and artists in the 1980s and 1990s, and the successful negotiation of the increasingly difficult economic realities of professional theater production in the twenty-first century. As this list attests, a comprehensive history of Karamu would require its own monograph. In this chapter, I highlight a few of Karamu's achievements in each decade of its existence as an example of how black theater both reflects and shapes the evolving cultural politics of urban arts programming. I also articulate the local and national import of this enduring institution.

The Progressive Era

When Russell and Rowena Jelliffe founded what was first known as the Playhouse Settlement and later as Karamu House, there were many other settlement houses in various Cleveland neighborhoods that served the city's poor immigrant communities. Hiram House (1896), Goodrich House (1897), Friendly Inn (1897), Alta House (1900), and the Cleveland Music School Settlement (1912) were some of the settlement houses already in existence when the Jelliffes arrived in Cleveland in 1915.[1] While many of these settlements would eventually serve Cleveland's African American residents, none

Fig. 1. Exterior of Karamu House. Photograph by Les Hunter.

of them had integrated programming in 1915.[2] In her book, *Black Neigh-bors: Race and the Limits of Reform in the American Settlement House Movement 1890–1945*, Elizabeth Lasch-Quinn states, "The settlement house movement grew out of an awareness of the severe conditions facing newcom-ers to the city. While it attempted to address the needs of white immigrants, it largely ignored the parallel situation of African Americans when they began to replace whites in settlement neighborhoods."[3] Lasch-Quinn writes, "The majority of settlement houses either excluded blacks, conducted segregated activities, closed down completely, or followed their former white neighbors out of black neighborhoods."[4] In his 554-page dissertation, "A History of the Karamu Theatre of Karamu House, 1915–1960," Reuben Silver's description of the racial prejudice of the Cleveland settlement communities is commensu-rate with Lasch-Quinn's general characterization of the attitudes and policies of white settlement houses across the nation. "Negroes were not welcome at most of the settlement houses . . . even some in or near mixed neighbor-hoods. Spokesmen for Goodrich House and Hiram House, for example, felt that admitting Negroes to membership would lower the standards of their institutions, and these well-meaning administrators would refer their Negro applicants to Playhouse Settlement, consciously or unconsciously perpetuat-ing segregation."[5] The YMCA of Cleveland was also notorious for excluding blacks. In his *Black Americans in Cleveland: From George Peake to Carl B. Stokes*, Russell Davis writes, "The history of the relationship of the YMCA to black individuals in the Cleveland Area had not been pleasant. . . . During a period of 25 years before the Cedar Branch of the YMCA was opened, there was a determined [often thwarted] effort on the part of young black men to gain the privileges of membership in the YMCA."[6]

Several attempts by prominent African American residents of Cleveland to establish a settlement house that would serve the city's black residents failed, one by the renowned author Charles W. Chesnutt in 1905 and another by the Federation of Colored Women's Clubs in 1912.[7] Edna Jane Hunter, an African American nurse who moved to Cleveland in 1905, succeeded after many years of fundraising and gathering community support in opening what would become known as the Phillis Wheatley Association in 1911 as a residence and organization that would "provide a wholesome atmosphere and social protection" for young black women. After a series of moves and improvements in facilities, the Phillis Wheatley Association was finally able to offer "club and community activities," in 1919, and "thus the idea of providing a home for working girls was extended to offering recreation for residents and to becoming a force for good in the community."[8] Still an operational community center, the Phillis Wheatley Association sponsored theater activities through their dramatic club, the Aldridge Players, in the late 1930s and early 1940s.[9] These dramatic endeavors petered out as music became the association's primary artistic focus. From the 1930s onward, resources were concentrated on the Sutphen School of Music, an organization still in existence today that provides free and low-cost music and voice lessons to area residents.[10]

The exclusionary policies of the major settlement houses and the YMCA along with the significant economic difficulties black residents found in establishing and financially supporting their own social services organizations meant that there were very few neighborhood services available to Cleveland's black residents in the early 1900s. Silver credits Russell and Rowena Jelliffes' embrace of integrated settlement house programming and services to their progressive education at Oberlin College.[11] In this respect, the Jelliffes were a product of an education more committed to the idea of racial equality than was common among the white population of that time period. In other respects, they shared many characteristics with their fellow settlement house founders. They were from middle- and upper-middle-class families, they were white, and they were committed to a variety of other popular Progressive Era causes such as women's suffrage. These commitments manifested themselves in their social work and social vision. For their graduate work at the University of Chicago, the Jelliffes lived and did fieldwork at Chicago Commons and Hull-House, the latter being arguably the most influential American settlement house of the Progressive Era.[12] These activities undoubtedly influenced their decision to found a settlement house in Cleveland and provided a model for its organizational structure and programming.[13]

In her comparative analysis of theater at Hull-House in Chicago, Henry Street Settlement in New York, and Karamu House in Cleveland, Melanie Blood writes:

> A brief glance at the background of settlement and theatre directors demonstrates their middle class, western European bias. A true exchange between the privileged and working classes remained more an ideal than a reality in American settlements. The failure of the settlement ideal of mutual benefit, however, does not diminish the real achievements of settlement workers from the 1880s through the 1930s. Settlement theatres were powerful forces for individuals, communities, and sometimes the nation. . . . American settlements developed models for reform—particularly in arts, education, and civics.[14]

As was the case with other settlements, the founding of Karamu was the result of a negotiation between wealthy progressive benefactors, middle-class social workers, and working-class residents that remains common to the operation of American social services agencies and charities to this day. Because Karamu was a settlement run by white patronage for the benefit of a racially mixed clientele, racial dynamics were in play in addition to the class dynamics of the whites-only settlements.

Karamu began when the Jelliffes were invited by the Men's Club of the wealthy Second Presbyterian Church to operate a "betterment" project at Thirty-Eighth Street and Central Avenue.[15] This was during time when the richest Cleveland families were in the process of moving out of the city. Serving many of these families, the Second Presbyterian Church also chose to relocate away from the increasingly working-class surrounding neighborhood. In the seventy-fifth anniversary souvenir book of Karamu House, Shraine Newman describes the initial motivation for the settlement's founding.

> A prominent member of the [church] group, physician and philanthropist Dr. Peter Dudley Allen . . . challenged the group by saying, "I will give no money to move away from this area unless you plan a constructive force to continue in this community after you are gone." He further stipulated, "When you are ready to bring this force into reality, I suggest you go to Oberlin College and inquire if they have anyone who might be interested and ready to put that force into operation." He then pledged $5,000 as the nucleus to fund a survey of the area and to address any negative findings prompted by the survey.[16]

After making an initial visit to the area in the summer of 1915, the Jelliffes accepted the position offered to them by the church and moved into the cottage in the backyard of the main house at 2241 East Thirty-Eighth Street.[17] The main house became known as the Playhouse Settlement because it was next door to Grant Playground, the municipal park where many of the activities of the settlement took place.[18]

In 1915, the neighborhood surrounding the settlement was occupied by African American, Jewish, Syrian, and Italian residents and was "more white than Negro," with a black population of approximately 25 percent.[19] Because of discriminatory housing practices, black residents were concentrated in this neighborhood.[20] In 1910 African Americans made up only about 1.5 percent of Cleveland's total population, and by 1920, about 4.3 percent of the total population.[21] The rise in the African American population of the city during this time is generally attributed to the cutting off of immigration from Europe during World War I and the consequent migration of African Americans to Cleveland and other industrial northern cities to take advantage of job opportunities that had hitherto been closed to them. Silver recalls the Jelliffes referring to one three-month period in 1918 when "the colored population of Cleveland doubled."[22] African American arrivals to Cleveland were confined to the central city. The neighborhood surrounding the settlement experienced a population explosion and the corresponding problems associated with overcrowding. This area became known as "the Roaring Third."[23] Unlike other settlement houses that either closed or set up segregated activities as black populations replaced immigrant populations, the Jelliffes saw their arrival at the beginning of the rapid transformation of the neighborhood as "providential."[24] They were committed from the beginning to establishing a settlement that served the interests of all of the neighborhood's residents regardless of race, creed, or color.

At first, the Jelliffes offered the usual settlement activities: sports, dancing, citizenship, boxing, cooking, knitting, sewing, childcare, a community library/reading room, game rooms, and the use of a telephone.[25] "By 1919, the settlement had outgrown its tie to the church and formally became the 'Neighborhood Association,' an independent entity with its own trustees and a charter member of the Welfare Federation and the first Community Chest."[26] Rowena Jelliffe began a children's theater program, first on the playground during the summer months and later in the auditoriums of neighborhood schools, using theater as a means of education and betterment by nurturing children's creative talents. Silver includes a 1917 review of the Playhouse Settlement's children's production of *Cinderella* by Ormond A. Forte for the local black newspaper the *Cleveland Advocate* as an example of the impact the playhouse's integrated theater programming made on the public.

> I beheld black children, brown children, white children—all mixed up in a glorious commonality—all joyous, rollicking, delighted, care-free . . . Soon the play "Cinderella" was announced, and in came the characters. There was a Colored mother, one white and two Colored

daughters—one of the latter being "Cinderella." Prince Charming [played by a girl] was white, his herald—who during the play,
patiently knelt to unlace the "long boots" of Colored "Cinderella"—
was also white. The two stage carpenters—whose big job was to
move a small table on and off the stage, were of different races, too,
thus completing the wonderful color scheme.[27]

The children's theater programming was directed first by Rowena Jelliffe
and later by settlement house personnel such as Genevieve Davis, Murtis
Howard, and Rose Griffiths.[28] Employing what would now be considered
colorblind casting, the children's theater program began Karamu's practice
of integrated theater programming open to all who wished to participate.

Inspired by the children's theater activities, a group of young adults led
by three brothers, Joseph, Ralph, and Lawrence Findley, formed the Dumas
Dramatic Club in 1920.[29] The group was named after Alexandre Dumas *père*
and *fils*, the celebrated French romantic novelists and playwrights known to
have African heritage.[30] The original membership of the adult drama group
was primarily black but was directed, up until the 1970s, by the white leadership of the settlement. The girls' activities staff worker Rose Griffiths was
the director of the Dumas group's first public performance in 1921 and continued on as main director of the group until 1923. Lillian Heydemann, a
former professional actor, served as the group's head coach from 1923 to
1926, and Rowena Jelliffe directed both the children's and adults' groups
from 1926 to 1946, at which point Reuben Silver was hired as a full-time
drama director.[31] Silver remained director of all theater activities until 1976,
when he was fired as a result of the organization's desire to have African
Americans in the leadership roles of what had long since become a predominantly black organization.[32]

The early repertoire of the Dumas Dramatic Club consisted primarily of "standard little theatre plays,"[33] that is to say, plays written by white
playwrights featuring white characters depicting serious dramatic fair not
represented on Broadway but of burgeoning interest to many of the newly
formed literary-minded theater organizations across the country.[34] The plays
were cast without regard to race. Silver suggests that Rose Griffiths's choice
in production material was largely a result of plays she was familiar with
and had participated in as a student at Ohio Wesleyan University and not so
much a result of any particular educational or social philosophy.[35] Silver contrasts this approach with that of Rowena Jelliffe, who consciously chose to
cultivate theater at the settlement as an educational and horizon-expanding
activity.[36]

In the documentary *The Progressive Era*, historian Eric Rauchway states,
"Progressives like Jane Addams set out to civilize the immigrant workers and
the immigrants came and took away from it what they wanted."[37] The good
but often naïve and sometimes condescending intentions of social workers

from backgrounds quite different from the people they served frequently led to conflict in many of America's settlement houses. This dynamic was present at several key moments in Karamu's history as well. The goals of the settlement's leadership sometimes came into conflict with the goals and aims of the settlement's clientele. In his dissertation, Silver describes one of these conflicts. "The core of the Dumas Dramatic Club was Negro. These were, after all, people who had been friends and who looked for continued social activity as much as for theatre."[38] Apparently there was a disagreement between the founding club members and Griffiths and Rowena Jelliffe. At least one of the Findley brothers was asked to leave the group because of his interest, as Silver put it, in being, "over-eager and self-centered in regards to what Mrs. Jelliffe calls 'the nasty little business of "what part can I do in this play?"' rather than thinking of the production and the attendant experience as a whole."[39] An actor's desire for a sizeable part to show off and develop his or her talent is hardly a character flaw. However, it was seen as such by Griffiths and Jelliffe because of their respective goals in ensemble building, education, and uplift. Undaunted, Joseph Findley Jr. left the Dumas Dramatic Club and founded the Vagabond Players, which, although short-lived, received favorable press in the black newspaper the *Gazette* in 1923 and 1924.[40] This disagreement shows that in some instances, the settlement members had different priorities and goals than the settlement's leaders and that these differing priorities created conflict. This particular instance also documents the tensions involved in many settlement houses where the purpose of the theater activities vacillated between being entirely for recreation and pleasure, to serving educational aims, to exploring sociopolitical concerns, to serving as a professional vehicle for the participating artists. In her comparative analysis of three theater programs in early twentieth-century settlement houses at Karamu, Hull-House, and Henry Street, Melanie N. Blood documents disagreements about the nature and purpose of theater activities at all three institutions, articulating how each institution created its own unique blend of professional and social practice.[41] In general, at Karamu and elsewhere, theater activities started as primarily recreational and moved to existing as professional or semiprofessional artistic entities over the course of several decades.

There is no doubt that by offering social and recreational services to Cleveland's African American residents, by hiring African Americans into staff positions, and by producing integrated theatrical programming, Karamu was in the cultural vanguard of the Progressive Era, pioneering integrated arts programming that was decades ahead of its time. The conflicts that arose based upon the differing backgrounds and expectations of the settlement's management and clientele showed that while the institution was unique in its inclusivity, it was not yet equitable in terms of the power dynamics of the organization, operating as it did on a patron-based charity model where wealthy white donors presumed to know what was in the best interests of the organization's multiracial working-class members.

The Harlem Renaissance

Karamu's early history also intersected with the Harlem Renaissance and the corresponding national interest in producing what were known at the time as folk plays. In their seminal anthology *Black Theatre USA*, James V. Hatch and Ted Shine describe the folk play as "one with a rural setting where the characters possessed little formal schooling, confronted poverty, race, and sexism, and spoke in a dialect peculiar to their region. A general feeling prevailed that the folk plays, by dignifying the people's struggles, extended a kind of egalitarian democracy to the rural people."[42] This early twentieth-century genre of literature was the result of several cultural factors. First, there was an interest in folk plays as part of the expression of nationalist folk movements in Europe, particularly Ireland. Many American theater artists drew inspiration from the 1911–14 American tours of the Abbey Theatre, whose productions were both innovative and controversial.[43] In her book *The Harlem and Irish Renaissances: Language, Identity, and Representation*, Tracy Mishkin examines the parallels between the American discovery of Irish folk theater, much of which was written in dialect and depicted the lives of the poor, and the interest and cultivation of Negro folk plays during the Harlem Renaissance, which were also written in dialect and featured poor rural protagonists. Mishkin points out that it was not just Irish American writers like Eugene O'Neill and Ridgely Torrence who were inspired by John Millington Synge and the Abbey Theatre tours but also James Weldon Johnson, who urged "the colored poet in the United States" to do "something like what Synge did for the Irish . . . [and] find a form that will express the racial spirit by symbols from within rather than symbols from without."[44] A great admirer of James Weldon Johnson's work, Rowena Jelliffe cultivated a lengthy correspondence with the poet and cited him as one of the primary inspirations for Karamu's eventual decision to produce this genre of literature. The Jelliffes would frequently consult with Johnson regarding their theater programming, asking, "Does this [production or course of action] make sense for the future" and "Is this solidly conceived?"[45]

The popularity of what were known at the time as Negro folk plays was also undoubtedly a result of the Great Migration and the subsequent curiosity of audiences in the North regarding the cultural life and experiences of African Americans coming up from the South. As in previous waves of theater history, white writers felt free to capitalize on popular interest in Southern black culture by creating representations of black folk life for the stage, whether or not they had any knowledge or understanding of this culture. Hatch and Shine write about this practice, stating, "The Irish folk theatre impetus entered the Negro theatre through the plays of Ridgely Torrence, a white writer. On the eve of the United States entry into World War I, April 5, 1917, at the Old Garden Theater in New York, Emily Hapgood presented Torrence's *Three Plays for a Negro Theater*."[46] Torrence's three plays, *The*

Rider of Dreams, *Granny Maumee*, and *Simon the Cyrenian*, were incredibly popular. Paul Green, another white writer, won the Pulitzer Prize in 1927 for his play featuring a Southern black protagonist, *In Abraham's Bosom*. Thus began an era lasting from the late teens through the mid-1930s, when white writers gleaned significant popular, literary, and financial rewards from theatrical works depicting poor Southern African Americans while black theater artists, particularly writers and directors, toiled in relative obscurity.[47]

Most folk plays offered sympathetic portrayals of the rural poor. However, the depictions of African Americans in Negro folk plays, particularly when written by whites, were also intertwined with racial stereotypes from the minstrel and vaudeville traditions. When a touring production of Eugene O'Neill's play *The Emperor Jones* came to Cleveland in 1922, several members of the Dumas Dramatic Club attended, despite protests from the black community and newspapers that the play trafficked in damaging stereotypes. Silver describes the reception to *Emperor Jones* by the black community of Cleveland as "praise for Gilpin [the leading actor], damnation for the play."[48] Hazel Mountain Walker, one of the club's most active members, stated, "It was his [Gilpin's] excellence that permitted me to see it objectively."[49] The response by Cleveland's black community to this play was split between distrust of the characterization of black people and black culture by white playwrights such as O'Neill and an appreciation for the showcasing of the professional talent of gifted African American actors such as Charles Gilpin and Rose McClendon.

As documented in many historical accounts, the Dumas players attended the touring production of *The Emperor Jones*, met with Charles Gilpin backstage afterward, and invited him to attend one of their rehearsals. The actor did so and donated fifty dollars (worth approximately seven hundred dollars today) to the group in support of their endeavors, encouraging them to "learn to see the drama in your own lives."[50] This poignant piece of theater history documents the efforts of African American theater practitioners like Gilpin to support the work of black theater ensembles, despite and perhaps especially because of the fact that the most richly compensated black performers of that time felt financially compelled to work with white arbiters of black cultural material. In honor of the actor and his charge, Karamu's adult drama group changed their name from the Dumas Dramatic Club to the Gilpin Players.

By the mid-1920s, a growing frustration regarding the recognition of white artists' success with ostensibly black cultural material led many prominent African American writers and intellectuals to offer their own interpretations of the Negro folk play. Hatch and Shine write, "The folk movement in America, as in Europe, came down from the top. W. E. B. Du Bois (PhD Harvard), Alain Leroy Locke (PhD Harvard) and James Weldon Johnson (Law Degree, Columbia) labeled, interpreted, and produced the literature."[51] Disgusted with literary material depicting blacks with "symbols from without, such as the mere mutilation of English spelling and punctuation,"[52] James Weldon

Johnson published his masterful poetry collection, *God's Trombones*, in 1927. Karamu later adapted this work for the stage under the direction of Terrence Spivey.[53]

Cognizant of the writings of W. E. B. Du Bois, Alain Locke, and James Weldon Johnson, Rowena Jelliffe developed a lengthy correspondence with each of these famous authors on the subject of the Negro folk play.[54] African American members of the Gilpin Players such as Hazel Mountain Walker, Elmer Cheeks, and Olive Hale drew inspiration from Charles Gilpin's performance and also witnessed touring productions of the New York–based African American theater company the Lafayette Players on at least two separate occasions, in February and June 1924.[55] Gilpin's personal challenge to the Dumas group, Jelliffe's cultivation of a correspondence with the leaders of America's black intelligentsia, and the group members' own experience witnessing the power of black performance applied to black subject matter that was dramatic (rather than comedic or musical) all combined and contributed to the group's decision to start to produce literature featuring black characters.

From 1925 onward, the Gilpin Players produced plays featuring black characters by both black and white writers.[56] The shift in subject matter was gradual, moving from producing European and European American little theater plays, to Negro folk plays by white authors, such as Ridgely Torrence's *Granny Maumee* (1925) and *Simon the Cyrenian* (1927) and Paul Green's *In Abraham's Bosom* and *The No Count Boy* (1928), to plays by black authors such as Willis Richardson's *Compromise* (1925), Zora Neale Hurston's *Sermon in the Valley* (1931), and Arna Bontemps and Countee Cullen's *St. Louis Woman* (1933). In the mid-1930s the organization began its incredibly prolific period of collaboration with Langston Hughes, producing his plays *Little Ham*, *When the Jack Hollers*, and *Troubled Island* in 1936; *Joy to My Soul* in 1937; *Front Porch* in 1938; and *Mulatto* in 1939. This evolution entailed an investment in a progressively more daring dramaturgy that expanded representations of African American life on stage.

Active ensemble members in the late 1920s included Elmer Cheeks, Laburda Ellis, George Guinn, Olive Hale, Mayme Jackson, Arthur Spencer, Arthur Talbot, Hazel Mountain Walker, Brownie Woodford, and Fitzhugh Woodford.[57] Active Karamu members during the 1930s included Paul Banks, Sherman Brown, William Cooper, Jesse Firse, Festus Fitzhugh, Edna Forte, August Grist, Mabel Ingram, William Johnson, John McMorries, Harper Paulsen, Irene Reese, Frank Warner, and Frances Williams.[58] Starting in 1927, Karamu received press coverage from the city's leading newspaper, the Cleveland *Plain Dealer*, an indication of the high regard this amateur company was able to cultivate as a serious and important artistic force in the city.[59]

While the quality of Karamu's productions and the talent of the community center's members were widely acknowledged, productions of Negro folk plays and other works that portrayed poverty and vice were not always warmly received. For instance, the Gilpin Players were frequently lambasted in the African American newspaper the *Gazette* for producing racially unflattering works that were seen as damaging to a public image of racial uplift.[60] The players sometimes countered criticism of their choice of dramatic material through public statements and letters to the editor, such as the following by Jesse Firse, published on March 23, 1935, in the *Gazette's* rival newspaper, the *Call & Post*:[61] "The Gilpin Players are primarily a race organization and have striven and will continue to strive to merit the approval and support of their people."[62] Firse felt called to defend the Gilpin Players' sociopolitical orientation in one of the city's black-owned newspapers in response to the harsh critical reception of Karamu's 1935 production of the prounion, prointegration, and antilynching play *Stevedore*, which was written by white playwrights Paul Peters and George Sklar and which the *Gazette* described as "rotten, vile, and blasphemous."[63] Despite the fact that the *Gazette's* editor Harry C. Smith was a leading activist and proponent of antilynching and antisegregation efforts, the inclusion of the word "goddamn" and other profanities in *Stevedore*, the play's criticism of capitalism, and its white authorship all combined to offend him and other African American conservative Christians, who joined together in an unsuccessful effort to censor Karamu's production.[64] This incident shows that the trajectory of the Gilpin Players' production history was not conflict free and that the decision to begin to produce plays by or about African Americans with pointed portrayals of poverty, vice, and outspoken leftist politics were frequently protested from both inside and outside the black community. These conflicts over content and subject matter reveal the political, cultural, and spiritual diversity of Cleveland's black community during this time.

Langston Hughes's Karamu Residency

During the 1930s, Karamu premiered several plays by prominent African American writers and intellectuals. Karamu's largest contribution to African American theater history during this era is undoubtedly the fruitful collaboration between the settlement and Langston Hughes. Langston Hughes moved to Cleveland with his mother in 1915. He attended Cleveland's Central High School from 1916 to 1920. As a teenager, he participated in the youth activities of the settlement, making particular use of the settlement's library and serving as a volunteer youth art teacher.[65] In *The Black Cultural Front: Black Writers and Artists of the Depression Generation*, Brian Dolinar writes, "Karamu can boast that it discovered Hughes years before the Harlem Renaissance."[66] After living in New York and gaining literary fame as one of the brightest lights of the Harlem Renaissance, Hughes returned to Cleveland in 1935 after his mother was diagnosed with breast cancer in order to help care for her.[67] He accepted a position as "resident playwright" from Rowena

Jelliffe and spent considerable time in Cleveland during the next four years, which are often referred to as the "Langston Hughes Period."[68] This period of close association was important to both the writer and the theater and forged an enduring bond between the two. Dolinar writes, "For the rest of his life, he maintained a relationship with Karamu and frequently stopped to see the Jelliffes when he was passing through the Midwest on reading tours."[69] When I toured Karamu House, I was shown the room that Hughes frequently used as his lodgings when passing through Cleveland on personal or professional business. Hughes remained a lifelong supporter of the theater and during the latter part of his life frequently lent his name and provided his literary works to fundraising efforts on the theater's behalf.

Hughes's Karamu residency is significant in that it overlaps with a time in which he was breaking free from the constraints of white patronage and seeking to "become a professional writer, making my living from writing."[70] Given the incredible popularity of his play *Mulatto*, which premiered on Broadway in 1935, ran for an entire year, and toured for two more years, the idea that theater might serve as a source of financial and intellectual independence was certainly plausible. Although the plays that premiered at Karamu during the late 1930s did not turn out to be his most popular or financially successful, they did serve several important historical purposes. First, they allowed Hughes to work out templates for his more successful literary works, such as the immensely popular Simple stories Hughes first wrote as serial pieces for his regular column in the *Chicago Defender* and later anthologized as best-selling novels.[71] Second, the Karamu residency provided Hughes workshop opportunities involving a stable and dedicated cadre of black actors who helped Hughes to develop and explore a theatrical vocabulary unfettered by the commercial constraints of Broadway. Finally, his Karamu experience inspired Hughes to found his own black theater companies (the Harlem Suitcase Theater in New York, the New Negro Theatre in Los Angeles, and the Skyloft Players in Chicago), which provided him the opportunity to produce work under his direct control.[72]

The benefits of this collaboration were equally great for Karamu. The dramatic material supplied by Hughes during this time helped Karamu explore African American plays that were more multidimensional and theatrically innovative than the work they had previously produced. Hughes's association with the theater also corresponded with a time when the artistic material of the theater was becoming more explicitly political, including content that the theater shied away from in previous and subsequent time periods. The organization's association with Hughes, whose national reputation was already largely recognized, lent the theater much-needed support and legitimized its claim of being one of the most influential and impactful black theaters in the country.

Hughes brought to Karamu significant theatrical training and a new aesthetic culled from several prior theater experiences. Hughes had worked at

Hedgerow Theatre in Pennsylvania, which inspired him to write his most celebrated play, *Mulatto*, in 1930.[73] He traveled in the Soviet Union in 1932, where he met with and witnessed the work of Vsevolod Meyerhold and Nikolay Okhlopkov.[74] He had also recently created leftist political theater inspired by his travels in the South, out of which he wrote the plays *Scottsboro, Limited* (published in 1931 in the magazine *New Masses*) and *Angelo Herndon Jones* (which won the *New Theatre* magazine contest in support of the National Committee for the Defense of Political Prisoners in 1936).[75] Hughes drew from these diverse theatrical influences during his Karamu residency, and Karamu provided him with the opportunity to hone his dramaturgy in a nurturing and supportive artistic environment.

Karamu's production of Hughes's dramaturgy began in 1931, when the theater began preparations to produce the folk comedy *Mule Bone*, a collaboration between Hughes and Zora Neale Hurston. Unfortunately, the production was cancelled due to a disagreement between Hughes and Hurston over the details of authorial credit.[76] Hughes had previously invited Karamu to produce both *Mulatto* and *Angelo Herndon Jones*, but Karamu was not yet ready to produce such controversial work and declined both of these scripts. Thus, the first fully produced play by Langston Hughes at Karamu was also the author's first solo comedic endeavor, *Little Ham*. It was the most popular play of Hughes's residency and was staged by the settlement on three separate occasions from 1936 to 1938.[77]

Little Ham focuses on the romantic entanglements of a Harlem shoeshine and numbers runner, "Hamlet Hitchcock Jones."[78] Although the play is set during the 1920s in Harlem, Hughes's biographer Arnold Rampersad wrote that the inspiration for *Little Ham* came from Hughes's bemused observation that many of his former Central High School classmates were doing significantly better economically than he was due to their participation in Cleveland's "numbers racket."[79] A light comedy, the play chronicles Hamlet Jones's quest for financial independence and love, both of which he ultimately finds in Tiny, an ironically named entrepreneurial beauty shop owner.[80] The original production opened on March 24, 1936, and featured a cast of forty-three including Festus Fitzhugh as the title character and Irene Reese as Tiny.[81] Described in the press as "hilarious" and "vivid and tangy," the play served as a comedic balm for its Depression era audience.[82] Writing about the production's enthusiastic reception in Cleveland, Rampersad contrasted the positive response to *Little Ham* with the Gilpin Players' rejection of Hughes's play *Angelo Herndon Jones*, a dramatic vignette inspired by the life of the Atlanta-based African American union organizer Angelo Herndon. "Black audiences wanted to laugh at little Hamlet Jones, not to agonize with *Angelo Herndon Jones*."[83]

In addition to being witty and comedic, *Little Ham* was also structurally innovative. Dolinar asserts that Karamu's production of *Little Ham* "gave Hughes a place where he could further experiment with the performative aspects of African American humor and speech."[84] "The character Little Ham is clearly a prototype of the latter Jesse B. Semple. Both are urban folk creations who espouse a common-sense view of the world, are quick to engage in witty banter, and embody the blues sentiment of 'laughing to keep from crying.' "[85] The play was also innovative in its setting and plot. The plot culminates with the characters participating in a Charleston contest set in a Harlem dance hall. The incorporation of a live jazz band and dancing into the action of the play was unusual for its time and made a favorable impression on audience members and newspaper critics alike.[86] Marjorie Witt Johnson had founded the dance program at Karamu in 1935, and her choreography was incorporated into this and many other plays done by Karamu during the 1930s.[87] Praising the innovative structure of the play, the drama critic for the Cleveland *Plain Dealer*, William McDermott, stated the play was "something probably unique in the history of American theater."[88]

Encouraged by the success of this comedy, Hughes quickly followed *Little Ham* with *When the Jack Hollers*, which was cowritten with Arna Bontemps and premiered two months after the inaugural production of *Little Ham*. This play attempted to merge the folk play and protest drama genres. Set in the South, the play follows a conjure woman named Aunt Billie (played by Hazel Mountain Walker) and her assistance in affairs of the heart. The horrific conditions of sharecropping are juxtaposed with comedic representations of the Klan as ineffectual, which Joseph McLaren described in *Langston Hughes: Folk Dramatist in the Protest Tradition* as "not true to the realities of the day."[89] Rampersad characterized the play as an attempt "to break new ground in using humor as a political weapon in an area, the South, where social reality was apparently too savage to readily admit it. . . . [The play] ends with a happy reconciliation of poor blacks and whites united against the bosses, as well as a loving union of various couples hitherto at odds with one another."[90] Perhaps because of its mixing of genres or the offhand way in which the play depicted the Klan as something to be laughed at rather than feared, the production was markedly less popular than *Little Ham*.[91] *When the Jack Hollers* was never restaged at Karamu, and although there was interest in the play from several divisions of the Federal Theatre Project, none of these queries succeeded in yielding any further productions.[92]

Hughes returned to serious drama for his third production at Karamu. *Troubled Island* opened November 11, 1936. The play was inspired by Hughes's trip to Cuba and Haiti with the visual artist Zell Ingram, whom he met at Karamu in 1931.[93] *Troubled Island* is a historical drama set immediately after the Haitian Revolution that focuses on the life and death of the Haitian general and revolutionary leader Jean-Jacques Dessalines. Members of the Gilpin Players assisted Hughes in the editing and revision of this play just as they did for other original work produced during the 1930s such as Arna Bontemps and Countee Cullen's *St. Louis Woman*.[94] According to Reuben Silver, *Troubled Island* featured a cast of "sixty-five characters, and

Karamu's dance group was spurred into even greater activity and growth by their participation in this historic drama."[95] The lead was played by William Johnson, who had also played the lead in *Stevedore* and whose talent and interest in serious, political theater prompted K. Elmo Lowe and Rowena Jelliffe to hire him as director of Cleveland's interracial unit of the Federal Theatre Project later that same year.[96]

The large casts for *Little Ham* (forty-three) and *Troubled Island* (sixty-five) give a sense of the popularity of the Gilpin Players during the 1930s and the high participation rate of neighborhood residents in the settlement's drama and dance programs. Rampersad's account of this time in Hughes's life acknowledges the historical importance of Karamu House and the distinguished honor Clevelanders felt in having Hughes as the theater's playwright-in-residence. Rampersad claims, "The opening of *Troubled Island* was the glittering highlight of the black Cleveland season. Sponsored by the local chapters of the Alpha Kappa Alpha sorority as the first production of the sixteenth Gilpin season, the premiere brought out of the community a Depression-defying montage of tuxedos, fur coats, and gorgeous evening gowns. . . . The production itself was . . . accounted a general success."[97] Rampersad's comments indicate that the settlement house continued to operate during the 1930s as an important social venue for the city's black residents.

Troubled Island was reworked and adapted many times both before and after its Karamu production. Variously titled *Emperor of Haiti* and *Drums for Haiti*, these adaptations culminated in *Troubled Island: An Opera*, a collaboration with the composer William Grant Still. Its 1949 production was the first time a composition by an African American composer was presented by an American opera company.[98] Karamu's participation in the production and development of this work contributed a major chapter not only to the diversification of American theater but also to American opera, whose staging practices, particularly in regards to blackface performance and the trafficking of racial stereotypes, have lagged significantly behind the antiracist efforts of other branches of the American performing arts.[99]

Hughes often worked on a number of different projects simultaneously, and 1937 yielded several finished dramas. One of these was the comedy *Joy to My Soul*, which premiered at Karamu in April 1937. *Joy to My Soul* adhered to similar comedic conventions as *Little Ham* and was another popular success. The play depicts a naïve Texan who checks into the Grand Harlem Hotel in Cleveland and becomes the target of several different con artists. Roy Stewart played the main character, Buster Whitehead. Irene Reese played the charlatan psychic, Mrs. Klinkscale, and Dorothy Smith played Wilmetta, the cigarette girl Buster falls in love with.[100] Other clients of the hotel include a "Ladies Drill Corps," which executes several drill performances throughout the play, and a satirical representation of a black fraternal society, the "Knights of the Royal Sphinx."[101] In response to some of the mixed newspaper reviews that found the play funny but rather shallow and "crude," Rampersad reported that "Blacks enjoyed the references to Cleveland" and "Hughes reasoned that many whites in the audience simply did not catch the jokes, especially those about life in a black hotel, that set blacks howling."[102] Hughes had written much of *Troubled Island* while in residence at Cleveland's Majestic Hotel, and *Joy to My Soul* can be read as a kind of good-natured roast of that establishment.[103] With a jazz venue, cocktail lounge, and more than two hundred rooms, the Majestic was Cleveland's leading African American hotel throughout the 1930s and 1940s, and many of its features were referenced in the production of *Joy to My Soul*.[104]

That same year, at the urging of Rowena Jelliffe to write something in a more serious vein, Hughes wrote the brief vignette *Soul Gone Home*. The play was never produced but won a literary contest and was published in the July 1937 edition of *One Act Play* magazine.[105] This play is often interpreted as a reflection of the difficult relationship between Hughes and his mother, whom he struggled to financially support.[106] In his biography of Hughes, Rampersad writes, "As moved as he was by her illness, Langston needed to get away from his mother. . . . Instead of leaving her, Hughes vented his anger in a macabre little play, 'Soul Gone Home,' in which a dead son sits up at his wake to confront his mother, evidently a cheap whore, with charges of hypocrisy and negligence."[107] Although the plot that Rampersad describes sounds quite dark, the play is actually very comedic with lines such as, "If I'm lyin', I'm dyin'" and "damn your hide, you ain't even decent dead."[108] Hughes emphasized that the play was "NOT a heavy tragic sentimental play. It is a TRAGI-COMEDY, with the accent on the comic elements in the boy's role, who is haunting his mother as much for fun as for spite."[109] Although the play depicts the brutality of poverty and the negative effect it has on the relationship between a mother and son, it also sympathetically portrays both characters. Hughes represents the mother as someone who is generally good-hearted and did the best she could do under her circumstances as an impoverished single parent. Like his relationship with his own mother, *Soul Gone Home* is more nuanced and loving than it first appears. Although the play ends with the mother cursing her son's mean-spiritedness, she determines to buy him some flowers "if I can pick up a dollar tonight."[110] This ending slyly equates Hughes's own support of his ailing mother through his not yet financially stable writing career with the fictional mother's desperate attempts to support her son through prostitution. The combination of tongue-in-cheek comedy and pathos is what makes the play distinctive.

Soul Gone Home also illustrates Hughes's talent in crafting witty dialogue and offering multidimensional and engaging portrayals of African American working-class characters. For example, after the son berates his mother, he asks her to hand him a comb before the undertaker arrives because "I don't want to go out of here with my hair standing straight up in the front, even if I is dead."[111] This intimate moment between mother and son hits the reader on two levels: there is the surface comedy of the moment, but there is also the simple yet touching depiction of the son's attempt to preserve his dignity, even in death. The combination of a realistic depiction of poverty alongside the humorous ways in which Hughes's characters inhabit and cope with this poverty is a signature component of Hughes's dramaturgy and literary legacy, a powerful style he developed while in residence at Karamu.

By 1938, Karamu had sufficiently recovered from the 1935 controversy surrounding the production of *Stevedore* that the Gilpin Players felt ready to again tackle a play exploring the relationship between black Americans and union organizing. Hughes's play *Front Porch* opened in December 1938. The play focuses on a young, middle-class black woman's choice between two suitors: a warehouse worker/labor organizer named Kenneth, who is currently on strike for better wages, and J. Donald Butler, a graduate student who dreams of returning to the South to open a school and buy a home. Harriet, the young female protagonist, prefers the handsome, passionate, and broke Kenneth, while her mother encourages the intelligent but conventional J. Donald. As is the case in Lorraine Hansberry's seminal play *A Raisin in the Sun*, which was written two decades later, the juxtaposition of two ideologically distinct male suitors in *Front Porch* allows the play to explore various attitudes toward integration, striving, and political activism.

Hughes was overcommitted at the time of writing *Front Porch*. He had already started the Harlem Suitcase Theater, which was taking up a substantial amount of his time, as well as working with the composer James P. Johnson on the opera *De Organizer*, which depicts the struggle to form a union between black and white sharecroppers in the South.[112] Because of these commitments, he was late in providing the final act of the play. Rampersad writes: "There is some question as to whether the last act arrived from Langston on time. Two different versions of the same act exist, along with a note from Hughes to the effect that the actors balked at his original ending, which was very unhappy, and requested something more pleasant. Rowena Jelliffe remembers the situation differently. 'Finally there was nothing for me to do . . . but to write the last act myself.'"[113] In her introduction to *Front Porch* in *The Collected Works of Langston Hughes*, Leslie Catherine Sanders states that Rowena Jelliffe's happy ending "averted problems caused by the similarity of the story to events in the life of the person she had cast in the leading role."[114] In Hughes's ending, Harriet dies from an illegal abortion she has been pushed into having by her mother, who is terrified that Harriet will face the same hardships and poverty from which their family has only recently escaped. "Hunger and rooming houses, and stopped-up sinks and no money, and roaches and bedbugs and worry and children a man can't feed—can kill love! . . . You won't have that child Harriet!"[115] Like *Angelo Herndon Jones*, which was rejected by the Gilpin Players because the cast of characters included prostitutes, *Front Porch* seems to have offended the moral sensibilities of the group.[116]

In Hughes's ending, the strike is broken, Kenneth is fired, and Harriet dies as the result of a backstreet abortion. In Rowena Jelliffe's ending, Harriet changes her mind about having the abortion, the strike is victorious, Kenneth is cleared of criminal charges, and Harriet's family finally accepts him, with the erstwhile implacable and antilabor mother stating, "If the workers are going to run the town, I think I'll call up Mr. Smith and join that Teachers' Union!"[117] Both versions of the third act are included in *The Collected Works of Langston Hughes*, with Hughes's version listed first and Jelliffe's version appended as "an alternative ending which may be used instead of preceding 3rd Act—for those preferring a happy conclusion."[118] Whether for personal, logistic, or aesthetic reasons, Rowena Jelliffe's ending was the version performed at Karamu in 1938. The play as a whole was certainly ahead of its time in terms of the realism with which it depicted middle-class black concerns. Despite the less controversial ending of the produced version, the play received mixed reviews ranging from "adroitly written" and "intelligent" to "tepid," "nondescript," and "hewing to Caucasian standards."[119]

The last Langston Hughes play staged by Karamu during the 1930s was the 1939 production of *Mulatto*. *Mulatto* depicts the conflict between Colonel Tom, a white plantation owner, and Bert, his black son, who kills his father out of anger after his father refuses to acknowledge him. Bert then commits suicide before a pursuing lynch mob can reach him. *Mulatto* was a popular success when it opened on Broadway in 1935. It broke a record for the longest-running nonmusical play written by an African American, a record that held until the production of Hansberry's a *Raisin in the Sun* in 1959.[120] Despite its commercial and popular success, the play was not a critical success. Having reluctantly agreed to allow the Broadway producer Martin Jones to rewrite part of the script for greater commercial appeal, Hughes was unhappy with the addition of what he saw as a gratuitous rape scene involving the main character's sister at the end of the play. Rampersad writes that Hughes felt humiliated by the negative press of opening night, much of which "questioned . . . his basic competence as a playwright."[121] In addition to the artistic differences between himself and Jones, Hughes encountered numerous other problems with the producer, from racial slights and microaggressions to legal disputes over royalty payments, which were repeatedly delayed and only paid after a series of legal battles and arbitration by the Dramatists Guild.[122]

The negative experience Hughes had with Jones and the Broadway production contrasts sharply with the long-standing, collaborative relationship he had with Karamu. In an interview with Reuben Silver in 1961, Hughes articulated the importance of this relationship. "I probably would have started a Karamu somewhere if there wasn't one to do my own plays. . . . I wanted to see how they looked done live, and I wanted to experience learning from them . . . a playwright in the theatre can learn a very great deal through production. In fact, that is practically the only way you do learn."[123] The kind of playwright development that Hughes mentions is only possible with a theater that values and understands the writer's artistic purpose. It is clear that Jones neither valued nor understood Hughes's artistic vision in terms of what Hughes was trying to achieve with *Mulatto*. When Karamu staged the play in 1939, the theater worked with Hughes to produce the "poetic tragedy" that Hughes had originally intended, rather than the "sex melodrama" Jones had parlayed into a commercial success.[124]

Hughes's preference for the community theater is supported by the fact that the playwright had offered *Mulatto* to Karamu in 1930 before it was picked up by Jones and Broadway, but the theater had been "unwilling to accept it . . . perhaps they considered it too controversial."[125] By 1939, however, the theater had produced many political and socially challenging plays such as "*Stevedore, Peace on Earth, Turpentine*, [and] *Darker Brother*" as well as Hughes's own *Front Porch*.[126] These plays were all considered very provocative, as was *Mulatto*, which prompted an anonymous letter to the editor in the African American Cleveland newspaper the *Call & Post*. This letter stated, "All Negroes are not the Langston Hughes type, and we are striving to progress and not go back. . . . Such a show should be shut down or burn[t] down. . . . Please investigate such trash."[127] A fire did, in fact, damage Karamu's theater building beyond usability the following October.[128] The cause of the fire was unknown, and arson was suspected but never proven.[129] Karamu was not able to rebuild until after the completion of a successful capital campaign in 1949, although it did produce touring productions at other venues throughout the 1940s despite many of its participants leaving to serve in the army during World War II.[130] After the fire, perhaps because of it or perhaps owing to a political climate increasingly dominated by what would become known as McCarthyism, the repertoire of Karamu House became decidedly less controversial, focusing, in the main, on the standard works of the emerging American regional theater movement, which were overwhelmingly by white playwrights.

Although the 1939 production of *Mulatto* was the end of Hughes's residency with the theater, he continued to support the activities of the settlement for the rest of his life. Historian Andrew Fearnley called attention to Hughes's fundraising efforts on behalf of the theater during the 1940s, writing, "If he wasn't supplying contact details for the rich, famous, and influential friends he had made in the course of his career, Hughes was sending letters of support encouraging prospective backers, occasionally serving as something of a Greek chorus to their fundraising efforts."[131] In addition to praise and fundraising, Hughes also encouraged the leadership of the settlement to produce more work by black writers and to provide more opportunities like those he had enjoyed and learned from during his residency in the 1930s. In his 1961 interview with Reuben Silver, for example, he offered a gentle admonishment to the director.

I would like to see this theatre be what a regional theatre might be in Texas or Oklahoma—what the folk theatre was—primarily for the Negro playwright. . . . I simply see no reason why Karamu or any other theatre primarily in a Negro neighborhood would do rehashes of Broadway plays which the Playhouse in Cleveland does—which come on tour here anyway. . . . I think it is most interesting that Karamu has done such a variety of productions, but I do feel that for this reason: for the lack of such a theatre anywhere else in America or the world—a theatre that could do superb productions of material primarily American Negro in origin or orientation, ought to do so. . . . I would think that since Karamu is located primarily in a Negro neighborhood, and its whole growth has been from the Negro community upward and outward, that the more responsibility it has towards its original ethnic base.[132]

This kind of constructive criticism by the theater's most famous participant reveals Hughes's effort to nurture black theater through the championing of plays that speak directly to the cultural experiences and histories of the organization's company members and audiences. This advice was heeded, and from the late 1960s onward, Karamu again focused primarily on African American dramatic material.

Hughes's constructive criticism of Karamu was always done carefully and in the context of his overall admiration for the Jelliffes and the organization they created. He expressed this appreciation most clearly in a poem he composed on the occasion of the Jelliffes' retirement in 1963. "And so it is / With those who make / Of life a flower, / A tree, a dream. / Reproducing (on into / Its own and mine/ and your infinity) / Its beauty and its life / In you and me."[133] Karamu was extremely influential and important to Hughes's development as an artist. The plays he wrote during his residency (many of which were unpublished prior to the printing of his complete collected works) were innovative, far ahead of their time, and creatively staged and edited by Karamu's member artists. These amateur artists succeeding in nurturing the talent of one of America's most beloved literary giants.

The Federal Theatre Project

The other important way that Karamu contributed to the development of African American theater in the late 1930s was through its participation in the Federal Theatre Project (FTP), one of the four artistic branches of the WPA, the government relief program created to financially support unemployed Americans during the Great Depression. The FTP operated from 1935 to 1939. FTP units were segregated, with sixteen Negro units, most of which were staffed with white leadership with the aim of getting these units "the federal money that was coming to them."[134] The most famous Negro unit, the New York unit, was co-run in its first year by African American actor Rose McClendon and white stage director John Houseman.[135] The segregation of the FTP units reflected the larger racial parameters of theater production in America during this time, namely, white artists could freely participate in and often dominated black theater endeavors, while black artists were completely barred from participating in white theater endeavors. This unequal racial dynamic applied strongly to the various iterations of the Cleveland units of the FTP.

The Cleveland FTP originally had two producing groups. One was overseen by K. Elmo Lowe, associate of the Cleveland Playhouse, who ran the activities of the "main Repertory Unit" at the Carter Theater in downtown Cleveland.[136] The other FTP group consisted of Karamu House members. Reuben Silver writes that the "Playhouse Settlement became a cooperating arm of the Cleveland Federal Theatre Project" and that Rowena Jelliffe organized "WPA #8118, popularly called, 'The Community Lab Theatre,' " under the direction of William Johnson, one of the leading actors of the Gilpin Players.[137] Unit 8118 was housed at Karamu and supported by the settlement's staff and membership. In her master's thesis, "The Contributions of the Gilpin Players of Karamu Theatre to Cleveland's Interracial Unit of the Federal Theatre Project," Denise Christy writes that "Cleveland's interracial unit was the only one of its kind in the United States," and "the other Federal Theatre units were either entirely white or black."[138] While not exactly true, for most of the Negro units in the FTP included white artists, the Community Lab theater unit was, to my knowledge, the only explicitly identified interracial unit of the FTP. This explicit naming was, no doubt, a result of the ethos of Karamu, where integration was a stated and cherished value of the settlement. As Christy writes, "The philosophy of the Gilpin Players carried over into the W.P.A. theatre."[139]

Reuben Silver gives a brief summary of the plays William Johnson directed in 1936 and for which he and the rest of the participants in unit 8118 were paid through FTP funds: "*The Big Top*, a product of a Karamu writing workshop group; *United We Eat*, a sharecropper drama; *No Left Turn*, a short play on the social life of a Negro; *Fowl Play*, a one-act farce; *Peace on Earth*, the powerful Maltz-Sklar 'agit-prop' play; a revival of [John Charles Brownell's] *Brain Sweat*. . . ; Rudolph Fisher's *The Conjure Man Dies*; and [Andre] Obey's *Noah*."[140] The FTP unit under Johnson's direction was more favorable to the African American participants in the Gilpin Players than the production conditions under the settlement house in two key respects. First, the participants were paid for their work, which was by this time widely acknowledged to be professional in quality. Second, Silver states that from 1920 to 1946, the acting personnel of the Playhouse Settlement were "almost completely Negro."[141] Despite this fact, the drama directors of the group remained white until the 1970s. Therefore, Rowena Jelliffe's suggestion of William Johnson as the director of the Community Lab FTP was a departure from the settlement's precedent of white management of black theatrical labor. Johnson was a talented member of the Gilpin Players and did an admirable job, garnering praise, offering free attendance to the community, and outpacing the volume of production of Cleveland's "main" (white) repertory unit, for whom "things did not go quite so smoothly."[142] With the combined administrative support of the FTP and Karamu, Johnson was able to bring to life a brilliant example of what state-sponsored black theater could look like in America. This method of artistic production was engaged in service to the community and also supported and sustained black artists, both as leaders and participants. Karamu's support for this more equitable form of black theater production should be applauded and noted for its historical import.

Unfortunately, WPA unit 8118 was short-lived due to federal funding cuts and the consequent decision that the two Cleveland units should merge in order to conserve funds.[143] In his history of Cleveland theater, *Showtime in Cleveland*, John Vacha states only, "In the end a single new children's theater was formed largely from the members of discontinued Repertory Unit."[144] In *Beyond Civil Rights*, John Selby's book on the first fifty years of Karamu's history, the author states that "word of the [interracial] unit reached someone in Washington, and in October of 1936 the ax fell."[145] Neither of these accounts captures the racism that the Community Lab unit faced locally and the ugliness that followed. Denise Christy quotes from a lengthy letter by Minnie Gentry, one of the actors of the Community Lab unit who had also appeared in numerous Karamu productions before moving to New York and achieving significant success as an actor working on Broadway, in television, and in film.[146] According to Gentry:

> We were an interracial group, and our performances were well attended. . . . There was another Federal Theatre Project in Cleveland at that time. It was all white. We were notified that the two groups would have to merge as the program would not support two theatre groups in Cleveland. The Carter Theatre, which was located downtown on Euclid Avenue, was leased and we were to report there on our next working day. When we arrived the white group had formed a human chain at the entrance, and were shouting "We will not work with niggers!" Finally a government official arrived, and we entered the theatre. The angry whites on one side of the theatre and our interracial group on the other. A vote was taken and the nays won. Members of our group and I were transferred to the Cleveland Department of Recreation.[147]

Reuben Silver also includes this incident in his dissertation, stating:

> In November of 1936, WPA #8118 was dealt a low blow. Despite its interracial makeup, and Karamu's interracial origins, Cleveland's

Federal Theatre project was ordered to segregate and re-form, with the added affront to the Negro performers that they be relegated to the State's Recreation Project and paid for "recreation" activity, not theatre work. When the nineteen actors protested this arrangement as a slight to their abilities, they were dismissed, and the Community Lab Theatre was abolished.[148]

This controversy does not appear in *Showtime in Cleveland*, nor does the community effort that was made on behalf of unit 8118, nor the reforming of the "bi-racial Federal Theatre Group" unit as WPA 13008 on February 19, 1937.[149] In "Writing the History of Karamu House: Philanthropy, Welfare, and Race in Wartime Cleveland," Andrew Fearnley states,

> Clevelanders generally liked to believe that they lived in one of the nation's most tolerant cities . . . these popular assumptions have remained largely in place even today. . . . Yet beneath the surface, tensions seethed in Cleveland, just as they did in nearby Chicago and Detroit. Discriminatory practices and segregation occurred there just as much as in other northern cities. The difference was that in Cleveland, like in Chicago a few years later, the municipal authorities worked hard to conceal such incidents from public view.[150]

While the achievements of Karamu are well-known, the resistance to those achievements is not common knowledge and has been, in some cases, deliberately left out of the historical record. Fearnley provides an example of this when he writes, "Just as residents of the nearby township of Brecksville, Ohio, had opposed the settlement's summer camp in the early 1930s, the Gilpins faced equal resistance, details of which can only be found tucked away in private records."[151] Minnie Gentry's letter to Denise Christy is one such record. Gentry's letter provides a vivid, firsthand account of local opposition to the integrated branch of Cleveland's FTP. It reveals the fact that the decision to eliminate the integrated branch was not initiated by the national or regional office of the FTP, as stated by Vacha and Selby, but was the result of deliberate, exclusionary racist action on the part of the all-white repertory unit.[152] Although the repertory unit's desire to remain all white was supported by both the regional and national office of the FTP, the onus of this action falls squarely on the local population and its significant racial prejudice. It is important to note that the racist actions of the repertory unit were rewarded; they did not have to integrate, and they were allowed to continue working and being paid, while the black actors whom they excluded were not. Omitting this incident masks the ways in which white supremacist actions have economically disadvantaged artists of color. Including details like these in historical records is vital to contextualizing and explaining the economic difficulties black theater production has faced and continues to face in arts ecologies that often deny the reality of racism while continuing to perpetuate it.

As Christy and Silver document, Karamu and its allies fought their exclusion from the FTP. Leveraging their political and social capital, they were able to reform the integrated branch of the FTP the following year.[153] WPA unit 13008, also known as the Civic Repertory Theatre, was directed by Gerald Davidson, a white playwright whose play *Fresh out of Heaven*, an adaptation of *Uncle Tom's Cabin*, was staged by Karamu in February 1937.[154] William Johnson performed as an actor in unit 13008 along with Lloyd and Minnie Gentry, Ethel Henderson, Mildred Coleman, Jack Stewart, Margaret Williams, William Day, Fred Carlo, and Elmer Brown.[155] Davidson came from a dance background, and the two plays he directed for this unit of the FTP, Edmond Ronstad's children's play *Chantecler* in March 1937 and Irwin Shaw's expressionistic antiwar drama *Bury the Dead* in May and again in July 1937, both incorporated modern dance into the plays' story lines.[156]

An important figure associated with both Karamu and the FTP was Shirley Graham (later known as Shirley Graham Du Bois after she married W. E. B. Du Bois). Graham had two of her plays produced by Karamu in 1939 and 1940. Graham had served as a director of the Negro FTP unit in Chicago and was involved in both of that unit's most famous productions: Theodore Ward's *Big White Fog* and a jazz adaptation of a Gilbert and Sullivan opera, *The Swing Mikado*, the latter being one of the biggest commercial successes of the entire FTP and for which, unfortunately, she received no credit.[157] Trained as a musicologist with an undergraduate and master's degree from Oberlin College, Graham had an enduring friendship with Rowena Jelliffe, who "steered [her three-act opera] *Tom Tom* to the Cleveland Opera" in 1932.[158] *Tom Tom* was an extravagant display of music and pageantry including a cast of over two hundred singers that played to great critical acclaim before an audience of thousands as part of the Cleveland Opera's annual open air summer performance festival.[159] Although not produced by Karamu, the opera featured many Karamu members as performers, including Festus Fitzhugh as one of the lead dancers.[160] Just as Langston Hughes found in Karamu a warm and receptive home to experiment with drama after some initial success in the (mostly white) commercial theater world, so did Shirley Graham. Karamu enthusiastically produced her play *Coal Dust* in April and May 1939 and *I Gotta Home* in February and March 1940.[161] Karamu also produced Graham's play *Track Thirteen* as a radio drama in March 1942. Rowena Jelliffe counted Graham as one of the top black dramatists of the day, comparing her talent to that of Langston Hughes, Zora Neale Hurston, and Owen Dodson.[162] Unlike Hughes, Graham was not able to overcome the many prejudices (both racist and sexist) that hindered her career as a theater artist. Her treatment during the productions of her plays at Yale was particularly egregious.[163] After struggling for over a decade to establish herself in the field of theater, Graham turned to the political activism for which she is better known today. Her three plays for Karamu, a sweeping labor drama, a light comedy, and a mystery, each have a richness and diversity of style and subject matter that make clear how underappreciated Graham's talent was.

Coal Dust was perfect for Karamu in that it was a prolabor play that focused on the efforts of striking coal miners and depicted the potential for solidarity between blacks and whites, a recurring theme that was often dramatically represented by the integrated troupe. It also crossed class lines, depicting "brotherhood" between the working-class black protagonist, Brick, and the white daughter of the mine owner, Leslie Clayton, who turns out to be his half-sister. The play is similar to Langston Hughes's Mulatto in its tragic ending—seeking revenge for his terrible treatment, Brick attempts to kill his father by trapping him in the coal mine. Unlike Mulatto, in Coal Dust the father and son reconcile with one another before their ultimate demise.[164] In his dissertation, Reuben Silver takes particular note of Richard Beatty's set design for Coal Dust as an outstanding accomplishment. The set included twenty-eight scene changes and the realistic representation of a coal mine onstage.[165] Although it received mixed reviews, Rowena Jelliffe thought it was well written and well balanced, stating, "It has a [good] deal of artistry," making its point without being "too obvious."[166]

Fire and War

Shirley Graham's association with Karamu was somewhat disrupted by the 1939 fire that rendered the settlement's theater unusable. After the 1939 fire, Karamu productions were sporadic and out of necessity consisted largely of touring productions along with a few productions at welcoming host venues such as the Brooks Theatre of the Cleveland Playhouse and the theater in Eldred Hall at Case Western University. Many other venues, including the municipal Cain Park Theater, which had been built by WPA workers, refused the Gilpin's request for performance space.[167] When Rowena Jelliffe appealed to the mayor for the right to use this public space, she was denied.[168] Andrew Fearnley writes, "While it was common knowledge that the Gilpins had been offered use of the Brooks Theater and Eldred Hall, few knew of the venues from which they had been turned away."[169] Fearnley suggests that records of these refusals are only found in the private correspondence of individual Karamu members because city leaders deliberately sought to obfuscate their practices of racial discrimination. Karamu members themselves only publicized instances of racial discrimination if they thought it would be helpful in achieving their goals. Otherwise, they preferred to express their frustrations in private, seeing the public projection of acceptance and achievement as more useful to their aims. This strategy probably aided in helping to establish and maintain Karamu as an important and cherished part of the Cleveland arts community, but it also obfuscated the true nature of the race relationships of the city.

One benefit of touring was that the settlement was able to forge connections with other sympathetic artists and organizations, both in and outside of Cleveland. The Karamu dance troupe toured during this time, for example, performing for appreciative audiences at the 1940's World Fair in New York City. The 1940 Karamu production of Shirley Graham's *I Gotta Home* also toured. In addition to playing at Eldred Hall in Cleveland, it was performed at Oberlin College as a benefit for the local Phillis Wheatley Community Center and later toured to Akron, Ohio, as part of the Association for Colored Community Work.[170] *I Gotta Home* focuses on the financial straits of an earnest preacher and his family's efforts to keep his church position and thus their home. It satirizes the greed and hypocrisy of certain members of the congregation and provides a happy if ironic ending when the preacher's sister arrives and is able to win the money needed to meet the church's financial needs by gambling at the horse track. In a letter to W. E. B. Du Bois, Graham describes this play as "a comedy . . . frankly written to lighten people's hearts and make them laugh."[171] An archival photograph of the Eldred Hall production features Karamu veterans Minnie Gentry and Jesse Firse as two of the principals in this production.[172]

Karamu would likely have been able to sustain a robust touring and guest artist production schedule had operations not been disrupted by America's involvement in World War II. The settlement had to cancel the planning for full productions of Shirley Graham's *Track Thirteen*, Langston Hughes's *Sold Away*, and Owen Dodson's *Doomsday Tale* in the 1941–42 season because of the sudden loss of personnel, both men and women, who left Karamu to enter or support the armed services.[173] Andrew Fearnley points to the high demand for employment in industries such as steel production and manufacturing during the war years as having an additional detrimental effect on Karamu activities during this time. Fearnley states that "frequently [Karamu] staff and members had to reduce the hours they could spend at the settlement."[174] The changes brought about by the war, combined with not having a functional performance space of their own due to the 1939 fire, severely curtailed the activities of the settlement, which offered no major productions from 1942 to 1945.[175]

In lieu of producing theater, Karamu's personnel turned their attention to fundraising during the war years. After failed capital campaigns in the late 1920s and the 1930s, the settlement was ultimately successful in achieving its 1939 fundraising goal of $500,000 (a value equivalent to $9.9 million in 2022) by the end of the 1940s.[176] The success of this campaign resulted in the building of the complex that is still inhabited by the organization at Quincy Avenue and East Eighty-Ninth Street today. Karamu achieved this feat despite the sharply rising costs of building materials and related construction charges during the 1940s, which reportedly went from $195,000 in 1941 to $480,000 in 1947.[177] While the official opening of the new site was October 1949, the building was done in several stages, beginning with the 1945 construction of the childcare building, which was also used for visual art and drama purposes.[178] In 1946, Gerald Marans was hired as the first professional director of the drama program to work in this temporary space, which emulated the arena style of staging coming to prominence in the nascent regional theater movement.[179]

It was on account of the fire and capital campaign that the organization as a whole changed its name in 1940 from the Playhouse Settlement of the Neighborhood Association to Karamu House, in honor of the theater that had been damaged by the fire. The individual groups that were part of the settlement also changed their names at this time, from the Gilpin Players to Karamu Theatre, from the Modern Dance Group to the Karamu Dancers, and from Chippewa Valley Camp to Camp Karamu.[180] These name changes were partly a way of processing the losses from the fire, which included original African artwork and African-inspired artwork created by the settlement members, and partly an attempt to draw public attention to the capital campaign. The name "Karamu" had been proffered by Hazel Mountain Walker, who found the word in a Swahili dictionary during the 1920s. Throughout the 1920s and 1930s, the name "Karamu" referred to the performance space at the corner of Thirty-Eighth and Central Avenue, which served as the organization's main theater from 1927 until it burned down in 1939.[181] Karamu's current slogan, "Karamu: A Joyful Gathering Place," includes a rough translation of this word.[182]

Karamu achieved the construction of its current buildings through the efforts of many individuals. Donors for the 1940s campaign included the children of the settlement, youth from nearby Central High School, church groups, sororities, and arts and sports organizations that put on and participated in benefit concerts and other fundraising events. There were also local and federal government grants and major foundation support. The Rockefeller Foundation provided $70,000 contingent upon the settlement raising $260,000.[183] It subsequently provided another $100,000 grant in 1955 to add an additional building to the existing campus.[184] The settlement received a federal grant of $42,000 contingent upon the construction and operation of a daycare facility to help facilitate women's necessary entry into the workforce during World War II.[185] Public figures such as Eleanor Roosevelt and Langston Hughes worked on behalf of the campaign, delivering speeches and written endorsements of Karamu and publicizing the need for new facilities to support it.[186]

Upon the successful completion of the new facility in 1949, which included both an arena and proscenium stage, theatrical activity markedly increased. The construction of the new buildings coincided with the hiring of Benno Frank in 1949 as Karamu's musical director. Frank, who was both German and Jewish, had directed opera at the Hamburg State Theater before fleeing Germany and working in Yiddish theater and opera in Palestine and New York. He served in the United States Army from 1943 to 1945 and was appointed chief of theater and music for the United States military government in Germany during the occupation and reconstruction period from 1945 to 1948.[187] In this capacity, Frank assisted with Bertolt Brecht's return from exile.[188] During Frank's tenure as Karamu's musical director, from 1949 to 1968, the organization annually produced several operas and musicals in addition to nonmusical plays, children's theater, and dance. Frank also held a simultaneous and equivalent position at the Cleveland Playhouse. Because of Frank's expertise in opera and musicals, these styles of theater dominated Karamu's repertoire in the 1950s and 1960s.

Colorblind Casting and Cultural Diplomacy

Most of the operas and musicals produced by Karamu during the 1950s and 1960s were not written by African Americans, nor did many feature black characters or story lines. The decision to hire Benno Frank and to produce classical European and American opera may have been influenced by the success and example of Marian Anderson, who was a regular correspondent with the Jelliffes and served as a cosponsor, along with Eleanor Roosevelt, Langston Hughes, James Weldon Johnson, and Ethel Waters, of a touring exhibition of Karamu visual artists in 1942.[189] The relationship between Anderson and Karamu, combined with the prominence and skill of Frank, facilitated the launching of many Karamu members' professional careers as opera singers during the 1950s and 1960s. Among such members was Zelma Watson George, who performed the title role in Karamu's production of Gian Carlo Menotti's *The Medium*, an opera about an alcoholic con artist and supposed psychic who begins to believe her own chicanery. George performed the opera sixty-seven times at Karamu and was hired for a New York production that ran for 102 performances.[190] In her obituary in the *New York Times*, Wolfgang Saxon writes that George was "the first black woman to take a white role on Broadway."[191] Although Karamu had practiced colorblind casting since its inception, it was during the 1950s that African American artists from the settlement were able to parlay these roles into professional opportunities elsewhere.

John Selby writes that "Karamu's success with *The Medium* so pleased the composer that Mr. Menotti gave Rowena stage rights to *Amahl and the Night Visitors*, which at Karamu as well as on television, makes an annual return in the holiday season."[192] *Amahl* depicts a visit from the biblical magi, who stop by the home of a poor Italian boy on their way to visit the Christ child. The title character, who is handicapped and walks with the aid of a crutch, is miraculously healed at the end of the performance. Despite the geographic implausibility of an Italian home being on the route of the magis' pilgrimage to Bethlehem, *Amahl and the Night Visitors* was a smash hit. It was the first opera ever commissioned for television and premiered live on NBC on

Christmas Eve in 1951. NBC broadcast the work every year from 1951 to 1966.[193] It was the second Menotti opera performed at Karamu with African American actors cast in the lead roles. There is an archival publicity photograph from the 1952 Karamu production of this opera that features a young actor, Robert Redus, costumed as Amahl, smiling down at Raymond Cress, a five-year-old described as "Cleveland's Easter Seal boy."[194] Both boys carry crutches, Redus's clearly a stage prop and Cress's clearly functional. The caption for the photograph reads, "Karamu is donating net proceeds from this week's performance of the Menotti opera to the Society for Crippled Children, sponsors of the Easter Seal sale."[195] This image of a white physically disabled child looking up admiringly at an older black child is striking in that it is a reversal of the common depiction of black youth as the recipients of white charity. The height, age, and ability of the older child frame him as the giver rather than the receiver of philanthropy.

Like *The Medium* and *Amahl and the Night Visitors*, all of the operas and musicals at Karamu during the 1950s and 1960s used colorblind casting with African Americans (who made up the majority of the settlement's membership) regularly playing the leading roles. Some other representative works of the 1950s and 1960s include *Carmen Jones, The Mikado, Lost in the Stars, Carousel, Blood Wedding, Three Penny Opera, The King and I, South Pacific, Cosi Fan Tutti, The Abduction from the Harem, Paint Your Wagon,* and *The Most Happy Fellow*.[196] Karamu also produced Langston Hughes's musical *Simply Heavenly* in 1959 after Karamu member Melvin Stewart was cast in the New York premiere in 1957. Participation in these operas and musicals helped the professional careers of many performers such as Clayton Corbin, Isabelle Cooley, and Victoria Harrison, all of whom had success either on Broadway or in opera.[197] Corbin expressed his appreciation for the training he received at Karamu as follows: "People spend $600 for a training course of a given number of weeks that doesn't give them one-third of what can actor can obtain for a $1.50 yearly membership card at Karamu."[198] Another example of the professional success of Karamu members during this time period occurred when Karamu members Leesa Foster, Sherman Sneed, Howard Roberts, and John McCurry were cast in the 1952 touring production and 1953 Broadway production of *Porgy and Bess*.[199] Emmy Award–winning television actor Robert Guillaume "moved to Cleveland to play Billy Bigelow in the Rodgers and Hammerstein musical *Carousel* at Karamu House."[200] Guillaume achieved early success in New York operas and musicals such *Porgy and Bess, Purlie,* and *Guys and Dolls*, works much like those produced at Karamu, before landing one of the principal roles in the television series *Soap*, which led to the spin-off featuring the character he played, *Benson*.[201] Ron O'Neal, star of the 1972 hit film *Superfly*, spent six years performing at Karamu after witnessing the organization's 1958 production of the musical *Finian's Rainbow*.[202]

Under the direction of Reuben Silver, the nonmusical plays of the 1950s and 1960s included classics such as *Lysistrata, Summer and Smoke, Golden*

Boy, Our Town, Death of a Salesman, and *Twelfth Night*.[203] Most of these works also used colorblind casting. Some, such as *Lysistrata*, were adapted to depict black cultural settings. As they had in the past, Karamu also produced plays that were not written by African Americans but that featured African American characters such as Dorothy Heyward's *Porgy* (with Dubose Heyward), Carson McCullers's *Member of the Wedding*, Lillian Gale's *Sun on the Water*, and the musicals *Set My People Free, Finian's Rainbow*, and *Jamaica*.[204]

Works by black writers during this time period included J. Harold Brown's cantata *The African Chief*, Langston's Hughes's *Street Scene* and *Shakespeare in Harlem*, Louis Peterson's *Take a Giant Step*, William Branch's *A Wreath for Udomo*, Lorraine Hansberry's *A Raisin in the Sun*, and Wole Soyinka's *The Swamp Dwellers* and *The Trials of Brother Jero*.[205] Karamu was the first theater to produce Soyinka's plays in the United States.[206] In addition to the 1964 Cleveland performances of Soyinka's plays, the group traveled to Denver to perform these plays at a conference on African Leadership in Higher Education at the University of Denver, which the playwright and future Nobel laureate attended.[207] This wide variety of plays, operas, and musicals continued into the 1970s, when the repertoire began to reflect more of the aesthetics and aims of the black arts movement.

Also of note during the 1950s and 1960s was Karamu's participation in arts diplomacy during the Cold War. Karamu served as an example of integration to foreign dignitaries and was frequented by representatives of various entities such as the State Department, the Institute of International Education, and UNESCO, all of which sent emissaries to Karamu House during this time period. Reuben Silver writes, "In 1952, three hundred foreigners from fifty countries visited the House; and in the 1957–58 season, that figure jumped to 546."[208] In Karamu House's seventy-fifth anniversary souvenir book, Shraine Newman quotes from Frances Bolton's 1951 address to the House of Representatives regarding Karamu's function as a cultural diplomat.

> Our State Department, recognizing and appreciating Karamu House as one of our greatest examples of a working democracy, has sent foreign students to Karamu from all parts of the world. They will carry the Karamu message to all nations. Thus, our Cleveland Karamu House has become not only a thrilling art center in a great cosmopolitan industrial city, but also the symbol of what life in a free country has in store for all of its people."[209]

Silver similarly articulated three purposes for these kinds of visits. First, to demonstrate "an integrated, democratic society . . . which may serve as an antidote to the distorted impression many foreigners have of our racial policies"; second, to give "a brighter view of American cultural standards than the one given by most of our exported movies"; and third, to show "the successful existence of a cultural institution in no way state-supported or controlled, but rather maintained privately, by a great many individuals who believe in a better community."[210] These aims are decidedly different from the social aims of both the era before, which included the vision and hope of a national theater, and the era that would come after, with its insistence on acknowledging the depth of the social, economic, and racial disparities at the root of the civil rights and Black Power protest movements. The relationship between Karamu and the State Department clearly demonstrates changes in the political landscape and Karamu's changed relationship to both the local and national government superstructure. Karamu was only one of many institutions during this time linked to the State Department and was invited, at least twice, to tour outside of the United States as a cultural ambassador. Individual Karamu members such as Zelma George and Langston Hughes also participated in State Department–sponsored tours abroad during the 1950s.[211] A participant in the federally funded FTP during the 1930s and accused on multiple instances of producing communist propaganda, it is highly ironic that Karamu and its members served as ambassadors for the State Department and as an example of privatized arts funding during the Cold War. This pivot in mission and marketing shows how the institution has survived by adapting and recontextualizing itself and its work in response to changes in the surrounding sociopolitical environment.

The Civil Rights Movement

During the 1960s, the civil rights movement perfectly dovetailed with Karamu's core philosophy of integration. Karamu wholeheartedly embraced the civil rights movement as the political expression of the driving ethos of its organization. An archival photo dated August 27, 1963, from the Cleveland Press titled "Karamu Goes to Washington" depicts Russell Jelliffe with a group of Karamu members preparing to board one of twelve buses the settlement arranged to bring Clevelanders to the March on Washington.[212] In 2018, Karamu president and CEO Tony Sias found Martin Luther King Jr.'s signature in the theater's September 1963 guest book while going through some of the organization's archival materials. King was hosted by Karamu member Zelma George and her husband Clayborne George while in Cleveland for a speaking engagement at the Olivet Baptist Church, which is located across the street from the theater. Prior to his speaking engagement, King received a tour of Karamu from the Georges. The theater now displays a photograph of Martin Luther King Jr.'s visit to Karamu along with his guest book signature in the theater's main lobby.[213] Coretta Scott King, who attended Antioch College as an education major, was also associated with Karamu and had worked as a youth counselor at Camp Karamu during the summer of

1946.[214] Karamu saw its identity and mission as intrinsically aligned with the civil rights movement, and its staff and members felt that the larger society around it was finally starting to reflect the guiding ethos of the organization. In 1966 Rowena Jellife stated, "We saw our function a long time ago and felt confirmed in our conviction that this was the kind of society that all people of this nation should consciously build, that is the unique quality of our country."[215] Proponents of integration in turn celebrated Karamu as a positive illustration of what an integrated arts education model could achieve in the inner city.

A specific example of Karamu's influence on and participation in the civil rights movement can be found in the career of the stage director Gilbert Moses. Moses participated in Karamu activities as a child and as a teenager. In the 1950s he performed under the direction of Ann Flagg, the children's theater director whom he described as "a great transmitter of love and the power of self-potential, self-discipline, and self-control through the process of creating a character, a prop, or a costume."[216] An archival photograph shows a young Gilbert Moses performing on the Karamu stage in 1960.[217] In 1963, after attending Oberlin College, Moses was one of the three cofounders, along with John O'Neal and Doris Derby, of the Free Southern Theater, an educational and cultural effort that worked in tandem with the Student Nonviolent Coordinating Committee and other civil rights efforts to extend integrated educational and cultural opportunities to black Americans in the South.[218] The most active period of the Free Southern Theater was 1963–68, but the company remained in existence until 1980. In a letter from 1963 that serves as a preface to *The Free Southern Theater by the Free Southern Theater*, Moses writes, "The South . . . is not unassailable. . . . I think the basic ugly cause here is the absence of cultural exposure and thought. I'm going to attempt to begin a theater here."[219] The first two plays that the Free Southern Theater produced were Martin Duberman's *In White America* and Samuel Beckett's *Waiting for Godot*, which toured primarily in Mississippi but also in select towns and cities in Alabama, Louisiana, and Georgia. Like Karamu, the Free Southern Theater began as an integrated group of activists but became a predominantly black organization during the latter part of its existence. Clearly inspired by Moses and the work of the Free Southern Theater, Karamu produced *In White America* in May and June 1966, signaling the organization's alignment with the dramatic materials and efforts of other theaters directly associated with the movement.[220]

Karamu, since its founding and continuing on to the present day, has always been an integrated organization run and patronized by individuals of different races. Up until the 1960s, however, the top leadership of the organization was exclusively white. A sea change occurred after the Jelliffes' retirement in 1963, although this change was not immediately evident.[221] The Jelliffes' first successor, James Olcutt Sanders, a progressive white Quaker who served as the executive director of Karamu from 1963 to 1965, was much like the

Jelliffes in philosophy and background. When Sanders left the organization, Karamu program director Edward Lander served as acting executive director until J. Newton Hill was hired in 1966.[222] J. Newton Hill was the first African American executive director of Karamu and served in that position from 1966 to 1969.[223] Hill had been dean of Lincoln University in Pennsylvania, the prestigious historically black college attended by Langston Hughes and Thurgood Marshall. There, Hill directed the Lincoln University Players, a member group of the Negro Intercollegiate Dramatic Association.[224] His leadership at Karamu thus linked the theater activities of historically black colleges to the dramatic efforts of community centers like Karamu. With the hiring of Hill, Karamu was finally able to move away from a model of white patronage of black artists and educators to an organization that put into practice more fully the ethos of equality it had expressed for over fifty years.

In 1967, Hill's stately Cleveland Heights home was bombed while he and his wife were asleep in their bedroom. This crime was one of many racially motivated acts of violence in that neighborhood during the late 1960s and was widely reported in the local and national press.[225] The Hill family was one of many black families subjected to terrorist acts during the 1960s after moving into predominantly white, previously inaccessible neighborhoods, not just in Cleveland but all across America. Although Hill and his wife were unharmed, they eventually relocated to New York, where Hill taught African art and English at New York University and Bronx Community College.[226] The violence directed toward J. Newton Hill shows the formidable resistance to the assertion of equal rights by Cleveland's black residents during the civil rights movement, a violence that victimized Karamu just as it victimized many other black businesses and individuals.[227]

Black Power and the Black Arts Movement

In 1967, Carl Stokes became the first African American mayor of a major urban city. His election signified a change in the political landscape of Cleveland and an increase in the political power of Cleveland's black community. The historian Leonard Moore wrote about the significance of Stokes's election.

> Between 1967 and 1971 Cleveland mayor Carl B. Stokes transformed the energy of the civil rights movement into a local model of black political power. As the first black mayor of a major urban center, Stokes ushered in the next phase of the civil rights movement, political power. By linking the civil rights movement and black political activism, Stokes occupied the key role in what was perhaps one of the greatest accomplishments of the black freedom struggle: the entry of African Americans into the political mainstream.[228]

Like many other black residents of Cleveland who wanted direct representation and a seat at the table of local political and social organizations, at Karamu, it became clear that many of the organization's black artists wanted more control and power over their own creative endeavors. In the documentary *Karamu: 100 Years in the House*, Woodie King Jr. describes the change in attitude on the part of the black members of Karamu, asking, "Look, why don't we just do this stuff ourselves and do it the best we can?"[229] The privileging of self-determination and self-representation that was central to the Black Power movement had started to gain traction within the organization.

Kenneth Snipes, executive director of Karamu House from 1969 to 1975, articulated Karamu as a self-consciously black-led and black-focused institution. Snipes is included in a 1975 *New York Times* article that explored the nuances of black theater philosophies during this time. The article quotes Snipes as characterizing Karamu's history of white leadership as a "tradition that started from somebody else's perspective."[230] Snipes was the first to articulate Karamu as a black theater, and he markedly increased the production of plays by African Americans during his tenure. At the same time, he continued to work with Reuben Silver as director of the theater program. Snipes had participated in theater programming previous to his appointment as executive director of the organization, for example, by creating the projections for the 1965 golden anniversary Karamu season, and he clearly respected Silver's work as a director.[231] Silver remained theater director during Snipes's administration, but Karamu produced noticeably more works by black playwrights during this era, such as LeRoi Jones/Amiri Baraka's *Dutchman* (1969), Derek Walcott's *Dream on Monkey Mountain* (1972), Charles Gordone's *No Place to Be Somebody* (1974), and *Hamlet Jones*, Silver's adaptation of Langston Hughes's *Little Ham* (1975), as well as works written by white playwrights that expressed the racial and economic frustrations of the times, such as the musical *The Me Nobody Knows* (1972) and *Slow Dance on the Killing Ground* (1970). Future executive director Margaret Ford-Taylor, who at the time worked as an administrative assistant at Karamu House, also wrote and directed two of her original plays, *I Want to Fly* and *Hotel Happiness*, at Karamu in 1973.[232]

In 1976, Lois P. McGuire was hired as the first African American female executive director of Karamu. Specializing in visual arts, McGuire had served in a variety of administrative capacities at Karamu and was a founding member of the Ohio Arts Council and Cleveland Area Arts Council.[233] McGuire "found it inappropriate to have a white director for a black theater," and the most controversial action she took during her time as executive director was to relieve Silver of his position as director of theater programs. In the documentary, *Karamu: 100 Years in the House*, Dorothy Silver, Reuben Silver's wife and fellow Karamu House staff member and theater artist, recounted her remembrance of Silver's dismissal. "The then executive director belatedly decided that a black person should be in Reuben's position. I was in the office and heard that discussion and she said, 'I have nothing but praise for the work you've done. I just think it's time for a black person.' "[234] In the same documentary, Roger Jelliffe, Russell and Rowena's son, stated that Silver was "fired because he was white."[235] These commentaries reveal the tensions involved in this transition and the resistance on the part of the white staff and trustees to the idea that black leadership was important to both the ethos of the time and to an organization that had become a predominantly black cultural institution but that had never had a black theater administrator.

In addition to the hurt feelings of the current and former white leadership of Karamu, who did not necessarily grasp the importance of self-determination and self-definition intrinsic to the black liberation movement, the more substantial problem facing Karamu during the 1970s was the related issue of retaining funding sources in the absence of well-connected white management. Woodie King Jr. alluded to this when he stated, "When Karamu felt the need to bring in African American directors of both the theatre and the settlement house, it did not bode well with the philanthropic community."[236] Shraine Newman wrote, "Many individuals, both white and black, could not accept what was perceived as extreme radicalism" and noted that after the retirement of the Jelliffes "eleven changes in executive leadership occurred" within a span of twenty-five years.[237] These frequent changes indicate the difficulties involved in attaining the level of support needed to keep the organization afloat. Karamu's fundraising ability was also hurt by the exodus of middle- and upper-class African Americans out of the neighborhood as a result of easing housing restrictions and the de facto segregation that had previously concentrated the city's entire black population in the central city. As Newman put it, "Blacks with financial means could now participate in those arenas heretofore denied them" and were less likely to associate with Karamu as strongly as they had in the past.[238] The 1973–75 recession and inflation crisis also made fundraising for Karamu programs that much more difficult.

Despite these social and economic challenges, Karamu persisted. The organization was supported in part by the Karamu Foundation, which had been set up by Russell and Rowena Jelliffe prior to their retirement. City and state arts board grants also aided the organization. In the late 1970s, Karamu received federal funds allocated through the Comprehensive Employment, Education, and Training Act (CETA), a federal jobs program similar in nature to the WPA that funded many of the black theaters of the 1970s including Concept East and Spirit of Shango theaters in Detroit, the New York–based Black Theatre Alliance, and Penumbra Theatre Company in St. Paul, Minnesota.[239] The authors of the Urban Institute's research and policy study "Investing in Creativity: A Study of the Support Structure for U.S. Artists" found that the CETA program of the late 1970s was "a catalyst for the creation of many arts organizations and a valuable source of steady income for many artists."[240]

In keeping with Karamu's gravitation toward a black arts movement aesthetic and approach, Lois McGuire hired Mike Malone as Silver's replacement in 1977.[241] Malone was a graduate of Georgetown University and had cofounded the Duke Ellington School of the Arts, a performing arts high school in Washington, DC, in 1974.[242] Malone was a particularly talented choreographer and musical theater director. He led the DC Black Repertory Dance Company and served as director of musical theater at Howard University. At Karamu, he discovered Langston Hughes's script for *Black Nativity* in the organization's archives and in 1979 began producing the play as an annual holiday classic. Although *Black Nativity* premiered in New York in 1961 (the 1991 Karamu production of *Black Nativity* was directed by the original New York director, Vinnette Carroll), it did not become a perennial offering at many black theaters across the country until the 1980s.[243] Malone was partly responsible for the show's renewed popularity, and the gospel play became known as one of his directing specialties. For the rest of his career, Malone directed *Black Nativity* at various theaters including Chicago's Congo Square Theatre. He was in rehearsals for his fourth production of the work there when he passed away in 2006.[244]

Professionalization

In 1981 Karamu House received a $53,000 grant from the US Department of Education to "implement programs that will help school desegregation in the cultural sense."[245] Karamu created two original productions using these funds. The first was a compilation of "slave narratives, slave songs and dances" titled *The Way It Was*, with a set design featuring a Reconstruction-era cabin and a corresponding visual art and photography exhibit. This production was directed by future executive director Margaret Ford-Taylor and was presented in celebration of Black History Month. The second educational play, *Dreams, Dreams, Play My Dreams*, was a compilation of writing from the Harlem Renaissance by Langston Hughes, Claude McKay, and Jean Toomer and songs from the Eubie Blake musical *Shuffle Along*. This production accompanied *The Way It Was* and was directed by Mike Malone.[246]

Buoyed by funds from the Department of Education, CETA, and the Cleveland Foundation, Karamu announced the formation of its professional company in December 1981. Mike Malone had been contemplating this move since his hiring in 1977, and he and the Karamu board finally felt that the organization could support such an endeavor.[247] The formation of the professional company reflected Karamu's desire to financially support its artists. The implementation of black leadership and the paying of a wage to its working artists (most of whom were black) addressed some of the racial and economic inequalities inherent to the organization. The Karamu Company, as the professional group was known, was conceived of as a complement rather than replacement of the community arts and service components of Karamu House.

The first production of the professional company was Hansberry's *A Raisin in the Sun*, which starred Minnie Gentry as Lena. Gentry had also performed the same role in the 1961 production directed by Reuben Silver, which was billed as the first off-Broadway production of the work.[248] Film and television actors Ron O'Neal and Al Fann shared the role of Walter Lee in the 1961 production, and a young Anthony Chisholm played Walter Lee in Karamu's 1981 production.[249] The second production of the professional company was *Eyes*, a musical adaptation of Zora Neale Hurston's *Their Eyes Were Watching God* by Mari Evans. This production starred Rhetta Hughes as Janie, the protagonist of Hurston's early twentieth-century feminist/womanist masterpiece.[250]

The third production of the professional company was an adaptation of Shakespeare's *The Taming of the Shrew*.[251] This production was done at a time when professional theaters did not generally cast artists of color in classical European works. African American actors were at a distinct economic disadvantage compared with their white counterparts because Shakespearean plays were and remain the biggest professional employment vehicles for actors working in nonprofit theater in the United States.[252] Janet League, who played Kate in the Karamu production of *Taming of the Shrew*, commented on the lack of opportunity for artists of color to participate in Shakespearean works during that era. "Even though there is a lot of work out there, there is not that much opportunity for blacks, especially in the classics. There never has been."[253] In 1986 Actors Equity Association (AEA) published a four-year study that supported this common knowledge. AEA reported that "over 90 percent of all of the professional theater produced in this country—from stock and dinner theatre to the avant-garde to Broadway—was staged with all-Caucasian casts."[254]

During the production run of *The Taming of the Shrew*, Karamu's newly appointed executive director William Lewis fired Mike Malone. Lewis and Karamu's board of directors found the professional company costlier than anticipated and noted that some community members resented the fact that some of the artists in the professional company were hired from out of town.[255] Several shows were cancelled when nine members of the cast protested Malone's firing. The play resumed under the direction of the program coordinator for arts education, Charles Briggs, after a meeting between the actors and Karamu management sufficiently convinced the performers to return to the production.[256]

After Malone's dismissal, Lucia Colombi was named interim artistic director and served in that position from 1982 to 1984.[257] Colombi, the daughter of a prominent local Italian American surgeon, was a former student of Silver's and had been a youth participant in Karamu's programs. After graduating from Kent State, Colombi returned to Karamu to work with the children's theater program.[258] She directed several notable Karamu productions prior to her appointment as interim artistic director. In 1975 she directed Karamu's production of *The Great White Hope*, whose cast included James Pickens Jr. During the 1976–77 season, she directed Karamu's production of Athol Fugard, John Kani, and Winston Ntshona's South African play *Sizwe Bansi Is Dead*, which also featured James Pickens Jr.[259] In 1979, Colombi founded Cleveland's Ensemble Theatre. Like Karamu, Ensemble Theatre practiced colorblind and nontraditional casting. Colombi ran the two theaters concurrently during her time as interim artistic director of Karamu. At Karamu, Colombi directed Leslie Lee's *Colored People's Time*, Michael Gazzo's *A Hatful of Rain*, and an original adaptation of Euripides's *The Trojan Women*.[260]

Ensemble Theatre has partnered several times with Karamu in coproductions such as Pearl Cleage's *Bourbon at the Border*, presented at the Cleveland Playhouse in 2008. In 2010, Karamu, Ensemble Theatre, and Akron's Weathervane Playhouse collaborated in a production of *The Great White Hope* in an effort to garner public attention for the movement to posthumously pardon Jack Johnson, the legendary African American boxer who is the subject of the play.[261] Ensemble Theatre and Karamu partnered again in 2017 with the production of Rajiv Joseph's *The Lake Effect*, which was presented at Karamu House. These coproductions reflect the overlapping history and mission of the two theaters.

During Colombi's tenure as interim artistic director of Karamu, the theater reverted to its former identity as an integrated community theater endeavor interested in producing a variety of plays from playwrights of diverse cultural backgrounds. Even when Karamu was identified more strongly as a black theater organization under the leadership of Snipes and McGuire, Karamu's staff was still composed of both black and white working artists. This fact shows that the difference between Karamu's articulation of itself as a multiethnic institution or a black-focused institution consisted primarily of whether or not the center had black leadership for both the parent organization and the theater program. From the 1970s onward, the production choices of both articulations of Karamu included a predominance of work by black playwrights.

In 1984, the African American playwright Don Evans was hired as the artistic director of Karamu's theater programs. Evans was an active participant in the black arts movement and a founding member of the Black Theatre Network.[262] His popular play *One Monkey Don't Stop No Show* had recently premiered at Crossroads Theatre Company in 1981.[263] Evans's other plays include *Sugarmouth Sam Don't Dance No More*, *It's Showdown Time* (an adaptation of *The Taming of the Shrew* set in a black cultural context), *A Love Song for Miss Lydia*, and the biographical musicals *Mahalia* and *Louis* about Mahalia Jackson and Louis Armstrong. Evans held advanced degrees from Temple University and taught African American studies and theater arts courses at multiple colleges and universities in his home state of New Jersey, including Princeton.[264] Eileen Morris, artistic director of Houston's Ensemble Theatre, described Evans as "a charming, smart, thoughtful and creative man that had a great style. . . . His characters provide a real opportunity for sharing truth, passion, and love, all of which make up our lives."[265]

In an interview with drama critic Tony Mastroianni during his second season at Karamu, Evans articulated his concept of Karamu's social and racial identity. "Evans doesn't like to hear Karamu labeled a black theater (which it is) or an interracial theater (which it was). He prefers to call it, 'the only American Theater in the country. It's open to all people and most of our theaters are not. . . . We are interpreting works that reflect American society, which is an interracial society.' "[266] Having experience with the black arts movement initiatives of the 1970s and also with classical works and the effort to open up productions of European classical works to people of color made Evans a great fit for Karamu's multiple and sometimes conflicting identities. The 1985–86 season reflected these various theatrical legacies with productions of Leslie Lee's *First Breeze of Summer*, Evans's own plays, *One Monkey Don't Stop No Show* and *Louis*, Ed Bullins's *In the Wine Time*, Marcus Hemphill's *Innocent Black and the Brothers*, Ray Aranha's *Orphans and Cannibals*, and Bertolt Brecht's *The Threepenny Opera*.[267] Evans directed many of his own plays during his tenure as artistic director of Karamu, which lasted from 1984 to 1988. In addition to the works listed above, Karamu produced *The Trials and Tribulations of Staggerlee Brown* in 1984, a 1985 original adaptation (with Jorge Lopez-Ruiz) of the Gilbert and Sullivan musical *H.M.S. Pinafore* set in a West Indian locale, *One Monkey Don't Stop No Show* in 1985, and *It's Showdown Time* in 1987.[268] Not since Langston Hughes's plays were produced in rapid succession had Karamu devoted so much time to one playwright. During his time at Karamu, Evans also had his play *Sweet Daddy of Love (Or, What Goes Around)* produced by Crossroads Theatre Company in 1985. This production featured Minnie Gentry as one of the play's principal characters.[269]

In 1985 Evans invited Woodie King Jr. to direct a Karamu coproduction with Oberlin College of Loften Mitchell's *Tell Pharoah*, "a multimedia cantata that tells the story of Harlem as a focal point for the history of blacks in America."[270] In residence at Oberlin, King conceived of this production as a way to reflect the close relationship between Karamu and Oberlin (the alma matter of the Jelliffes and many other Karamu artists). In a news feature about this production, King spoke about his respect for Karamu and the artists Karamu cultivated: "If you study black theater, you must be aware of Karamu. So many famous figures. . . . I had my first long discussions with Langston Hughes, Fred O'Neill, Malcolm Boyd, Sidney Lamer at Karamu. I came to the 1965 golden anniversary. It was a training school for a group of my friends, actors like Minnie Gentry, Robert Guillaume. I've kept in touch with each of the directors and remained very close to Reuben and Dorothy Silver."[271] *Tell Pharoah* was underwritten by a grant from the Gund Foundation that was intended to bring black drama to Cleveland high schools. This grant helped Karamu contribute to its educational mission and enabled the production to serve as a college-recruiting tool. According to King, "So many minority students don't even know that Oberlin exists. That's really why I've come."[272] The Cleveland *Plain Dealer* listed an audience of fifteen hundred students, who, thanks to the Gund grant, were able to attend the Karamu production free of charge.[273]

In 1987, Evans returned to his faculty positions at Trenton State College and Princeton, from which he had taken a leave of absence in order to work at Karamu.[274] He continued to work for Karamu over the next several years as a consultant and guest director. In February 1988 Evans directed the local premiere of August Wilson's *Ma Rainey's Black Bottom*. A decade later he would participate in the seminal Black Theatre Summit "On Golden Pond," at Dartmouth College, which followed and explored the views expressed by Wilson regarding the support and maintenance of African American theater companies in his famous speech *The Ground on Which I Stand*.[275]

In 1988 Margaret Ford-Taylor was appointed executive director of Karamu after the death of the previous director, Milton C. Morris.[276] At the time of her appointment the Cleveland *Plain Dealer* reported, "Karamu has faced serious financial problems in the past few years that threatened to close the institution. Ford-Taylor said her task is to rebuild Karamu."[277] Ford-Taylor had participated in Karamu programming and worked as a staff member in various capacities for seventeen years before being named executive director. As an artist, Ford-Taylor was the recipient of two Emmy Award nominations, as a writer of the television special *The Second Reconstruction* and as an actor for her role as Ida B. Wells in *American Women: Echoes and Dreams*. As an administrator, Ford-Taylor had served as the artistic director of the Afro American Cultural Center in Buffalo, New York, where she had directed numerous plays over a twelve-year period.[278]

During Ford-Taylor's tenure as Karamu's executive director, she launched a capital campaign with the aid of businessman Arnold Pinkney, congressman Louis Stokes (brother of former Cleveland mayor Carl Stokes), city council representative Kenneth Lumpkin, and Cleveland mayor Michael White.[279] In a 1989 feature on the organization, Ford-Taylor stated that Karamu had a fifteen-person staff that "swells during theater season when directors, choreographers, actors and artists gather to put on shows" and that the organization still operated social services outside of its theater activities such as programs for the elderly and a daycare facility.[280] Financially maintaining the organization through the 1990s proved to be a major challenge despite the support Karamu received from the city, local foundations, and the National Endowment for the Arts (NEA). There were several changes in board leadership, and in 1993 Karamu leased some of the space in its facility to Bank One, with the stated desire to help provide financial services "tailored for low and moderate income customers" but also presumably to increase its earned income revenue.[281] In 1994 Karamu faced a $100,000 deficit and almost closed. In a news article that doubled as a financial appeal, Margaret

Ford-Taylor is quoted as saying, "The theatre hasn't increased its budget since 1982, although it has greatly expanded its programming" and that the organization needed $50,000 to make it through the summer.[282] Ford-Taylor was able to raise the immediate funds needed, but the organization continued to accumulate debt. In 1996, Ford-Taylor was released from her position as executive director as a stipulation of the Cleveland Foundation, which oversees Karamu's trust fund, when they granted Karamu's request to reduce the fund's principal by $250,000 to pay off the dependent organization's debt.[283]

Feminist and Womanist Theater

Despite the financial challenges she encountered, Margaret Ford-Taylor had a lasting impact on Karamu as a leader and an artist. She contributed greatly to a decade that placed greater emphasis on the production of work by African American women. In 1989 she directed an ensemble of six African American women portrayed by Brenda Butler, Connie Blair, Amonica Kirkpatrick, Barbara Reaze, Evelyn Whatley, and Rena Sims in P. J. Gibson's character-driven drama *Long Time since Yesterday*. *Plain Dealer* drama critic Marianne Evett praised Ford-Taylor's direction of the play. "The ensemble of women onstage set off real fireworks. . . . As director, Ford-Taylor orchestrates the growing tensions; the play gathers such emotional steam that you forget about its flaws while you watch the heat rise onstage."[284] In 1991 Ford-Taylor directed another all-female cast, Ntozake Shange's *for colored girls who have considered suicide when the rainbow is enuf*. This production was one of three in the organization's history. Kenneth Daugherty had first directed the play at Karamu in 1980.[285] Ford-Taylor's 1991 production "doubled the usual size of the cast."[286] The 1991 production ran in repertoire with Charles Fuller's *A Soldier's Play* (directed by Sarah May), which featured an all-male cast. Evett noted that the women's play was "impressionistic, presenting vivid emotional moments through short poetic monologues," while the men's play was "clearly structured" and "moves relentlessly toward a solution."[287] These observations are in keeping with theories of feminist theater of the time. For example, Sue Ellen Case's 1988 seminal text *Feminism and Theatre* explores the cultural feminist idea of "a women's form—a feminine morphology"[288] distinct from and rejecting of the traditional linear plotline as "a male form," that is, "phallocentric, reflecting the nature of the male's sexual physiology."[289] While cultural feminist theories have largely fallen out of favor, the play *for colored girls* has not. Karamu produced *for colored girls* again in 2004 under the direction of Terrence Spivey. This production handed one of the cast members, Nina Dominique, a best actress award from the Cleveland Theater Collective.[290]

Ford-Taylor also hired several women guest directors during her tenure at Karamu who produced outstanding work. Caroline Jackson-Smith's

1992 adaptation and direction of the poetry volume *The Women of Plums: Voices of Slave Women* by Delores Kendrick was one such production.[291] Jackson-Smith took many of the individual pieces in the poetry collection and wove them together with an ensemble of women, combining the poems with song and dance to create "celebrations of black women who endured and triumphed over pain and found themselves stronger."[292] The performers, Conni Blair, Kwanza Brewer, Cathy Clifford, Ebani Edward, Tanya Dione Haithcock, Evelyn Irby-Whatley, Renee Mathews-Jackson, Cassandra McCree, Joyce Meadows, Chelsea Mosley, and Joyce M. Rice, were praised as "uniformly excellent. Separately, they give individual and distinctive voices to the characters they portray. Together, they form a superb acting ensemble."[293]

Sarah May, who served as theater manager and frequent director from 1990 to 1997, also directed many significant productions at Karamu during this time period and was often praised by reviewers for her strong directing choices, particularly her arresting stage pictures. In 1992 she led a Karamu/ Dobama coproduction of Frank Galati's stage adaption of John Steinbeck's *The Grapes of Wrath*.[294] In 1994, she directed a contemporary interpretation of Orson Welles's 1930s adaptation of Shakespeare's *Macbeth*. Welles's version was set in 1800s postrevolution Haiti and was one of the most famous productions of the FTP. May's *Voodoo Macbeth* used guns and other modern props to portray the struggle for political power in contemporary Haiti.[295] This production was likely inspired by a retrospective of works from the WPA in 1992 that was a collaboration among the Cleveland Art Museum, Cuyahoga Community College, and Karamu. The retrospective featured a production of another famous FTP play, *The Swing Mikado*, that was directed by former Karamu artistic director Mike Malone.[296] Sarah May has also directed three other Dobama/Karamu coproductions: Athol Fugard's *Playland* in 1994, Anna Deveare Smith's *Fires in the Mirror* in 1995, and Tony Kushner's *Caroline, or Change* in 2008.[297] Like Lucia Colombi's association with Karamu and Ensemble Theatre, May's association with Dobama and Karamu has yielded excellent coproductions that have engaged both theaters' core audiences.

A historically significant contribution that May made to Karamu's repertoire was her direction of the Langston Hughes–Zora Neale Hurston collaboration *Mule Bone*, which was originally intended to have its premier at Karamu in 1931. As previously mentioned, the production was cancelled after Hughes and Hurston had an argument over authorial credit.[298] Although the 1996 Karamu production was not the play's premiere (it premiered at Lincoln Center in New York in 1991), the Karamu production had significance in that it tied the contemporary practice of theater at Karamu to the organization's important historical legacy.[299]

Mule Bone is a romantic comedy set in rural Florida. Reviewing the show for the *Plain Dealer*, Linda Eisenstein wrote, "This isn't your average community theater ensemble. The cast is chock-full of dozens of Karamu's most capable veteran character actors and singers, who make each part funny and real. . . . Karamu has lavished love, attention and top-notch resources on *Mule Bone* and every bit shows."[300] Cast members for this production included Niles River, Kyle Primous, Sonya Leslie, Rob Robinson, Charles Bevels, Grant Banks, Hassan B. Rogers, Kathy Bibbs, J. C. Thompson, Jimmy Walker Jr., Shraine Newman, Safiyyah Hakim, and Jaietta Jackson.[301] Just as Alice Walker had helped to revive scholarly and popular interest in Zora Neale Hurston during the 1970s and 1980s, Karamu's production of *Mule Bone* brought a largely forgotten piece of Hurston's work back into public view and discussion in the 1990s.[302] Margaret Ford-Taylor's leadership and the cultivation of other female playwrights and directors at Karamu during the 1990s increased the showcasing of black women's stories in Cleveland's arts ecology, further diversifying both the content and production practices of Karamu in a way that dovetailed with feminist and womanist concerns of the time period.

Honoring August Wilson

In addition to works written or directed by women, the 1990s at Karamu also featured many productions of plays by August Wilson. Caroline Jackson-Smith directed *Joe Turner's Come and Gone* in 1991 and *Jitney* in 1999.[303] Margaret Ford-Taylor directed *Fences* for Karamu in 1992, for which she received the following praise: "Director Margaret Ford-Taylor totally understands the play; portrayals are honest and moving."[304] Gary Darnell Anderson directed *The Piano Lesson* in 1993.[305] Karamu alumnus Bill Cobbs directed *Two Trains Running* in 1995, which featured Broadway actor and Negro Ensemble Company member Charles Brown in the role of Memphis.[306] Since the 1990s, Karamu has produced several more productions from Wilson's twentieth-century cycle. Caroline Jackson-Smith returned to Karamu to direct the 2007 production of *King Hedley II*.[307] Michael Oatman directed *Gem of the Ocean* in 2012, and Terrence Spivey directed the second Karamu production of *Joe Turner's Come and Gone* in 2015.[308] This extensive list shows that Karamu has made the production of August Wilson's work a mainstay of its repertoire. In this respect, Karamu is like many other contemporary African American theaters that have been drawn to the richness and cultural specificity of August Wilson's work. Just as the ubiquity of Shakespeare productions in the United States has helped to maintain the professional practice of white actors and predominately white theater institutions, the immense popularity of August Wilson's work in the regional theaters, on Broadway, and in black theater organizations during the 1990s and 2000s has helped to provide support and regular employment for black performers, who often move among these three types of organizations on a contract basis. Black theater institutions such as Karamu have also benefited from the name recognition of August Wilson and his plays' ability to draw sizeable audiences. A fervent defender of black theater institutions, August Wilson and his literary and institutional legacy will be covered in further depth in the following chapter, which focuses on how Wilson transformed the arts ecology of Pittsburgh, his hometown.

The Terrence Spivey Era

When Gerry McClamy replaced Margaret Ford-Taylor as executive director of Karamu House in 1997, she did not immediately hire an artistic director but "concentrated her efforts on regaining economic viability."[309] In 2003, McClamy and the board of directors felt confident that the organization had returned to relative financial security. After a national search, they hired Terrence Spivey as Karamu's artistic director, a position he held from 2003 to 2016. During this time, Spivey markedly increased the theater's local and national prominence. In an article for the online publication Cool Cleveland, Anastasia Pantsios credited Spivey with "restoring its [Karamu's] luster with exciting new productions and attracting a horde of new actors, directors, and playwrights as well as encouraging others who had left to return. Productions there became must-sees. . . . He also worked tirelessly to network outside Cleveland, attending conferences and events in the black cultural and theater community to make it aware that Karamu was still a force to be reckoned with."[310] Former County Commissioner and Ohio State legislature representative Peter Lawson Jones, who was a Karamu member in his youth, stated, "The greater Cleveland community owes Terrence Spivey an enormous debt of gratitude for the thought provoking and entertaining theatrical offerings he has brought us. Karamu owes him a debt that can never be satisfied. . . . I am forever obligated to my 'brother' for rekindling, when I thought it had long been extinguished, my passion for the performing arts."[311] Jones performed in many Karamu productions during Spivey's tenure, including *Bourbon at the Border* (2008), *A House with No Walls* (2009), *The Great White Hope* (2010), *From Breast Cancer to Broadway* (2010), *Ruined* (2011), *Ceremonies in Dark Old Men* (2014), and *The Colored Museum* (2016).[312] As a former member of Karamu during his youth, Jones's assessment of Spivey's impact on Karamu includes a knowledge and appreciation for the organization's past as well as its present.

In a telephone interview with the director, Spivey spoke about his respect for Karamu and how he was drawn to Cleveland from New York to work for the organization.

> I started as a guest director for Karamu. They brought me in during the winter of 2003 to do *Little Tommy Parker's Celebrated Colored*

Minstrel Show, Carlyle Brown's piece. . . . I was there for six weeks, and they observed my workmanship. I got a chance to see the glory of Karamu. When I saw that sign on the outside of the building that said Karamu House, tears just flowed down my face. . . . By the third or fourth week, the administration had heard from the actors that, "yes, this guy is cool, he allows us to create." I came back with my family to see the closing performance and they were shocked that a guest director would do that. I said, "I love art and I want to see how the play had grown." So, they asked me to come on as the artistic director. That was Fall 2003.[313]

In 2004 and 2005 the theater won "a spate of awards, from such organizations as the Cleveland Theater Collective, the Black Theatre Network, and the Ohio Alliance for Education," as a result of his leadership.[314] Spivey was voted "Best Theatre Honcho" in 2005 by Cleveland Scene, which proclaimed him "a master at blending interesting productions that speak to the African American experience while also offering a welcoming hand to everyone else. During the past season, outstanding shows such as *Bee Luther Hatchee* and *Johnnie Taylor Is Gone* combined entertainment—sharply drawn characters and taut, precise timing—with thematic messages in ways that haven't been seen on East 89th for quite some time."[315] In 2009 Spivey was invited to become a member of the National Theatre Conference, an organization that includes directors and playwrights of national prominence. He was also featured in *American Theatre* magazine in an article entitled "Terrence Spivey Energy Source," which highlighted Karamu's productions of Derek Walcott's *Dream on Monkey Mountain* (2006), Ossie Davis's *Purlie Victorious* (2007), William A. Parker's *Waiting 2 End Hell* (2008), and Thomas Gibbons's *A House with No Walls* (2008), all of which were directed by Spivey.[316] In 2011, he was given a proclamation by the mayor and the city of Cleveland, and in 2013, Karamu received the prestigious AUDELCO award.[317] In 2015 Spivey delivered the keynote address to the national annual conference of the United States Institute for Theatre Technology (USITT) as part of its focus on diversity efforts within American theater.[318]

Over the thirteen years of his tenure as artistic director, Spivey produced over seventy shows, at least half of which he directed. During this time, he learned about Karamu's important history from theatergoers, artists, and the organization's administration. "I have met many people in the lobby at Karamu. For twelve years after every show I would be there every day, to greet the community. The shows ran for sixteen performances for four weeks, four shows a week. That's how I learned so much more about Karamu. Patrons would tell me about legendary people who had come through. It holds a special place in the community's heart."[319] Following the Karamu tradition of producing a wide range of African American dramatic literature, Spivey concentrated his production choices on historic as well as contemporary work.

When I say "black theater" I mean not just Lynn Nottage and
Suzan-Lori Parks or Dominique Morisseau or Katori Hall and other
contemporary black playwrights but the classics, like Steve Carter,
Alice Childress, and Richard Wesley. Who's going to preserve their
works? I mean, they're barely studied in schools so who's going to do
Alice Childress's work? *A Raisin in the Sun*, the great August Wilson,
yes, his plays will be done but there are also others. Who's going to
produce Theodore Ward's *Big White Fog*. . . . We want to stage and
study our classics as much as *Death of a Salesman*.[320]

It was for this reason that Spivey chose to produce Lonne Elder III's 1969
play *Ceremonies in Dark Old Men* on the Karamu stage in 2014. "We need
to do more black classics so these young folks can learn about those before
us. When we staged *Ceremonies in Dark Old Men*, most patrons didn't
know how old the play was. They thought it was new. Some patrons asked
me, 'where's the playwright?' I said, 'See how relevant it is? See how fresh
it is?' "[321] Spivey's comments illustrate one of the vital functions of African
American theaters. While regional theaters or multiethnic theaters might do
one or two plays written by African Americans in a season, they will never
be able to match the depth and complexity of an African American theater
that offers a full season of both contemporary and classic African American drama. Spivey's selection of lesser-known plays such as Karamu's 2004
production of John Henry Redwood's *No Niggers, No Jews, No Dogs*, a
play about racism and anti-Semitism in the segregated South, nicely complemented better-known and more widely produced plays such as the 2011
production of Lynn Nottage's Pulitzer Prize–winning play *Ruined*, which
chronicles the lives of women traumatized and exploited during the civil war
in the Democratic Republic of Congo. Although Spivey did not direct either
of these works (Redwood's play was directed by Hassan Rogers; Nottage's
play was directed by Caroline Jackson-Smith), as artistic director, he was
responsible for selecting the productions and broadening the scope of the
dramatic literature presented under his leadership. [322]

In addition to producing published playwrights, Spivey also helped hone
the talent of emerging African American playwrights by providing them with
development opportunities. Under his leadership, Michael Oatman became
Karamu's second playwright-in-residence, Langston Hughes being the only
other writer to carry that title in the organization's hundred-year history.
Oatman's first play, *Not a Uterus in Sight*, a play that "concerns a black
FBI agent in a future where Roe versus Wade has been struck down," was
written during his time as an MFA student at Cleveland State University.[323]
His play *The Chittlin Thief* won the African American Playwrights Exchange
award for best comedy in 2008, and his play *Warpaint* was a finalist for the
Kennedy Center's Best Short Play award in 2009.[324] In 2010, Karamu pro-
duced Oatman's *Eclipse: The War between Pac and B.I.G.* The production

was directed by Tony Sias and was featured in a *New York Times* article that included an audio slideshow narrated by Oatman about the life of Tupac Shakur and his intentions regarding the production of the play.[325] In 2011 Oatman won the Cleveland Arts Prize Emerging Artist Award for Literature.[326] Oatman also directed several productions during his time at Karamu including August Wilson's *Gem of the Ocean* in 2012 and Don Evans's play *One Monkey Don't Stop No Show* in 2014.[327] In a press interview Oatman stated, "Under the mentorship of Karamu's artistic director Terrence Spivey, I have matured as a man and as an artist in that institution. Without that place or that man, I simply would not exist. I love them both beyond words."[328]

Spivey also supported professional new play production as a part of the youth theater activities of Karamu House. Michael Oatman wrote his 2011 play *You Got Nerve*, about the Cleveland School for the Arts, for Karamu's youth program. Nicole Kearney began a series of ten plays for Karamu's youth theater program focused on teaching African American youth important moments in black history. Kearney's play, *The Little Boy That Shook Up the World: The Emmett Till Story*, was produced by Karamu's youth theater program in 2005.[329] In 2006 Karamu produced Kearney's *Breaking Barriers: The Little Rock Nine*, about the teenagers who integrated Little Rock Central High School in 1957.[330] *Foot Soldiers for Freedom*, about student civil rights activists during freedom summer, was produced by Karamu in 2009.[331] In response to an article featuring Terrence Spivey in 2016, Kearney commented, "Terrence gave me my start. . . . The career I have is because of his guidance, support and opening up Karamu House for me to grow and learn. I'm forever thankful to Terrence and wish him continued blessings on his new journey."[332] Kearney's Karamu productions were part of a robust youth program that included a summer theater camp that served "100 to 150 children," which furthered the educational and community-building mission of the organization.[333]

Recession and Financial Crisis

Despite this excellent programming, Karamu soon faced another financial crisis. Prior to Spivey's arrival, Gerry McClamy had run Karamu in a Spartan-like manner in an effort to keep the organization financially afloat. Seeing the need for greater artistic output, McClamy hired Spivey, who was praised for increasing both the quantity and the quality of Karamu's productions.[334] The larger and more professional production season Spivey oversaw naturally required more resources. McClamy managed these financial challenges well, but after her retirement, the organization struggled. Gregory Ashe was hired first as interim executive director of Karamu House in 2006 and then was renewed as permanent executive director in 2007. Ashe had previously served as the president of the Boys and Girls Club of Cleveland. In an interview with the *Plain Dealer* in 2010, Ashe spoke of the importance of Karamu to the community.

> If Karamu House walls could talk they would speak of the thousands of children that have learned new words, numbers and colors, and how to draw, paint, sing, dance, and be good citizens. They would echo with the laughter of children and adults of all ages. They would tell you about the triumph and excitement felt after a successful audition, the camaraderie after a big show, the tears and frustration that often accompanies the pursuit of excellence and the pure joy of a standing ovation. They would regale you with stories about scores of amazing people that were nurtured and encouraged.[335]

It is clear from this description that Ashe valued Karamu's history as a social and educational service center equally with its function as a community-based theater. Spivey praised Ashe in his *American Theatre* feature in 2009, stating that Ashe was "doing an exceptional job, [and] we have been able to raise funds through different venues. The past three shows in 2008, in spite of the economic crunch, managed to generate enough money to cover expenses."[336] Ashe, for his part, praised Spivey: "Terrence's wonderful ability to bring a play to life is appreciated both internally and externally by audiences and critics."[337] However, as the global financial crisis wore on, Karamu began to have serious financial difficulties. The fact that Ashe was new to his position at Karamu made the task of financially managing the organization through the eye of this storm that much harder.

At first, it seemed as though the organization could manage these difficulties. Karamu received several major grants in 2009–12, including a $100,000 "Engaging the Future" multiyear grant from the Cleveland Foundation for 2010–13 that was designed to attract new audiences.[338] Karamu also received a $10,000 grant from the NEA to mount a 2010 production of the Mary Weems play *Closure*, which tackled the issue of the recession directly through a plot centered on objects left in foreclosed homes. *Closure* featured legendary dancer, actor, and Karamu alumna Dianne McIntyre.[339] While these grants supported specific programming at Karamu, the regular operations budget of the organization dwindled during the recession. In 2009, other major Cleveland arts organizations such as the Cleveland Museum of Art ($50,000), Cleveland Public Theatre ($50,000), and Cleveland Playhouse ($25,000) all received NEA grants to "support the preservation of jobs that are threatened by declines in philanthropic and other support during the current economic downturn."[340] In retrospect, Karamu could have greatly benefited from such a grant.

Black theater organizations are usually small to midsize entities with operating budgets under $5 million. They do not have the staffing capacity of the larger regional theaters, orchestras, and art museums, which have full-time staff positions dedicated to fundraising and development and several experienced grant writers on salary. Unequal staffing in grant writing and development further disadvantages smaller organizations when they compete for the same local and national grants as the larger entities. In July 2017, the Helicon Collaborative study *Not Just Money: Equity Issues in Cultural Philanthropy* found that although "arts foundations and non-profit leaders are increasingly aware of diversity, equity, and inclusion issues in the non-profit cultural sector . . . funding is getting less equitable."[341] Arts organizations of color are underfunded in nine out of ten of the cities with the largest arts ecologies. In these nine cities, the percentage of grant money and philanthropy received by arts organizations devoted to nonwhite artistic and cultural work is significantly less than the percentage of the population that is nonwhite in those cities.[342] The study found that

> the distribution of arts funding nationally is actually getting more concentrated in the hands of the institutions that already have the most resources. Just 2 percent of all cultural institutions received nearly 60 percent of all contributed revenue, up approximately 5 percentage points over a decade. The 2 percent cohort is made up of 925 cultural groups that have annual budgets of more than $5 million. (NCCS) These organizations are symphonies, opera companies, regional theatres, art museums, ballet companies and other large institutions—the majority of which focus primarily on Western European fine arts traditions. While most of these institutions have made sincere efforts to broaden participation in the past decade, their audiences remain predominantly white and upper income (NEA Research Report #57).[343]

This dynamic is certainly in play in Cleveland. In the case of Karamu, the Cleveland Foundation provided Karamu a $100,000 grant to hire and train a development officer in 1994 and a multiyear grant that culminated in $60,000 for a marketing and finance manager in 2010.[344] These numbers, while certainly helpful, pale in comparison to the approximately $10 million operating budget of the Cleveland Playhouse and other "elite" arts organizations with whom Karamu must compete for grant money.[345] If Karamu had four or five development staff members trained in grant writing like these larger institutions have, it may have foreseen the need to shore up its financial base and apply for the grants that helped to shepherd the larger institutions through the financial crisis. Because Karamu did not have the staff power, the financial reserves, or the number of wealthy patrons of the larger Cleveland arts institutions, the recession hit the organization particularly hard.

In 2011 Anastasia Pantsios published an article on Cleveland Scene that detailed various disagreements among the leadership of Karamu, including the resignation of half of Karamu's board of directors.[346] Accusations were made that funds earmarked for production purposes went to operational support.[347] Gregory Ashe resigned in 2013 and was replaced by Patricia Egan, who served as the interim executive director for two years. Egan's consulting fee was approximately twice what Ashe's salary had been, which did not help the organization's financial outlook in the short term.[348] In 2014, the United Way, which had been contributing $120,000 per year to Karamu's operating budget, dropped the organization due to its decision to focus exclusively on poverty prevention efforts. At this point the organization's cash reserves dwindled to $2,000.[349] The board of directors embarked upon a strategic planning initiative that was ultimately paused in favor of a national search for a permanent executive director who would play a crucial role in any organizational realignment.[350] Tony Sias was part of the strategic planning committee and was encouraged to apply for the executive position. He did so and was hired as president and CEO of the organization in 2015.[351]

Sias described his history with Karamu as follows:

> The first time I came to Karamu was in the summer of 1992. I was finishing my MFA at Ohio University. I got a residency at the Cleveland Playhouse to finish the work. That was in June of 1992. I graduated and shortly thereafter came to Karamu. I was asked to do some coaching with one of the actors in the musical *Swing Mikado*. Theater legend Mike Malone was directing the show. I think Mike had taught at Howard for some time by then. That was the beginning of my experience here as an actor and director. My first show [as an actor] here was a show called *Oak and Ivy* about Paul Laurence Dunbar. So from 1992 to about 2002, I worked here regularly as an actor and director.[352]

Prior to his appointment as president and CEO of Karamu, Sias had served as director for arts education for the Cleveland School District, where he had worked in various capacities for fifteen years. Sias stated that his biggest task in his new position at Karamu was to "complete the strategic planning—to set the stage for a holistic new vision at Karamu—aimed at producing the next 100 years."[353]

This goal was particularly challenging given the financial situation Sias inherited. To address the organization's finances, Sias and the board of directors laid off fifteen staff members, "13 full time employees and 2 part timers," including artistic director Terrence Spivey, in late February 2016.[354] Karamu also closed its daycare facility and temporarily suspended its after-school programs.[355] *American Theatre* magazine reported, "In his review of the theatre's finances, Sias looked at each of Karamu's four product lines: early childhood development, arts education, theatre, and community programs. He said he uncovered some 'numbers that were breathtaking,' and concluded that the status quo was not sustainable."[356] Since its founding, Karamu had always been a multiservice organization. Sias believed that economic necessity and a changed cultural landscape required a refocusing of the institution's mission and energies. When I interviewed him, he stated that the organization now had three main service lines, "theatre, arts education, and community engagement."[357] The daycare building was vacant, and it was explained that it would eventually be refurbished to serve another purpose. When the daycare opened in the middle of World War II, there were no quality childcare facilities in the neighborhood and its construction was subsidized by a federal grant designed to help women enter the workforce as part of the war effort.[358] In his article for *American Theatre* magazine, Christopher Johnston stated that the decision to eliminate Karamu's daycare program in 2016 was easier than some of the other cost-saving measures the organization adopted because "families could enroll their children in other, high-rated programs in the community."[359] By implementing these reductions, Sias signaled that his leadership would prioritize economic feasibility. In a 2016 interview with Cleveland Scene, Sias reiterated this intention, stating, "What I'm committed to is operating this institution as a sound business. And one of the things we have to get to is a sustainable financial model."[360]

For his part, Terrence Spivey stated that although he was not expecting to be laid off, he was "hoping and praying for Karamu's continued success" and was "going to enjoy the freedom to create where I can."[361] One of his most significant post-Karamu projects was his direction of *Objectively/Reasonable: A Community Response to the Shooting of Tamir Rice 11/22/14* for Playwrights Local. Although this was not a Karamu production, it featured many of the artists Spivey had worked with at Karamu and was deeply invested in the local community and social justice.

Objectively/Reasonable came about through an original commission and development process at Playwrights Local. The play consists of a series of monologues created from interviews conducted by the playwrights with community members regarding their reactions to the shooting of Tamir Rice, the twelve-year-old boy who was killed by police in a Cleveland public park in 2014. Part of what motivated Spivey to participate in this project was witnessing other black theaters around the country participate in the Black Lives Matter movement. During a telephone interview with the director, Spivey explained:

> I'll never forget that when the Ferguson protests were going the National Black Theatre in New York was having forums on how art can express the unjust. I am very daring and open. It's not about being political; it's about letting art speak out as it did during the black arts movement. I let him [David Todd, the artistic director of Playwrights Local] know that my approach was going to come out very strong and express the frustration the community . . . "in your face style," breaking the fourth wall, black power theater. He said, "Yeah, go for it."[362]

The script was created by five local playwrights. The team included two black playwrights: Michael Oatman, who had recently served as playwright-in-residence at Karamu, and Lisa Langford, a Harvard University graduate and actor as well as playwright, whose work has appeared at Playwrights Horizons, La Jolla Playhouse, and Actors Theatre of Louisville, as well as locally at the Cleveland Playhouse and Dobama Theatre.[363] The other three members of the playwriting ensemble were white and included Playwrights Local artistic director David Todd, who was the play's conceiver and editor; Tom Hayes, Playwrights Local's managing director; and Michael Geither, Playwrights Local company member. The play included monologues from both adults and children expressing their hurt, anger, and sadness. It spoke viscerally to the Cleveland community and was attended by some of Rice's surviving relatives. Its original production ran from August 18 to September 4, 2016, and featured a cast of ten: Ashley Aquilla, Kaila Benford, India Burton, Samone Cummings, Ananias Dixon, Kali Hatten, LaShawn Little, Brenton Lyles, Jameka Terry, and Nathan Tolliver. The play was voted "most socially significant play of 2016" by Cleveland Critics Circle and was so popular it was restaged and ran from February 17 to March 11, 2017. The cast for the revival consisted of Samone Cummings, Kali Hatten, Christina Johnson, LaShawn Little, Joshua McElroy, Mary-Francis Renee Miller, Phillia, Corin B. Self, and Nathan Tolliver. The revival production also participated in several outreach and touring performances to local high schools and nearby universities such as Shaker Heights High School and Oberlin College.[364] *Objectively/Reasonable* was a beautiful example of how theater can help to reflect and shape the cultural politics of the city. The production was a means of collectively processing the trauma of Rice's death for Cleveland residents and raising awareness about excessive police force and violence directed at African American youth in the city. In this way it not only reflected the sociopolitical realities of the city but also contributed to working to transform these realities.

Rebuilding and Planning for the Next Hundred Years

Back at Karamu, the organization took what Sias described as "a pause" to complete strategic planning, recuperate, and financially realign the organization. Evidence of the reduced administrative capacity of the theater after the layoffs came in April 2016 when the organization temporarily lost its nonprofit status due to the 2015 paperwork required to renew that status being lost and never received by the IRS.[365] After an administrative scramble, Karamu's nonprofit status was restored in July and retroactively applied to the previous season.[366] The rest of the summer was spent preparing for the 2016–17 season and for a major building renovation, which was funded through a $1.8 million state grant.[367]

The theater renovation, conceived of during the strategic planning period, was designed to serve both theatrical productions and the community-engagement component of Karamu's programming by providing a theater space with modern projection capabilities and seating that would be more attractive to rental groups and well as upgrades that could provide adequate meeting space for social gatherings and cultural celebrations. Sias explained that the renovation of the theater was designed to maximize the use and versatility of the space, hopefully contributing to greater earned income in the future. "We see ourselves as a convening organization so that people from the community, whether it's minorities in business or service organizations like the Links or the Kappas, fraternities and sororities and service organizations can all come in and use Karamu as a place for conversation and dialogue."[368] Some examples of how Karamu's renovation has enabled diversified programming include the addition of a summer film series, line dancing sessions, and a local visual arts residency program.

Sias's position at Karamu incorporates the function of both the managing/executive director position and the artistic director position that are most commonly found in American nonprofit theaters. As a professional artist with a long connection to Karamu and an arts administrator with over a decade of experience, Sias is uniquely qualified to make artistic decisions such as season selection and the hiring of contract artists in addition to his administrative duties regarding financial planning and organizational management. The combining of these roles is a unique and innovative response to the financial challenges the organization faced and the formidable skill set that Sias brings to the job.

The first play produced by Karamu under Sias's leadership was Sheldon Epps's *Blues in the Night*, a musical directed by Reggie Kelly. Kelly described his history with Karamu in a local radio show broadcast after the play's opening weekend.

> I began at Karamu at the age of nine. I was just a young boy riding my bicycle up and down the street. I used to run into Karamu to get water from the water fountain. One day they said, "Little boy, you just can't be running up here getting water, you should get in a class." That's where the journey began and the journey has been God filled and God sanctioned. Karamu House is my home. I grew up there. I met my mentors there, Mike Malone and the incredible Dianne McIntyre, those are world-renowned teachers that have placed many, many artists on the world stage. I was blessed from an early age to have those folks in my life. My relationship with Karamu has been long. I've been involved in two dance companies there and have directed maybe thirty plays there. . . . I had left Karamu about thirteen years ago to continue my journey but Tony Sias, the new President and CEO of Karamu, who is a good friend, called me and

said "Reggie, I'm President of Karamu House now and I need you."
[The production of *Blues in the Night*] has been a wonderful journey;
it's a delightful cast. . . . The play is beautiful. It's a wonderful tapes-
try of black music that we just love singing.[369]

In a review for Cleveland Scene, Christine Howey wrote, "The first show
of the new regime is promising evidence that this grand institution is beginning its second hundred years in high style."[370] India Blatch-Geib, the costume
designer for the production, won the 2016 Critics Choice Award for best
costume design, showing that the technical design and quality of the production was as appreciated as the acting and singing.[371] The other productions
of the 2016–17 season included *Sister Act*, the musical, directed by Sheffia
Randall Dooley; *Rasheeda Speaking*, an office drama written by Joel Drake
Johnson and directed by Sarah May; *Repairing a Nation*, a play about repa-
rations and the Tulsa race massacre written by Nikkole Salter and directed by
Margaret Ford-Taylor; and a non–traditionally cast production of *You Can't
Take It with You*, directed by Fred Sternfeld as a tribute to Karamu's beginnings as an interracial theater company. The season honored Karamu's past
not only in its diverse selection of plays but in its inclusion of former Karamu
directors and staff like Margaret Ford-Taylor and Sarah May.

The 2017–18 season included the plays *Simply Simone: The Music of
Nina Simone*, created by Robert Neblett and David Grapes; *The Lake Effect*,
by Rajiv Joseph, a coproduction with Dobama Theatre; an original *Holiday
Jazz Revue*; *Sassy Mamas*, by Celeste Bedford Walker; *The Adventures of the
Black Girl in Her Search for God*, by Lisa Codrington; and *Passing Strange*, a
musical by Stew and Heidi Rodewald. When asked which productions under
his leadership have stood out the most, Sias mentioned *Blues in the Night*
and *Simply Simone*. Where *Blues in the Night* received rave reviews, *Simply
Simone* was more of a popular favorite. Sias explained the appeal of this
production to Karamu's audience.

> A couple of critics panned it, but the community fell in love with it.
> It was a success comparable to our *Black Nativity* or *God's Trom-
> bones*. People that come to our theater said, "This is the best thing
> I've seen at Karamu. You have got to bring this back." So sometimes
> critics have an opinion and they're entitled to it, but audiences feel
> differently and that show really spoke to the spirit of Karamu. The
> audiences were diverse because Nina Simone, as an artist and activist,
> she just crossed both generation lines and culture lines.[372]

In response to the positive audience reaction to this musical, Sias scheduled
a remount of the production for the 2018–19 season. The 2018–19 season
also included *Letters from Zora*, a one-woman show written and performed
by Vanessa Bell Calloway, a Karamu alumna and film and television actor

with credits including *Coming to America, What's Love Got to Do with It*, and *Southside with You*. In an interview published in the Cleveland *Plain Dealer*, Calloway stated, "It feels great to be back home and at Karamu. It feels just right."[373] By bringing back artists such as Calloway, Margaret Ford-Taylor, Sarah May, and Reggie Kelly as guest directors and performers, Sias consciously created a connection between Karamu's past and his vision for the organization's future.

As a complement to the main-stage programming listed above, Karamu has also instituted a social justice series in association with Case Western Reserve University. At least two of Karamu's plays each season will be part of that series, and Case Western University's Social Justice Institute will provide speakers and panelists for talk backs and other forms of audience engagement.[374] Karamu has also entered into a formal agreement with Dobama Theatre regarding regular coproductions.[375] These endeavors aim to attract a larger and more diverse audience and to deepen audience engagement with plays that speak to contemporary social issues.

Arts education, the third arm of Karamu's services, resumed programming in 2017, and Karamu has plans to further expand its educational initiatives in the future. Karamu currently provides performance space to arts groups such as Cleveland School for the Arts and also runs its own after-school, weekend, and summer arts education programs. Karamu is also listed as a community partner with the local public elementary school.[376] The Cleveland school board is considering building a new K–8 facility across the street from Karamu to facilitate joint arts education and programming for its students.[377] Karamu's role in contributing to arts education classes and educational enrichment opportunities is vital to serving the artistic and cultural needs of the youth living in the Fairfax neighborhood and elsewhere across the city. Arts education for youth, which Karamu has participated in since its founding over a hundred years ago, is another way that this theater company shapes the city of which it is a part. This has become especially critical in the last decade, when much of K–12 arts education has been eliminated from the public school curriculum in urban areas.[378]

In terms of long-term planning, Karamu's staff and board of directors are seeking to replicate municipal efforts to revitalize neighborhoods through arts programming that have been successful in other areas of the city. Joy Roller, Karamu's development director, spoke to me about her previous work in this area and of Karamu's plans to be "an anchor institution" in the economic revitalization of the Fairfax neighborhood.

> I was the executive director of a thirty million–dollar economic development initiative called the Gordon Square Arts District. . . . We created an arts and entertainment district out of an old run-down neighborhood on the west side of Cleveland. . . . My specialty is arts as economic development. How to use the arts to really build economic

development in a neighborhood that can help improve the quality of life for the neighborhood and for the citizens. . . . So how are you going to do that? It's important, as I did in Gordon Square, not to just look at it as a one-off organization or effort. We [Karamu] are an anchor of a neighborhood. We are an anchor of a community.[379]

Sias expanded on this idea of being an anchor organization for economic development with a few plans Karamu has to draw more of the community into Karamu and to serve more of its basic needs.

We are located in a food desert, and there's a plethora of opportunity here. We are literally one and a half blocks from the Justice Center where hundreds of people go to work and visit. Sitting in the heart of Fairfax, people say we're in the backyard of the Cleveland Clinic. I tell them, "No, the Cleveland Clinic is in our front yard, because we've been here much longer than the clinic has been here. Part of my vision is to increase the earned revenue by creating a coffee shop that would be able to do coffee in the morning, lunch, snack in the afternoon, and a preshow cocktail or postshow cocktail or appetizer. When we get those patrons in here, what will happen is that we can market all of our events and have giveaways and things of that nature. I'm not necessarily interested in getting into the food and beverage business, but I could see contracting with a local caterer or a pastry shop or renting space out to such business and being able to have a diversified revenue stream as well as helping to serve the needs of the neighborhood.[380]

On my tour of the building, Sias showed me the space Karamu formerly used for a kitchen and reception gathering place as an ideal venue for a future coffee shop or restaurant. On May 7, 2019, the Cleveland Foundation announced the awarding of a $2 million grant to Karamu to facilitate Sias's vision. The grant funds construction for "revamped lobbies, an audience lounge, an art gallery, a neighborhood bistro, and an outdoor plaza on Quincy Avenue," supporting Karamu's role "as a cultural, social and educational anchor in Fairfax, a low-income, majority black neighborhood."[381] In this respect, Karamu is following the lead of other theater and arts organizations that have focused on urban placemaking in addition to arts programming.

Sias and Roller also both mentioned the development of 105th Street, which is currently under construction and is being widened to more speedily connect Interstate 77 and 490 to the Cleveland Clinic and University Circle neighborhood. Sias explained the project as follows: "There's this development happening at 105th Street and it's called Opportunity Corridor. At one point there was going to be a freeway there that would have driven over the city so suburbanites could miss coming through the city on their way to University Circle and the Cleveland Clinic."[382] Protests during the 1960s prevented the merging of the two freeways by destroying the low-income housing stock between them, but city planners were recently able to get approval for a three-mile, 35-mile-per-hour boulevard that would connect them. The boulevard has been marketed as a compromise that would ostensibly both speed traffic and allow for economic development in the Slavic Village, Kinsman, and Fairfax neighborhoods.[383] This development project remains controversial and was temporarily blocked by city council member T. J. Dow, who argued "the redevelopment wouldn't benefit the residents of his community."[384] Sias sees the project as potentially beneficial to drawing greater traffic and interest to Karamu House.

> They called it Opportunity Corridor because it would be engaging residents from the respective communities to be a part of the economic engine of this connector. We are a quarter of a mile away from that. Also, Fairfax Renaissance Development Corporation is about to build diverse housing in this community . . . market rate, affordable, and mixed income to serve the Cleveland Clinic med students and those who are in the diverse salary ranges that work there. So, I see Karamu as part of all that, part of the economic development of this community and as a place where people can go who want to be in a walking community. We have something great to offer in this footprint.[385]

My discussions with Sias and Roller, which ranged from Karamu's plans to take advantage of recent development efforts, to ways of serving the existing poor and working-class residents of the Fairfax neighborhood, speak to the diverse economic influences and social forces that are currently affecting and changing many urban African American communities.

When I asked Terrence Spivey how he thought the programming of Karamu reflected the specific nature of Cleveland's black neighborhoods and arts ecologies, he brought up August Wilson's play *Radio Golf* as an example of a play that mirrored the reality and challenges of the Fairfax neighborhood. "Though most of the black playwrights produced here [at Karamu] are not from Cleveland, their works reflect different slices of African American life such as domestic problems, police brutality, racism, gentrification. Works of August Wilson are popular, such as *Radio Golf*, which I staged at Ensemble Theatre. That play tackles gentrification. The theater patrons related [the play] to past and present goings on with Cleveland Clinic."[386] Like the fictional scenario depicted in *Radio Golf*, in Cleveland hopes for better opportunities and living conditions for African Americans are mixed with criticisms of gentrification and the displacement of current residents and businesses. In the case of Opportunity Corridor, the projected "pockets of vitality" created at various intersections along the boulevard and in the proposed green "bike and hike" spaces come at the expense of "63 homes and multiunit dwellings, sheltering 95 families," "13 companies," and one church, all of which will need to be relocated.[387] As a hundred-year resident of the city, Karamu and its leadership are in the difficult position of honoring the neighborhood's past, serving its current residents, and preparing to be a part of what will clearly be a somewhat different future. Hiring Roller as development director and aligning Karamu with recent trends toward arts-based economic development undoubtedly helped it to secure the $2 million grant from the Cleveland Foundation, $400,000 of which is earmarked for educational and community-engagement projects that will serve current youth and adult neighborhood residents. $1.6 million will fund the placemaking construction projects that may appeal to future and perhaps wealthier individuals in addition to Karamu's current clientele.[388] By forging these partnerships, Sias has succeeded in financially bolstering the institution, reporting in May 2019 that Karamu "achieved a $300,000 surplus in 2018 and expects to finish in the black on a $2.2 million operating budget."[389]

Karamu's history has shown it to be an incredibly resilient organization. It has weathered many storms, and the community it has created has repeatedly rallied to sustain it. The key to Karamu's longevity has been a mixture of innovative change at crucial points in its history combined with the cultivation of enduring relationships with its members, many of whom experienced Karamu as children and went on to become artists, patrons, and civic leaders in advantageous enough positions to be able to advocate for and enrich the organization through their time, talent, or financial resources. Writing about Karamu in his seminal text *The Impact of Race: Theatre and Culture*, Woodie King Jr. states:

> If we don't celebrate our past, our history, we cannot really understand or appreciate our future. If we cannot see or understand Karamu's contribution to the place we call Cleveland, Ohio, and to our country, we all are blind and in serious trouble. It was to institutions like Karamu that we looked in the past for that leadership; we most certainly are going to look to Karamu in the future. But what will the African American theatre of tomorrow be? And what will it be about?"[390]

Examining the accomplishments and challenges Karamu has experienced in its long history can help us honor the extraordinary achievements of this institution and also identify the areas in which the production of theater in America might become more equitable and more sustaining to individual African American artists, black communities, and the larger arts ecologies in which black theaters operate.

Chapter 2

✦

The Legacy of August Wilson
Black Theater in Pittsburgh

Easily the most recognized, produced, and lauded African American play-wright to date, August Wilson and his ten-play twentieth-century cycle loom mythically large over the city of Pittsburgh, his hometown. The Hill District, the black neighborhood in which Wilson grew up, serves as the setting for nine out of the ten plays in this famous series. Wilson sprinkled the geography of the neighborhood throughout these plays with references to Wiley, Bedford, and Centre Avenues, which figure prominently in his works. His Pittsburgh friends and neighbors also inspired many of his characters. For example, Wilson modeled the character of Troy Maxson, the protagonist of *Fences*, on Charley Burley, a prizefighter who was Wilson's neighbor during his childhood.[1] In addition to celebrating the people and places of Pittsburgh in his plays, Wilson also worked as a participant and champion of Pittsburgh's black theater institutions. Although he achieved unparalleled success on Broadway and in predominantly white, behemoth regional theaters, he remained committed to supporting the local black theaters of his hometown. Wilson recognized that sociological issues affect both the content and material conditions of production and patronage. He devoted a substantial amount of his professional capital to advocating for African American control over the means of theatrical productions involving black cultural material. His did this in myriad ways, most famously in his seminal speech *The Ground on Which I Stand* and by advocating for the hiring of black directors for the production of his plays and any film adaptations of his work.[2] His support and participation in Pittsburgh's African American theater institutions is a lesser-known component of his activism and legacy. The aim of this chapter is to rectify this by examining the history of the black theater institutions that were influenced by his participation and patronage. Looking at the history of these institutions and their relationship to the larger arts ecology of Pittsburgh reveals a largely grassroots, sociopolitically engaged practice of black theater that has combatted the persistence of racial inequalities and shaped the city by asserting the presence and artistic voices of the city's black residents.

Over one hundred years after the establishment of Pittsburgh's most famous museums, libraries, and symphonies, racial inequalities continue to persist in the city's expression and funding of the arts. Pittsburgh was one of the cities featured in the Helicon Collaborative's 2017 research study *Not Just Money* because Pittsburgh is among the top ten cities in America with the highest levels of giving to the arts. Helicon found that although culturally specific arts and cultural organizations make up 12 percent of the total nonprofit arts and culture organizations in Pittsburgh, they receive just 2 percent of the total foundation funding dedicated to this sector.[3] African Americans make up approximately 25 percent of the population of Pittsburgh, making this inequality that much more staggering. As recently as 2014, negative public comments in response to newspaper articles reporting on the financial troubles of the August Wilson Center exhibited the attitude that African American artistic practice should not receive any public financial support.[4] These often blatantly racist remarks ignore present and historic racial inequalities in arts funding and the pointed exclusion of African Americans from the city's artistic philanthropy over the course of many decades.[5]

The current arts ecology of Pittsburgh is tied to the historic footprint of steel and other heavy manufacturing industries and to several subsequent waves of urban redevelopment that until recently have not benefited and in many instances further victimized the city's African American population.[6] For decades, the charitable institutions and cultural foundations that were built from the industrial wealth of the city largely ignored the African American population that provided a significant portion of the labor that produced their wealth.[7] Although Pittsburgh has had a robust theatrical presence since its founding, segregationist policies entirely excluded African Americans from participating in the flagship performing arts institutions of the city until the mid-1950s.[8] Nonetheless, Pittsburgh has a rich history of African American theatrical practice. Important early twentieth-century African American dramatic groups such as the Olympians, the Kay Dramatic Club, the Urban Players, and the Negro Y Playhouse were supported through the 1920s, 1930s, and 1940s by local churches, women's clubs, and neighborhood branches of the Urban League and Centre Avenue YMCA.[9] These black theater practitioners were either entirely ignored or pointedly excluded by the greater theater and philanthropic community of Pittsburgh during the first half of the twentieth century. For example, the Olympians were barred from participating in the Drama League of Pittsburgh, despite multiple petitions for admittance.[10]

Notwithstanding these challenges, black theater in Pittsburgh continued. Following the neighborhood development model of the 1920s and 1930s, the most prominent theater group featuring African Americans during the 1940s was the Curtaineers, an interracial troupe operating out of the Irene Kaufmann Settlement House. This group produced theater in the Hill District from 1943 to 1958.[11] Much like Karamu House in Cleveland, the Curtaineers were supported by a settlement house originally funded and operated by white (in this case Jewish) neighborhood residents in a community center that became, like the neighborhood surrounding it, predominantly African American. The Curtaineers employed nontraditional casting practices designed to combat racial stereotypes.[12] The Freedom Readers, an interracial readers theater group established in 1965, was likewise dedicated to promoting integration and expressing the ethos of the civil rights movement.[13]

Although August Wilson would later develop an admiration for the work of previous generations of black theater practitioners in Pittsburgh, he was not aware of their practice when he founded Black Horizons Theatre with Rob Penny in 1968.[14] Because of the institutional longevity of Karamu House, there was more interaction between the different generations of black theater practitioners in Cleveland than there was in Pittsburgh. In Pittsburgh, there have been a greater number of black theater endeavors operating for shorter periods of time. August Wilson was involved in at least five of these institutions, each of which has revealed and contributed to the sociopolitical realities of the city of Pittsburgh in different ways.

Black Horizons

August Wilson began his artistic career as a poet, not a playwright. Wilson and his friends Rob Penny, Nick Flournoy, Chawley P. Williams, and Maisha Baton were part of a poetry collective that became increasingly more community based and politically active. Pittsburgh historian Laurence Glasco stated that these poets "called themselves 'Poets in the Centre Avenue Tradition' because they were writing poetry that reflected the atmosphere and the people on Centre Avenue. So, August wasn't the only one who was interested in the community and the people in the community as a source of something they could make into poetry and theater."[15] Rob Penny deeply admired Amiri Baraka, and like Baraka, became more explicitly political in both the content and performance of his poetry and playwriting as the 1960s wore on. Both Penny and Wilson gradually moved from poetry to theater, which Baraka touted at the time as a more immediate, revolutionary art form. Glasco described Penny's admiration for Baraka and the activist work he was doing in conjunction with his poetry and theater.

> Rob really moved August into black consciousness and black power in the midsixties. Baraka, who was Rob's idol, said they needed to shift from poetry into theater because theater is a more powerful way of reaching the masses and raising consciousness. . . . August remained thinking of himself primarily as a poet, but he was intrigued by Rob's entreaty that they should establish a theater that would be a consciousness-raising force in the black community.[16]

Fig. 2. Poets of the Centre Avenue tradition, backstage at Kelly's Bar, 1982. *Left to right,*
Chawley P. Williams, Rob Penny, August Wilson, Maisha Baton, and Nick Flournoy.
Photograph by Mark Clayton Southers for the *Pittsburgh Courier*. Courtesy of Mark
Clayton Southers.

In tandem with the concerns and actions of black power initiatives, Wilson
and Penny founded Black Horizons Theatre (BHT) in Pittsburgh in 1968
out of the need to blend artistic and political practice.[17] According to original company member and lead actor Sala Udin, BHT was a decidedly black
nationalist endeavor. As a young man, Udin had participated in the civil
rights movement as a freedom rider. When he returned to Pittsburgh, he was
involved in the black liberation movement as a community organizer and
activist. In a telephone interview, he described how the work of the theater
intersected with his activism.

> It was a political and civic instrument and institution first and an
> artistic institution secondarily. That's also true for those of us who
> were members of the theater. We were political first. We used theater
> as an instrument in our political work. We didn't start out being art-
> ists for the sake of being artists. We were political for the sake of
> black liberation, and we used theater in the service of that goal. I
> often have to explain that to people. Since August Wilson became
> such a recognized Broadway star, he gets mixed in with the arts world

as though he were initially or primarily an artist. He was initially and primarily an activist in the black liberation movement and recognized, as we all did, that theater enhanced our political work.[18]

Udin further articulated the function of poetry and later drama in the activist work of the black liberation movement of that time.

[The Centre Avenue poets] added a very strong component to the community meetings and political meetings whenever they were there. Our community meetings might open up with three or four poets, then we would go into the meat of the meeting, and then we would close with a couple poets. So, they became a part of the political organizing in that way. Eventually, as African consciousness increased, we began to integrate more African culture into our political work so rather than just poets, there might be poets and drumming and dancing and African clothing and African language. It became much more theatrical, artistic, and African.[19]

Elva Branson, who was a member of BHT and served as artistic director of the organization in its later years, similarly recalled the character of the early theater as "primarily political, associated with the university crowd, and the Pan African nationalist movement of the 60's and 70's. The impetus for our work was consciousness-raising within the black community, promoting solidarity, instilling pride in our collective American experience as well as our African heritage (of which most of us were just becoming aware)."[20] It is clear from these testimonials that the theater was a multidisciplinary expression of black liberation ideology that combined poetry, theater, dance, and music. Penny's plays in particular blended conventional dramaturgy with musical interludes and stylized movements that were organized into "pulses" rather than scenes.[21]

Another way the founding of the theater connected to the Black Power movement was through the support it received from the University of Pittsburgh's Black Action Society (BAS). During the 1960s and early 1970s, the black nationalist community, BHT, and the Black Studies Department and Student Action Society at the University of Pittsburgh were all intertwined. Sala Udin described his participation in each of these groups and how they were all related to one another.

I was an organizer and community leader of the black nationalist/ black liberation movement during that time, during 1968 and 1969. I was closely involved with the black student organization on the campus of the University of Pittsburgh, which was largely composed of the Black Studies Program [later known as the Black Studies Department] and Black Action Society. The Black Action Society was the student body organization. At that time, there was a very strong integration of the movement in the community and the black community on campus. That was because it was the black liberation movement in the community that approached the university and demanded the creation of the Black Studies Program and the black student organization. So, when they were finally created, the black liberation movement from the community was present every day and very much involved in the organizing and shaping of both the Black Studies Program and the Black Action Society.[22]

The BAS provided much of the financial support, audience base, and company membership for BHT. Curtiss Porter, emeritus chancellor of Penn State Greater Allegheny, was one of the student leaders of BAS during the late 1960s and early 1970s. He recounted the founding of the theater and its association with the student group.

> With the success of the BAS being allocated a budget from the university, and my own election by my peers in BAS to "Program Committee Chairman," I saw the control of my budget as an opportunity to raise awareness generally on campus and in the community by bringing in speakers and artists, and we brought in many. . . . One of the first artists we sponsored was LeRoi Jones/Imamu Amiri Baraka. He was breaking new ground in combining the poetic, the musical and the theatrical in a winding and enthralling theatrical performance art. . . . We also brought Ed Bullins who was beginning to gain notice as [part of] a new generation of "Black" playwrights. There was at this time a general discussion throughout the national Black community, about a new Black Consciousness, a new "Black aesthetic." [Rob] Penny, [August] Wilson, and I had long conversations on these matters. When we hosted Baraka, Barbara Ann Teer, and Ed Bullins—they stayed in the community, at our homes and we talked theatre.[23]

According to Porter, exciting guest visits from the nation's top black theater professionals inspired the BAS to support the founding of a black nationalist theater in Pittsburgh.

> When the opportunity came, with the resources at hand to establish a theatre institution, I, along with two of my BAS brothers sought out Rob [Penny] and August [Wilson] to begin the conversation in earnest about developing a Black theatre group that would operate within the framework of this developing Black aesthetic. It turns out this would become the Black Horizons Theatre. Officially, myself, Anthony "Tony" Fountain, the Political Action Committee Chairman of the BAS, and E. Philip McKain, met with Rob Penny and August

Wilson at a Community Action Program (CAP) office on Chauncey
Street in Pittsburgh's fabled Hill District, where Rob worked, to discuss and agree to establish a theatre that would be funded by BAS
program funds. I thought to call it "Black Horizons Theatre." Rob
thought he could secure A. Leo Weil school auditorium for our performances though his CAP connections, and he did. A Leo Weil school
was the first home of the BHT which perfectly suited our purposes of
being of the University and in the Community.[24]

As indicated by Udin and Porter, the theater was supported by a combination
of black nationalists from the community and university student activists and
artists. This was by design and adhered to the community-based focus of the
black arts movement.

The support that BHT received from the BAS and Black Studies Department at the University of Pittsburgh greatly helped to sustain the theater and
the artists involved in its operations. After the establishment of the Black
Studies Department, several company members became departmental faculty
and vice versa, including the playwright Rob Penny and the choreographer
Bob Johnson. Johnson was an original cast member of the musical *Hair*.
Shortly after he was hired by the University of Pittsburgh, he founded the
dance troupe Black Theatre Dance Ensemble. Johnson also worked as a
theater director in addition to being a choreographer and founded several
other theater and dance companies including Theatre Urge, which operated
in Pittsburgh during the late 1970s and early 1980s. Johnson became a friend
and frequent collaborator with August Wilson and Rob Penny and directed
several successful productions of *Jitney* in Pittsburgh in collaboration with
Wilson in 1982 and 1983.[25]

Like many other theaters founded during the black arts movement, BHT
was inspired by the manifestos and plays published in the 1968 "Black Theatre" special issue of the *Tulane Drama Review*. Laurence Glasco stated,

It was fortuitous that the *Tulane Drama Review*'s special black theater edition with Larry Neal's famous essay had just come out; the
plays that were included in that edition were already there, ready
to be staged. In addition, Rob went home and knocked off a couple
of plays of his own. During that first year they put on plays out of
that *Tulane Drama Review* special edition, and they also put on Rob
Penny's plays, *Dance of the Blues Dead* and *Deeds of Blackness*.[26]

Ideologically and practically, BHT was a theater of the black arts movement,
self-articulated as part of the cultural arm of the black liberation movement.
The founding of black theaters and black studies departments during the
1960s and 1970s were linked in that they were both part of a larger effort
to create, as Larry Neal so eloquently wrote in the 1968 special issue of

the *Tulane Drama Review*, "a cultural revolution in art and ideas."[27] The Black Studies Department at Pitt directly challenged an education system exclusively based on European cultural patrimony at the expense and neglect of the cultural patrimony of a quarter of the city's residents. The founding of BHT was another specific response to the paucity of African American cultural representation in American arts and education. The Black Studies Department and BAS enthusiastically supported the theater because the students saw the theater as an extension of the consciousness-raising ideologies they were studying in class and an avenue that enabled them to put those ideas into practice outside the classroom in the community.

Although BHT was inspired by and produced well-known plays from the black arts movement, such as Amiri Baraka's *Black Mass*, the theater's enduring dramaturgical legacy is undoubtedly the local focus of its original work. The simultaneous development of local playwrights and the exploration of an artistic voice crafted specifically in reaction to life in Pittsburgh's black neighborhoods is what makes BHT's dramaturgy distinctive. Rob Penny and Curtiss Porter wrote several original plays that were included in the early years of the theater such as Penny's *Dance of the Blues Dead* and *Deeds of Blackness* (produced during the first season) and Porter's *Evolution to Revolution* (produced during the second season). This emphasis on depicting the minutiae of black life in Pittsburgh came out of Wilson and Penny's participation in the Centre Avenue Poets. Exploring and celebrating the specificity of Pittsburgh's black neighborhoods and their cultural life remains a defining feature of black drama in Pittsburgh today. The 2018 site-specific production of August Wilson's play *King Hedley II* at his childhood home on Bedford Avenue and the cultivation and showcasing of local playwrights by the Pittsburgh Playwrights Theatre Company are two examples of this enduring legacy.[28]

Located in the Hill District and supported by the University of Pittsburgh, BHT actively sought to engage the local black community in several other neighborhoods and locations throughout the city. Elva Branson clarified that in addition to the elementary school in the Hill District, BHT performed in a variety of different venues and tried to stay as mobile and flexible as possible. "[Our work] spoke to the community via whatever venue was available. We performed a lot at festivals, did street theater, went into bars up and down Centre Avenue and did impromptu improvisational theater that reflected on the issues of the times. We traveled to colleges in the tri-state area for their black arts festivals, which was also a new idea, born of the times."[29] While focused on the issues and culture of the Hill District, BHT also sought to make connections with other black communities. Laurence Glasco recalled that BHT was "very aware of what was happening elsewhere. They would go to Chicago, they'd go to Cleveland, they'd go to Newark and pick up ideas. They really felt they were part of a broader process."[30] Curtiss Porter remembers a significant trip the company took to Oberlin College, which was financed by the BAS, as well as several international undertakings the company made. He identified Bayo Oduneye, who served as the artistic director of the National Troupes of Nigeria from 1991 to 2000, as an important connection between BHT and African artists active in the Pan-African movement of the 1960s and 1970s.[31] Porter stated:

> Mr. Oduneye worked with Black Horizons Theatre. He was instrumental in introducing Rob Penny and myself to Nigeria's iconic playwright Wole Soyinka, whom we met in Nigeria. Mr. Oduneye worked on sets with BHT while studying at Carnegie Mellon (then Carnegie Tech). In a Black Studies sponsored trip to Nigeria and Tanzania, Bayo served to guide us to make connections with African theatres and universities. BHT was well ahead its time, having Pan African connections with theatre [makers] on the African continent and in the Caribbean. Through Bayo and Soyinka, we also got closer to Barbara Ann Teer's National Black Theatre, which at the time, was deeply connected to Soyinka and other Nigerian artists, notably, Twins Seven Seven [the renowned painter and musician] and Fela Ransome-Kuti [the renowned musician]. It was a heady time![32]

These recollections indicate that although the theater was based in and interested in expressing the black life and culture of Pittsburgh, it saw itself as part of a larger national and international practice of black theater and it participated in black theater endeavors in other cities with sizeable black populations in the United States and abroad.

Structurally, BHT operated as a collective, with members serving and rotating through multiple roles. Sala Udin was the lead actor and political organizer and also served for a time as codirector with Curtiss Porter. Rob Penny was the resident playwright and also directed on several occasions. Curtiss Porter wrote plays and operated as producer and the company's main liaison to the University of Pittsburgh and its resources. Although August Wilson was the de facto director from 1968 to 1969, Laurence Glasco states that he was referred to as "Mister Everything" and also worked on costumes, sets, and lighting, in addition to directing and soliciting funds.[33] This experience undoubtedly helped Wilson later in his career when he transitioned to professional playwriting. He knew the mechanics of theatrical production because he had participated in every aspect of theater making at BHT. He later used that knowledge to craft plays that took full advantage of the theatrical medium.

As was the case with many other artistic institutions founded during the black arts movement, BHT was generally distrustful of "white money."[34] In his 1968 essay "The Black Arts Movement," Larry Neal provided a cautionary tale regarding dependency on government and foundation funding by detailing the withdrawal of financial support from Amiri Baraka's Black

Arts Repertoire Theatre School by what Neal described as "War on Poverty bureaucrats."[35] In Pittsburgh, Sala Udin recalled that "we were inclined to operate on our own resources. . . . We operated out of our own pockets and the little bit of money we were able to hustle out of tickets sales, which we were determined to keep very inexpensive. Therefore, ticket sales contributed only a small amount to the cost of running the theater."[36] The fact that BHT largely self-funded their theater initiatives and kept ticket sales purposely low demonstrates their commitment to keeping art accessible and insepa- rable from the community, a fundamental tenet of the black arts movement. In keeping with these principles, August Wilson and others would try to aug- ment ticket sales by soliciting contributions from local black businesses and churches. One such appeal by Bob Johnson is quoted in a 1970 news feature in which he states, "The black bourgeoisie, the black middle-class man must come forth and support the culture in order for it to be alive."[37] For the most part, however, these contributions were small and sporadic. The do- it-yourself model of operating and fundraising was difficult to sustain and led to burnout among the most active company members. By 1969 August Wilson was exhausted and relinquished the directorship of BHT to Frank Floyd Hightower, a photographer and playwright, who ran the company for a year before moving to Philadelphia.[38] Sala Udin and Curtiss Porter then ran the company until 1972, when they invited Elva Branson to become artistic director.[39]

Because Branson was one of the few members of the collective with formal theater training, she was deeply respected by the rest of the group. She had been a theater major at Pitt and found in BHT "an outlet to work and grow under the influence of such seasoned artists and forward thinkers as Rob Penny, Sala Udin, and Curtiss Porter."[40] Curtiss Porter remembers her direc- tion of Rob Penny's play *Centre Avenue: A Trip* during the 1970–71 season, which was coproduced with the University of Pittsburgh, as one of the high- lights of the company's repertoire. Porter stated that this production was the "first all-Black casting of a play at the University's theatre. It was produced under the auspices of the DBCERD [Department of Black Community Edu- cation Research and Development]/BLACK STUDIES."[41] Branson described this production as "a favorite" and noted that the collaboration between BHT and the University of Pittsburgh was "a precursor to [the establishment of] Kuntu [Repertory] Theatre."[42] *Centre Avenue: A Trip* celebrated the main commercial thoroughfare of the Hill District as the heart of the neighbor- hood's black community and used the kinds of jazz motifs and pulses for which Penny was well-known.

As part of her artistic vision for the company, Branson tried to broaden the focus of the work done at BHT and include a wider variety of artistic perspec- tives. "[When] I became the Artistic and Executive Director of the company, I had the opportunity to bring in Claude Purdy, Dr. Maisha Baton and August Wilson [who had previously taken a hiatus from the company], all of whom had a broader artistic vision and experience that influenced me as an artist as well as the direction in which I took the company."[43] Maisha Baton was a poet who had been active with the Centre Avenue Poets before becoming involved in BHT as a playwright.[44] Claude Purdy had studied experimental theater in Europe and Africa previous to his arrival in Pittsburgh in 1968 and would spend his career directing a variety of works by both black and white playwrights across the country in black and regional theaters.[45] In Pittsburgh he acted and directed for BHT and later City Theatre as well as the Pittsburgh Public Theater. Branson introduced Wilson to Purdy while at BHT, and the two became lifelong friends and collaborators.[46]

The programming of BHT began to decline by the mid-1970s as several black theater initiatives began in other neighborhoods and many members such as Branson, Purdy, and Hightower moved out of Pittsburgh to pursue their careers in other cities. In 1972, August Wilson, Rob Penny, Ron Pitts, and Mary Bradley founded the Ujima Theatre in the Hazelwood neighborhood after Penny and Wilson were invited to organize theater programming at a local community center.[47] Pitts, who went on to found the Ujima Theatre of Columbus, Ohio, describes the history of the original Pittsburgh company as follows: "Pitts, Wilson, Penny and another friend, Mary Bradly [sic] began Ujima in an effort to raise money for community recreation activities in the Hazelwood housing projects. They solicited and received help from the history department of the University of Pittsburgh, and with that collaboration, put on a drama production that raised $10,000. Ujima's success helped to quell some of the negative unrest in the community at that time, particularly among youths."[48] "Ujima" is a Swahili word that is translated into English as either "life" or "collective work and responsibility" and is one of the seven principles of Kwanza.[49] The Ujima Theatre was intended to be very much like BHT, with a focus on black nationalism but operating under the umbrella of community center programming. Although committed to community action and empowerment, Penny and Wilson had some growing pains in their new role as youth mentors. For example, Laurence Glasco recalled a series of disagreements between Wilson, Penny, and the youth they were hired to direct.

> August and Rob asked the kids, "What would you like to put on?"
> The kids wanted *Superfly*, which was popular at the time. Rob and
> August were not at all interested in *Superfly*; it was everything they
> hated—it certainly lacked the sort of black consciousness they wanted
> to instill. But the kids were insistent, so Rob and August made a deal
> with the kids. They said, "OK, we'll do *Superfly*, but after that you've
> got to be in the plays that we want to put on," which were their black
> nationalist plays and the plays that Rob was writing.[50]

Penny adapted the plot of *Superfly* to include a stronger antidrug message, and Wilson cast youth from the community center in the major roles. Pitts cites this production as the beginning of his theatrical career.[51] The popularity and financial success of *Superfly* underwrote the rest of the youth programming of the center. Pittsburgh Playwrights Theatre's artistic director Mark Clayton Southers remembers having a conversation with August Wilson about this experience when he asked for Wilson's advice on generating audience interest.

> I said to him, "August, how do we get our people in here? How do we get butts in the seats?" and he said, "Yay, well, you know, we were doing stuff over in Hazelwood, we wrote a play called *Superfly* and everybody came out. The place was packed to the rafters, and then we would pass out flyers for our next play, something we really wanted them to come see." So basically, they had to do stuff that appealed to pop culture to get the people in the door and then say, "Hey, by the way, come back and see this piece next time." That's what he and Rob Penny attempted to do to get an audience.[52]

The production of *Superfly* accomplished two things: it raised a significant amount of money for the community center, and it provided an opportunity for Wilson and Penny to advertise their own plays and works that were more reflective of their own artistic aesthetic.

Unfortunately, the black nationalist aesthetic Wilson and Penny were committed to was much less well received than *Superfly* had been. Glasco cites audience lack of interest in the company's original plays as the reason for Penny and Wilson's eventual abandonment of the Ujima Theatre. "*Superfly* was a huge success. . . . Then they put on their own plays and everybody hated them . . . they thought they were boring. They were these political message plays, and the audience didn't want it. August and Rob were thoroughly frustrated by that, so they ended up quitting."[53] Glasco links this learning experience to Wilson's professional development as a world-class playwright.

> I think August learned something from that, that the Baraka-type theater doesn't cut it with the public. It works for a small, select group of people that are already cultural nationalists or oriented in that direction, but for the broader community, it just doesn't work. I think that one lesson he learned was that there wasn't a market for agit-prop theater. There was a market when they catered it toward college students who were already primed toward a black consciousness, but just to go into the larger community, it didn't work.[54]

Glasco suggests that Wilson retained his commitment to black power ideology but was able to create a dramaturgy based primarily in realism that was more accessible to a broader audience than the abstract, political theater that was popular during his time at BHT. Glasco also referenced Wilson's play

Two Trains Running as another example of the difficulties Wilson personally encountered while promoting black nationalist ideas and activities during this time period.

> When Sterling hands out flyers for the Malcolm X rally, Holloway dismisses him by saying, "I remember when Malcolm didn't have but twelve followers." And, when Sterling says the rally aims to promote black power, Memphis launches into a tirade about the foolishness of "black power niggers" who "don't know what they doing themselves." That incident is based on August's experience handing out flyers for the Malcolm X rally at the New Granada Theater in February 1968.[55]

In this play and many of his later works, Wilson includes a variety of political perspectives in an interwoven ensemble-based realism that was much more successful with his audiences than his black nationalist plays and poetry had been. It is the multiple perspectives and attitudes toward the political ideology of black nationalism combined with the fine attention to realism extrapolated from his personal experience in *Two Trains Running* that provide much of the nuance and artistry of this play. The play is also a reflection of the history of Pittsburgh during the 1960s and the period when Wilson was active with both the black liberation movement and BHT.

By the time Elva Branson took over the leadership of BHT in 1972, "The 'revolutionary theater' concept was giving way to more of a simple artistic reflection of the black experience, which I loved. Think Ed Bullins and August Wilson. More *A Raisin in the Sun* than *The Dutchman*, if you follow me."[56] Branson's comments suggest that toward the end of BHT's tenure, the politics of the company had expanded to include a wider variety of expressions of black subjectivity more in line with the content of many African American theaters today. Branson and Purdy left Pittsburgh in 1974 to pursue their theater careers in Los Angeles, at which point BHT faltered.

It is clear from these first-person accounts that BHT was central to the assertion of African American rights and representation in Pittsburgh during the late 1960s and early 1970s. From the creation of a Black Studies Department at the University of Pittsburgh to the use of that department to bring black art to the campus and broader community, the individuals that were part of BHT created new opportunities for Pittsburgh's black residents to stake a larger claim in the city's educational system, assert and cultivate the city's African American artistic and cultural resources, and use those resources in service of political transformation and efforts toward the achievement of greater representational power. Clearly influenced by the major players of the black arts movement and by New York artists in particular, Wilson, Penny, and the other artists from BHT also saw the value of their own local culture and created an enduring body of work specifically focused on Pittsburgh.

They both represented and participated in the artistic, educational, and political work that transformed their city and asserted the presence, power, history, and culture of Pittsburgh's black communities.

Kuntu Repertory Theatre

By 1974 BHT and Ujima Theatre had exhausted the energy and financial resources of their remaining core members. It was therefore quite fortuitous that Dr. Vernell A. Lillie was hired as a faculty member in the Black Studies Department at the University of Pittsburgh. Sala Udin recalls that

> By [19]74 we were about broke. So, when Vernell Lillie came to town and said that she intended to begin a theater company . . . it allowed us to let Black Horizons die, knowing that a black theater company was going to continue the work. . . . By that time, I was also burnt out personally. The theater was taking a lot more time out of my political activities than I would have preferred so I was glad to take a rest from the theater work and declined to get very much involved with Kuntu Repertory Theatre. I certainly had no intention of being as involved in Kuntu as I was in Black Horizons, so I was glad that Vernell Lillie came to town.[57]

Lillie was able to secure free performance space from the university and subsequently founded Kuntu Repertory Theatre. Her colleague, Rob Penny, whose plays she greatly admired, served as the company's playwright-in-residence. Penny's presence in a leadership and founding position for both BHT and Kuntu Repertory Theatre provided a substantive link and continuity of purpose and aesthetics between the two organizations.

In October 1974, Vernell Lillie directed a stage reading of Rob Penny's play *Little Willie Armstrong Jones* for an invited audience at the Department of Black Community Education Research and Development.[58] The following April, Kuntu Repertory Theatre was launched with a fully staged version of the play as its first official production, which took place in the Stephen Foster Memorial auditorium.[59] The Stephen Foster Memorial building, built in 1937, is dedicated to the archive and memorial of the nineteenth-century Pittsburgher who became the first professional American songwriter by making his name and fortune composing songs predominantly in the genre of blackface minstrelsy. The Foster building houses the University of Pittsburgh's two main theater spaces. In his essay "Blackface Minstrelsy and Jacksonian Ideology," Alexander Saxton writes that Foster should be considered one of the four founders of blackface minstrelsy in America given his role as the "major white innovator of minstrel music."[60] In "Whitewashing Blackface Minstrelsy in American College Textbooks," Joseph Byrd described Foster's treatment of slave life in his musical compositions as "both sentimental and highly misinformed," noting that Foster's hugely popular success made him a "master painter of a land that never was, where cheerful darkies and benevolent masters lived—literally—in harmony."[61] The original second verse of Foster's "Oh! Susanna," a song still frequently taught to schoolchildren today, includes the lines "I jumped abroad de telegraph / And trabbled down de riber/De lectric fluid magnified/And killed five hundred nigger."[62] These lyrics illustrate how minstrel songs perpetuated racial hatred and indulged in fantasies of racial violence against African Americans in addition to romanticizing the institution of slavery. In recognition of its racist content, the city of Pittsburgh removed a statue featuring Foster towering over a grinning barefoot black man playing a banjo, who was referred to as "Uncle Ned" (a character in one of Foster's songs), from the park across the street from the memorial in 2018.[63] The fact that the Stephen Foster Memorial building still honors a man who profited off of exploiting black stereotypes, that Kuntu Repertory Theatre performed in this space for over thirty years, and that the Theater Department of the University of Pittsburgh still uses this building today reveals a shocking and abiding lack of racial sensitivity and restorative justice. It also serves as a particularly vivid example of how African American artistic practice often abuts and rubs against white performance practices and spaces invested in the erasure and distortion of African Americans' lives and experiences.

Despite and clearly in opposition to the legacy of the name on the building out of which Kuntu operated, the company endeavored to perform multidimensional black drama created by and directed toward Pittsburgh's African American population. In his review of Kuntu's inaugural production of *Little Willie Armstrong Jones* for the *New Pittsburgh Courier*, Ron Suber described the play's titular character as "a nightclub owner in the Hill District who is [too] hung up in his own dream of himself, by himself, and for himself for a loving marriage."[64] Donus Crawford played the title role, and Tredessa Dalton portrayed Willie's long-suffering wife Estelle. Like *Centre Avenue: A Trip*, *Little Willie Armstrong Jones* delighted audiences by dramatizing the hopes, dreams, and problems of Hill District residents. The three-hour play included jazzy riffs and movement segments choreographed by Bob Johnson. In an article covering the 1977 remount of the play, Ethel M. Parris described the structure of the play as "arranged in three movements and pulses. The action is spontaneous and grows out of the frustrations and moods of Little Willie, and the complexities centering around his life: his relationship with his pregnant wife, Estelle; his mother, brother; friends and enemies."[65] *Little Willie Armstrong Jones* continued BHT's practice of mixing drama, music, poetry, and politics. The play was dedicated to several former members of BHT including Sala Udin, Curtiss Porter, and August Wilson.[66]

Through his collaboration with Lillie, Rob Penny found an artistic home that supported the development and production of his work for the rest of his life. Kuntu would average one to two productions of Penny's plays each year for the entirety of its thirty-eight-year existence. An underappreciated contributor to the black arts movement, Penny's body of work includes over three hundred poems and thirty plays, many of which were staged at other influential theaters of the time including Spirit House, New Federal Theatre, and ETA: Creative Arts, in addition to being produced locally by BHT, Ujima Theatre, and Kuntu Repertory Theatre.[67] Like August Wilson, Penny's work focused on the African American residents of Pittsburgh. Unlike Wilson, Penny continued to live and work in the community that artistically inspired him. In Kuntu, Penny found what few playwrights ever do, a nurturing and permanent artistic home that allowed his work to grow and flourish. Given the fact that 75 percent of the plays produced in America are written by white male playwrights, it is a tremendous asset for African American playwrights to find theater institutions where they can establish an ongoing relationship that results in multiple production and development opportunities.[68] Providing substantive playwright development opportunities and nurturing the creation of plays that specifically focus on Pittsburgh is an important legacy of the Kuntu Repertory Theatre.

In addition to producing the works of Penny and other local writers, Vernell Lillie took a particular interest in exploring African performance practices and theories. Paul Carter Harrison's seminal collection *Kuntu Drama: Plays of the African Continuum* was published in 1974 and served as inspiration for the aesthetic Lillie envisioned and cultivated. In his preface to *Kuntu Drama*, Oliver Jackson writes, "The play is the ritualized context of reality. . . . In this theater there is no separation between audience and actors. The mode is the event."[69] In her 1977 interview with Ethel Parris, Lillie paraphrased Jackson by stating, "The concept of Kuntu in theater is that the audience and performers act as one. The audience will respond verbally to situations that they experience, that are performed by the actors; audience become one with performers."[70] Here Lillie associates the common practice of black audiences "talking back" and verbally engaging with the action on stage as it unfolds with the African-inspired theories of dramaturgy put forth by Jackson and Harrison. In 1979, Penny and Lillie self-published *Kuntu Magazine*, for which Lillie wrote an essay further defining her use and understanding of the concept of kuntu. She cited the works of Janheinz Jahn, Oliver Jackson, and Paul Carter Harrison in her explanation. After glossing each of the previously mentioned authors' works, Lillie described kuntu as "the event rather than the play, or the art object or the poetry. . . . It uses cultural traditions drawn from the African continuum. Kuntu employs the power of the word, images, and sound to change, to reveal, and to support Black life styles and systems. It is an action modality."[71] Lillie strove to put into practice Harrison's urging that "there is a future for the black theater when we begin to accept Africa as the source that gives expression to our walk/dance, talk/song."[72] At Kuntu, Lillie developed a form of theater self-consciously modeled on African performance traditions rather than Western concepts of the well-made play. The theater produced on Kuntu's stage reflected "the cultural tradition of Africa in which the artistic creation in dance/movement, drama, music, visual arts, and words are entwined as a single unit. The aesthetic and philosophical base of Kuntu drama flows from the mores, rituals, and traditions of West Africa, Nubian, Kush, and Ancient Kemet (Egypt)."[73] In this sense Kuntu continued the effort common to many theaters of the black arts era to create a stage reality grounded in African and African American culture in form as well as in content.

Lillie thought Rob Penny's work was "an excellent example of Paul Carter Harrison's description of Kuntu drama" and worked tirelessly to put Harrison's theories into practice in the work produced under Kuntu Repertory Theatre's umbrella.[74] Shortly before her retirement, Lillie expanded upon these ideas in an article that was published on the theater's website.

> The accomplishment that Dr. Vernell Lillie is most proud of is the development of the Kuntu Canon of literature. The Kuntu Canon consists of literature that has several dimensions, including the absence of a single protagonist and antagonist, the co-existence of humor and seriousness and the presentation of (past, present, and future) as a single unit. The Kuntu Canon seeks to capture the essence of Bantu and West African culture through the implementation of a structure around a community that is responsible for defining the essence of life, enforcing what has been set forth as the rituals and traditions of this culture, and preserving these traditions so that they may be passed from one generation to the next.[75]

This detailed dramaturgy explicitly differentiated itself from dominant forms of European theater, for example, from the legacy of Aristotle's *Poetics* in European-based dramatic literature with its formal proscription against the mixing of comedy and tragedy.[76] Kuntu literature also rejected much of American literature's focus on a single protagonist and the much-codified conventions of "the hero's journey."[77] In Kuntu dramatic literature, "Every person in the story has a story which is told in the work, not just the story of the protagonist and the antagonist."[78] This description demonstrates a commitment to an ensemble approach explicitly tied to the theater's community-strengthening aims. "The mission of Kuntu is to examine Black life from social, political and historical perspectives and to highlight the aspects of theater that both entertain and educate, moving actors and audience members to personal growth and social change."[79] In this respect, Kuntu followed two of the primary precepts of the black arts movement, namely, that black artists should look to African forms for artistic inspiration and that the art created should always be in service of community building.

The community that Kuntu Repertory Theatre created included members of all ages and abilities. In an article with the *Pittsburgh Post-Gazette*, Sala

Udin stated, "Some people thought Kuntu wasn't professional because it primarily used students as acting and directing personnel."[80] The theater defined its company membership as follows: "Kuntu's diverse membership includes students from area high schools and colleges, as well as community members and professional theatre artists."[81] Labeling Kuntu a semiprofessional or amateur theater misses the point of its mission and relies upon the strict separation of professional and nonprofessional theater that was contrary to the community-based, utilitarian, and Afrocentric ethos of the company. Kuntu worked with students but also with many professional artists such as Lillie, Penny, Esther Rolle, Mark Clayton Southers, and Joyce Meggerson-Moore.[82] Part of Kuntu's mission was to advance the careers of professional African American artists, particularly playwrights, but also to provide artistic training and performance opportunities to African American students and others in the community. "Beyond its main stage programs, Kuntu is anchored in this community through ten to twenty touring productions of plays and collages for campus groups and [visits] to colleges, universities, community organizations, social service centers and state and federal prisons. . . . Kuntu offers free acting classes throughout the year to students, the community, and theatre professionals."[83] The deliberate mixing of ages, abilities, and skill sets among participants in Kuntu's programming reveals a commitment to the community-building work that was so important to black institutions during the black arts movement. The primacy of the education programs of many contemporary black theater companies is part of the legacy of this commitment.

As a community service, Kuntu also offered "psychodrama workshops for the training of actors, teachers, social workers, and as a strategy for the social growth of seniors and children."[84] Lillie was known as an expert in the use of psychodrama as a form of social work. She described the methodology for her course Social Growth through Psychodrama at the University of Pittsburgh as follows:

> It's an action modality. A way of teaching literature and life experience through tools developed by J.L. Moreno. . . . Moreno developed these tools in Vienna when he was a student of Freud. He was opposed to the Freudian method and he was watching young kids in the park. If you really think about it, your kids do psychodrama all the time. It's an action way of looking at your issues. You bring the characters that are in your life and you interact with them. . . . My primary use of psychodrama is teaching literature and my secondary use is to teach theatre. . . . My other use of it is to assist social workers and how they read individuals. . . . We learn from observing others so why not [use these observations to] teach us how to interact in terms of intra and interpersonal skills. Why not teach ways that we can practice making decisions and implementing decisions and problem solving?[85]

Psychodrama was used as a tool in many of the black theaters of the 1970s and 1980s including Penumbra Theatre Company in St. Paul, Minnesota, and Living Stage Theatre Company in Washington, DC.[86] As such, Kuntu was part of a larger practice of black theatrical production during that time that focused on the intersection of art, social work, and group therapy.

During the 1970s and 1980s, Vernell Lillie, Rob Penny, and Bob Johnson all created formidable theatrical events and performances under the auspices of the University of Pittsburgh's Black Studies Department. A brief gloss of some of the other black theater endeavors of the 1970s and 1980s in Pittsburgh gives some idea of the rich cultural and artistic climate of Pittsburgh during this period. Bob Johnson's company Theatre Urge ran alongside of and sometimes in collaboration with Kuntu Repertory Theatre in the 1970s and early 1980s. Notable Theatre Urge productions included a series of one-act plays produced in 1976 that featured *The Owl Killer*, by Phillip Hayes Dean, directed by August Wilson; *Baltimore*, by Anna Deveare Smith, directed by Bob Johnson; and *Hello Out There* by William Saroyan, also directed by Bob Johnson. The 1977 Theatre Urge production of *The Fabulous Miss Marie* by Ed Bullins, directed by Bob Johnson, was also a hit. In June 1981, Bob Johnson directed *Black Happening* by Kelly Marie Berry along with *Tears, the Living Children* by Maisha Baton. *Black Happening* featured Vernell Lillie in the role of Mama and Linda Wharton in the role of Jessie. In her playwright's notes, Berry stated that her inspiration to write the play came out of frustration over the lack of complexity in the portrayal of black women characters onstage.[87] The artists involved in these productions show that there was considerable overlap among BHT, Kuntu Repertory Theatre, and Theatre Urge.

The 1980s also featured a number of black theater achievements and activities in Pittsburgh that overlapped with the artistic personnel and aesthetics of Kuntu Repertory Theatre. For example, the Wilkinsburg Arts Council established the Wilkinsburg Arts Theatre in 1986. Although not explicitly a black theater company, many of the productions were written, directed, and performed by black artists. Notable productions included Ossie Davis's *Purlie Victorious* (1988), several annual productions of Langston Hughes's *Black Nativity* during the late 1980s and early 1990s, Lonne Elder III's *Ceremonies in Dark Old Men* (1989), Douglas Turner Ward's *Happy Ending* and *Day of Absence* (1990), and Ntozake Shange's *for colored girls who have considered suicide when the rainbow is enuf* (1993). Prominent local black actors in Wilkinsburg Arts Theatre productions included John Wanamaker, Milton Thompson, Ron Pitts, Bob Gore, Elva Branson, Deborah Norrell, Cheryl El, Victoria Bey, and Linda Hunt. Many of these artists were also active in both BHT and Kuntu.[88]

Under the umbrella of the Allegheny Repertory Theatre, Bob Johnson and Beryl Berry codirected Pittsburgh's first production of August Wilson's play *Jitney* in 1982. Featuring Sala Udin, Curtiss Porter, Ron Pitts, Milton E. Thompson, James R. Darby, Montae Russell, and Gwendolyn Perry, the play was "a smash hit."[89] In Christopher Applegate's review, "Allegheny Rep's Latest Gamble Pays Off," Applegate writes:

> Co-directors Bob Johnson (of the Pitt Black Studies faculty) and Beryl Berry have latched onto the truth in Wilson's writing and guided their fine cast through the script with an unerring hand. And the cast, incredibly enough, glides through the emotionally demanding play without so much as the faintest glimmer of dishonest staginess. It seems unfair to single out individual actors in such a tight, consistent ensemble company, but Sala Udin's Becker (the owner of the cab company) is compassionate, complex, and wonderfully human. Milton E. Thompson Jr. is a scene stealer as the argumentative and unpredictable Turnbo, and Curtis [sic] Porter brings quiet dignity and magnetic stage presence to Doub, one of the drivers.[90]

Wilson attended the November 12 and 13 productions and participated in the postshow "Playwright forum."[91] Due to the great success of the 1982 production, Bob Johnson and Berry remounted the play in 1983 under the auspices of "Beryl Berry Productions."[92] Claude Purdy replaced Sala Udin as Becker, and Greg Kinney and Tony McElroy portrayed Doub and Booster. The rest of the original cast remained the same. Covering the second production of *Jitney* for the *Pittsburgh Courier*, Timothy Cox wrote, "In *Jitney*, you get the opportunity to witness a real-life situation, presented by actors who lay it on you in a straight-forward manner. Unlike TV or some movies, they talk like black folks really talk—not super-cool or like Caucasian clones. *Jitney* IS for real."[93] It is clear from these reviews that Bob Johnson and Berry's production of *Jitney* provided black Pittsburghers with the pleasure of seeing one of their neighborhoods dramatically represented and the culture of 1970s Pittsburgh expertly rendered by Wilson's rising star through the talents of his friends and artistic collaborators.

Kuntu Repertory Theatre also collaborated with leading black theater practitioners from other cities. For example, Woodie King Jr. and the New Federal Theatre began to work with Kuntu in the 1980s. New Federal produced Rob Penny's play *Who Loves the Dancer?* in New York in 1982 under the direction of Shauneille Perry. Penny's blending of a variety of artistic forms—theater, dance, and music—is evident in Mel Gussow's review of the production for the *New York Times*.

> Deep in the second act . . . Mr. [Giancarlo] Esposito releases his emotions—and lithe body—in a dance, gradually building into an intuitive expression of his free creative spirit. When dealing with an artist on stage, it is always dangerous to show that art in action, but Mr. Esposito easily meets that challenge. . . . The work sprawls over 24 short scenes, but it has an inherent honesty, and in Shauneille

Perry's production, the evening is filled with conviction. . . . Characters become atmosphere: a streetcorner quintet of young doowop singers harmonizing on songs written by two of their number.[94]

Kuntu Repertory Theatre produced the same play in Pittsburgh in 1985. A press release for this production describes the action as follows. "*Who Loves the Dancer* is set in the Hill District, 1956. A teenager aspires to a professional dance career, but is opposed by his mother and taunted by members of a youth gang. The boy must prove his manhood, emotionally and physically."[95] The play was directed by Vernell Lillie, choreographed by Bob Johnson, and featured a cast of fifteen.

In 1988, the New Federal Theatre produced another of Penny's plays, *Good Black Don't Crack*, about an overworked and underpaid middle-aged mother struggling with her children, romantic relationships, and a boss who sexually harasses her. An excerpt from this play provides an example of Penny's poetic diction. "There goes a great lady. What is she doing in a jungle? The Hill's a messed-up place for a lady, . . . Great old black lady. She got two suns under her armpits. She taught me something about women. And a hell of a lot about myself."[96] The play is unique in that it centers around the life of an ordinary, less-than-perfect middle-aged woman trying to cope with the challenging circumstances of her life. The New York production was reviewed by the *New York Times,* which credited the following performances.

> The cast, under Claude Purdy's direction works hard at involving the audience. Fern Howell provides a sympathetic reading to Dalejean, and Mel Winkler is quite good as Jake, her lecherous employer. Kenneth J. Green, a native of the Lower East Side who trained at Henry Street, gives a fine performance as James Jr., Dalejean's son, who wants to become a Black Muslim. With Amber Kain, who plays his younger sister Janet, Mr. Greer has a very funning scene in which he tries to recite the Muslim credo. . . . Mr. Purdy keeps the action moving smoothly.[97]

Kuntu produced *Good Black Don't Crack* three times, in 1974, 1991, and 2007. The press release for the 2007 production stated, "Although the play was written in 1974, Dalejean's story remains as timely as ever. The way Dalejean negotiates life's challenges demonstrates the axiom 'good Black don't crack.'"[98] Cast members for the 2007 production included Victoria Bey as Dalejean and Ron Pitts as Jake, the role he originated in 1974, as well as Kimberly Ginyard, Les Howard, Tyrone Johnson, Teri Bridgett, Lamar "Quest" Field, Jada Ginyard, Rodra Burruss, Alexis Dixon, and Sahara Nzongola.[99]

Another Kuntu production that involved collaboration with nationally recognized black theater practitioners was the 1984 production of *A Raisin in the Sun*, which featured Esther Rolle as Lena Younger. The show was guest directed by Elizabeth Van Dyke, who also performed her one-woman show *Love to All, Lorraine* as part of Kuntu's twenty-fifth anniversary celebration of the premiere of Hansberry's seminal play. *Love to All, Lorraine* was codirected by Van Dyke and Woodie King Jr. and was presented in Pittsburgh on April 2, 1984. *A Raisin in the Sun* had a three-week run, from April 7 through April 21, 1984. Postshow discussion panelists for these two productions included Glynn Turman, who portrayed the role of Travis in the original production, and Robert Nemiroff, Hansberry's widower. Local actors included Marcia Jones as Ruth, Donus Crawford as Walter Lee, Felecia Marie Bell as Beneatha, Lamont Arnold as George Murchison, Norman Upsher as Joseph Asagai, Jacques Taylor as Travis, Milton Thompson as Bobo, and Frank Koe as Karl Linder. Kuntu remounted both productions again for the 1999/2000 season as part of the company's twenty-fifth anniversary season.

In an interview with the *Pittsburgh Press*, Rolle, who was an original member of the Negro Ensemble Company, stated that she accepted the role because "I have convictions about struggling young black organizations trying to do a thing of worth and I like what Kuntu is representing here. That caused me to make up my mind to do it."[100] Rolle criticized the depiction of black Americans on television at that time, including the widely successful series in which she starred, *Good Times*, which ran from 1974 to 1979. In this series, Rolle played the role of Florida Evans, for which she was nominated for a Golden Globe Award for best actress in a musical/comedy in 1975. After successfully lobbying the producers to provide her character with a husband because she thought it was important to have the television series depict a two-parent black family, Rolle became displeased about the frivolous development of the series, especially the depiction of the Evans's son J.J. as a layabout. "[*Good Times*] wasn't up to my qualification of what my show should be like. . . . I was put here for something more than being just a jackass to please any one group of people. . . . I would love it much more if there were a black show that was more on the dramatic side or truthful to what our lifestyle is about. I resent making every black TV series comedic and with no worth."[101] This biting criticism of her own television show reveals the bind black performers were in at that time. The financially lucrative roles were frequently stereotypical and unfulfilling. Realistic portrayals of black life languished from neglect or were produced by exhausting the personal resources of the artists who felt inspired to bring them to the public. Kuntu Repertory Theatre's production of *A Raisin in the Sun* is a perfect example of this harsh reality. Vernell Lillie and Renee Berry Mack coproduced the show. Writing about the financial encumbrances of the production, the *Pittsburgh Press* stated, "Ms. Lillie is still left looking down the barrel of a $25,000 commitment" and quotes Lillie as saying, "I feel so strongly about this project. I figure if nobody else comes forward I'll just have to bankroll it myself."[102]

This would not be the last time that Lillie would take on significant personal financial debt in order to financially sustain Kuntu productions and activities. In 1989, the *Pittsburgh Post-Gazette* reported that Lillie "used her teaching salary as collateral to obtain the advance from the university" and "planned to mortgage her house to buy the airline tickets and provide lodging for the group" to attend and perform at the Edinburgh Fringe Festival.[103] These personal financial sacrifices are an example of how Lillie and many other African American theater artists have "made a way out of no way" in order to bring the artistic projects they believe in to life.[104]

Despite these financial constraints and setbacks, Kuntu continued to produce many significant productions throughout the 1980s. In 1987, Kuntu produced August Wilson's *Ma Rainey's Black Bottom*, which was the first such production of the work in Pittsburgh. Susan Smith praised Donald Marshall's portrayal of the main character as "a far more engaging Levee than Broadway's Charles S. Dutton. A likeable smart-mouthing Levee, Marshall . . . initially shows none of the self-destructive anger or neurosis that undoes Levee, but is still able to make the transition into the tortured murderer who feels betrayed by God and his brothers."[105] The rest of the cast included Bob Gore, Milt Thompson, Mark Turner, and Maria Kersey as Ma Rainey. Kersey's portrayal was praised for her "brassy manner that captures well the indomitable spirit of the woman."[106] Gladys Starr-Goodman and Pamela Hart's period costumes were also noted for their artistry. Wilson attended Kuntu's production in a show of support for the theater.[107] He had directed Ed Bullin's play *In New England Winter* for Kuntu back in 1977 and remained a staunch supporter of Kuntu throughout the duration of the company's existence.[108] By cultivating ongoing relationships with nationally known artists such as Woodie King Jr., Esther Rolle, and August Wilson, Kuntu provided valuable educational opportunities for students at Pitt and the greater Pittsburgh community to both see and participate in a national practice of black theater.

Vernell Lillie's interest in African-inspired dramaturgy and poetics led naturally to Kuntu's production of many plays exploring African diaspora identities and cultures. Kuntu productions during the 1980s included Nigerian Wole Soyinka's *The Strong Breed* (1983), Ghanaian Ama Ata Aidoo's *Dilemma of a Ghost* (1988), and Jamaican Trevor Rhone's *Two Can Play* (1989). *The Strong Breed* was directed by Harvey Johnson, a Pittsburgh native who had previously worked at Karamu House in Cleveland, before returning to Pittsburgh to pursue a master's degree in drama from Carnegie Mellon. The Kuntu production of *The Strong Breed* was his directing final project.[109] The play received positive reviews, with Christopher Rawson of the *Pittsburgh Post-Gazette* writing, "Guest director Harvey Johnson has put together what is almost an all-star cast of local black actors. Kelvin Shepard (Iman's [*sic*] father) is especially fine. Lamont Arnold (Eman) does well in a part that is largely underwritten. With only a few exceptions, all the other actors succeed in difficult parts."[110] Montae Russell played Ifada, the disabled boy whom Eman protects from persecution. Russell appeared in many Kuntu productions as a student at the University of Pittsburgh and went on to a successful television acting career, appearing as a regular on the TV series *ER*.

While the *Strong Breed* focused primarily on male characters and the relationship between fathers and sons, *Dilemma of a Ghost* and *Two Can Play* explored women's experiences. *Dilemma of a Ghost* contrasted African American and Ghanaian gender norms, and *Two Can Play* dealt with cultural misunderstandings between Jamaicans and African Americans. Lillie's direction of *Dilemma of a Ghost* corresponded with Ama Ata Aidoo's 1988 visit to Pittsburgh to take part in the African Literature Conference at the University of Pittsburgh. Speaking about what drew her to Aidoo's play, Lillie stated, "It's a beautiful slice of life play observing how people exist in Africa, what their traditions are."[111] Actors included Don Marshall, Pamela Hart, and Elva Branson. The *Pittsburgh Press* provided the following succinct summary of the play's main action. "In the play, a young man from Ghana's Fanti [Fante] tribe marries an Afro-American woman and takes her home to live with his family. The traditionalists don't know what to make of this woman."[112] In this play, as in many of her other works such as *Anowa* and *The Girl Who Can*, Aidoo creates independent, intelligent, and free-thinking female characters who challenge the status quo.[113] One of the most prominent advocates for African women's rights, Aidoo served briefly as minister of education in Ghana and established a foundation to support educational opportunities for Ghanaian girls.[114]

Two Can Play also focused on intercultural misunderstandings and differing gender expectations. The promotional materials for Kuntu's production of *Two Can Play* states, "Rhone [the playwright] takes his audience through a delightful journey of self-discovery through a Jamaican couple who confront and redefine familial roles and expectations, who challenge American immigration policies, and who demonstrate saliency. The setting is in Kingston, Jamaica in Rollington Town during the national political unrest of the 1970s."[115] The *Pittsburgh Press* stated that the play "portrays a down to earth look at a married couples' reassessment of their relationship while fleeing Jamaica for the United States."[116] Bob Gore, who played the role of Jim Thomas, told Michael Winks of the *Pittsburgh Press*, "I think it [the play] uses women's liberation to talk about who is free in society and what does it mean."[117] Andrida McCall, who played Gloria Thomas, said, "She [Gloria] finds out things are just as 'free' in Jamaica as they are in the United States, and that your problems follow you wherever you go."[118] Like *Dilemma of a Ghost*, *Two Can Play* explored issues of sexism, cultural differences, and geopolitical power dynamics between the United States and other countries with significant black populations. As such, these two plays communicated themes of intersectional feminism far ahead of their time.

Throughout its history, Kuntu remained deeply committed to developing black writers, forging connections between local playwrights and leading literary figures from outside the region. In June 1991 the theater hosted a black writers conference featuring Amiri Baraka, Lucille Clifton, Woodie King Jr., and August Wilson. Ntozake Shange gave the keynote address. The *Pittsburgh Press* noted that the conference, which was dedicated to Sterling Brown, included "a series of workshops on fiction, poetry, playwriting, criticism, folk tales, newspaper writing, small presses, writing for children and getting published."[119] Bob Johnson's dance ensemble presented the dance theater piece *African Sunrise*, and August Wilson chaired a symposium entitled "Threats to Black Existence and How Writers Can Respond."[120] This ambitious programming involved many local and national black theater artists. As such, the Black Writers Conference affirmed the theater's support and development of local writers and highlighted the relationship between the Kuntu Repertory Theatre (led by Vernell Lillie) and the Kuntu Writers' Workshop (led by Rob Penny).

Throughout the 1990s, Lillie continued to produce the works of Rob Penny and other notable Pittsburgh playwrights. A wonderful contribution to local history was Penny's play about the Pittsburgh Negro League baseball teams, *Among the Best: The Pittsburgh Crawfords and the Homestead Grays*, which premiered at Kuntu in 1993 and was restaged during the 2008–9 season. The *Pittsburgh Post-Gazette* described the play as follows: "The play gathers Josh Gibson, Satchel Paige, Cool Papa Bell, Buck Leonard and Ted "Double Duty" Radcliffe at Greenlee Field in the Hill District, where they contemplate the impact Jackie Robinson and the integration of the Major Leagues had throughout their careers. Their struggle parallels the disappointment of young Kemiya, a girl who has been rejected by a local male baseball team."[121] Pittsburgh's Negro League teams featured many talented African American baseball players, and this play shines a light on their achievements and the many instances of discrimination that hampered their careers. While August Wilson's *Fences* focused on the negative impact of racism on a fictional baseball player, Penny chose to dramatize the lives of the real-life men who lived through this period of history.

In addition to Penny's works, Kuntu also produced BHT original company member Frank Hightower's play *Lifting* in 1999. In his program notes, Hightower "credits his becoming a playwright to his association with such poets and playwrights as Rob Penny, Nick Flournoy, Charlie [*sic*] P. Williams, and August Wilson. The essence of their work has an enduring quality. To him they represent the true "poetics" of his world."[122] Hightower also cited Maisha Baton, Valerie Lawrence, William Mayfield, Ann Sawyer Berkley, and Rob Penny from the Kuntu Writer's Workshop as other important influences on his work and ethos. *Lifting* had been previously produced by ETA: Creative Arts Foundation in Chicago in 1997. A press release for the Pittsburgh production described the plot and meaning of the play's title.

> *Lifting* is a drama set in Pittsburgh just after World War II. It is the story of Buford Kincade (Wali Abdullah), a bar owner torn between his love for Mavis (Nyjah Moore), a blues singer weighing a return to the road with a young blues guitarist, and Minnie (Tracy Turner), his widowed sister-in-law, who grieves for a son killed in the war. . . . *Lifting* refers to the transforming power of the blues that inspires these people to carry on through their pain and suffering to find hope in love.[123]

Lifting was one of a series of plays at Kuntu in the late 1990s and early 2000s that focused on blues and jazz musicians. The production was directed by Eileen J. Morris, artistic director of Houston's Ensemble Theatre, who frequently guest directs at black theaters in Pittsburgh and who served as the managing director of Kuntu from 1999 to 2006.[124]

Morris's direction of *Lifting* was sponsored by the Woodie King Jr. Professional Director and Producer series. The cast featured Mark Clayton Southers, Mayme Williams, and Ronald Goode in addition to Abdullah, Moore, and Turner. Morris's director's notes for this production provides an example of the emphasis Kuntu productions placed on social transformation and community healing.

> Frank Hightower, playwright, has gathered us together in a time and place where we can evaluate our own freedom, our own needs, our own burdens. Each character hungers for love, for a need for nurturing, for release from "the kind of madness as, Old Folks say, that comes from slavery." There is nothing in the world more powerful than the spirit. This is our own true self. When we tap into the power, knowledge, and wisdom of self, we can fulfill our purposes in life with grace and ease. The thunder within the play represents an African metaphor that reconnects us to the ritualistic energy within. This poetic transformation enables us to bear witness to the "lifting" that is needed.[125]

Here, Morris emphasizes the connection between the individual stories conveyed through the play's narrative and the aims of Kuntu to explore African-inspired performance forms and rituals as a means of community strengthening and healing.

Kuntu concluded the 1998–99 season with another play about black musicians, William Mayfield's *Sing Black Hammer*. The play won the 1990–91 Theodore Ward Prize for playwriting administered by Columbia College in Chicago and was subsequently produced at Columbia in 1991. Mayfield, an electrician by trade before beginning his playwriting career, was the first Pittsburgher to win the prize. He was followed by Javon Johnson, who won the 1999–2000 contest with his play *Hambone*, and Mark Clayton Southers, whose play *Ma Noah* won in the 2003–4 competition.[126] *Sing Black Hammer* is set in 1964 and follows the relationship between a Detroit mill worker and a waitress with dreams of a singing career. Prospects go down for the mill worker after he moves to Pittsburgh and suffers a mill accident, while the waitress's star rises as she and her friends are offered a recording contract with Motown. The play offers a touching portrait of the ambitions of youth and of dreams both deferred and realized. John Hayes praised the high quality of Kuntu's production in his review of the play for the *Pittsburgh Post-Gazette.*

> The show is well cast. Wali J. Abdullah is new to the stage, but he's a natural actor born to play this leading role. . . . Kevin Brown provides both comic relief and some of the play's most dramatic moments, with charisma to spare. Jonathan Berry is affable in a brief but important role, but keep an eye on up-and-coming Andre Sharpley, a young Point Park College drama student who turns his supporting part into one of the show's best. Teri Bridgett is delightfully unlikable as a penny-pinching slumlord with a secret, which she shares in a well-penned scene with a workaholic bartender, well played by Nathan James. Kuntu veteran Brenda Marks blends excruciating insecurity and overwhelming passion for her music and her man as the soon-to-be-diva Miss D. Her backup singers, JaSonta Roberts and Shaunte Grigsby, act well and belt out some delightful a cappella tunes.[127]

Nathan James later achieved a varied and well-recognized career as an actor in HBO, ABC, Netflix, and Hulu films as well as a writer lauded for his one-man show *Growing Pains* and for "Superiority Fantasy," his contribution to *Hands Up: Seven Playwrights, Seven Testaments*, the New Black Festival's artistic response to the killing of Michael Brown and the emergence of the Black Lives Matter movement.[128] The developmental opportunities afforded to James, Mayfield, Hightower, Southers, and numerous others demonstrate the commitment Kuntu had to cultivating the talents of wide swaths of the local black community, not just students but also tradesmen like Mayfield and Southers who were able to embark on successful second careers in the theater thanks to the opportunities and training they received by participating in Kuntu productions.

Throughout the 2000s, Kuntu continued to focus on playwright development. The 2002–3 season was dedicated to "mentors and protégées" and presented paired works by Chadwick Boseman and Sybil Roberts, Javon Johnson and August Wilson, and Mark Clayton Southers and Rob Penny. This season, along with several retrospective seasons dedicated to Rob Penny and to the playwrights who influenced him, demonstrated the company's strong and continued investment in playwright development as a primary focus of its mission. Other notable themes and productions from the 2000s include the 2003–4 season, which was dedicated to "exploring the West" and featured five plays focused on African American cowboys and buffalo soldiers. There were also several seasons dedicated to exploring the lives and legacies of black musicians, including the 2007–8 season, which was dedicated to "Blues, Gospel, and Jazz Poetics."[129]

After Dr. Lillie retired from the University of Pittsburgh in 2010, Kuntu lost access to the University of Pittsburgh's theater spaces. Lillie sold land she had inherited in order to keep the company financially afloat, but after two years of presenting work at various rental locations, including the public library in Homewood, the financial burden became too great and Kuntu ceased operations.[130] Fortunately, Elva Branson and Mark Clayton Southers had started companies that continued the commitment to African American theater production that BHT and Kuntu had exemplified. Branson and Southers had begun their careers in the community-based theater practices of BHT and Kuntu. While appreciative of the opportunities and aesthetics developed in the black theaters of the 1960s and 1970s, both artists sought to create companies that would offer more professional developmental and financial support for Pittsburgh's African American artists. New Horizon Theater, started by Branson in 1992, and Pittsburgh Playwrights Theatre Company, started by Southers in 2003, both currently serve the Pittsburgh arts ecology by producing high-quality African American drama.

Pittsburgh Playwrights Theatre Company

Although Pittsburgh Playwrights does not categorize itself explicitly as a black theater company, the majority of the work it does promotes and sustains the African American performing arts community. The theater's founder, Mark Clayton Southers, described Kuntu's artistic director, Vernell Lillie, as "my theater mom" and stated, "She's the one that got me into theatre and gave me opportunities."[131] A former steel mill worker, Southers participated in a variety of artistic activities that led him to the decision to found a theater. He was a photographer and a poet before beginning to practice theater, and it was as a photographer for the *Pittsburgh Courier* that he first met Dr. Lillie and became involved with Kuntu Repertory Theatre. Southers participated in many aspects of theater production while at Kuntu. "I did over a dozen plays with them [as an actor]. They produced one of my plays, *Ashes to Africa*. I've directed for them; built sets for them. That was my training ground. She [Lillie] was a giving person, [and also] adamant about folks giving their best and being prepared."[132] After gaining experience with Kuntu, Southers went on to do professional work first as an actor, then as a playwright and director.

August Wilson was another important influence on Southers's theatrical development. Wilson helped Southers develop his craft as an actor and had a direct impact on Southers's decision to branch out into playwriting and directing.

> I met August Wilson a few different times. I really got to know him in 1998, when I met him in South Africa where I was performing as an actor. . . . We really got to know each other and would hang out, and he listened to some of my poetry. I hung out with him again that same summer at the Edward Albee Theatre Festival in Valdez, Alaska, and he encouraged me to write for the stage and talked about starting a theater company. As our relationship grew, we talked more and more about it. When I met him, I was just writing poetry, but I grew to love the art of playwriting.[133]

August Wilson's mentorship of Southers during a time when Wilson was winning Pulitzer Prizes and working with the largest regional theaters and on Broadway illustrates the playwright's continued support of local, grassroots black theater initiatives and the lifelong commitment he made to helping other black theater artists succeed.

After working with Wilson in South Africa and having some success with his plays being produced in other cities, Southers hit an artistic wall.

> I found that it was very difficult to shop scripts with African American themes in a predominantly white theater world, especially in Pittsburgh, where the theater vibe is 99.9 percent white. It's hit or miss, if you don't hear from anybody, you don't get your work produced. But I found that every time I sent my work out to other cities, they got picked up right away. My first three plays got picked up by the first three places I sent them to. ETA theater in Chicago produced my very first play. The next play I wrote went to Dayton Future Fest, and my third play got picked up in Chicago at Columbia University; it won their theater award prize. So I realized I wasn't getting that same type of action in Pittsburgh, in my own hometown. I thought, "OK, the work must be OK if it's getting picked up in these different places," so the problem was Pittsburgh. I realized that I would have to create my own space.[134]

The opportunity came when the Penn Theatre, where Southers had participated in a play reading workshop, closed and its space became available.

> [The Penn Theatre] did about six plays a year. They were a small, scrappy theater and the word got out that the guy was shutting it down. So, I called him up. I worked at the steel mill at the time, so I had some income. . . . I went to look at the place and it wasn't bad. . . . I was so excited about it because the possibilities were

endless. He told me what he wanted for it and I countered his offer and we agreed on a deal and I took a home equity loan out on my house and I bought him out. . . . It was a nice space. . . . It was a turnkey operation so I got it and was like, "OK, now I've got to do a play." I founded the theater so I could produce my own work. My thinking was that if I was a carpenter, I would want to have a workshop; if I was an auto mechanic, I would want to have a garage; well I wanted to be a playwright. I wanted to get out of the steel mill and pursue the arts full time, and this was a way to do it. So, I took a home equity loan out and made it happen. That was fourteen years ago, and it hasn't been a mistake.[135]

Pittsburgh Playwrights Theatre Company's first season opened with August Wilson's *Ma Rainey's Black Bottom* in March of 2003. Wilson attended the production in a show of his support for the theater.[136] In addition to Wilson, Southers produced three other plays by African American Pittsburghers in the company's inaugural season: Rob Penny's *Boppin' with the Ancestors*; his own script, *When the Water Turns Clear*; and Javon Johnson's *Hambone*; along with two theater festival showcases of shorter works, Midsummer Night's Chamber Theatre and the first annual Theatre Festival in Black and White.[137]

Although Pittsburgh Playwrights Theatre produces a significant body of work by African American playwrights, Southers does not categorize it as an exclusively black theater.

I want to start out by saying that I do African American theater, but I don't consider us an African American theater in a true sense where the mission is to uplift black culture. Our mission is simply to produce plays by Pittsburgh playwrights. I do put an emphasis on producing African American playwrights. That has always been one of my objectives, and it is evident from our seasons. We do a good body of African American work, a good percentage, and we apply for grants that are geared toward the African American community because our work supports that. However, I don't go under the moniker of an African American theater company for several reasons. One, just because I'm African American, people will say, "Oh, this is a black theater company," because they're not used to seeing that. People don't say "white theater company," they just say "theater" because it's the norm, white theaters get to carry that moniker, that they're the norm, because of privilege, if you know what I mean? So, I'm like, "Hey, I have a theater company. I founded a theater company, and I'm African American, and I'm going to do things that appeal to me." I want to enlarge the audience from the black community and get them more involved with being theater patrons, and

I need to offer work that's going to attract them. At the same time, I'll expose folks to plays by Caucasian playwrights, because we do plays by Pittsburgh Playwrights. If you look at plays by, let's just call it white theater companies, generally, they may do one African American play every other season, not even every season. Some more progressive ones will do one every season. I'm the opposite of that. I'll do a play by a white playwright every season. If I do a season, I might have three African American plays and one white play. Every once in a while, it will be split right down the middle depending on the strength of the work.[138]

Southers's point about wanting to challenge the assumption that a non–culturally specific theater would automatically produce only or primarily European American works provides an example of the positive effect companies with African American artistic directors have on the diversity of American theatrical practice. When African American artistic directors are hired at non–culturally specific theaters, their interest in work from their own and other cultures in addition to white culture is often assumed and reflected in the programming of the organizations they head. This has been true for African American artistic directors at leading regional theaters such as Lloyd Richards's tenure at Yale Repertory Theatre, George Wolfe's directorship of the Public Theater, and Sheldon Epps's time as artistic director of the Pasadena Playhouse.[139] The fact that African American artistic directors are rare is a real problem for an inclusive American theater practice. Like the directors just mentioned, I see Mark Clayton Southers's philosophy of diversity as similarly invested in the notion that African American artists have a clear place in any American theatrical organization that seeks to reflect the cultural expression of the people in the cities in which these organizations reside, from which they receive civic funding, and to which they in turn provide opportunities for education, entertainment, and civic engagement.

In addition to showcasing his own and other local playwrights' work, Southers has created programming specifically designed to diversify and desegregate Pittsburgh's theater audiences. The company's Theatre Festival in Black and White is the main way he accomplishes this. Southers explained that the idea for this festival came to him in a dream.

I had this little dream where I was standing up against the wall in a theater looking at the audience's profile and they were cracking up, they were having a good time and the lights were dim and they were looking toward the stage. I couldn't see the stage. I just saw them, and it was a mixed audience, something you very rarely see in Pittsburgh. You see it now sometimes because of some of the initiatives we've taken, but . . . if you go to the big arts establishments in Pittsburgh, the audience is ninety-eight or ninety-nine percent white and you can pick the black folks out. But this audience in my dream was mixed. It was reflective of something that was better than what we had.[140]

This vision of an integrated audience led him to create programming specifically designed to attract such an audience.

I thought maybe we could do a black play and white play in the same evening and [thus] get a black crowd and a white crowd and it morphed into me doing eight one-act plays and we called it the Theatre Festival in Black and White. We took four plays by black playwrights and four plays by white playwrights, and we ran them over a two- or three-week period. . . . The point was to mix it up.[141]

In addition to selecting diverse plays and presenting them together on the same playbill, Southers sought to expose the theater artists he worked with to artists of other cultural backgrounds.

We set it up so the black plays were directed by white directors and the white plays were directed by black directors and that really cranked it up a notch. That really got people working with each other who weren't used to working with each other. You can imagine how crazy it was. There were white folks who had never worked with black folks in their whole lives; they had never been exposed. That was not so much the case for us, you know; we interact with them more than they interact with us. You would think it would be balanced, but it's not. We're used to them, we can mimic them because we live in their world, basically. It's just the way things are. Of course, there was some head-butting going on, people getting used to the different ways people do things, but it's been successful from day one.[142]

Southers's leadership provided the artists involved with an opportunity to participate in a truly intercultural theater experience, along with all the associated challenges and opportunities it involved. His point that white artists are less used to working for black artists than vice versa illustrates just one of the many ways in which black theatrical leadership is beneficial and can be used as a tool for dismantling racism in multicultural communities. In 2015, the company recognized some of the city's other ethnic populations when it produced a multicultural edition of the annual festival that featured artists of Asian and Indian backgrounds. Innovative in both its premise and execution, Pittsburgh Playwrights Theatre produced some version of this festival of one-act plays every year from 2003 to 2016. This programming helped to reshape the arts ecology of Pittsburgh and desegregate both audiences and previously distinct groups of artists.

Another way Pittsburgh Playwrights Theatre has helped to both reflect and shape the arts ecology of the city is through site-specific performances of August Wilson's work in collaboration with the August Wilson House in the Hill District. Wilson's childhood home at 1727 Bedford Avenue is now a historical landmark. The August Wilson House is managed by Wilson's nephew Paul Ellis and financially supported by a number of foundations and individuals including the actor Denzel Washington. Ellis founded the Daisy Wilson Arts Community as an umbrella organization to manage programming at the house and to "celebrate the literary and personal legacy of August Wilson and serve as an arts center to nurture the historic Hill District community and arts practitioners and scholars influenced by his work."[143] In 2016 Southers directed *Seven Guitars* in the backyard of the August Wilson House, which was the original inspiration for the play's setting. The 2016 production featured Ty Barrow, Jonathan Berry, Teri Bridgett, Kevin Brown, Jamilah Chanie, Wali Jamal, and Leslie Ezra Smith.[144] Many reviews for this production commented on the powerful acting and the significance of the setting. For example, Wendy Arons wrote, "How much this production gains from its setting: knowing that people may well have had conversations and conflicts much like those depicted in the play *on this very spot* raises the stakes of its issues in a deeply satisfying and provocative manner. Indeed, I'm not sure I've ever found the play's representation of structural racism and the ways in which the deck is stacked against black men to be so resonant."[145] In 2018 Southers also used the backyard of the August Wilson House to stage *King Hedley II*, which is the sequel to *Seven Guitars* set in the same location forty years later. Mark Clayton Southers, Monteze Freeland, and Dennis Robinson Jr. directed a cast featuring Rico Parker, Karla Payne, Sam Lothard, Etta Cox, Wali Jamal, Sala Udin, and Dominque Briggs. In his review for *Pittsburgh in the Round*, Jason Clearfield wrote, "Seeing a play at August Wilson's actual home is beyond a privilege. It is absolutely necessary. . . . Here we look upon a people of a devasted area as they plumb relics for opportunity and find only the betrayal of a nation. . . . I can't stress this enough: it is remarkable to see this play in this setting, to feel it there."[146] The dilapidated state of neglect of the August Wilson House, whose interior at the time of these productions was still uninhabitable and awaiting renovation, communicated the economic needs and desperation that drive the action of the play. The performance of this play in the neighborhood it depicts, where many black Pittsburgh families have lived for generations and where the median household income is half of what it is for the rest of the city, underscored not only the economic hardships of the neighborhood but also the deep history and sense of connection to place its residents feel.[147] The sense of placemaking and place marking was palpable and commented upon by every review of the production.

Pittsburgh Playwrights Theatre continued this practice of place marking in 2019, when it again collaborated with the August Wilson House to

Fig. 3. Pittsburgh Playwrights Theatre's 2016 site-specific performance of *Seven Guitars* in the backyard of August Wilson's childhood home at 1727 Bedford Avenue, the setting that inspired the play. Photograph by Chris Chapman.

produce *Gem of the Ocean* on an outdoor stage in the vacate lot at 1839 Wylie Avenue, the address Wilson provides in his plays for the house of his fictional matriarch Aunt Ester. In a television interview with *Pittsburgh Live* before the premier of the company's production of *Gem of the Ocean*, Southers explained the significance of this location. "This is 1839 Wylie. All August Wilson fans know that it's talked about in several of his plays. Its Aunt Ester's fictional home. There used to be a school on this property, and August traversed through here many times. He chose to place her home on this perch, on this hill because you can see so much of the Hill [District] from this location."[148] This production of *Gem of the Ocean* was directed by Andrea Frye and featured Chrystal Bates, Candace Walker, Jonathan Berry, Kevin Brown, Les Howard, Wali Jamal, and Marcus Muzopappa. In a nod to the importance of Aunt Ester's character as the cycle's matriarch, the production and design team was an all-woman endeavor. It was produced by Ashley Southers and managed by Shanita Bivins, with music, lighting, scenic, costume, hair, and makeup designs by Kathryn Bostic, Angela Baughman, Latrice Lovett, Diane Melchitzy, Kim Brown, and Cheryl El-Walker, respectively. The master electrician was Madeleine Steineck, and the fight director was Lisa Ann Goldsmith.[149] In a review for *Pittsburgh City Paper*, Alex Gordon wrote:

> Not all stories are better experienced in their literal setting, but for a piece this richly bound to and inspired by its location, the approach is incredibly powerful. The set is so effectively insular, so at odds with

its surroundings, that it feels that Ester could, if she wanted, snap her fingers and detach the room from its soil and send it sailing into the sky. That doesn't happen, but what does is almost equally fantastic, unbelievable, and affecting.[150]

Here Gordon is referring to the spiritual journey to the city of bones that Aunt Ester facilitates at the end of the play. His review links the importance of the site of production to the ritual of theater and the healing power of the religious experience depicted in the play. All three of these site-specific performances not only provided audiences with the pleasure of seeing the actual locations that inspired Wilson's dramaturgy, but they were also a conscious effort on the part of the August Wilson House and Pittsburgh Playwrights Theatre to use art to bring resources, attention, and artistic services into the Hill District as a means of community strengthening and community support.

Although Pittsburgh Playwrights Theatre Company has produced important site-specific productions in the Hill District, its permanent home is in the downtown Cultural District. The development of the Cultural District was part of a series of late twentieth-century urban renewal efforts designed to transform the downtown landscape and shift Pittsburgh's economic dependency from an industrial to a technology- and service-based economy. In their book, *SynergiCity: Reinventing the Postindustrial City*, Paul Hardin Kapp and Paul J. Armstrong use Pittsburgh as a positive example of an American city that has reinvented itself. Citing eight metrics—climate and terrain, housing, health care, transportation, education, the arts, recreation, and economic outlook—Kapp and Armstrong point out that Pittsburgh has been rated America's "Most Livable City" four separate times by Rand McNally's *Places Rated Almanac* (twice), the *Economist*, and *Forbes* from 1985 to 2010.[151] Kapp and Armstrong argue that Pittsburgh's success is "the result of a realistic assessment of assets and problems, imaginative long-range economic regional planning, a shared vision, a tradition of successful public-private partnerships, involvement of concerned private organizations, authentic citizen participation, strategic investment, organized feedback and evaluation, and patience to stay the course."[152] This quotation implicitly references the three major redevelopment projects the city of Pittsburgh has undertaken since the 1940s: Renaissance I, Renaissance II, and Strategy 21. Each of these projects has largely excluded African Americans and, in the case of Renaissance I, specifically victimized black residents who lost homes and businesses in the Lower Hill District as a result of the construction of a sports arena that was short-lived and eventually demolished. Writing about Renaissance I in *Race and Renaissance: African Americans in Pittsburgh since World War II*, Joe Trotter and Jared Day claim, "In Pittsburgh and Western Pennsylvania, as in other urban centers across the country, urban renewal programs destroyed whole communities, especially those dominated by low-income families."[153] The inclusion of African American arts organizations in the Cultural District is one effort to bring some of the rewards of urban redevelopment to the quarter of the city's population that has least benefited from them.

The one million square feet of property in the fourteen-block stretch of downtown that comprises the Cultural District is managed by the Pittsburgh Cultural Trust. The Cultural District includes the majority of the city's historic theaters, all of which were renovated as part of city redevelopment projects during the 1980s and 1990s. The trust sees itself as a "national model of urban revitalization through the arts,"[154] and its website boasts of attracting "2,000,000 visitors annually generating an economic impact of $303 million."[155] The Pittsburgh Cultural Trust thus employs a neoliberal framework that characterizes art as one of the economic engines of the city. "Using the arts as an economic catalyst, The Pittsburgh Cultural Trust has holistically created a world-renowned Cultural District that is revitalizing the city, improving the regional economy and enhancing Pittsburgh's quality of life."[156] In 2004, Janis Burley Wilson, the former vice president of strategic partnership and community engagement at the Pittsburgh Cultural Trust, attended the Theatre Festival in Black and White at the Pittsburgh Playwrights Theatre, was impressed with the quality of the work she saw, and invited the organization to occupy one of the spaces managed by the trust. The company moved to 542 Penn Avenue in 2005. In 2011, the company moved again, into the more affordable penthouse at 937 Liberty Avenue, and then in 2020 to a storefront location at 819 Penn Avenue. A modest organization in an area dominated by the largest art institutions in the city such as the Pittsburgh Symphony, the Pittsburgh Ballet, and the Pittsburgh Public Theater, Pittsburgh Playwrights Theatre Company is now part of the portfolio of downtown arts organizations that lease and receive marketing support from the Pittsburgh Cultural Trust. The other major African American arts institution that is part of this district is the August Wilson Center for African American Arts and Culture (later renamed the August Wilson African American Cultural Center).

The August Wilson African American Cultural Center

For years, city planners and arts and culture advocates envisioned the construction of a flagship African American arts center located on the edge of the Cultural District. In 2009, that dream was realized when Pittsburgh honored the legacy of August Wilson by opening the August Wilson Center for African American Culture, a sixty-five thousand square foot impressive structure featuring an approximately five hundred–seat theater and several gallery spaces, meeting rooms, dance studios, and classrooms.[157] The building's construction cost $43 million and was supported by Pittsburgh's major philanthropic foundations, its city council, and its urban redevelopment program.[158] The August Wilson Center was emblematic of the desire to create and sustain

African American cultural institutions that can compare in size and stature to the largest predominantly white arts institutions in major US cities and also of the challenges that have historically faced African American art institutions and those who endeavor to support them. The center's history is a particularly dramatic example of the issues involved in building and sustaining such institutions. I see the financial problems the August Wilson Center encountered early in its history as partly the result of the national recession, which hit during its construction, and partly the consequence of two divergent strands of arts production that contributed to its creation. Examining each of these influences helps to understand the mission, operations, challenges, and eventual success of this unique organization.

The August Wilson Center materialized out of Wilson's dream for autonomous, well-funded, black theaters in every American city with significant black populations. In his seminal 1996 speech to attendees of the annual conference of Theatre Communications Group, August Wilson called for greater financial support for large-scale African American theater institutions.

> In terms of economics and privilege, one significant fact affects us all in the American theatre: Of the 66 LORT [League of Resident Theatres] theatres, there is only one that can be considered black. From this it could be falsely assumed that there aren't sufficient numbers of blacks working in the American theatre to sustain and support more theatres. If you do not know, I will tell you that black theatre in America is alive . . . it is vibrant . . . it is vital . . . it just isn't funded.[159]

In this speech Wilson criticized the funders of the regional theater system for supporting predominately white theater institutions to the detriment and exclusion of black theaters.

> Black theatre doesn't share in the economics that would allow it to support its artists and supply them with meaningful avenues to develop their talent and broadcast and disseminate ideas crucial to its growth. The economics are reserved as privilege to the overwhelming abundance of institutions that preserve, promote and perpetuate white culture. That is not a complaint. That is an advertisement. Since the funding sources, both public and private, do not publicly carry avowed missions of exclusion and segregated support, this is obviously either a glaring case of oversight, or we the proponents of black theatre have not made our presence or needs known. I hope here tonight to correct that.[160]

In the more than twenty years since Wilson delivered this address things have only gotten worse in terms of the economics and patronage of black theater in the United States. Wilson's point, that African American artistic practices have never been supported in American cities to the level that European theater arts have been, remains emphatically germane. On the twentieth anniversary of Wilson's speech, Rob Weinert-Kendt wrote in *American Theatre* magazine, "The landscape for black theatres . . . is by many measures more treacherous now . . . while there are more LORT theatres than there were 20 years ago, there is not even one in that size range that is black identified."[161] The establishment of the August Wilson Center in downtown Pittsburgh was a direct response to Wilson's challenge by the civic leaders of his hometown. Its creation and continued operation represent a valiant attempt to do black theater and other African-based arts on a large scale, to assert the civic value of black culture, and to demonstrate support for black artistic practice on par with the level of public and private support that the city's operas, symphonies, ballets, art museums, and white theater companies receive.

August Wilson was himself a product of two very different systems of theater productions: the local, community-based black theaters that included Pittsburgh's BHT and Kuntu Repertory Theatre and St. Paul's Penumbra Theatre Company, as well as the consortium of large regional theaters in conjunction with commercial Broadway transfers that conferred upon Wilson his celebrity status.[162] August Wilson could not have become the great American playwright he is currently acknowledged to be without both of these systems of production. He explicitly referenced this in *The Ground on Which I Stand*, in essence asking the latter to more fully support the former. A look at the creation and maintenance of the August Wilson Center reveals some of the tensions between these two different ways of producing art and the challenges involved in trying to blend the historic, community-based practice of African American theater with more recent neoliberal models of arts tourism and art as a catalyst for economic development.

A variety of artists, local politicians, and foundation leaders contributed to the founding of the August Wilson Center. In their case study on nonprofit arts management, "Saving the August Wilson Center," Anne Ferola, Jennifer Ginsberg, and Martice Sutton wrote, "For years, Pittsburgh's African American citizens explored ways to celebrate and showcase their vibrant community. . . . Among the first attempts was the Homewood Art Museum, which presented community arts programming in various locations but was never able to raise funds to build a permanent home."[163] The Homewood Art Museum is also mentioned by journalist Elizabeth Bloom in her summary of the early trials and tribulations of the August Wilson Center. Bloom includes her interview with Emma Slaughter, one of the Homewood Art Museum's founders, as evidence of disagreement over the location of the August Wilson Center. Slaughter and other supporters of the Homewood Art Museum advocated for placing the center in a predominantly black neighborhood such as Homewood or the Hill District. Others, including Wilson's long-time friend and collaborator, Pittsburgh city council member Sala Udin, wanted the location centrally located within the Cultural District.[164] This disagreement over place reveals the tension between the two systems of production and consequent visions of African American art making in which August Wilson participated.

Neighborhood-based arts programming is significantly different in both size and scope from what I will refer to, for lack of a better term, as magnet programming. Magnet programming is usually housed in a large, centrally located building that communicates, often through neoclassical architecture or the innovative designs of renowned contemporary architects, the fact that the institution is an illustration of the city's financial and cultural might. Magnet programming seeks to be recognized as "world class" by hiring artistic and administrative leadership from national or international searches and either implicitly or explicitly subscribing to a mission that aims to bring great art and culture to the city and its residents. Regional theaters, symphonies, ballets, and opera all operate on this model, and until the 1970s, the artistic material produced by these institutions was almost exclusively of European origin.[165]

Neighborhood arts programming, on the other hand, has always been decidedly process rather than product oriented. Most frequently housed in utilitarian community centers, neighborhood-based arts programming focuses primarily on arts education, youth programs, and the ability of neighborhood residents to participate in the creation and dissemination of the work produced and showcased in that venue. The theatrical companies of neighborhood-based arts institutions are usually semiprofessional, although several of the flagship theaters from the black arts movement such as Karamu House and Penumbra Theatre Company transitioned to fully professional companies as their reputations grew. While both magnet and neighborhood institutions now engage in arts education, a neighborhood institution's focus on arts education is either primary or equal to its professional productions, while a magnet institution's engagement in arts education is always secondary.

African American arts organizations are overwhelmingly of the neighborhood type, for both practical and philosophical reasons. This is true in Pittsburgh as well, where all of the other African American theater institutions discussed in this chapter have grown out of the community-based neighborhood model. Larry Neal articulated some of the philosophical reasons for this in his seminal manifesto on the black arts movement: "The Black Arts Movement is radically opposed to any concept of the artist that alienates the artist from his/her community."[166] Neal and other black arts practitioners and theorists explicitly questioned the value of a magnet-style approach to arts production and lauded the neighborhood approach as politically useful and personally transformative.

On a practical level, African American art has overwhelmingly been cultivated and produced within a neighborhood arts programming model because African Americans have historically lacked the capital to create and sustain magnet-sized institutions. While Neal and Slaughter express a preference for the neighborhood model of arts programming, there are many African

American artists that seek the financial support, career opportunities, and broader recognition that working in the magnet system provides. August Wilson is one example of an artist that chose to work within the magnet system, despite his ideological objections to that system, for reasons of career development including the greater resources, recognition, and dissemination of his work that such a system afforded. Wilson's championing of smaller-budget neighborhood-based African American theaters combined with his call to establish large, well-funded magnet-style black theaters illustrates his recognition of the value of both forms of artistic production.

A core part of my efforts as an African American theater historian has been to call attention to the diversity of black theatrical practice and to expose the social inequities that hinder African American theatrical production. While I believe that the neighborhood approach to African American theatrical practice has been the lifeblood of black theater, I don't believe it is nor should be the only expression of black theater. I find the goal of creating large, centrally located African American arts institutions that produce in the magnet mode entirely reasonable, and in a city like Pittsburgh, where one-fourth of the citizens are black, entirely appropriate and worthy of the full support of civic leadership and foundations that already support a plethora of other magnet-style arts institutions that produce work derived from European cultural lineage. This is not a criticism of Slaughter and other proponents of the neighborhood model. Neighborhood-based arts institutions are equally valuable, necessary, and underfunded. Pittsburgh should have well-supported African American arts institutions in black neighborhoods in Homewood and the Hill as well as in the Cultural District. The challenges in establishing economically stable institutions in both strands of art production speak to persistent and entrenched racial inequities in the arts ecology of the city.

As one of the main planners and supporters of the August Wilson Center, Sala Udin spoke to me about the long process of its establishment. It was clear from our conversation that the center would never have been built without key advocates on the city council. Udin spoke about the importance of having African American leadership on the city council, not just for this art project but for all kinds of issues regarding racial justice and accountability. He stated:

> One of the things I enjoyed about city council was that it gave us the opportunity to create institutions and legislation that directly spoke to issues that we could only protest about before. All of the time from the sixties to the nineties, we protested police brutality, for example. Once I got on city council and took up the issue of police brutality and created a citizen police review board that could subpoena police officers to come before a community board and defend themselves against accusations of police abuse . . . that was a whole lot different than protesting outside with picket signs.[167]

In addition to working toward police accountability, Udin used his position on the city council to build support for the creation of a large-scale African American arts center.

> Around the time I was first elected, there was the momentum of the Million Man March. There were African American museums and cultural centers sprouting up all over the country, and we wanted to have an African American cultural center here in Pittsburgh. I wanted to use my position on city council and also to use my position as a city council representative to the Urban Redevelopment Authority, the development arm of city government. I sat on their board as a member of city council. So, we started exploring the creation and establishment of an African American cultural center. That was in ninety-seven . . . We started raising money, and we used the Urban Redevelopment Authority that I sat on to provide us with the kind of administrative undergirding and infrastructure that an organization like that needs. . . . By 2005 . . . we had the business plan in hand, and we were ready to build a building.[168]

The location of the center in the Cultural District was a self-conscious statement on the part of its supporters of the relevance and import of black culture not only for black people but for the city as a whole. Former board member Dr. Mona Generett made this point when she stated that the center's vision was to "enrich and enlighten the culture of the entire Pittsburgh community. To achieve that mission, it must be in the heart of the city—accessible to the greatest number of patrons, regardless of race."[169] After chronicling the myriad ways African Americans had been either victimized or ignored by Pittsburgh's twentieth-century redevelopment projects in their book *Race and Renaissance: African Americans in Pittsburgh since World War II*, Joe Trotter and Jared Day write, "The movement to create a state-of-the-art African American cultural center also underscored the many ways that black people moved out of the shadows of the city's revitalization."[170] Both of these statements frame the size and location of the center as a political act, a demonstration of mainstream support for the value of black art within the larger arts ecology of the city of Pittsburgh and the sweep of its twentieth-century postindustrial development.

The design and construction of the center's building was in line with the aims of a magnet-style arts institution—expensive, innovative, and meant to impress. Allison Williams, a prominent African American architect from the Bay Area who contributed to the design of the Lawrence Berkeley National Laboratory Facility and the San Francisco International Airport, won a competition to design the center. Transforming a triangular block that included a strip club and an adult bookstore (both demolished under eminent domain), Williams's architectural firm, Perkins + Will, created a building with an abstract, modern design. The curvilinear apex of the building's triangle serves as a representation of a dhow or *jahazi* sailing ship, the type of vessel traditionally used along the Swahili coast for trading goods and ferrying people. The ship motif emphasized the center's purpose of bringing African culture into the Cultural District and downtown area.[171] In a feature for the online architectural magazine *ArchDaily*, Perkins + Will described the 328-foot glassy façade of the structure as a "giant picture window framing the constant transformation, evolution, and influence of African culture, active and glowing proudly from within."[172] This lofty description clearly demonstrates the purpose of a magnet-style arts institution: to communicate cultural sophistication and a sense of awe. August Wilson's widow, Constanza Romero Wilson, made a similar point at the center's opening ceremony in 2009 when she stated:

> I am honored to be back in Pittsburgh again. I came here frequently with August. Every time we walked through the city he would make many otherwise unremarkable places come alive for me. . . . Before he passed August knew that Pittsburgh planned a project of great scope with his name attached, but this beautiful building, the magnitude of this project, this city's championing of African-American culture would have made his heart simply dance with pride and joy.[173]

The richly symbolic form of the building, along with its high-quality construction materials and intricate design, attests to its function as a political and cultural statement. Just as the architecture of civic buildings such as city halls communicates a sense of gravitas concomitant with the legal proceedings that occur within them, the architecture of magnet-style performance spaces seeks to communicate their importance as preeminent cultural institutions.

The interior of the building was designed to functionally accommodate a variety of different forms of artistic and community expression. Like many of the historic theaters in the Cultural District, the building serves as a venue for multiple local arts organizations as well as touring productions and exhibits. In an interview with the *New Pittsburgh Courier*, Williams spoke about designing the building as an iconic work of art in service of multiple uses. "The building is meant to be a neutral and flexible stage that allows the center to take on issues that surround our culture through art, music, politics, theatre and dance. . . . It's a new icon, a new landmark. It has an importance, a movement and influence beyond the site."[174] Williams's statement here connects the form and function of the building. The flexible space Williams describes above includes "a 486-seat proscenium theater, 11,000 gsf [ground square feet] of exhibit galleries, a flexible studio . . . and an education center.[175] Many news articles and individuals have criticized the planners of the August Wilson Center for failing to plan for the financial sustainability of the building and organization that owned it. However, the initial plans for the building included revenue-generating components such as a restaurant and boutique hotel on top of the existing structure. The building was designed to accommodate the construction of hotel and restaurant space, but development agencies were unable to secure an investor for those additions, which were subsequently left off. In an interview with Debra Erdley and Adam Smeltz for *Trib Live*, Williams stated, "I think the need to proceed with the center as a first-phase cultural facility was their critical mission. They did not want to jeopardize that while awaiting the fantasy of a developer who might not have shown up for years."[176]

Construction began in 2007 and took two years to complete, during which time the financial crisis hit. Sala Udin described the financial effect the recession had on construction costs.

> When we broke ground in 2007, we did not know that we were at the beginning of an economic crisis. That economic crisis affected the price of construction, labor, and materials and what we had thought was going to be a thirty-million-dollar project increased in cost by twelve million dollars. We had to decide, do we abandon this project, because it took everything we had to raise thirty million dollars. We knew that we couldn't raise another twelve million so we had to choose between abandoning the project or borrowing twelve million dollars. We decided to put our last political muscle behind the effort to borrow twelve million dollars to finish the project.[177]

Shortly before the building opened in 2009, the original board that had raised the initial money for the building rotated off and a new board of directors took over with over $11 million of debt. The center's initial executive director Neil Barclay, who had been hired in 2003 and had participated in the initial fundraising efforts, also left the organization shortly before the grand opening in 2009 to take a position with the Atlanta Black Arts Festival. Marva K. Harris, retired senior vice president of PNC Bank, served as interim executive director, overseeing the grand opening of the building in 2009 and staying on until the board completed a national search for a permanent executive director in 2010.[178]

Under Harris's leadership, the August Wilson Center commissioned the Aunt Ester cycle to celebrate its inaugural season. The Aunt Ester cycle was a series of four performances inspired by August Wilson's matriarchal character. It was "recognized as the top cultural event of the year by the *Pittsburgh Tribune*."[179] The series included the presentation of two touring productions of August Wilson's plays: St. Louis Black Repertory Company's production of *Gem of the Ocean*, directed by Andrea Frye, and Penumbra Theatre Company's production of *Radio Golf*, directed by Lou Bellamy. The third production, *Two Trains Running*, was helmed by Pittsburgh Playwrights Theatre Company and directed by Mark Clayton Southers. The fourth production, *Women of the Hill*, was an original oral history performance piece curated by Ping Chong and Talvin Wilks.[180] For *Women of the Hill*, Wilks and Chong interviewed over fifty women and then selected six of them to share their family histories and relationship to the neighborhood. Wilks and Chong curated their separate stories and combined them into one cohesive performance. Of the six performers chosen for this project, only one was a professional artist, Kimberly Ellis, aka Dr. Goddess, who also happened to be August Wilson's niece.[181] The other performers included Pittsburgh police detective Brenda Tate, realtor Phillis Daniel Lavelle, office administrator and community volunteer Marlene Scott Ramsey, retiree Norma J. Thompson, and Carnegie Museum archivist for the Teenie Harris photography collection Charlene Foggie Barnett.[182] In her essay, "Celebrating the 'Historical' Community through Different Voices: Ping Chong and Talvin Wilks's *Women of the Hill*," Yuko Kurahashi writes, "*Women of the Hill* provides the participants with a tool to remember, 'document,' and share what has been rarely recorded in mainstream history."[183] Kurahasi also points out that many of the audience members shared the memories and experiences of the Hill District recounted in the play and were therefore "able to participate in this 'reclaiming' project with the participants."[184] With this production, the center made a valuable contribution to the local community through the commissioning of a theatrical performance deeply connected to and celebratory of Pittsburgh's black community.

In 2010, the board of the August Wilson Center hired André Kimo Stone Guess as its executive director. Guess had successfully led the Jazz at Lincoln Center program in New York from 2000 to 2006 and was optimistic that the center's debt could be paid off over time. Guess is quoted in the *Pittsburgh Post-Gazette* in 2010 as saying, "We've raised 500,000 from the African American community in the three months I've been here . . . every space is rentable. We have corporate events here, anniversaries and birthday parties, even movie scenes being shot."[185] By the end of 2010, the board of directors had received pledges of $2 million to pay down the debt and there was a general air of optimism that the rest of the money could be found. By mid-2011, Guess was less optimistic, stating, "We've had our fair share of challenges" and pointing out that "the operating costs of this facility is $750,000."[186] In an email exchange with the former director, Guess said that his greatest challenge during his time in Pittsburgh was "the financial burden that was on the institution. The operating budget was at a deficit and there was an eleven million-dollar bullet mortgage that was coming due approximately 18 months after my arrival."[187]

During his tenure, Guess received several programming grants from local foundations and developed an innovative arts program spanning four distinct arts disciplines. He hired Sean Jones as the center's musical director, Mark Clayton Southers as the theater director, Cecile Shellum as the visual arts director, and Greer Reed as the dance director. Robust local programming in addition to touring shows and rentals were a core part of Guess's vision for the center.[188] With this organizational structure, Guess created something truly unique. He stated, "At the time there was nothing in the world that celebrated black music, dance, theater and visual arts in one place."[189] Significant programming continued into 2012. For example, Mark Clayton Southers brought in Tre Garrett, artistic director of the Jubilee Theatre in Fort Worth, Texas, to direct Marcus Gardley's acclaimed play *Every Tongue Confess*, and Cecile Shellum curated the impressive exhibition *Strength in the Struggle: Civil Rights* in partnership with the African American Museum of Philadelphia, the Smithsonian Institution, and local visual artists and organizations.[190] This programming provided the city with world-class, high-quality arts experiences typical of magnet-style arts production that served the mission of the organization and the vision of its founders admirably.

However, by mid-2012, it was clear that the center would not be able to meet its financial obligations. Mark Clayton Southers described the overwhelming financial burden facing the center during that period.

> We had a really good program going, the problem was they [the center] had a seven million–dollar debt and were paying fifty-six thousand dollars a month in payments. There would be benefactors in the community that would write checks and different foundations would help out, but it got to a point where the funds just ran out and the whole thing collapsed. It was like Mr. Guess had an eleven million–dollar noose around his neck. He did manage to close the gap and get it down to seven million.[191]

With unpaid bills piling up, Guess left at the end of his contract in July 2012. The remaining staff was laid off in early 2013, and by September of 2013 "the building was forced into foreclosure."[192] There was developer interest in purchasing the property and building a luxury hotel there, but there was strong community opposition to the center falling into the hands of a for-profit commercial entity. Speaking about the original founders, Sala Udin stated, "[We] inserted ourselves back into the process enough to get three foundations to agree to put up the money to save the center and not allow it to be purchased at fire sale cost and turned into a hotel."[193] In "Saving the August Wilson Center," Ferola, Ginsberg, and Sutton add that the larger community also rallied together in a last-ditch effort to save the center. "Independent citizens held 'Community Conversations' with more than seventy key stakeholders throughout Pittsburgh, encouraging public support to save the center. African American Pittsburghers, speaking out in the center's defense, included August Wilson's niece Kimberly Ellis, Reverend Harold Lewis of Calvary Episcopal Church, and Tony Award–winner Billy Porter. A town hall meeting in the Hill District was standing room only."[194] On November 3, 2014, after a series of legal proceedings and negotiations, Dollar Bank, one of the center's main creditors, purchased the property at a sheriff's sale. The next day, the Heinz Endowments, the Pittsburgh Foundation, and the R. K. Mellon Foundation purchased the deed to the building free of all liens for $7.9 million.[195] On the date of the final sale, Dollar Bank issued the following statement.

> The Sheriff Sale was an action taken by Dollar Bank to ensure clean and free title to the property so that the purchase of the property by the Foundation could take place. . . . Dollar Bank is pleased that the opportunity for the Center to pursue its mission with sound financial support and in a debt-free building is now at hand. . . . They also wish the organization much success moving forward with formulating their business plan and for their planned 2015 reopening.[196]

The process of clearing the building's debt was thus one that was supported by individual community members, local businesses such as Dollar Bank that were both creditors and charitable contributors to the center, the major foundations and players in Pittsburgh's philanthropic community, former and current board members, and local elected officials, all of whom were interested in the preservation and continuation of the center.

The three foundations that purchased the deed to the building established a new board of directors for the center that consisted of Maxwell King, Grant Oliphant, and Scott Izzo, the chief executives of the three foundations, along with two local African American businessmen, Michael Polite and Richard W. Taylor. The organization was renamed the August Wilson African American Cultural Center to differentiate it from the earlier nonprofit. Ferola, Ginsberg, and Sutton quote Oliphant as stating an eventual goal of "two African American led nonprofits: [one] to maintain and operate the facility, the other to fill it with deeply relevant African-American programming."[197] In the meantime, the board contracted out the programming of the center to the Pittsburgh Cultural Trust with Janice Burley Wilson, the Pittsburgh Cultural Trust's vice president for strategic partnership and community engagement, who spearheaded programming for the center from 2015 to 2017. Programming during this time consisted of a mix of large-scale income-generating dance and music rentals and smaller, more intimate visual arts exhibitions and education programs. Most but not all of the programming for the center during this time featured artists of African descent.

Significant touring productions and exhibitions brought in by the Pittsburgh Cultural Trust during this time period included dance performances by Philadanco, Ailey II, and Urban Bush Women. A notable example from visual arts was Brazilian photographer Angélica Dass's 2015 exhibition "Humanae/I Am August," which presented giant-sized portraits of hundreds of local residents against matching flesh-colored backgrounds labeled with specific Pantone color descriptions. On her artist's website, Dass wrote, "During the year-long AWC [August Wilson Center] Recovery Conversations in the community, 'I am August,' became a rallying cry of artists, community leaders, and friends of the AWC. The overwhelming sentiment was that people wanted to see bold, dynamic programming that reminded everyone that the Center, like August Wilson, is for everyone. Humanae/I am August accomplishes this."[198] The first theatrical performance presented in the reopened building was August Wilson's *Piano Lesson*. This production, a collaboration between the Pittsburgh Cultural Trust and Pittsburgh Playwrights Theatre, opened in November 2015. The play was directed by Mark Clayton Southers and featured local actors Wali Jamal, Karla Payne, Kevin Brown, Garbie Dukes, Monteze Freeland, Edwin Lee Gibson, and Brenda Marks. In a review for *Trib Live*, Alice Carter wrote, "There could be no better way to reignite theater in this space than with a play by Pittsburgh native playwright and Pulitzer Prize–winner August Wilson, performed, designed, and directed by Pittsburgh-based theatre artists."[199] It was also fitting that the first play presented in the newly reopened space was one that focuses on the struggle of an African American family to hold on to a cherished piece of property that is irreplaceable and invaluable, a piece of property whose possession and use connects the family to their past and leads to their spiritual transformation. One cannot help but draw a parallel between the significance of the piano in August Wilson's play and the struggle to establish, maintain, and retain the August Wilson Center as both a cherished possession and a medium for the artistic expression of African American Pittsburghers.

The programming and management structure put in place by the new board of the August Wilson Center was successful in financially stabilizing the organization. As evidence of their confidence in Janice Burley Wilson, the board of directors hired her as the center's new CEO and president in 2017 after the completion of a national search. Now directly employed by the center, Burley Wilson has continued to work with local community partners as well as bring in touring productions and rentals. At the time of Burley Wilson's hire in 2017, Michael Polite quoted the operating budget of the center as $1.2 million with another approximately $1.2 million dedicated to programming.[200] For a large, multidisciplinary arts organization, this is a very modest programming budget. For comparison, the Andy Warhol Museum (also located in Pittsburgh) has an annual operating budget of approximately $6 million. The operating budget of Penumbra, the high-caliber professional African American theater company located in St. Paul, Minnesota (a similar, midsized city), is approximately $2 million for a production season of four to five plays. The small programming budget for the August Wilson Center in 2017 meant that the organization could not, on its own, produce a full season of theater, music, dance, and visual arts exhibitions and had to continue to rely heavily on rentals, coproductions, and the community partnerships and support Burley Wilson had forged during her time at the Pittsburgh Cultural Trust.

While 2017 featured many rentals and coproductions, in 2018 the August Wilson Center was able to expand its programming significantly. Highlights from 2018 include the ninth annual Pittsburgh International Jazz Festival, a series Burley Wilson brought with her from the Pittsburgh Cultural Trust, and the second annual Black Bottom Film Festival, an initiative begun in 2017. Theater offerings during 2018 included a touring solo performance by Anna Deavere Smith as well as Malik Yoba's one-man show *Harlem to Hollywood*, in association with the New York-based company Hi Arts (formerly known as the Hip Hop Theater Festival).[201] Greer Reed, who had headed up the dance programming of the center prior to its closure, offered a weekly community dance class. Pearl Arts, Hill Dance Academy, and Afro American Music Institute also have partnerships with the center, either offering classes or presenting work.[202] Visual art exhibitions from 2018 included *Abstract Minded: Works by Six Contemporary African Artists*, featuring works by Osi Audu, Nicholas Hlobo, Serge Alain Nitegaka, Odili Donald Odita, Nnenna Okore, and Elias Sime; Naomi Chambers's solo show *Communal Future; Lest We Forget*, a collection of art objects and artworks from James Kidd; and *Darkness Giving Light*, a collection of art from the Braddock Carnegie Library curated by Latika Ann as part of the August Wilson Center's curatorial mentorship program. By slowly expanding the programming of the center and building partnerships with other arts organizations, foundations, and sponsors, the board and Burley Wilson have been able to build upon and more than double the 2017 budget of the August Wilson Center. Burley Wilson reported the center's 2019 budget as "close to $7 million."[203] This budget puts the organization on par with many of the other larger downtown arts organizations of the city.

As the operations of BHT, Kuntu, Pittsburgh Playwrights, and the August Wilson Center have shown, black theater has a long and distinguished history in Pittsburgh. Each of these institutions has uniquely benefited from its association with August Wilson and also helped to further his legacy. While the remaining black theater institutions in Pittsburgh still encounter challenges and work tirelessly to economically support the important work they produce, it is inspiring to take note of what these institutions and their predecessors have collectively accomplished. It is also promising to see the larger arts ecology of the city participate more directly in supporting and sustaining black theatrical activity, often in conjunction with the continued celebration of the life and legacy of August Wilson. It is clear that August Wilson and the institutions he championed have shaped the city, delving into and presenting the rich history of African American Pittsburghers and pushing toward a more equitable practice of artistic representation and arts productions in the larger Pittsburgh arts ecology.

Chapter 3

✦

Displacement and Resilience

Bay Area Black Theaters

Long considered a locus of personal and political freedom, the San Francisco Bay Area is home to a variety of African American performing arts institutions including theater, dance, and solo performance companies dedicated to expressing African American artistic aesthetics. This chapter will focus on Black Repertory Group (BRG), a community theater in Berkeley, and the Lorraine Hansberry Theatre (LHT) and African-American Shakespeare Company (AASC), both professional companies based in San Francisco. While there has been some overlap in each of these companies' activities and personnel over the course of their existence, the missions of these organizations are quite distinct. As such, they offer different strategies for expressing African American subjectivity and increasing the autonomy and participation of African Americans on the American stage. Before addressing their specific programming, however, it is necessary to examine the unique urban ecology in which they operate.

San Francisco has experienced two major waves of gentrification and displacement since the beginning of the twenty-first century. In 2014, San Francisco surpassed New York and became America's most expensive city.[1] As middle- and working-class people were priced out of neighborhood after neighborhood, community groups fought against the economic forces that have decreased the diversity and vitality of the city. The historically Latinx Mission District was the primary focus of this conflict, most famously symbolized by the Google bus protests of 2013 and 2014.[2] According to the Anti-Eviction Mapping Project, from January 1, 1997, to November 24, 2015, the Ellis Act (the legal precedent that allows California landlords to evict tenants of a particular property in order to convert said property into another business use) has been used 4,190 times to evict tenants in the city of San Francisco.[3] Just as working-class people of color were displaced from their homes, so were arts organizations, many of which lost their leases and were forced to relocate or close altogether.[4] This period of hypergentrification mirrored previous waves of displacement from which black communities suffered.[5] Understanding these waves of displacement is key to understanding the ecology of the city and the place African American cultural arts organizations have within it.

Historically, San Francisco's black neighborhoods were established when African Americans came to the West Coast in significant numbers during the 1940s to take advantage of the shipping and industrial opportunities created by World War II and the subsequent economic boom. Because of racism, restrictive housing covenants, and affordability, in San Francisco, Seattle, and Los Angeles, African Americans often moved into Japanese American neighborhoods whose inhabitants had been forcibly removed and interned during the war.[6] In San Francisco, this neighborhood is known as the Fillmore, or more expansively, the Western Addition. After the end of World War II, many Japanese Americans returned to the Fillmore, and these two communities coexisted for twenty years until two urban renewal projects, A-1 and A-2, displaced more than thirteen thousand of the neighborhood's lowest-income residents.[7] In "The Racial Triangulation of Space: The Case of Urban Renewal in San Francisco's Fillmore District," Clement Lai details how predominantly black organizations such as the Western Addition Community Organization, later known as the Western Addition Project Area Committee, and Freedom House fought against the displacement of low-income African Americans and the destruction of low-income housing. These community organizations legally challenged the redevelopment projects in court and in public throughout the 1960s and 1970s. The work of these community organizations, along with changes in urban redevelopment policy, stalled the completion of A-2, which was officially sunset in 2008. Nevertheless, Lai claims that the early displacement of housing and individuals, along with the construction of the Geary expressway, "effectively destroyed the city's most significant African American and Japanese American neighborhoods."[8]

According to census data and the Anti-Eviction Mapping Project, the black population of San Francisco decreased from 13 percent to 6 percent from 1970 to 2013.[9] This precipitous loss has been marked by historians, urban geographers, community organizers, and artists. For instance, in 2019 the film *The Last Black Man in San Francisco* received the Sundance Film Festival Special Jury Award.[10] In Oakland and Berkeley, traditionally thought of as the heart of the Bay Area's black community, African American residents have also been displaced.[11] In her article "Oakland Wants You to Stop Calling It 'The New Brooklyn,'" Susie Cagle writes that Oakland's black population has fallen 25 percent from 2000 to 2010 largely as a result of the foreclosure crisis and the consequent spate of flipped properties that are now too expensive for working-class Oakland residents but a bargain for middle- and upper-class San Franciscans moving out of a now unaffordable city.[12] These statistics show the incredible economic pressures involved in living in the Bay Area, where a six-figure salary is now considered "low income."[13] Despite these enormous economic challenges and the large-scale displacements of many people, the Bay Area retains a rich cultural history and continues the robust social and political activism that stems from the Black Power and free speech movements of the 1960s and 1970s. The activism of its citizens remains a defining feature of the area. These oppositional forces have shaped the accomplishments and challenges of the Bay Area's black theaters.

Black Repertory Group

As the oldest continuously operating black theater in the San Francisco Bay Area, BRG is decidedly rooted in a neighborhood and community-based organizational model. BRG was founded in Berkeley in 1964 by Birel and Nora Vaughn, who had recently moved from Vicksburg, Mississippi, to the Bay Area to escape persecution from the KKK during the civil rights movement. The theater was first housed in and supported by Downs United Methodist Church, where Birel Vaughn served as minister. Nora Vaughn, who had studied drama at the historically black college Alcorn State, served as the director of the church's drama program. After four seasons of directing holiday programs for the church, BRG expanded its programming beyond church services, performing the work of black playwrights in the community "at senior and recreational centers" and in outdoor parks.[14]

From the beginning, BRG was community based, using theater as a tool for individual empowerment and community strengthening. Its current mission emphasizes this focus. "Our #1 goal continues to be 'Keepers of the Culture,' by promoting and preserving our theatrical arts. By utilizing our theater stage and its related functions, we provide a platform to build self-esteem and pride within our participants, audience and community."[15] A community theater organization, BRG does not pay its participating artists and describes the "primary rewards" from participating in its programs as "psychic and human, providing therapeutic improvements in the morale of participants, both individually and collectively."[16] A list of the group's programs such as health education through theater, street kids at risk, summer theatrical arts day camp, and tutorial and cultural empowerment indicates its community focus. Drama critic Nancy Scott stressed this component of BRG's work in an article for the *San Francisco Examiner*. "For Mrs. Vaughn, the stage was not a museum. The preservation of black culture was always linked for her with preservation of the community; with bringing black youngsters in off the street into workshops; with finding a place for talented amateurs who longed to be professionals; and with giving voice to new black playwrights."[17] From its inception to the present day, BRG has been a theater inseparable from the neighborhood and community of which it is a part. The fact that BRG's facility has recently been used as a venue for Congresswoman Barbara Lee's town hall meeting on race in America, as a polling station, a comedy club, and a youth theater camp demonstrates its continued import to the East Bay black community and the carrying forward of its initial mission.[18]

The founding of BRG was part of a larger flowering of community-based arts and activism during the 1960s. The company's early programming complemented other local youth programs such as the Oakland Community School and the Free Breakfast for Children in Oakland program, both begun by the Black Panther Party, which sought to directly empower the black community in the Bay Area, paying particular attention to youth development and support.[19] BRG was established slightly before the major endeavors of San Francisco–based black revolutionary theaters such as Black Arts West, Culture House, and Black Educational Theater, which were organized by Marvin X and Ed Bullins as part of the Black Panther Party in 1966 and 1967.[20] BRG's tenure also overlapped with other influential black theaters in the Bay Area during the 1960s such as Aldridge Players West, which was housed in the Sutter Street YWCA in San Francisco and led by Henrietta Harris; the Haight-Ashbury settlement house, led by Charles Smith; and the North Richmond house, run by Dan Robbin.[21] These Bay Area theaters strongly contributed to the articulation of the black arts movement as the artistic arm of the Black Power movement. For example, Bullins was editor of the *Tulane Drama Review*'s 1968 "Black Theatre" special issue that crystalized the ethos and national practice of the movement, inspiring a generation.[22] Marvin X and Henrietta Harris were also contributing authors to that publication.[23] While not directly associated with any of these organizations, BRG describes its mission and practice as "kin to all of the black cultural movements and struggles."[24] Its affinity for the artists and causes of that time period continues. For instance, in 2017, Marvin X held a series of concerts and poetry readings at BRG.[25]

After years of performing in churches, senior centers, cultural houses, and parks, BRG established a storefront theater on Alcatraz Avenue in 1970.[26] The group named this space the South Berkeley Playhouse.[27] The first production in this space was Ossie Davis's *Purlie Victorious*, which depicts the accomplishments of a plucky and resourceful Southern preacher who successfully reclaims a land theft from a white plantation owner.[28] This play resonated with the experience of the Vaughns as members of the church working within the movement in Mississippi, and BRG restaged this production many times over the course of its history. For example, in 1972, the group performed the play as a benefit for the Martin Luther King Junior Middle School PTA.[29]

The repertoire of the company during the 1970s was diverse. The group produced many plays with religious themes such as Langston Hughes's *Tambourines to Glory*, James Weldon Johnson's *God's Trombones*, and James Baldwin's *The Amen Corner*. Alice Childress was also a favorite playwright, with Nora Vaughn directing *Wedding Band* several times in addition to producing multiple iterations of *Trouble in Mind* and *Wine in the Wilderness*. BRG also produced several of the more seminal works of the black arts movement including Phillip Hayes Dean's *Sty of the Blind Pig*, Lonnie Elder III's *Ceremonies in Dark Old Men*, and Steve Carter's *Eden*. In an interview with the *San Francisco Examiner* in 1979 Nora Vaughn described the production choices of the company as "theater the whole family can see, including grandmothers and children."[30] In this respect the repertoire of BRG was somewhat broader than some of the other Bay Area black theater initiatives of that time and perhaps for this reason outlasted them. The fact that BRG also never aimed to professionalize and from the beginning embraced its identity as an educational and amateur company also undoubtedly kept its production costs low and contributed to its survival.

During the 1970s, BRG operated concurrently with the San Francisco–based West Coast Black Repertory Theater (founded by John Cochran and Sandra Richards), Oakland Ensemble Theatre (founded by Ron Stacker Thompson), and Grassroots Experience Theatre Company (founded by John Doyle). These companies collaborated with one another and coordinated a three-day conference entitled Black Community Theater: Tools for Survival in 1974.[31] John Doyle would later direct three one-act plays by Ed Bullins for BRG in 1982.[32] One of the participating members of Black Repertory Theater and Grassroots Experience, Buriel Clay II, a playwright and professor of creative writing at San Francisco State University, would later found the Western Addition Cultural Center at 762 Fulton Street in San Francisco in 1978. Clay and other black theater practitioners worked with the city of San Francisco, which owned the building, and convinced it to cede the building to the neighborhood for use as a community center/cultural space. Both the building and the arts organization that manages it still exist today. Now known as the African American Art and Culture Complex (AAACC), this building is used today by four of San Francisco's contemporary black theaters. The theater space inside the building is named after Buriel Clay.[33]

The success of the black theater groups of San Francisco attaining a city-supported building in which to create black art motivated Nora Vaughn to seek out such a space in the East Bay. A 1979 *San Francisco Examiner* article reports that BRG had negotiated a "55-year lease for $1 a year with the city of Berkeley for a plot of vacant land in South Berkeley."[34] The group needed a new performing space because "the condition of the [Alcatraz] building was not up to standard" and was described by numerous drama critics from that era as cramped and "shabby."[35] After nearly a decade of fundraising and petitioning the city, BRG moved into its current home at 3201 Adeline Street in 1987. The building includes a 250-seat theater, community room, and dance studio.[36] Construction cost $900,000 in 1987 and was funded by the city and other community partners.[37] The group still operates out of this building today. The fact that the cities of Berkeley and San Francisco still directly fund and house black theater is a unique and laudable characteristic of the Bay Area arts ecology and a rare example of civic commitment to racial justice and equity in arts programming and practice.

Having a functional, affordable, and permanent home empowered BRG to expand its programming. Productions in the 1980s and 1990s continued to reflect the diverse tastes of Nora Vaughn. In addition to many repeat productions of *God's Trombones* and Alice Childress's plays, other significant productions included Abram Hill's *On Striver's Row*, Theodore Ward's *Big White Fog*, Langston Hughes's *Mulatto*, *Purlie* (the musical adaptation of *Purlie Victorious*), Samm-Art Williams's *Home*, and *The Prodigal Sister*, a gender reversed musical adaptation of the biblical story by J. E. Franklin.[38] Berkeley mayor Gus Newport proclaimed June 30, 1985, "Black Repertory Day," in honor of the company's twentieth anniversary.[39] In 1989, the group produced *Hubba City* by local literary giant Ishmael Reed.[40] In 1999, the group produced Marvin X's play about drug recovery *One Day in the Life*.[41] Productions by Marvin X, Bullins, Reed, and Franklin show that the repertoire of the group continued to include more politically pointed plays alongside church stories, musicals, and historical dramas. In the 1990s, BRG began to produce August Wilson plays, likely inspired by Claude Purdy's excellent 1989 production of *Joe Turner's Come and Gone*, which was coproduced by LHT and American Conservatory Theater in San Francisco.[42] BRG's 1990–91 season included two Wilson Plays, *Joe Turner's Come and Gone* and *Ma Rainey's Black Bottom*.[43]

After Nora Vaughn passed away in 1994, her daughter Dr. Mona Vaughn Scott took over the executive leadership of BRG. Nora Vaughn's grandson, Sean Vaughn Scott, is also a board member and currently the development director of the group. Throughout the 1990s, the group continued to be a core participant in the civic and artistic life of the Bay Area. In 1997, for example, the group performed as part of the thirtieth anniversary celebration of the Summer of Love in Golden Gate Park.[44] In 1998, BRG produced a developmental production of *Gethsemane Park*, a gospel opera or "gospra" set in an Oakland park that was written by Ishmael Reed the same year he won the MacArthur Genius Award.[45] Reed had originally been commissioned to develop the piece at the San Francisco Opera with Bobby McFerrin as composer. When these arrangements did not work out, Reed invested his own money in productions first with BRG in 1998 and later with LHT in 1999.[46]

Reed has remained a strong supporter of black theater companies in the Bay Area and is listed as a board member on recent tax documents of both LHT and BRG.[47] Reed came to the defense of BRG after the City of Berkeley considered defunding it following an unfavorable city audit in 1999. In an editorial published in the *San Francisco Chronicle*, Reed pointed out that with a very modest budget BRG "enrolled 100 kids, 20 of whom were homeless," in a production of *Da Wiz* in 1999.[48] Reed again defended the company in 2007 with another article in the *Chronicle*, "Black Repertory Theater and the Creation of Opportunities for Kids: Berkeley Group Soldiers On as Help from City and Developers Lag."[49] In this piece, Reed described a theater initiative involving students from a juvenile correctional institution and BRG's summer youth educational theater program. "With a budget of $28,000, the theatre hosted more than 100 children, keeping them all day so their parents could work, feeding them lunch, and ending the summer with a rousing performance of *The Lion King*, a production I found thoroughly enjoyable."[50] Reed's editorial was in reaction to a previous *Chronicle* article that quoted several East Bay artists and neighboring business owners who wanted to see the city cut off funding to the group and evict them, with statements such as "I don't believe anything Black Rep does couldn't be done in a church basement" and complaints that the theater's space could be put to better use by a professional company.[51] These neighbors' comments clearly demonstrated a low regard for the group's social service mission. Fortunately, at the city council meeting in which the continuance of the group's one dollar a year lease was debated, "a standing-room-only crowd of theater supporters packed the council's chambers . . . to urge the council to continue to support the company," and BRG's lease was renewed for another twenty-five years.[52] These news articles document an economically motivated effort to displace BRG from its home in an area that has now become prime real estate. The group's ability to renew its lease and stave off efforts to displace it indicates its community significance and the local support it has gathered over the course of several decades. It also provides an example of the economic and racial tensions arts groups in the Bay Area have faced during a period of hypergentrification.

In recent years, BRG has expanded its artistic practice beyond theater. Current programming includes stand-up comedy, poetry, film festivals, and a gospel music series that broaden the focus of the group from strictly theater to several related performing arts disciplines.[53] Like many contemporary theater companies that are branching out to include other popular forms of art and entertainment, the impetus to include these kinds of activities stems from the related goals of attracting broader audiences and increasing revenue from both rentals and ticket sales. Presenting these other arts activities is also one way to stay connected to the community and provide overlapping programming with religious groups and other black arts organizations and disciplines.

BRG continues to present and produce relevant and civically engaged live theater and performance. In 2006, for instance, the group presented a reenactment of the botched execution of Stanley Tookie Williams. The event was produced by Barbara Becnel and Shirley Neal as a protest of California's use of the death penalty during a time when its constitutionality was being debated in federal court.[54] Another significant performance art piece was presented in 2018 when the founder of the San Francisco–based Afro Solo Theatre Company, Thomas Robert Simpson, staged the one-man show *Courage under Fire: The Story of Elroy* as a tribute to his father who had survived a life lived under Jim Crow.[55] Mona Vaughn Scott has also written numerous plays for BRG's main-stage programming. In 2017, BRG staged

Unbought and Unbossed, Vaughn Scott's multimedia retrospective on the life and accomplishments of Shirley Chisholm. In association with this production, RBG sponsored a high school essay writing contest on the subject of Shirley Chisholm's contribution to democracy. The press release for the contest stated, "Before there was Hillary Clinton and Barack Obama, there was Shirley Chisholm. . . . Students are asked to research and analyze the career, motivations and legacy of Shirley Chisholm. Highlighting the correlations between her platform, beliefs, and the critical socioeconomic issues of today."[56] Carrying a cash prize of $1,000, this contest was a beautiful way to meld theater, civic literacy, and education.

BRG has also helped to tell the stories of African Americans from the Bay Area, publicly asserting the presence and history of the cities' black communities. For example, as part of its New Arts play development program, BRG presented two productions (in 2017 and 2018) of *Port Chicago 50* by David Shackelford and Dennis Rowe. This play, directed at BRG by J. D. Hall, examines the 1944 Port Chicago harbor accident that killed over three hundred people when African American navy servicemen were ordered to load explosive cargo onto military vessels without proper training, supervision, or safety measures. After the accident, surviving white sailors were given time off, while black sailors were ordered back to work before the completion of any safety review or inquiry. Fifty African American naval personnel were court-martialed following the accident for their refusal to continue work under these unsafe conditions.[57] The play tells the story from the perspective of one of the survivors, Freddie Meeks, who received a pardon from the navy in 1999 shortly before his death in 2003.[58] *Port Chicago 50* was performed twice in Berkeley in 2017 and 2018 and once in 2017 in Pittsburgh, California, a city near the Port Chicago Naval Station where the events of the play took place.[59] This production is an example of how BRG has continued to participate in the telling of Bay Area history through the art of theater. Telling these stories shapes the city by asserting the presence and history of a black population that has been displaced, maligned, and ignored. By continuing their work, BRG also makes space for the cultural expression of the black population that has managed to remain. All of its recent endeavors show that BRG has continued to be active and involved in the performing arts ecology of the Bay Area. The fact that the group is an amateur one in no way diminishes the impact of its accomplishments.

The Lorraine Hansberry Theatre

Stanley E. Williams and Quentin Easter founded LHT in 1981. Williams had previously performed as an actor with the Oakland Ensemble Theater, a flourishing black theater active during the 1970s. In an interview with the *San Francisco Examiner*, Williams stated, "I wanted to create a theater by and for black people, drawing from a pool of black actors, technicians, and writers, to deal with the issues that are important to black and Third World people."[60] Like many other black theaters of this era, Williams and Easter were inspired by the New York–based Negro Ensemble Company and saw that company's investment in and development of black talent as "a model."[61] Williams served as the company's artistic director, and Easter was the company's executive producer and manager. Overcoming numerous challenges, Williams and Easter succeeded in establishing a professional, influential, and enduring black theater in San Francisco that intersected with the careers of some of the Bay Area's brightest artistic luminaries such as Danny Glover, Ishmael Reed, Ntozake Shange, and Alice Walker.

Since its inception, securing adequate performance space has been one of the theater's greatest challenges. For the first five years of the company's existence, productions were presented at a variety of different spaces in San Francisco, including leasing space in the Mission District at 2940 Sixteenth Street during its first season, performing and participating in the artist colony at the historic Goodman Building in the Tenderloin during its second season, and spending several years producing in a cramped forty-seat space in the Trinity Episcopal Church in the Western Addition.[62] Despite venue constraints, the company was praised for "four full seasons of intriguing and challenging plays that almost certainly would not have been attempted by any other theater in the Bay Area."[63] The inaugural production of the company included two one-act plays, Wole Soyinka's *The Trials of Brother Jero* and Ali Wadud's *Companions of the Fire*, which had premiered at the Negro Ensemble Company the year before.[64] Both pieces were directed by Felix Justice. Justice wrote the play *Prophecy in America: The Life of Martin Luther King*, which was also staged during LHT's inaugural season.[65] Justice would later develop another work about Martin Luther King Jr. with friend and colleague Danny Glover as the touring production/speaking engagement *An Evening with Martin and Langston*.[66] Other significant early LHT productions included Steve Carter's *Nevis Mountain Dew*, which was directed by John Doyle in 1981, and Whitney J. LeBlanc's direction of Charles Fuller's *Zooman and the Sign* and Adrienne Kennedy's *Funnyhouse of a Negro* in 1983 and Lorraine Hansberry's *A Raisin in the Sun* in 1984.[67] Stanley Williams directed Ntozake Shange's *Boogie Woogie Landscapes* during the 1983–84 season and Derek Walcott's *Dream on Monkey Mountain* in 1984. In 1985, LHT produced an adaptation of Alice Walker's novel *The Third Life of Grange Copeland*, which was also directed by Williams. This selection of plays shows the wide range of the theater, whose seasons included a balance between male and female playwrights and between social realism and more experimental/avant-garde work, as well as plays with historical subjects presented alongside of contemporary dramas and world premieres.

The work that LHT produced also reflected the strong influence of San Francisco's counterculture and provides an example of African American

participation in that movement and that movement's cultural legacy. One of
the most celebrated plays of the company's early history was Robert Alexander's rock musical *Air Guitar*, which was produced in 1985 in collaboration
with San Francisco State University. It was directed by Clinton Turner Davis
with music by David Allen and Jabari Allen and Chor-Evelyn Thomas.[68] The
play follows the fantasy life of an accountant (played by Jesse Moore) who is
having a midlife crisis and is jealous of his son's ambitions to become a rock
musician.[69] The production was listed as one of the "year's ten best plays" by
the *SF Bay Guardian* and received local Dramalog awards for best new play,
direction, and musical score.[70]

A prolific playwright, Robert Alexander was inspired by both the hard-
hitting plays of the black arts movement and musicals such as *Hair*, which
he saw as a child growing up in the DC metro area.[71] In an interview with SF
Gate, Alexander discussed his various artistic influences.

> The militant playwrights that came out of the Black Arts Movement,
> Amiri Baraka . . . and Ed Bullins, primarily. They had a profound
> influence on me. . . . Their plays were politically charged but also very
> angry. Then, later I saw the San Francisco Mime Troupe and I saw
> that you could make strong political points, and be funny at the same
> time. . . . I saw that you could go a lot further with humor than you
> could with anger.[72]

As a result of these interests, Alexander was active with both LHT and the
San Francisco Mime Troupe. He considers former San Francisco Mime
Troupe resident playwright Joan Holden a personal mentor, stating, "I got
my first master's degree from the school of Joan Holden and my second
master's degree from the University of Iowa."[73] Alexander worked with the
San Francisco Mime Troupe for six seasons, assisting Joan Holden on the
creation of several scripts and serving as lead writer for plays such as *The
Hourglass* (1978), *Factwino vs Armageddonman* (1983), *The Mozamgola
Caper* (1986), and *Secret in the Sands* (1989).[74]

Started in 1959, the San Francisco Mime Troupe (SFMT) is the Bay Area
theater company with the longest and closest ties to the free speech movement,
antiwar efforts, and the countercultural scene of the 1960s for which the Bay
Area is well-known.[75] SFMT runs on a collective model and has been inten-
tionally racially diverse and inclusive since its founding. In the introduction
to *The Plays of the San Francisco Mime Troupe: 2000–2016*, Michael Gene
Sullivan writes, "Long before the word 'multicultural' entered the language,
the SFMT was a multiracial company to reflect the complexity of America's
present reality, and to state our hope for a multicultural, equitable, future."[76]
In 1990, LHT and SFMT coproduced *I Ain't Yo Uncle: The New Jack Revisionist Uncle Tom's Cabin*.[77] *I Ain't Yo Uncle* places Harriet Beecher Stowe
on trial for creating damaging racial stereotypes. The production humorously

deconstructs and subverts the well-known black caricatures that originated from Stowe's best-selling nineteenth-century novel. LHT's collaborations with SFMT and Robert Alexander reflect the overlap in mission between the two companies—namely, the use of art to dismantle racism, increase social equity, and embrace personal as well as political freedom.

Like BRG, LHT has also helped to tell the stories of African Americans in the Bay Area. A resident of Oakland, Robert Alexander's best-known work, *Servant of the People: The Rise and Fall of Huey Newton and the Black Panther Party*, reflects his interest in the history of black power in the Bay Area. The play premiered at St. Louis Black Repertory Company in 1995 and was subsequently staged by Atlanta's Jomandi Productions later in 1995, Chicago's National Pastime Theater in 1996, and Baltimore's Arena Players in 1996.[78] LHT also produced the play in 1996 under the direction of Stanley Williams. SFMT collective member Michael Gene Sullivan portrayed the title role. Four years later Sullivan would write his own one-man show, *Did Anyone Ever Tell You, You Look Like Huey P. Newton?* about the experience of being in *Servant of the People* and his own changing opinions and relationship to the ideologies of Newton and the Black Panther Party.[79] These productions offered a nuanced look at Huey Newton's life and politics from the perspective of the next generation of Bay Area black artists and activists.

LHT started another enduring relationship with a prominent playwright in 1984 when the company staged Ntozake Shange's *Boogie Woogie Landscapes*. Shange had been a part of the Bay Area art scene during the 1970s. Her seminal play *for colored girls who have considered suicide when the rainbow is enuf* was developed through a series of readings and performances throughout the Bay Area in late 1974 and early 1975 including venues such as the women's bar Bacchanal in Albany (near Berkeley) and Minnie's Can Do Club in the Haight-Ashbury neighborhood of San Francisco.[80] After Shange moved to New York in 1975, the play was picked up by Woodie King Jr. and the New Federal Theatre. Due to its success and popularity, it was transferred twice, once to the Public Theater, and then to Broadway, where it ran for over seven hundred performances and was catapulted into fame, becoming one of the most influential and enduring plays of the twentieth century.[81] In her article "Activists Who Yearn for Art That Transforms: Parallels in the Black Arts Movement and Feminist Art Movements in the United States," Lisa Gail Collins writes,

> A handful of courageous and visionary women claimed, drew from, and shaped both [the black arts and feminist art] movements, and perhaps no one was better able to do this than Ntozake Shange. . . . Shange, from her bohemian Bay Area vantage point, saw the quest for female imagery and the search for a black aesthetic as linked, like her accepted name [meaning "she who brings her own things" and "one who walks with lions"], which elegantly meshes the desire for

an African homeland so palpable in the black arts movement with
the desire for female self-reliance and bodily sovereignty so crucial to
women's liberation.[82]

An instructor teaching courses in women's studies at Sonoma State University at the time of *for colored girls* development, Shange commuted to her job
so she could live in the Bay Area and take African-based dance classes. Halifu
Osumare was one of her teachers.[83] In her essay, Collins describes Shange's
"hungry embrace of the rich resources of the period's (and the region's)
vibrant cultural movements."[84]

While LHT was not involved in the development of *for colored girls*, its
productions of *Boogie Woogie Landscapes* in 1984 and *Spell #7* in 1985
drew from and contributed to the robust and intertwined worlds of African
American theater and dance in the Bay Area from which Shange had emerged
and crafted her masterpiece. For example, Shange's teacher and friend Halifu
Osumare choreographed both *Boogie Woogie Landscapes* and *Spell #7* for
LHT. Like *for colored girls*, *Boogie Woogie Landscapes* is described as a
"choreopoem" and mixes dance, poetry, theater, and music together to depict
black women's thoughts and experiences.[85] Williams directed the piece, and
Idris Ackamoor, cofounder of Cultural Odyssey, served as composer and
musical director. The cast included a mix of professional dancers and actors
including Deborah Asante, Chery McClelland, Carla Hightower, Winifred
Cabiness, Donald Lacy, Todd Jackson, and Hassan Al Falak.[86] Some of the
brightest dance and theater luminaries in the Bay Area were also in LHT's
production of *Spell #7*, which was directed by Keryl McCord and choreographed by Halifu Osumare, with musical direction by Rob Robinson. The
cast included Rob Robinson, Clinton Vidal, Amara Tabor (now Amara
Tabor-Smith), Darold Ross, Baomi Butts-Bhanji, Niva Ruschell, Eloise Chit-
mon, Ronnie Britton, and Kimberley Anne LaMarque.[87]

While Shange was not personally involved in either of these two productions, she directly supported and collaborated with LHT on several
subsequent occasions. For example, she appeared in a benefit reading for the
company on a double bill with Ishmael Reed in 1986.[88] She also participated
as a performer in LHT's world premiere of her play *Three Views of Mt. Fuji*
in 1987.[89] In *Three Views of Mt. Fuji*, Shange portrayed the multicultural Bay
Area arts scene she was a part of during the early 1970s. Because the setting
of the play is San Francisco, it was fitting that Shange gave the opportunity
to produce the world premiere of this production to LHT. The play examines
"the lives of the post-beat poets of San Francisco," centering on the birthday
party of one of these poets and including a poetry reading as part of the play's
action.[90] In an interview with drama critic Rob Hurwitt, Shange explained
her motivation to write a play about the Bay Area's multicultural poetry
scene: "Anyone who works in San Francisco works in the shadow of the
Beats. . . . If we come after the beatniks and we're not hippies who are we?

. . . all different kinds of people: Puerto Rican nationalists, Filipino exiles, Chicanos who speak Spanish, Chicanos who don't speak Spanish, blacks who dance, blacks who don't dance, white people who don't like blacks, white people who think they're black people."[91] During the same interview, Shange described participating in this production as "coming back to the roots of my artistic soul."[92] Later in her career she would continue to praise the relaxed and fluid multicultural world of the Bay Area that she had participated in during the 1970s as something special and unique. In her 2007 interview with Will Power for *American Theatre* magazine, for example, she stated, "The Bay Area was one of the few places in the country that was truly and actively multicultural. When I wrote *for colored girls*, I meant it for all women of color. When I took that idea to New York, they took out all my Puerto Ricans, and when I wanted to include Asians, they looked at me like I had lost my mind!"[93] By writing and participating in the production of *Three Views of Mt. Fuji*, Shange honored the spirit of arts production in the Bay Area. She also used the production to renew her collaboration with Halifu Osumare, who served as the play's choreographer. Shange returned to LHT to perform *The Love Space Demands*, an "exciting theatre piece based on her poetry," in 1992 and *from okra to greens, a different kinda love story* in 2006.[94] *The Love Space Demands* was performed as a one-woman show by Shange in a four-day Bay Area appearance. The choreopoem *from okra to greens* is centered on the love story between a man and woman named after the titular soul food items and adapted from a series of poems Shange wrote during the 1980s. Stanley Williams codirected the piece with choreographer Danny Duncan.[95] These collaborations demonstrate the deep and abiding creative partnership that existed between Shange and LHT. While many other theaters have produced *for colored girls*, LHT is unique in its commitment to staging so many of Shange's other plays and poetic experiments.

The partnership between Shange and LHT is one example of how the organization has actively contributed to the practice of feminist and womanist theater. LHT's former artistic director Steven Anthony Jones emphasized the production of black women's work, pointing out that "because we are named for a great African American woman artist, every season we produce plays by African American women. Our other major area of focus is on issues of social justice as they relate to African Americans."[96] As Ntozake Shange did, LHT invests in the goals of both the black power and women's liberation movements. For example, in 1995 on the twentieth anniversary of the Broadway production of *for colored girls*, LHT produced the iconic choreopoem. This production was part of a celebration of International Women's Day that involved members of each of the three companies discussed in this chapter. The cast of LHT's 1995 production included Sherri Young, future founder of the AASC, whose role was described as "buoyantly performed."[97] The other performances featured Jan Crain-Hunter, Karen Polk, Payge, Deborah Edwards, Safi Tating, and Saun-Toy Latifa Trotter. After the performance,

Stanley Williams presented four prominent African American women with awards, one of whom was Mona Vaughn Scott, executive director of BRG, who had recently taken over direction of the company after her mother's passing. In 2018, AASC produced another acclaimed Bay Area production of *for colored girls*, demonstrating the persistent influence of this play in the Bay Area black community.[98] All of these productions show that Shange's work has brought together distinct strands of black theater production and feminist practice in the Bay Area, a phenomenon that has persisted from the 1970s to the present day.

Although LHT's productions throughout the 1980s and 1990s were recognized for their quality and contributions to local and national artistic and cultural movements, the venues they were presented in were often subpar. *San Francisco Examiner* and *Chronicle* drama critic Nancy Scott repeatedly remarked on the unfavorable production conditions under which the company made great art throughout the 1980s. Scott described the company's performance space at Trinity Episcopal Church as "probably OK for amateur theatricals . . . absolutely inadequate, in shape, acoustics and size, for the complex, varied, and sophisticated productions."[99] In "The City's Homeless Ethnic Theatres," Scott called attention to the lack of performance space for nonwhite theaters and the misleading narrative presented by a promotional brochure regarding the use of the city's Hotel Tax Fund.

> At first glance, I thought wonderful. We tax the tourists to help the artists and the artists are truly diverse in color and culture. My second thought was, wait a minute. Right now, as the publicity is rolling out for the 84–85 season, I cannot think of a single ethnic theater that has a home of its own. . . . I do not want to give the impression that I do not love the Hotel Tax Fund . . . when it was set up in 1961, it was the first of its kind in the country. I just want to point out that there is an ironic discrepancy between the self-congratulatory image of San Francisco as a city that welcomes ethnic diversity in theater and the grim reality for those that are trying to create ethnic theater.[100]

Scott's comments show that the challenges arts organizations of color have faced in securing and retaining production space go back well before the current period of hypergentrification. Her comments also reveal the complexity of the city art's funding and support system. In the Helicon Collaborative's recent study, San Francisco was the only city in the ten wealthiest urban arts ecologies that did not exhibit gross racial bias in its public and private arts philanthropy. The report states: "The notable exception to the general pattern is San Francisco, where two decades of intentional and collaborative efforts to boost mid-sized and smaller cultural organizations and increase cultural equity—by both public sector funders and private foundations . . . has led to funding distribution patterns that more closely reflect the city's demographic profile and the diversity of the local cultural sector."[101] While laudable, this lack of bias does not mitigate the fact that arts organizations of color still have extreme difficulty securing and maintaining performance and production space in the Bay Area. In her article, Scott mentioned LHT (then known as SEW Productions), Bayview Repertory Theatre Company, BRG, and Oakland Ensemble Theatre (all black theater companies); Asian American Theater and Theater of Yugen (Asian American companies); and Teatro Latino as examples of nonwhite theater organizations struggling to find and fundraise for adequate performance space. It is telling that many of these theaters no longer exist.

Fortunately for LHT, Stanley Williams and Quentin Easter realized their dream of securing a home for their theater in 1987 when they negotiated to lease and renovate a space in the YWCA building at 620 Sutter Street in the Union Square theater district. After raising $400,000, LHT secured the services of theater architect and set designer Gene Angell.[102] Angell designed many of the performance spaces in the Bay Area including Berkeley Repertory Theatre's thrust stage, California Shakespeare Company's outdoor theater, the redesign and renovation of Brava Theater Center in the Mission District and many others.[103] With renovations completed in 1988 and an operating budget of $400,000, LHT began two decades of theater production exploring black experiences from a variety of perspectives in a state-of-the-art space in the heart of the city's theater district.

For the next twenty years, LHT produced a rich variety of new plays by local and national playwrights like Robert Alexander and Roger Guenveur Smith, classic works from the black arts movement by playwrights such as Amiri Baraka, Joseph Walker, and Marvin X, and plays by women such as Glenda Dickerson, Ramona King, Vinnette Carroll, Marcia Leslie, Thulani Davis, Lynn Nottage, Regina Taylor, Rhodessa Jones, and Suzan-Lori Parks.[104] The first production in the new space was *The Resurrection of Lady Lester*, by Oyamo, a play about the musician Lester Young. It was directed by Claude Purdy, with music by Mary Watkins and choreography by Halifu Osumare. The cast included dancers from Osumare's company Citicentre Dance Theatre.[105]

Purdy had previously directed *Ma Rainey's Black Bottom* at American Conservatory Theater (ACT) in 1987. He returned to the Bay Area to direct a series of plays in the late 1980s for LHT. Immediately following *The Resurrection of Lady Lester* in 1988, Purdy directed a LHT/Eureka Theatre coproduction of George Wolfe's *The Colored Museum*.[106] He then directed a critically acclaimed LHT/ACT coproduction of August Wilson's *Joe Turner's Come and Gone* at ACT in 1989, featuring a powerhouse cast including Roscoe Lee Brown as Bynum, fellow Penumbra company member James Craven as Loomis, future LHT artistic director and previous Negro Ensemble Company member Steven Anthony Jones as Seth, acclaimed solo performer Anna Deveare Smith as Molly, and Delores Mitchell, Kimberley LaMarque, Mark

Daniel Cade, Scott Freeman, and Adilah Barnes as Bertha, Mattie, Jeremy, Selig, and Martha Pentecost, respectively. Amber Russ played Loomis's daughter Zonia.[107] This production is an example of how LHT participated in artistic collaborations of national significance at a time when August Wilson was using his artistic clout in service of building greater autonomy and power for black artists working within the regional theater system. Wilson helped to broker Claude Purdy's hiring at ACT and the affording of double billing to LHT, just as he did with Penumbra Theatre Company in St. Paul and the coproductions of Wilson's work that the company presented at the Guthrie Theater.[108]

At their best, these kinds of coproductions increase the resources and audiences available to smaller, culturally specific theaters that are better equipped to theatrically present black cultural life. At their worst, these partnerships reinforce a hierarchy of arts production where the largest, best-funded theaters (which are almost always predominantly white) act as satellites around which smaller, nonwhite theater companies must revolve and seek patronage. I have written about the problematics of this dynamic in my book on the Penumbra Theatre Company where I analyze Penumbra's collaborations with the Guthrie Theater.[109] Steven Anthony Jones spoke to me about the problematic dynamics of these kinds of partnerships in the Bay Area.

> ACT and LHT have a long history. . . . I have been a member of both institutions. . . . ACT has a wealth of space and facilities, and they occasionally make it available to smaller theaters. . . . In these kinds of partnerships, the smaller theater benefits from the very large subscription audience of the larger theater noticing you and that's a benefit, but it's not as big a benefit as you might think. . . . Right now, I'm more interested in collaborations among equals.[110]

Jones described these partnerships as fundamentally unequal because of the size and resources of the participating institutions. In 1984, ACT had a budget of $7 million and LHT had a budget of $400,000.[111] According to available Guidestar data, ACT had an approximately $20 million budget in 2016, while LHT had a $274,000 budget in the same year.[112] These data show that the economic discrepancy between these organizations has worsened, not improved, over the last thirty years. Because of these extreme economic differences, which are typical among large regional theaters and smaller nonwhite companies, collaborations are often fraught. Knowing this, August Wilson used his celebrity status to help elevate the power position of black theaters and black artists working in collaboration with well-resourced, largely white theater institutions.

Claude Purdy's 1989 direction of the LHT/ACT coproduction of *Joe Turner's Come and Gone* was riveting and described by the press as "perfect" and "stirring."[113] It inaugurated the production of August Wilson's work at

LHT. Over the next twenty years, the company produced many other Wilson plays such as *Fences* (1990–91 and 2007–8 seasons), *The Piano Lesson* (1991–92 and 2001–2), *Two Trains Running* (1993–94), *Jitney* (1998–99), *Ma Rainey's Black Bottom* (2000–2001), *Seven Guitars* (2002–3), *King Hedley II* (2003–4), and a second LHT production of *Joe Turner's Come and Gone* in 2006–7.[114] The second LHT production of *Fences* during the 2007–8 season was the last production to take place at its Sutter Street location. It is ironic that a play about making and keeping a home was the last production presented in the theater's permanent space.

LHT lost the home it had occupied for nearly twenty years when the building that housed the theater was sold in 2007 to the for-profit educational institution the Academy of Art University. There were public protests and boycotts of the Academy of Art, which nevertheless terminated the company's lease and turned its theater space into a student gymnasium.[115] Williams and Easter were convinced to sign away their lease renewal rights after being told that the building housing the theater would be gutted and they would displaced regardless of whether or not they signed. Seeing little recourse, they signed in exchange for two years of free rent. The building was not gutted, and in an interview with SF Gate, Easter stated, "The rent was never an issue for us. . . . We were told that the situation within the building meant that we could not exercise those [lease renewal] options, but that the owner would let us stay for another two years rent-free. We would never have traded away our right to stay for 10 [more] years for two years of free rent."[116] Former San Francisco mayor Willie Brown attempted to mediate an agreement between the theater and the Academy of Art that was ultimately unsuccessful.[117] The city of San Francisco has since sued the Academy of Art for "deliberate noncompliance" with numerous planning and zoning requirements, and many see the organization as a predatory for-profit company and real estate monopoly whose interests run counter to the public good.[118] Although protests and other efforts to keep LHT in its home were unsuccessful, these efforts showed resistance to the profit-driven displacements of the twenty-first century and support for the value of LHT as an important civic institution.

After several years of presenting work in temporary locations, Williams and Easter leased another theater near Union Square on Post Street in 2010. The company had to cancel the lease when both partners faced chronic illness and passed away later that year.[119] In 2011, the newly appointed artistic director Steven Anthony Jones announced that the theater had renegotiated a five-year lease at the Post Street theater. The company left the Post Street location in 2012, however, when it became clear that LHT could not afford the rent.[120] SF Playhouse, a midsized theater company with a $3 million operating budget, took over the lease and continues to operate out of this space today.[121] During a telephone interview I conducted with Steven Anthony Jones, the former LHT artistic director stated, "Sometimes, if you have a space, that can put you in the most perilous position. The model that works for larger theaters just does not work for smaller organizations. It is so expensive to maintain a space that it really only works for large theaters."[122] What happened to LHT is typical of many displaced individuals and organizations in the Bay Area. Once an individual or group loses a rental property within their financial means, it is nearly impossible to secure another comparable space because of San Francisco's skyrocketing rates of rental increase. This reality has displaced thousands of people over the past two decades, with low-income citizens, people of color, and artists disproportionately impacted by these changes. The devious way in which LHT was removed from its home reflects the myriad nefarious business practices of certain greedy landlords, who in the worst cases have resorted to arson in order to circumvent their tenants' rights and to exponentially increase the income they can garner from their properties.[123]

No longer able to take on the substantial financial responsibility of an ongoing lease in downtown San Francisco, the theater has sought to forge partnerships with other artistic and cultural institutions throughout the Bay Area. From 2008 to 2015, LHT partnered with major Bay Area theater companies and listed productions featuring African American playwrights as part of its "passport" seasons. The 2014–15 passport season consisted of eight productions, including two LHT productions: the annual gospel musical *Black Nativity* and *Thurgood*, a one-man show about the iconic Supreme Court justice that was performed excellently with Jones in the title role. The other five productions listed on the LHT website were produced by ACT, the Cutting Ball Theater, Marin Theatre Company, the Magic Theatre, SF Playhouse, and Just Theater in association with Shotgun Players. These were not coproductions but rather productions whose host theaters had ticketing agreements with LHT. Jones described this arrangement as follows: "Our subscription buyers would buy a ticket to see a play at Berkeley Rep[ertory Theatre] or Marin Theatre Company or ACT, and we would make a little bit of money from the sale and it allowed us to support some of the programming we were doing."[124] It was clear to me from looking at this season lineup that the company's ability to offer a full production season had been profoundly reduced since the loss of its permanent space and the death of its founders. My sentiment was echoed by drama critic Lily Janiak in her 2017 review "*Home*: A Too Rare Show from Lorraine Hansberry Theatre."[125] During our interview Jones acknowledged that the passport season did not adequately support the independence and financial strength of the institution. "We have stopped doing [the passport season] because it took up a lot of staff time and the other theaters got a little more tightfisted and it just became too difficult financially."[126] The passport seasons let LHT audience members know where work by black playwrights was being performed elsewhere in the Bay Area but did not support the financial health or programming of LHT in any significant way.

After several sparse seasons like this, Jones was able to eliminate the company's debt and secure affordable office and performance space at the AAACC. This arts center is located in the historically black Fillmore neighborhood. Because the city of San Francisco owns the building out of which the AAACC operates, the costs of office and performance space are substantially subsidized. The AAACC and its tenants are also directly supported by the San Francisco Arts Commission whose mission is to champion "the arts as essential to daily life by investing in a vibrant arts community, enlivening the urban environment and shaping innovative cultural policy" and whose vision includes "a San Francisco where the transformative power of art is critical to strengthening neighborhoods, building infrastructure, and fostering positive social change."[127] As rental and real estate prices have skyrocketed in San Francisco, the San Francisco Arts Commission has endeavored to support and subsidize historically important arts organizations that might otherwise be driven out of the city. The fact that the city owns two cultural arts centers in historically black neighborhoods, the AAACC in the Fillmore/Western Addition and the Bayview Opera House in Bayview/Hunter's Point, demonstrates a continued investment on the part of local government to support and facilitate the production of African American art in San Francisco. Taking advantage of the resources of city government, particularly in regard to facilities and performance space, has been key to the survival of the city's black theaters.

Aside from drastic changes in economics and the affordability of producing theater in the city of San Francisco, LHT has also navigated changes in the cultural demographics of the city and changing understandings of the legacy, function, and historical impact of black theaters. Jones spoke about these changes during our interview.

> When the theater started, the black population in San Francisco was larger and the theater also appealed to the black population in the entire Bay Area. Those theatergoers tended to support us and not attend the other theaters so much. The Mime Troupe attracted some of that audience . . . and all of the other theaters of color had their own representative audiences. That has changed. The Lorraine Hansberry Theatre's home audience is still primarily African American, but the African American population in the Bay Area has really shrunk. . . . Now, because everybody does black plays, the audience is also more dispersed among the different theaters.[128]

In many ways LHT is representative of the theaters that were founded in the second wave of the black arts movement during the late 1970s and early 1980s, all of which struggled after larger, predominantly white institutions began to produce black culture material in the late 1980s and early 1990s.[129] The displacement of the black population of San Francisco further dispersed LHT's audience base.

Despite these challenges, LHT remains uniquely able to serve the arts ecology of the Bay Area in ways that predominantly white and multicultural theaters cannot. During our interview, Jones and I discussed the continued importance of black theater companies and the legacies they leave. Jones saw the mission of LHT as part of the legacy of the Negro Ensemble Company, a company he was a member of and one of the most influential black theaters of the 1960s, 1970s, and 1980s.

> We are connected to the history of black theater in this country, and that history is fraught. We were almost seen as an adjunct to the theater, and that's wrong. Douglas Turner Ward wrote an article that helped to start the Negro Ensemble Company in the sixties, and he pushed the door open. Every single constituent theater, not just black theaters but women's theaters and theater for other people of color, they all owe a debt to Doug, all the voices that were struggling to be heard walked through the door that Doug opened. It informs the present in ways that are obvious and also not so obvious. The stories that were told more accurately reflected the conscious of the American theater because it included everyone. [The depiction of] Social inequality was always part of the American theater, so was the immigrant experience, but the voices of all Americans have not always been part of the American theater, and that is important to remember.[130]

Here, Jones conceptualized LHT as part of the lineage of the black theaters of the 1960s, and of the Negro Ensemble Company in particular. He reiterated the point that black theaters are necessary for the cultivation and continued support not only of black playwrights but also of black actors and designers who would otherwise work only occasionally at predominately white or multicultural theaters. Speaking of the service that LHT provides to the Bay Area artistic community, Jones stated:

> One thing that we offer to African American artists in the Bay Area is the Actors Equity Contract. We operate under the AEA Bay Area small theater contract, and for many actors, the place where they can join the union is here. The Negro Ensemble Company offered the same opportunity for many generations of actors, directors, and designers in New York City, and I count myself among them. So, the Lorraine Hansberry Theatre follows that tradition and still performs an important service [for black artists]. Many of the smaller theaters in the area do not offer an equity contract, so in that way we are still significant.[131]

When companies such as the Negro Ensemble Theatre were founded, there weren't many roles available to African American performers in the major regional theaters, and while the amount of African American plays produced by regional theaters has increased, they are still a minority of many companies' main-stage seasons. While most of the larger regional theaters have begun to include African American playwrights in their production choices, playwrights of color are still underproduced in relation to the size of communities of color in America's urban areas.[132]

Today, a jobbing black actor in San Francisco (as in most other American cities) often auditions for companies that have very few roles for African Americans. The greater the operating budget of the theater (which generally correlates with the number of productions the company is able to produce), the less racially inclusive its season usually is. For example, during the 2015–16 season, the four Bay Area theaters with operating budgets of $5 million or more (ACT, Berkeley Repertory Theatre, California Shakespeare Company, and TheatreWorks) collectively produced thirty-two productions.[133] Of those productions, only one was written by an African American playwright: Sarah Jones's one-woman show *Sell/Buy/Date*, which was produced by Berkeley Repertory Theatre. Six of the thirteen productions that featured African American actors were plays that specifically called for African American characters; the seven remaining plays were non–traditionally cast in the sense that they were written by white playwrights (such as Shakespeare) and/or had been previously produced with white actors (for example, David Auburn's *Proof*, which TheatreWorks cast entirely with African American performers in a concept production). These statistics starkly reveal the continued need for black theater companies. A black theater company that produces a season of plays entirely or primarily written by African Americans provides not only quantitative opportunities for African American playwrights, actors, and designers but also qualitative opportunities to take material from the artists' own cultural lineage and background and use it in the development and execution of their craft.

In San Francisco, the Asian and Latinx populations of the city are much larger than the African American population, and therefore the production of theatrical work from those communities is even more needed in terms of equitably representing the cultural pluralism of the city. Jones spoke about how LHT might contribute to the production of work that both reflected this makeup and gave greater voice to other underrepresented artists of color.

> San Francisco is an interesting city; in terms of race it is predominantly white and Asian. I have collaborated with the [Japanese American] playwright Philip Kan Gotanda, who lives in the Bay Area. We were interested in the connections between us, and Philip came up with this idea of "adapting from the fringe." He contacted me and asked if I would consider doing his play *The Wash* with African American actors, and I said, "Sure, but how would that work?" So, we had to figure that out. The play reflects the lives of Asian immigrants, and

we renamed it *The Jamaican Wash* and changed some things so it still reflected the lives of immigrants, it's just that these immigrants were now black people. We were both responding to the fact that plays like *The Glass Menagerie* and *Death of a Salesman* have been produced with black casts. We were sick to death of that because, are those authors underproduced or underrepresented? The answer is no, of course. Philip's play *The Wash* is a beautiful play that had its moment but then fell off the table. I was in Charles Fuller's *A Soldier's Play*, which is a murder mystery; it's a great play with great characters but no one does it anymore. No one brings those plays back and does them, not even black theaters. Another great play, *Home*, by Samm-Art Williams, is rarely done [LHT produced this play in 1984 and again in 2017]. In our Bringing Art the Audience reading series, we do new work and what I call "forgotten" plays. In both the Asian and black communities, we still have that problem. The theaters that do black plays want to do Lynn Nottage, Marcus Gardley, whatever's hot right now. You have your moment and then it disappears, whereas theaters will produce *The Glass Menagerie* ad nauseam. We artists of color are not continuously produced. No one is afforded that respect except August Wilson. Doing this collaboration with Philip allows our two communities to intermingle and also speaks to some of the issues facing both of our communities. In that way, the collaboration reflects the identity of the city.[134]

As Jones's example of the collaboration on *The Jamaican Wash* shows, black theaters are becoming more interested in exploring cross-cultural partnerships outside of a black and white binary, where African American experiences come into dialogue with artists and experiences from other minority communities. Given the population and cultural influence of the many different Asian American communities in the Bay Area, cross-cultural collaborations between black and Asian arts organizations have the potential to help black theater engage with a much larger audience base at the same time that it continues to explore minority issues and experiences.

LHT has also reached out to a wider geographical area in an effort to build its audience. For its Bringing Art to the Audiences program, LHT has offered a series of staged readings at African American cultural institutions across the Bay Area such as the Museum of the African Diaspora (MOAD) in San Francisco, the East Bay Center for the Performing Arts in Richmond, and the Oakland School for the Arts. Through this program, the theater forged partnerships with other African American arts organizations and operated in communities that have larger black populations. On February 20, 2016, I attended one of these events, LHT's reading of Britney Frazier's play *Dysphoria* at MOAD. The play featured a transgender main character struggling with suicide and drug addiction and was emblematic of the kind of work

Fig. 4. Steven Anthony Jones, emeritus artistic director of the Lorraine Hansberry Theatre, in conversation with the author following a performance of *Thurgood* at the University of the Pacific in 2017. Photograph by Gary Armagnac.

Jones feels called to produce. *Dysphoria* featured characters that reflected the struggles of San Francisco's many homeless and mentally ill inhabitants, citizens that are often explicitly excluded and harmed by public and private management of the city as an income-generating tourist attraction.[135] In this way, LHT's programming attempted to reflect the experiences of some of the most misunderstood, vulnerable, and victimized residents of the city.

In June 2017, Jones announced his retirement from LHT. Under his leadership the organization had eliminated the debt that accumulated as a result of the loss of its permanent home, attempts to remain in the Union Square theater district, and the instability brought about by the deaths of both cofounders. Jones had forged partnerships with other arts organizations in the Bay Area, and LHT now had affordable access to both office and performance space in the AAACC. He felt that it was "a good time for a new person to take over."[136] When I last spoke to Jones he said he was looking forward to having fewer administrative responsibilities and performing more as an actor, especially in one-person shows, like LHT's 2016 production of *Thurgood*, during which he commanded the stage for over two hours of riveting solo performance. He took on a similarly demanding project in late 2018 and early 2019 when he performed August Wilson's one-man show *How I Learned What I Learned*, which was directed by Margo Hall and coproduced and presented at the Buriel Clay Memorial Theater for LHT, in Mill Valley at Marin Theatre Company, and in Oakland for Ubuntu Theater Project, a collective of East Bay artists founded in 2012.[137]

In October 2017, LHT's board of directors announced that Aldo Billingslea would serve as interim artist director for one year during their search for a permanent artistic director. Billingslea is a deeply respected theater artist and frequent performer on Bay Area stages. He is also a faculty member and former associate provost for diversity and inclusion at Santa Clara University. In 2017 he won a Theatre Bay Area (TBA) award for acting for his role as Paw Sidin in California Shakespeare Company's acclaimed production of Marcus Gardley's *Black Odyssey* as well as a TBA directing award for LHT's 2017 production of Samm-Art Williams's *Home*.[138] Like Jones, Billingslea reiterated LHT's commitment to producing work by African American women in honor of the organization's namesake, having a playwright development program and process, and strengthening the stability of the institution.[139] In an interview with Lily Janiak for the *San Francisco Chronicle*, Billingslea pointed out that while LHT has had reduced programming since the loss of its founders, its success "shouldn't be measured just by the number of productions but also by their caliber."[140] Sometimes, by reducing programming, an organization is able to survive a financial downturn that might overwise lead to its demise. On the other hand, reduced programming makes it more difficult to attract funding. Too many cancelled productions and seasons can erode confidence, patronage, and audiences. Under Jones's leadership, the organization was able to eliminate its debt and come back from the brink of catastrophe. Following this period of austerity, excellent and regularly scheduled full productions were clearly needed to demonstrate the organization's continued relevance. Billingslea began this process with his finely wrought 2017 production of Samm-Art Williams's classic 1979 play *Home*. The production featured Myers Clark, Britney Frazier and Tristan Cunningham and earned positive critical reviews.[141]

In order to stage full productions, an organization obviously needs to have the financial means to do so. The fact that LHT has half of the operating budget today that it had in the 1980s is clearly troubling.[142] Recognizing the critical need for fundraising and increasing earned income, the LHT board appointed Stephanie Shoffner in July 2017 as executive director of the organization. Having previously served on LHT's board and worked in business and finance, Shoffner is "committed to financially reinvigorating LHT as it continues to transition, grow, and evolve."[143] In 2018, LHT hired Darryl V. Jones, a director, actor, and faculty member of the Theater and Dance Department at Cal State East Bay to serve as acting artistic director. Darryl V. Jones had recently directed Dominique Morisseau's play *Detroit 67* at the Aurora Theatre in Berkeley and also performed as an actor in Theatre

Rhinoceros's production of *Priscilla, Queen of the Desert*. Speaking about his intentions for programming at LHT, Jones stated that he would be undertaking far fewer staged readings so the organization could focus its energy and resources on resuming the presentation of full productions.[144]

Because LHT's operating budget is relatively small, Darryl V. Jones collaborated with other organizations in the Bay Area to mount several coproductions. In addition to collaborating with Marin Theatre Company and Ubuntu Theater Project on August Wilson's *How I Learned What I Learned*, LHT collaborated with Shotgun Players on the 2019 production of James Ijames's *Kill Move Paradise*. Partially in reaction to the police shooting of twelve-year-old Tamir Rice, the play is set in the afterlife and features a cast of young African Americans processing the trauma of their violent death at the hands of white supremacists and law enforcement. Directed by Darryl V. Jones, the play featured Trevonne Bell, Edward Ewell, Lenard Jackson, Dwaye Clay, and Keli'I Salvador.[145] It was performed at Shotgun Players' Ashby Stage in Berkeley. "We're doing partnerships with small and large companies in an effort to bring other artists into the fold and to continue to build our audiences and make more people aware of us and establish good working relationships with our peers."[146] These coproductions improved upon LHT's previous passport seasons in that they include LHT company members in positions of creative authority actively participating in the creation of the artistic work.

In addition to coproductions, Darryl V. Jones also saw room to reflect more of the multiethnic makeup of the Bay Area in LHT's productions. "We have such amazing talent here in the Bay Area, whether its African American, Latino, white, Asian, whatever. We want the theatre company to be a home for this talent. Right now, the job, for me, is reaching out to all kinds of artists . . . to continue to do theatre at its finest."[147] The cast of characters for Darryl V. Jones's first full production at LHT, A. Zell Williams's *The Urban Retreat*, required the kind of multigenerational and multiracial diverse talent pool that Jones described in his interview. The play was chosen by Aldo Billingslea as the outgoing artistic director and opened in March 2019. The playwright, A. Zell Williams, grew up in the Central Valley and received his undergraduate degree from Santa Clara University, where he studied with Billingslea before leaving California to pursue his career in New York.[148] The content of the play also has a California connection in that it is set in Marin County during a writers' retreat at a house formerly occupied by Jack Kerouac.[149] The play centers around Trench, a successful rapper in his twenties who enlists his former high school writing teacher, Chaucer Mosley, to ghostwrite a fictionalized and sensational memoir. Mosley convinces Trench to tell "his real story."[150] Jones spoke about directing the play for LHT. For him, the play is about "the power of words to heal," and he sees the heart of the play as "about black male mentorship . . . this man [Mosley] eventually becomes his [Trench's] mentor and gets him to live as his authentic self rather than in this thug image that was promoted by the record industry to sell records and make money."[151] The cast included Lenard Jackson as Trench, LaKeidrick Wimberly as Pooh Butt, Trench's manager, and Adrian Roberts as Chaucer Mosley. Publisher Maggie Farmer and her assistant were played by Miriam Ani and Emily Kristner. Bay Area spoken word artist Jamey Williams played Trench's friend Setty Rexpin and Mosley's estranged son Corey.[152] Both the subject matter and the characters of this play are meant to appeal to a younger audience, a demographic all theater companies are working hard to engage. The production was well received and serves as an example of how LHT continues to shape and disseminate artwork that tells the unique stories and cultural experiences of African Americans from the Bay Area.

African-American Shakespeare Company

As its name indicates, AASC produces primarily Shakespearean work. As such, it did not initially fit into my experience of black theater. As an African American theater scholar, I have generally studied and worked with organizations that are proponents of the "by, about, for, and near" mandate first expressed by the Krigwa Players in 1926, a group that included both W. E. B. Du Bois and Zora Neale Hurston. The playbill for the 1926 Harlem presentation of *Compromise*, *The Church Fight*, and *Broken Banjo* included the following manifesto, which has been foundational to the study and theorization of black theater ever since its initial publication.

> [A] new Negro theatre is demanded and it is slowly coming. It needs, however, guiding lights. For instance, some excellent groups of colored amateurs are entertaining colored audiences in Cleveland, in Philadelphia and elsewhere. Almost invariably, however, they miss the real path. They play Shakespeare or Synge or reset a successful Broadway play with colored principals. The movement which has begun this year in Harlem, New York City, lays down four fundamental principles. The plays of a real Negro theatre must be: *One: About us*. That is, they must have plots which reveal Negro life as it is. *Two: By us*. That is, they must be written by Negro authors who understand from birth and continual association just what it means to be a Negro today. *Three: For us*. That is, the theatre must cater primarily to Negro audiences and be supported and sustained by their entertainment and approval. *Fourth: Near Us*. The theatre must be in a Negro neighborhood near the mass of ordinary Negro people.[153]

This manifesto reveals the tensions and differences in ideologies and artistic practice between African American artists producing European or European American theatrical works and African American artists dedicated to supporting the production of black playwrights telling stories written about and featuring black people. The tension between these two practices has been continuously revisited in the seminal theoretical texts of African American dramatic theory and criticism. For example, in the 1968 "Black Theatre" special issue of the *Tulane Drama Review* Larry Neal famously wrote:

> We advocate for a cultural revolution in art and ideas. The cultural values inherent in Western history must either be radicalized or destroyed. . . . The motive behind the black aesthetic is the destruction of the white thing, the destruction of white ideas, and white ways of looking at the world. The new aesthetic is mostly predicated on an Ethics which asks the question: whose vision of the world is finally more meaningful, ours or that of our white oppressors? What is truth? Or more precisely, whose truth shall we express, that of the oppressed or of the oppressors? These are the basic questions. Black intellectuals of previous decades failed to ask them.[154]

Here Neal, like Du Bois before him, explicitly criticized other black artists and intellectuals for investing their energies in the production of cultural works originally created by white people. Both Neal and Du Bois called for the creation of a revolutionary art that explicitly divested from white cultural production in order to explore, discover, and articulate a self-consciously independent black politics and artistic aesthetic. Du Bois, Neal, and more recently August Wilson have all seen the participation of African American artists in the production of white cultural works as an impediment to the creation of a self-consciously articulated African American dramaturgy. In his 1996 address to Theatre Communications Group, Wilson famously stated, "We do not need colorblind casting; we need theatres. We need theatres to develop our playwrights."[155]

Each of these writers has eloquently argued for the production of original African American plays that express the unique sociocultural realities of black experiences. They have also advocated for the support and development of African American theatrical institutions as a means of enacting racial justice, and they have pointed out the searing racial inequities and operation of white supremacy within American theatrical practice. The importance of their legacy in articulating and inspiring African American artistic self-representation and the need to control the means of our own artistic production cannot be overstated. However, I have come to believe that it is a mistake to vilify the artistic practices of African American artists who choose to work with European forms in order to define the strengths and import of particular African American aesthetics or movements. I agree with Brandi Wilkins Catanese, who makes the argument that a variety of black performance strategies (including various kinds of nontraditional casting in plays written by Europeans or European Americans) can be racially transgressive.

> One of the objectives of this analysis is to advance a recuperative
> perspective on colorblind casting . . . that emphasizes its transcendent
> possibilities . . . colorblind casting may contribute to the multivalence
> of black subjectivity by insisting upon the relevance of black bodies
> and the intertext of black culture to a wider variety of narratives than
> are currently staged. . . . When colorblind casting allows black actors
> to take on the roles for which they would not otherwise be consid-
> ered and then gives way to a production process in which the black
> actors' intersectional identity is integrated into, rather than sacrificed
> to, the production, the practice does not abandon still urgent race-
> based political inquiry: instead, it acknowledges the multiplicity of
> the black subject as a political and aesthetic force . . . black performa-
> tivity must be allowed and required to account for its heterogeneity.[156]

To risk making an obvious point, because African Americans are Americans,
and as such have received an education that has been and continues to be
dominated by European arts and letters, it is not surprising that many African American theater artists use and identify with European literary works
in their artistic practices. This interest is not mutually exclusive of an investment in and use of African cultural forms or the creation and expression of
transgressive racial, social, and cultural subjectivities. Condemning African
American theater artists who use European artistic material is taking a rather
narrow view and limits the depth of recognition and theorization of the richness and variety of African American performance as it is currently and has
been historically practiced in the United States. The first known professional
black theater company in the United States, the nineteenth-century New
York–based African Grove Theatre, was, after all, dedicated to the production of Shakespeare.[157] In a similar way, AASC operates in many ways, not
least importantly in its own self-conception as a black theater. Its theatrical practice has complicated my view of what black theater is and is thus
a valuable contribution to a study that seeks to uncover the ways in which
black theaters reflect and shape the cultural politics of the cities in which they
reside. By pairing an analysis of the mission and cultural contributions of
BRG and LHT with AASC, I hope to show that these companies all contribute to socially progressive artistic practices that utilize black performance in
complementary rather than oppositional ways.

   According to its mission statement, AASC was founded in 1994 "to open
the realm of classic theatre to a diverse audience; and provide an opportunity
and place for actors of color to hone their skills and talent in mastering some
of the world's greatest classical roles."[158] In pursuing this mission, AASC is
following a long line of African American actors and production companies
that have used Shakespeare as their primary dramatic material. Shakespearean
productions featuring African American actors and/or produced by companies
with African American artistic leadership have a long and storied history in

the United States. The previously mentioned African Grove Theatre, which produced Shakespearean work during the nineteenth century in New York, is the first known professional black theater company in the United States and was deemed so transgressive that its actors and management were ridiculed, harassed, and imprisoned.[159] White supremacists forced the company to close, but not before the African Grove made an indelible mark on theater history and helped to launch the career of the famed Ira Aldridge.[160] A "classical" (i.e., European derived) repertory of theater production was also always a part of the curriculum of historically black colleges such as Howard and Morehouse both prior to and alongside the creation and dissemination of original African American dramatic literature. For example, while Howard faculty such as Alain Locke articulated the aims of "the new Negro" during the 1920s in the midst of the Harlem Renaissance,[161] the Howard Players continued to produce European dramatic literature including Shakespeare in addition to the production of original African American dramatic literature in service of the movement.[162] During the 1930s, the Negro theater units of the WPA-sponsored FTP staged adaptations of Shakespearean works such as the "voodoo" *Macbeth* in New York and *Romeo and Juliet* (*Romey and Julie*) in Chicago alongside original African American folk plays and plays of social critique.[163] In her analysis of the Negro units of the FTP, Rena Fraden writes, "Houseman [the director of the Harlem unit of the FTP] decided to set up two companies, one devoted to contemporary plays, presumably focusing on 'racial material,' and the other classical."[164] Angela Pao sees the 1930s classical FTP Negro unit productions as part of the legacy of contemporary African American theater companies dedicated to the production of classical work. "These adapted productions by all-black or predominantly black companies established a performance tradition that has been continued in the present by the work of the African American Shakespeare Company in San Francisco and the Classical Theatre of Harlem in New York."[165] Paul Robeson, arguably the most famous African American stage and film actor of the 1930s and 1940s, frequently performed the title roles in such works as *Othello* and *Emperor Jones* at the same time as he invested in original African American dramatic work and participated in civil rights and anticolonial efforts.[166] All of these examples show that there have been two simultaneous and at times overlapping threads in the development and practice of black theater in America: one that has concentrated on the production and support of new plays written by African Americans that speak to the cultural experiences and sociopolitical struggles of black life and another that uses an inherited legacy of European dramatic works in ways that self-consciously attempt to express these same subjectivities. Although the rhetoric of the first strand of artistic practice has frequently decried the second strand, many of the individuals and organizations from which this rhetoric has come have, in fact, participated in both traditions.

Historically, African American artists and institutions working primarily in the production of European classical work have faced significant hostility and censorship from white audiences and cultural critics who sought to deny their access to the cultural cachet of this art. African American practitioners of Shakespeare have also weathered criticisms from other African American artists and theorists such as those previously cited, who sought to distance themselves from European cultural dominance. The fact that African American productions of Shakespearean work have at different moments in time been received as transgressive, progressive, and accommodationist reveals a complex and changing relationship between race, literature, and performance. I will examine this relationship as it pertains to the programming of AASC and the place the organization occupies within the cultural ecology of the Bay Area.

AASC shares many of the same values and characteristics as other black theaters, including a desire to support the training and professional development of African American theater practitioners. The company's office is housed in the AAACC in the heart of what was once one of the most significant black neighborhoods of San Francisco and articulates its work as "at its core an African-American aesthetic, steeped in an American sensibility."[167] When I attended AASC's production of Antony and Cleopatra on May 9, 2016, at the Buriel Clay Memorial Theater in the AAACC, I could see the building's landlord and patron, city hall, in all the glory of its neoclassical architecture, looming in the distance at the end of Fulton Avenue as I drove into the complex's parking lot. I also observed several large, generic, low-income housing blocks with security bars on their windows and doors, a beautiful mural of jazz artists on the outside of the complex's walls, and a smaller, more recent mural paying tribute to Trayvon Martin on the wall of an adjacent building. As I entered the building, I noticed that the art gallery that is located on the ground floor of the AAACC was open, and I walked through a photography exhibit featuring local artist Jessica Cross and South African photographers Moeketsi Moticoe and Max Mogole that depicted scenes from a rural South African township. I then settled into my seat in the intimate two hundred–seat thrust theater. The audience in my rough estimation was approximately 50 percent black with the remaining 50 percent consisting of white and Asian patrons. I mention these details because in my experience, the environment in which a play is produced has a significant impact on the reception and construction involved in the meaning making of theatergoing. The environment of this production privileged African American culture and history in a decidedly cosmopolitan way in the sense that Kwame Anthony Appiah uses that word, as grounded in the specificity of place while at the same time in conversation with how a particular locality of place (in this case the Fillmore) sits in conversation with the larger world.[168] Although the space was clearly designated as a seat of black cultural authority, there was also clear evidence of an internationalism (the gallery exhibit, the Shakespeare play) that situated the production as participating in the staging of San Francisco as an international city.

In an interview I had conducted with Sherri Young early that week, the founder and executive director of the company described the neighborhood out of which the theater operated as an intersection of several cultures, both geographically and ideologically. In terms of geography, Young stated:

> We are located in Hayes Valley, so on one side there are the major institutions of the city such city hall and the San Francisco Opera; on the other side there are new trendy restaurants, the techie zone, I like to call it; and on our side there is low-income housing bordering the Fillmore/Western Addition, what has been called the Historic Jazz District, what was once known as the Harlem of the West. We are serving all these different communities.[169]

In terms of ideology, Young explained that her impetus to found the company was rooted in a cosmopolitan desire to make Shakespearean work that reflected more of the cultural specificities of African Americans. "I really started thinking about it in 1992–1993. At that time there was a colorblind casting initiative. I had just graduated from the American Conservatory Theater, and there was this big push to have more diversity on stage. But what was happening was a lot of the theater companies, they were putting bodies on the stage without really incorporating the culture as part of the production."[170] Here Young differentiates between colorblind casting and what she described in our interview as "culturally imbued" productions. Young posits the work of AASC as engaging with the specificity of African American culture rather than just ignoring it. In the productions at AASC, African American culture is used as a way into the text and themes of the Shakespearean work the company produces. "I wanted to attract . . . people who were curious about the classics but didn't necessarily feel invited to engage with that work, as well as some more adventurous audiences who were open to seeing the work done in a different way."[171] For example, Young recalled the incorporation of a stomp dance routine into AASC's production of *The Merry Wives of Windsor* as an example of the way the company used elements of black culture to enliven and communicate the themes and narrative of the play. "The critics didn't get it, but the black audience was laughing out loud. So, what we are trying to do is to make Shakespeare speak to a black audience. . . . White artists or critics don't always understand it."[172] This example shows that while the themes of Shakespeare might be universal, the understanding and interpretation of these themes are always filtered through the production team's and the audience's own cultural understandings.

In *The Problem of the Color[blind]*, Brandi Wilkins Catanese gives another example of the cultural specificity of Shakespearean work when she recounts an instance when she was preparing a scene from *As You Like It* and had been cast in the role of Rosalind. She points out the fact that Orlando's line "I swear to thee, youth, by the white hand of Rosalind" belies the oft-claimed universality of Shakespeare and reveals the text to be grounded in a white cultural background.[173] "I *got* Rosalind on so many levels, but because I didn't *get* at birth the same skin color that Shakespeare imagined for her, I was forever estranged from the character in ways that some of my classmates could never have understood, estranged through their very eyes as spectators who would respond to the dissonance between words and body in different ways."[174]

Catanese's experience here incorporates many nodes of the complexity of African American performance of "classical" work. First, the study of Shakespeare in particular and European literature in general is part of the experience of American education and therefore also part of the African American experience. Second, this literature is not universal, as indeed no literature can be; it is specifically grounded in certain historical time periods, places, and cultures, although it might have application or appreciation in other times periods, places, and cultures. Lastly, the performance of European works by African Americans often creates resonances and dissonances out of which particular racial and cultural realities of the moment of production become visible. With her example from *The Merry Wives of Windsor*, Young highlighted the ways Shakespearean plays can be adapted to more deeply resonate with African American audiences, while Catanese offered an example of her own understanding and "playing" with the dissonance created through her performance of an explicitly white role. Both examples resulted in extratextual meanings that caused the audience to think about the performativity and contemporary meanings of both race and culture. In my view, this is the value of nontraditional casting, not its so-called universality or even its function as a form of affirmative action, but rather, its potential to reveal how race and culture are made, read, and interpreted and how they might be reread and reinterpreted through a variety of transgressive staging practices that are attentive to rather than ignorant of or "blind" to current social and historical racial paradigms.

In their more than twenty years of existence, AASC has staged many productions of Shakespeare's plays, often set in explicitly black cultural contexts. A few examples include an early 1997 production of *As You Like It* that was set during the Reconstruction era in the South, a 1999 production of *Julius Caesar* set during the civil rights movement, a 2000 production of *Romeo and Juliet* set in Cuba featuring Latinx and African lovers, a 2001 production of *The Tempest* set in the Caribbean during carnival, and a 2017 production of *A Midsummer Night's Dream* set in Trinidad and Tobago. These productions sought to express black cultural subjectivity by changing the settings of the plays. The company has also experimented with more extensive adaptations of classical texts such as when it produced *MacB: The Macbeth Project* in 2002 and 2008 as the tale of an ambitious rapper willing to murder his way to the top. The witches became a Destiny's Child–like trio that "would rather be produced by MacB than Duncan," and the banquet scene was transformed into the filming of a music video.[175] In 2011, AASC produced a film noir–inspired version of *Twelfth Night* that was set in San Francisco's Fillmore District during the mid-1940s, when the neighborhood was known as the "Harlem of the West."[176] Directed by L. Peter Callender, this production featured an original jazz score by acclaimed composer and jazz musician Marcus Shelby.[177]

AASC has produced other European classics in addition to Shakespeare such as the ancient Greek plays *Oedipus Rex*, *Medea*, and *Lysistrata*, staged in 1997, 2006, and 2014. As with the Shakespearean work, it has also produced more extensive cultural adaptations of Greek plays. L. Peter Callender, in his first year as artistic director of AASC, staged Colin Teevan's *Iph* (a very contemporary translation of Euripides's *Iphigenia at Aulis*) as a coproduction with Brava Theater in 2010. In 2015, Rhodessa Jones directed an AASC production of Nambi E. Kelley's *Xtigone*, an adaptation of Sophocles's *Antigone* that depicts the deaths of Antigone's brothers as the result of gang violence rather than civil war. As these examples indicate, each AASC production of a European classic has used different means to tell the story of the original drama from a black perspective. Some productions altered the text, others altered the setting, and some were simply performed with black actors in an otherwise unaltered interpretation of the world of the play. As such, the ways these plays were "culturally imbued" varied dramatically. In order to more deeply analyze the cultural dynamics in play in these works, I will focus on two AASC productions that I personally witnessed, the 2016 production of Shakespeare's *Antony and Cleopatra* and the 2018 production of Tennessee Williams's *A Streetcar Named Desire*.

AASC's 2016 production of *Antony and Cleopatra* provided an excellent opportunity to examine how the company culturally interpreted a Shakespearean text. Since assuming the role of the company's artistic director in 2010 when founder Sherri Young decided to focus her energies on the management of the theater, L. Peter Callender, a Julliard trained actor, has performed as an anchor artist for several AASC productions in addition to his directing at least one AASC show per season. In AASC's production of *Antony and Cleopatra*, Callender portrayed Antony. Leontyne Mbele-Mbong played Cleopatra. The majority of the other roles were also played by African Americans including the roles of Pompey (Edward Neville Ewell) and Charmaine/Octavia (both played by India Wilmont). Ewell also portrayed multiple other characters including Lepidus and several messengers and ambassadors. Octavius Caesar was played by a Latinx actor, Steve Ortiz. Enobarbus, Antony's faithful soldier in arms, was portrayed by a white actor, Timothy Redmond. The production team included African Americans in the positions of technical director and sound designer (Kevin Myrick), assistant stage manager (Brian Snow), prop artisan (Brittany White), and technical assistant (Christopher Howard). The director (Jon Tracy), stage manager (Annye Bone), and costume designer (Maggie Whitaker) were white, and the fight choreographer (Durand Garcia) was Latinx.

Overall, there did not seem to be any particular overarching racial or cultural logic to the casting or production team choices other than casting the two largest roles with the company's veteran African American actors. There also did not seem to be any attempt to convey the ethnicities of the historical characters on which Shakespeare based this drama, such as the ethnic differences between the various Roman generals and soldiers, the Hellenistic Egyptian rulers, and the Egyptian attendants and populace. The production did not, therefore, attempt to adhere to historical accuracy or to portray a revisionist or restorative depiction of the ethnic specificities of the original setting. Neither did it explicitly translate the story from one particular cultural setting to another except for the fact that the modern dress and set design suggested a contemporary time period. As such, it was difficult to place in any clear nontraditional casting philosophy or paradigm.

In order to tease out the cultural meanings created by AASC's production of *Antony and Cleopatra*, I turn to the work of Angela Pao, who writes in *No Safe Spaces*,

> All more-or-less traditional dramatic theater productions refer to between one and three frames of reference: (1) the era of the author; (2) the era of the director/actor/spectator; and (3) the era of the fictional world of the play. These frames may all coincide . . . or all three may be different . . . the controversies generated by race-sensitive casting make it clear that the present time and place stand apart from other domains as a field of contested representation. . . . When arguments over casting practices themselves or the conditions under which they are employed have become heated and acrimonious, it has been whenever fundamental conceptions of twentieth- and twenty-first-century American society and culture are at stake.[178]

Pao suggests that many of the initial forays into colorblind and nontraditional casting in the United States were in Shakespearean plays precisely because of the cultural distance between Shakespeare's era and the contemporary moment of various theater companies' productions. She cites the greater controversies resulting from the casting of minority actors in modernist dramas of the twentieth and twenty-first centuries as evidence of the emphasis that audiences and critics place on the application of contemporary racial logic and cultural understanding rather than an expectation of adherence to the racial logic of the historical moment of a play's production. The racial dynamics of the era of the author and the play's original setting is less viscerally important to audiences the farther these eras are from the contemporary moment of production.

Because Shakespearean plays are particularly temporally and culturally removed from contemporary US culture, they have been some of the mostly successfully accepted non–traditionally cast American productions, despite the fact that many directors claim the contemporary relevance of the plays' themes. For example, in her analysis of the Oregon Shakespeare Festival non–traditionally cast 1996 production of *Coriolanus*, Pao quotes the director Tony Taccone (the former artistic director of Berkeley Repertory Theatre) and his assertion that "Shakespeare's legacy is all about: a way to imagine the past, to examine the present, to reinvent the future."[179] In Taccone's statement, the past and the future are both malleable, but the present remains fixed, something to be examined rather than transformed. In fact, all productions of Shakespearean works in the United States are both temporal and cultural translations; nontraditional casting merely calls attention to this fact in that it "exposes and destabilizes not just the normativity of all-white casting practices, but more significantly, the normativity of white social and cultural dominance, both of which could be taken for granted until the 1960s."[180] Seen in this way, the casting of minority actors in productions that had previously been cast with exclusively white performers transgressed and disrupted the erroneous depiction of contemporary American culture as exclusively and normatively white.

Among the major nontraditional casting paradigms, the emphasis on deconstructing whitewashed representations of American culture is known as "societal casting." Both Catanese and Pao refer to this practice when they cite the categories of nontraditional casting outlined by Clinton Turner Davis and Harry Newman in their transcriptions of the 1988 First National Symposium on Nontraditional Casting. Many scholars see this publication as seminal in establishing the theoretical foundations of nontraditional casting as it is currently practiced in the United States. In it, Davis and Newman define the following American casting paradigms:

COLORBLIND CASTING: Actors are cast without regard to their race or ethnicity; the best actor cast in the role.

SOCIETAL CASTING: Ethnic, female, or disabled actors are cast in the societal roles they perform in society as a whole.

CONCEPTUAL CASTING: An ethnic, female, or disabled actor is cast in a role to give the play greater resonance.

CROSS-CULTURAL CASTING: The entire world of the play is translated to a different cultural setting.[181]

In theory, these approaches are unique; in practice, these categories often overlap. For example, AASC's production of *Antony and Cleopatra* seems to fit best into both the colorblind and societal theoretical frameworks described above. The production was colorblind in the sense that the most experienced actors were cast in the largest roles and there was not any obvious racial cohesion to the depiction of particular families or nationalities (the brother and sister of the same family were differently raced, for example, and both Roman and Egyptian characters were portrayed by both black and white actors). The production was societally cast in terms of its depiction of a contemporary setting populated by people of various races in various positions of power and authority. That is to say, when understood as set in contemporary times, the racial logic of the casting was plausible in the sense that it did not violate the contemporary lived experience of race in the United States. For example, it is perfectly believable for the generals Antony and Octavius to be played by African American and Latinx actors as both African Americans and Latinos serve in significant numbers in the armed forces and have reached the rank of general. It is also plausible for half siblings from blended families to be visually identified and/or to self-identify as belonging to different races. Understood in this way, the AASC production engaged in a cross-cultural casting paradigm where the world/setting of the play was translated from ancient Rome and Egypt into a believable, contemporary, multiracial American milieu.

Because our society is not colorblind, when productions engage in colorblind casting, racial meanings are always read into the casting choices a company makes. Although the casting of AASC's production of *Antony and Cleopatra* did not convey any particularly overt racial logic or message (such as casting of all the Romans as white and all the Egyptians as black to reinforce the colonial dominance of the former over the latter, for example), the play was nevertheless interpreted through a racial lens. For example, in his review for KQED, John Wilkins sought to make connections between Callender's depiction of Marc Antony and Carl Lumbly's depiction of Ira Aldridge in the nearby SF Playhouse's production of *Red Velvet*, a play focusing on the work of the nineteenth-century African American Shakespearean tragedian. Wilkins interpreted the depictions of both characters as pushing against the racial strictures of their settings.

> As Callender's Antony falls, you can't help but feel his descent in racial terms when personified by a black actor. . . . What unites these two productions is the fear that race—or blackness, really—is a kind of performance that is always on the verge of disrupting everything around it . . . it is Antony's body that goes through the most profound transformations. In Egypt, he behaves as if he were a Greek god descended from the heavens to once again taste the pleasures of the earth; in Rome, he is less than human and more the personification of political will and power. Callender embodies both states so fully that you see traces of one in the other. It is as if Antony is suffering a psychic split right before us, constantly and without end.[182]

This description of racial double consciousness is the result of the reviewer interpreting Callender's performance through the lens of his own understanding of the strictures and impositions of contemporary black masculinity.[183] The original script exoticizes Cleopatra as "other" on the grounds of both gender and nationality; she is depicted as the sensual and impetuous female Egyptian foil to the strong, rational, and decisive Roman male, and Antony's infatuation with her is often cited as that character's "tragic flaw."[184] When a black actor personifies the role of Antony, Antony's character can also be interpreted as socially, culturally, and racially "other." As Wilkins's review reveals, Antony's downfall can also be read as an internal conflict rather than or in addition to a racial projection, a wrestling with two competing ontological states that are the result of the character's racial and social status. In this production, Antony's defeat is less a result of Cleopatra's corrupting influence and more the result of the impossibility of suppressing his nature in order to advance politically in a hostile sociocultural environment.

The casting choices of AASC's production of *Antony and Cleopatra* also communicated a sense of racial solidarity in that the greatest affinities occurred between characters portrayed by African Americans. The clearest example of this was the passionate love between Antony and Cleopatra, but a kind of respect and solidarity was also expressed in the cooler alliances between Antony and Octavia as well as between Antony and Pompey. In the scenes between Pompey, Antony, and Octavius, Ewell played his role so that Pompey spoke almost entirely to Antony, ignoring Octavius during the negotiation of their treaty. Music was also used to draw attention to the affectionate relationships among characters portrayed by African American actors. During our interview, Young stated that music was one of the ways AASC connected Shakespearean material to contemporary African American audiences. I saw evidence of this in the production of *Antony and Cleopatra* where upbeat, high-energy rock music was used both during the opening love scene between Antony and Cleopatra and in the party scene on Pompey's boat with the African American members of the cast dancing during the few moments of celebration and enjoyment in a play where the characters were otherwise reserved and restricted by their political responsibilities. Music was used as a way of letting off steam and supported an interpretation of the characters that were portrayed by African American actors as having a certain amount of camaraderie when in one another's company.

Another racial resonance that arose from the casting choices made in this production occurred during act 3, scene 13, where Antony comes upon Octavius's messenger, Thidias, kissing the hand of Cleopatra. In this scene, Antony falls into a jealous rage and has the messenger whipped. Shakespeare's text indicates that Thidias is taken away and whipped, but in AASC's production the scene was staged with Antony himself whipping Thidias; Callender took off his belt and stage whipped Neville Ewell (the actor portraying Thidias) before delivering the speech that communicates Antony's message of defiance to Octavius. For me, this moment of violence communicated several different racialized, gendered, and sociopolitical meanings. The action is meant to show the frustration of the conquered general, as evidenced by Enobarbus's line, "Tis better playing with a lion's whelp than with an old one dying."[185]

Both the beating and the kissing of Cleopatra's hand link sexuality to political power. When Cleopatra offers Thidias her hand, she refers in that moment to her previous romantic and political alliance with Julius Caesar in her apparent supplication to the authority of Octavius. Because of this reference, the kissing of Cleopatra's hand symbolizes not only her physical possession by Octavius as the emerging leader of Rome but also the political dominance and possession of Egypt (gendered as feminine) as part of the Roman Empire (gendered as masculine). The usurpation of masculine political authority was emphasized in AASC's production by the age differences between Callender and Ewell. Antony is the "old lion," whereas Thidias, Octavius's young messenger, is the "whelp" referred to by Enobarbus. While Antony is able to defend his political and sexual territory during that moment, the audience knows he has been defeated and will shortly be driven out of Egypt and Cleopatra's arms. If Thidias had been cast with a white actor, the whipping scene would have had different resonances for an American audience in terms of the racial dynamics of political authority. The whipping of Thidias showed Antony's action to be a vengeful and impotent attempt to reinforce his dominance and political position through an act of violence perpetuated on a younger, more vulnerable person of lower class rather than on the true object of his anger, the out-of-reach and victorious Octavius. The injustice of the whipping not only expressed the "don't blame the messenger" sentiment of the original text, but because both characters were played by black actors, this act also illustrated a violation of the racial solidarity that had been expressed elsewhere throughout the production.

These examples show how the racial, gender, and political resonances of the text can intersect with contemporary interpretations of these dynamics. The sociopolitical significances created through casting and performance are not always explicitly stated in American Shakespearean productions, but they are always read in relation to the cultural background of the present by both the production team and the audience. For example, Pao cites Oregon Shakespeare's 1996 production of *Coriolanus* as a production that used casting to reflect on the contemporary intersections of race and economics in America. Pao cites Taccone's published director's notes as framing the play as an exploration of "class warfare,"[186] while a personal interview with Derrick Lee Weeden, the African American actor cast as Coriolanus, revealed that the director did discuss the use of casting to convey "the thematic resemblance between the family of Coriolanus and inner-city African American families, in the tangled threads of social alienation, matriarchal family structure and masculinity expressed through acts of violence."[187] Perhaps, as a white director, Taccone did not feel comfortable publicly addressing the racial dynamics produced by his casting choices, or perhaps the emphasis on colorblind casting at the time of production in the regional theaters prevented him from explicitly framing the racial connotations of his production choices.

Similarly, the white director of AASC's production of *Antony and Cleopatra*, Jon Tracy, also pointed out the class dimensions rather than the racial resonances of his dramatic interpretation of the play in his director's notes. Tracy chose to emphasize class and the corruptive influence of political power as two of the production's most dominant themes.

> Like all of us fundamentally lost souls that are actually terrified by the power we've attained, they [Antony and Cleopatra] try to detach and find some sense of utopia where the above rules don't apply. But because we have all subscribed to the fallacy of classism, the world needs them to act. . . . *Antony and Cleopatra* is the story of what happens when leaders yearn to be the very humans they ran away from all those years ago in hopes of attaining a sense of legacy that, it turns out, is as mythological as the process they built to attain it.[188]

These notes suggest that the production's focus is primarily upon the dehumanizing consequences of wielding political power rather than any particular portrayal of racial hierarchy or racialized political experiences. However, the racial resonances that resulted from the casting choices (whether intentional or not) linked the performance of social power to the experience and interpretation of racialized positionalities. In this way the production mirrored the larger social and economic forces at work in the city of San Francisco today. While class has been at the forefront of the consciousness of San Francisco residents as the city has been transformed into a playground for the superrich, the decimation of the city's black resident population has shown that issues of class and race are always intersectional.

In addition to Shakespeare, AASC has also produced a variety of other European and Euro-American classics. For instance, L. Peter Callender directed Tennessee Williams's *Cat on a Hot Tin Roof* with an all-black cast in 2013. He returned to Williams's work in the 2018 AASC production of *A Streetcar Named Desire*. This production was an example of cross-cultural casting in that all of the characters, with the exception of Eunice (played by Kim Saunders), were African American. These casting choices depicted the subject of the play as a Southern African American family rather than a Southern white one. The cast for this production was excellent, with Santoya Fields playing a grounded, open, and caring Stella; Jemier Jenkins playing sister Blanche as laughably self-centered and pretentious but still pitiable; and Khary Moye appropriately playing Stella's husband Stanley as a bully with a chip on his shoulder. The entire cast admirably communicated the emotional resonances and dysfunctional family dynamics of the original story in this production, which received rave reviews. Writing for *Theatrius*, Gilad Barach declared the production "a masterpiece," writing, "L. Peter Callender's *Streetcar* goes beyond 'desire' to examine gender, alienation, class conflict, and sexual exploitation. . . . The mostly African American cast masterfully gives new life to Williams' attack on class privilege, challenging traditional U.S. prejudices and bullying."[189] In a review for the *San Francisco Chronicle*, Lily Janiak wrote that the production gave black actors the opportunity "to fight the cosmic fights—for love, home and family, for autonomy, imagination and artistry—that we still give mostly to white characters."[190] While I disagree that these opportunities do not exist in drama written by and about African Americans, AASC's production of *Streetcar* showed that the family dynamics at the center of Williams's play are fairly easily translated into other cultural contexts.

While the emotional heart of this production was very strong, the larger social and historical references of the original text were more difficult to translate into a black cultural context. Presenting a non–traditionally cast twentieth-century American work is much more fraught than producing an ancient text because the cultural realities of the play are so much closer to the lived experience of the audience and production team. For instance, in *A Streetcar Named Desire*, an important part of the plot is that Stanley is Polish American and Stella and Blanche are the descendants of French Mississippi plantation owners. There are numerous instances of Blanche calling Stanley a Polack and other ethnic slurs in Williams's script, which partially fuels Stanley's hatred for Blanche and his desire to dominate and humiliate her. Casting all these characters as African American fundamentally changes the racial and cultural dynamics of the original text. In order to translate this story into a black cultural context, the lines referring to Stanley as Polish were cut. By focusing on other components of the characters' identities and personalities, such as highlighting differences in dressing habits and education, the cast was still able to convey the fact that Blanche thinks she is better than Stanley and that Stanley resents this. While the experience of being looked down upon for being Polish does not translate well into a black cultural context, other ethnic references in the original text were retained. One of the lines that got the most laughs on the evening I attended this production occurred during the date scene between Blanche and Mitch. In this scene Mitch (earnestly played by Fred Pitts) questions Blanche about her family name: "It's French isn't it?" Jemier Jenkins's performance of Blanche's response, "of French *extraction*," was hilarious and instantly recognizable to a black audience familiar with the pretentiousness of African American Creole families who emphasize their French heritage over their African heritage. In this way, the attitude of the Du Bois sisters regarding their ethnicity translated very easily into a black context.

The lines referring to Belle Reve, the sisters' family home and former plantation, worked less well in this production. This was the only part of an otherwise excellent show that struck me as out of place. In AASC's production, Stanley still asks Stella about "our plantation" and Blanche still refers to it as a "beautiful dream."[191] Although a percentage of free blacks in the South did own plantations and enslaved people throughout the operation of slavery in the United States, I found black actors voicing nostalgic references to plantations in a play set during the 1940s jarring.[192] Specifically, I found it unbelievable that an African American in the twentieth century would refer to a plantation as "a beautiful dream." These references reveal the fact that Williams's characters were originally written to represent the white descendants of slaveholders. In my opinion, these lines, like the lines referring to Stanley's Polish ancestry, should have been cut or otherwise dealt with. If racially specific references are not dealt with in culturally translated productions, either through editing or performance practices that in some way acknowledge the changed dynamics of these references, then the audience becomes disoriented or otherwise taken out of the action of the play. The difficulty in dealing with the inherent racism ingrained in the original white characters' backgrounds, ingrained in the South and in our country as a whole, provides a counterexample to the notion of the classics being universal. Every story is culturally specific. This does not mean that cultural translations of these stories should not be done, just that these specificities must be addressed if a production is to operate as a work of social realism or social critique.

Having long produced European and European American classics, in 2012, AASC expanded its programming to include classic plays by African American dramatists as well. The company's first production by an African American playwright was Lorraine Hansberry's *A Raisin in the Sun*, arguably the most iconic and widely produced piece of African American dramatic literature. L. Peter Callender directed the production, which featured Eleanor Jacobs as Lena, Todd Risby as Walter Lee, Leontyne Mbele-Mbong as Ruth, Siaira Harris as Beneatha, and Savion Green as Travis. The production of other African American classics followed, including George Wolfe's *The Colored Museum*, codirected by Callender, Velina Brown, Michael Gene Sullivan, and Edris Cooper-Anifowoshe in 2016; and August Wilson's *Jitney*, directed by Callender in 2017. In 2018, AASC produced Ntozake Shange's *for colored girls who have considered suicide when the rainbow is enuf*. This production was directed by Elizabeth Carter. In 2019, AASC produced Leslie Lee's play about the Tuskegee airmen, *Black Eagles*, which was presented at the Marines' Memorial Theatre and directed by L. Peter Callender. Each of these productions was critically acclaimed and well attended. The expansion of AASC's programming into the realm of African American literature came during a period of lower output for LHT, making these productions an even more needed and welcome expansion of black theater offerings in the Bay Area.

In 2015, AASC sought to make connections between the black community of the Bay Area and other minority groups when it coproduced Torange Yeghiazarian's *Isfahana Blues* with Golden Thread Productions, a Bay Area company dedicated to the presenting works "from or about the Middle East that celebrate the multiplicity of its perspectives and identities."[193] Inspired by the life of the playwright's mother, prerevolutionary Iranian film actor

Vida Ghahremani, and by the Duke Ellington Orchestra's 1963 tour to Iran, *Isfahana Blues* imagines a meeting between one of the members of Duke Ellington's band and a famous Iranian film actor. L. Peter Callender played the American musician Ray, and Ghahremani played Bella, the character inspired by her own life. Ghahremani's character acts as a kind of narrator, looking back at her time as an actor and nightclub owner in prerevolutionary Iran. Sofia Ahmed played the younger 1963 version of Bella, and Marcus Shelby composed original music for the production.[194] The result of two years of collaboration between the two companies, this production was an amazing example of two minority theaters creating something unique and bringing to the American stage voices and stories that are rarely represented.

In 2019, AASC received one of six Audience (R)Evolution grants from Theatre Communications Group in partnership with Afro Solo, SFBATCO (San Francisco Bay Area Theatre Company), and Cultural Odyssey working together as member organizations of the African American Theatre Alliance for Independence (AATAIN).[195] The grant supports the hiring of youth to help create theater experiences geared to their generation as part of a national effort to increase the generational diversity of theater audiences. AATAIN's successful grant application evidences the benefit of black theaters working together to support one another and build the critical mass necessary to compete with much larger organizations. For example, California Shakespeare Theater, another recipient of the grant, has a budget of approximately $5 million.[196] By pooling administrative resources and demonstrating the collective importance of these culturally specific organizations, AATAIN was able to successfully compete with an organization with ten times the budget of some of its member groups. In addition to the three companies named in the grant, LHT, Push Dance Company, and AAACC are also members of AATAIN. Afro Solo describes AATAIN as "an alliance of like-minded Black arts organizations working together to enhance the cultural landscape of San Francisco."[197] As such, AATAIN is part of an innovative strategy to increase the power of black theater companies that could serve as a model for similar collaborations in other cities.

Of the three organizations covered in this chapter, AASC is the most financially secure, thanks largely to the savvy management of its founder Sherri Young. According to the company's Guidestar profile, its 2019 revenue was approximately $1.1 million.[198] It is clear that Young has spent years carefully cultivating AASC's audience and donor base, gradually expanding the work produced by the organization beyond the most well-recognized and popular forms of theater to include new productions in addition to classical work.

The operation of San Francisco's black theaters supports the representation and participation of African Americans within the arts ecology of the Bay Area. As real estate prices have soared and the black population of the city has dwindled, these theaters have survived by taking advantage of resources such as the city-owned AAACC and efforts by agencies and foundations such as the San Francisco Arts Commission to stabilize and maintain arts organizations of historic and community-based importance. Under the AATAIN alliance, they have pooled resources to attract national grants, successfully competing with major regional theaters with budgets many times their size. Bay Area black theaters have created partnerships with each other and with other arts institutions and populations that are more widely represented in the city's current cultural demographics. They have engaged with telling the stories of Bay Area black citizens and communities, showing how black people have contributed to the larger culture and identity of the city. Located in the city that most starkly reflects the widening chasm between rich and the poor, these theaters' histories and continued practice serve as a reminder of the importance of race-conscious theater in a world that disproportionately impacts communities of color when economics rather than civic engagement drives municipal development.

Chapter 4

✦

In the Mecca

Atlanta-Based Black Theater Production

The Atlanta arts ecology is unique in a variety of ways. First and foremost, Atlanta has been majority black for several decades.[1] Since the civil rights era, Atlanta has also been the seat of black wealth and political power in the South.[2] Although Atlanta has certainly been shaped by racism and exhibits the economic problems and neglect of the working class (many of whom are African American) typical of contemporary American neoliberal cities, it is also undoubtedly a metropolitan area where African Americans have been able to participate in higher education, stake out valuable real estate, run multinational corporations, and harness the critical mass needed to wield substantial political power at the city and county levels.[3] Atlanta's first black mayor, Maynard Jackson, is credited with creating "more African American millionaires" than "any other public official, black or white."[4] In "Maynard Jackson: Creating a Bully Pulpit for Black Business," Derek Dingle writes:

> As mayor of Atlanta during the 1970s and again in the '90s, he used his office to level the playing field for African American entrepreneurs and, as a result, bolstered the city's black middle class. . . . Jackson established a national model for creating access to contracts for black businesses that was emulated by mayors in other major cities like Detroit, Los Angeles, Boston, and Chicago."[5]

The city's "boosters" boast that Atlanta has had "40 consecutive years of progressive black mayors."[6] This fact is provided as evidence of the rightness of the city's "black mecca" moniker and its continued attractiveness to African American professionals and entrepreneurs seeking economic opportunity and a supportive community where "black people are getting things done."[7] For example, in a 1996 *Essence* article that was published at the height of the "new migration," Joy Cain proclaimed, "This is the place where people of color with good ideas can find people of color with money to invest in them."[8] Stacey Abrams's recent competitive bid to become the first black

157

governor of Georgia, and the first black female governor of *any* state, is an indication of the continued power and legacy of the political influence of Atlanta's black community.[9]

In this chapter I examine the history and contributions of three significant Atlanta theater institutions: Jomandi Productions, which operated from 1978 to 2002; Kenny Leon's True Colors Theatre Company, founded in 2002; and the Atlanta Black Theatre Festival, founded in 2012. The history of these three institutions intersects with the transformation of the Atlanta metro area into a flourishing economic and cultural hub centered around black experience. Looking at the production history of these three companies shows how black theater in Atlanta is intertwined with black political power.

Jomandi Productions

Jomandi Productions was founded in 1978 when Thomas W. Jones II and Marsha Jackson created the company in memory of Jones's father who had been a prominent physician and contributor to the establishment of the Morehouse Medical School during his tenure as a Fulton County deputy commissioner of health.[10] The founding of Jomandi thus intersects with the legacy of the consortium of historically black colleges located in Atlanta. Morehouse, Spelman, and Clark Atlanta universities have each nurtured generations of African American educators, entrepreneurs, political leaders, and artists.[11] Until the 1970s, black theater in Atlanta was primarily produced by this consortium of historically black colleges. Jones recalls that "if you went to Morehouse or you went to Spelman, you went to the AU [Atlanta University] Center. That was where you had a night out particularly in the late sixties and seventies."[12]

The work of Carlton W. Molette and the late Barbara J. Molette provides one example of the rich theatrical practice that was nurtured and created at Atlanta's consortium of historically black colleges and universities. Faculty members of Spelman and Clark Atlanta University, the Molettes participated in the theaters associated with the civil rights movement (the Free Southern Theater) and the black arts movement (the Negro Ensemble Company) and brought the artistic arm of these movements to bear on the work they did with Atlanta's historically black colleges. The Molettes' first collaborative play, *Rosalee Pritchett*, was produced in 1970 by Atlanta's Morehouse-Spelman Players and then was picked up by the Negro Ensemble Company in 1971. The play was remounted by the Negro Ensemble Company in 2017 for its fiftieth anniversary season. *Rosalee Pritchett* was also produced by the Free Southern Theater and several other university theaters.[13] The Molettes collaboratively wrote *Black Theatre: Premise and Presentation*, a treatise on black theatrical practices as "an expression of culture and a means of communicating values."[14] They also produced the Atlanta University Summer

Theatre program, which operated for many years and influenced a generation of African American youth in the Atlanta area. For all of these efforts,
they were honored with "the Black Theatre Network's Lifetime Membership
Award in 2012, the National Black Theatre Festival's Living Legend Award
and the Ethel Woolson Award for Legacy in 2013, and the Atlanta Black
Theatre Festival's Legend Award in 2016."[15]

While the Molettes were part of the first generation of African American
artists coming out of the black arts and civil rights movements, Thomas Jones
considers himself and the company he founded to be "part of the second
generation of African American theaters" inspired by these same movements.[16] Jones was a student of Sonia Sanchez, one of the leading writers
of the black arts movement.[17] Under Sanchez's mentorship, Jones wrote his
first play, *Every Father's Child*, as a tribute to his father. *Every Father's Child*
was Jomandi's first production. Jones and his family wanted to use the ticket
sales from the production to contribute to an endowed scholarship at Morehouse in honor of his father. The name Jomandi was chosen as an acronym
that incorporated components of each of the four surviving family members'
names.[18]

Jones saw the interdisciplinary nature of the performance works Jomandi
created over the next twenty-four years as deeply inspired by the earlier practices and aesthetics of artists from the black arts movement. In an *Art Works*
podcast produced by the NEA, Jones explained this influence.

> [I] Studied with Sonia Sanchez, who was also . . . someone who I
> deeply admired in high school . . . [I] read all of those poets, [Amiri]
> Baraka and Nikki Giovanni and Sonia Sanchez and Haki Mad-
> hubuti . . . the whole litany of Black Arts poets, and particularly those
> that were coming out of Broadside Press in Detroit. . . . A lot of our
> early work was looking at theater in a nontraditional context, was
> really kind of exploring form and structure and kind of getting inside
> of it, and I think a lot of that developed because we were such stu-
> dents of the black arts movement and there was so much of the idea
> of redefining theater, theater coming into a community, theater . . .
> particularly from an African American aesthetic, using and conjoin-
> ing all of the different elements, music and dance and poetry . . . that
> theater didn't have to be linear or the four chairs and a table, that
> you could begin exploring and playing with form . . . that theater
> was multidisciplinary, or that performance was multidisciplinary. . . .
> I think a lot of our early work in Atlanta, at Jomandi, was beginning
> to continue that exploration.[19]

In a 1986 feature in *Ebony* magazine, co–artistic director Marsha Jackson
similarly characterized Jomandi's aesthetic. "Jomandi involves various disciplines in the rendering of dramatic work. People find that they are uniquely

drawn not only by what we do, but by the way we do it."[20] Rooted in the tenets of the black arts movement, Jomandi's aesthetic sought to break down artificial divisions between performance practices and directly engage in the life of the community from which it came and in which it was performed.

By Jones's estimate, there were around ten other black theater companies operating in Atlanta as part of the flowering of the black arts movement when Jones and Jackson first founded Jomandi in 1978. "There was Atlanta Renaissance Theatre, there was Theatre without Walls, there was Just Us, there was Composition, there was Jomandi, and there was the People's Revival Theatre. There were just a whole host of theaters that were being born out of a sense of having a mission within a community and having a vision. . . . So, we were born out of that tradition."[21] In order to differentiate themselves from the other theater companies in the area, Jomandi focused on new plays and ensemble-developed performances.

> We were doing stuff that was, as they said, "avant-garde." That was just everybody's word for it, because it was probably the only word they had. We were doing a lot of company development work. We were doing a lot of multidisciplinary work. We were doing a lot of ensemble-based work. We were doing a lot of adaptations of things. . . . We weren't doing standard fare. *Raisin in the Sun*, you know, *Ain't Misbehavin*, those plays that were part of the popular canon were already being done by other companies. . . . A lot of our early work was really being developed from writers; either we were developing new writers or working with a handful of writers that didn't have access. We were creating a whole body of new work.[22]

Using a black arts–inspired aesthetic, Jomandi presented over 250 productions in its twenty-four years of existence, including many original works.[23] Jones explained that Jomandi was an important developmental space for many artists who later received critical acclaim and professional notoriety. "A lot of artists came through our doors. A lot of writers came through our doors. Much like Penumbra was August Wilson's [early] home, we were a home to Jeff Stetson. We were a home for Alonzo Lamont. I gave Kenny Leon and Drew Cohen their first directing jobs. . . . Tyler Perry used to stand backstage in the nineties and watch our shows."[24] Just as Jones and Jackson had gotten their start through the mentorship of an earlier generation of African American artists, many of Atlanta's contemporary theater artists such as Kenny Leon and Tyler Perry developed their craft working for and attending Jomandi Productions. In his memoir, Leon writes, "During the time when I was working at the Academy [Theatre], I also did regular work for two black theater companies, Jomandi Productions and Just Us Theatre . . . we focused on the work of black writers, and it was a chance for me to stretch beyond the improv and community work and more mainstream stuff."[25] Leon's statement here supports Jones's assertion and points out the interdisciplinary and original nature of much of the work that Jomandi produced outside of the "mainstream" of traditional theater production.

Thomas Jones's 1988 solo show *The Wizard of Hip, Or, When in Doubt, Slam Dunk* provides an example of Jomandi's own unique artistic aesthetic. This production innovatively combined spoken word, hip hop, and solo performance. An excerpt from this piece gives a sense of Jones's effort to, "break down the walls of what theatre can be."[26]

> I just want to be where the truly hip be, hang there where the hip hang, speak with a sculptured hip tongue, surround myself in an ultra-phonic quadrapletic euphoric, surreal and unique hipness. . . . Somebody give me a Beat. . . . We're on our own beat. Hep me . . . what is hip? . . . as in the wonderment of where do I belong in the grand circuit of the moment.[27]

In this work, Jones combines hip hop and stand-up comedy with the "structure and depth of theater."[28] In an interview with the *Atlanta Constitution*, Jones described the play as "an expressionistic odyssey, a stream of consciousness through life's phases, spiced with 'my particular madness.'"[29] He created and performed the role of "Afro Jo" as a kind of theatrical alter ego and everyman that allowed him to mix many autobiographical experiences from his own life with larger social musings in a high-energy theatrical tour de force. Primarily comedic, *The Wizard of Hip* expressed black middle-class experiences that were eminently relatable to Atlanta audiences. "This is who I am. A middle-class black man. No apologies."[30] The play was incredibly popular. It was restaged in 1990 and also toured nationally, enjoying positive reception in both Washington, DC, and New York. *New York Times* critic D. J. R. Bruckner describes the show's overall aesthetic as "the kind of good-humored, wise, hip storytelling that makes most of Mr. Jones's thoughts about life so fresh and memorable."[31] *The Wizard of Hip's* latest revival in August 2017 at Metro Stage in the DC area was described by Debbie Minter Jackson as "a kind of time capsule glimpse of who we were and from whence we've come, from the zany mind of one of the most talented and creative performers around."[32]

Jomandi's co–artistic director Marsha Jackson also achieved major success as a writer and performer during her tenure at Jomandi. Like Jones, Jackson was a former student of Sonia Sanchez. She wrote, directed, and performed in many Jomandi productions in addition to serving as the co–artistic and managing director of the company. She wrote at least five plays for the company including *Witchbird, Josephine Live!, Dunbar Fantasy*, and *Sisters*.[33] Her most popular play, *Sisters*, a more traditionally structured play than *The Wizard of Hip*, premiered in 1986 at Jomandi and was restaged as part of the National Black Arts Festival at the Academy Theatre in Atlanta in

1988.[34] That same year, Jackson starred opposite Denzel Washington in the Broadway production of Ron Milner's *Checkmates*, which also starred Ruby Dee and Paul Winfield.[35] After its second Atlanta production, *Sisters* toured nationally, including an off-Broadway production in 1990 at the Joyce Theater in New York.[36]

Sisters takes place in an Atlanta office building and juxtaposes the life experience of a corporate executive and that of an office cleaner, both African American women, who learn from and bond with one another when they are stuck in the building together during a power outage. With its direct depiction of the different economic realities of the two main characters, the play spoke to the widening economic gap in Atlanta's black communities, exploring some interesting ruminations on class, race, and gender. The play opens with Cassie, the janitor, singing Chaka Khan's hit song "I'm Every Woman" as she listens to her cassette player and vacuums the office of Olivia, an advertising executive. Cassie proceeds to mock Olivia's taste in "muzak" and superior attitude and pretensions. By the end of the storm that has caused a power outage in their office building and after several rounds of drinking, the two women form a friendship that reflects a solidarity rooted in black sisterhood. "This is for the sisters on the other end of the line. Those here and far away too."[37] Directed by Jones, Jackson played the role of Olivia, the uptight ad executive, and Andrea Frye performed the role of Cassie, the wise but overburdened office cleaner. The play explored the intersection of race and class with particular emphasis on the economic pressures faced by black women.

In a review of the 1991 Jomandi production of Valetta Anderson's play *She'll Find Her Way Home*, Dan Hulbert juxtaposes the multidimensional portrayals of black life and culture produced by Jomandi during this time period with the meticulously constructed and stilted representations of black middle-class experience portrayed on television during the late 1980s and early 1990s.

> While TV shows about middle-class blacks illustrate what might be called the triumph of assimilation, the theater is taking the deeper view. . . . Even among black comedies set in the present, the trend is for older, earthier characters to get in the last, wisest word. The working-class couple in *Checkmates* by Ron Milner; and the cleaning lady in *Sisters*, by Jomandi co–artistic director Marsha Jackson, have something to teach the know-it-all buppies.[38]

This focus on the intersection of race and class is not surprising given that Jomandi's existence corresponded roughly with the height of the reverse migration of African Americans to Atlanta and the intentional development of the city's black middle and upper classes. Because of this correspondence, its work was often highlighted as an indication of the rich black cultural expressions of the city. For example, in a 1996 *Essence* feature on Atlanta that sang the praises of the city, Joy Cain named Marsha Jackson as one of Atlanta's "sisters with clout," alongside news anchors, corporate executives, politicians, and Coretta Scott King.[39] Jomandi was also one of the local theater companies featured in the Olympic Arts Festival, which was produced during Atlanta's hosting of the 1996 summer Olympics.[40] For this international arts event, the company presented Jones's show *Hip 2: Birth of the Boom*, a sequel to his popular solo performance *The Wizard of Hip*.[41] This kind of press coverage framed the work that Jomandi did as part of the cultural sophistication and racial identity of the city.

When asked about the uniqueness of Atlanta's arts ecology during the height of Jomandi Productions, Jones heavily emphasized the impact of the city's black political leadership.

> In the midseventies you had Maynard Jackson. . . . With him came people like Shirley Franklin. With him came Michael Lomax. With him came Pearl Cleage. With him came David Franklin, who was Richard Pryor's first lawyer and Roberta Flack's lawyer. So, you had, for the first time, a kind of high-end, political movement coming out of the civil rights movement that was redefining, I think, the ecology of a city, because you now had black political leadership. Under Maynard Jackson, for example, came something called the Department of Cultural Affairs. That was a city-funded bureau that was tasked to create and administer and support a healthy arts community. So, from that came an initiative to take old, abandoned school buildings and turn them into art centers. Five art centers were created. One of them was the Center for Puppetry Arts. One of them was the Neighborhood Arts Center. One of them was called Arts Exchange.[42]

Jones also mentioned the CETA program, a 1970s federal employment program that paid salaries for city workers, including artists, that was administered through city governments.

> CETA funding [was] a way to employ artists, not only in these centers, but also within their own theater companies. So, you actually had the city underwriting employees working for arts institutions. Michael Lomax then created the Fulton County Arts Council, which was the funding agent and the funding engine for the National Black Arts Festival, which became this internationally renowned arts festival in its first 10 years. So, you had a kind of sensibility about art, that art had a function within a community, and that it was supported in a particular way, with these public/private partnerships.[43]

City and county resources underwrote or provided rehearsal and performance space, salaries, marketing, and touring opportunities.

> For example, Jomandi and another theater company, Just Us, we were recipients in 1979 or '80 of an arts block grant that came out of the county that enabled us to get an infusion of capital so that we could do the work that we wanted to do. So, I think that what was unique about the city, was that you had a sensibility from its political leaders and even from its corporate leaders that art, specifically art that came through the lens of African American artists, had a unique significance in the city and should be supported in a particular way.[44]

The city's black leadership worked to increase the national profile of local African American arts organizations as a kind of arts diplomacy, crafting the city's image as a cosmopolitan, majority black metropolitan area. "When you have Andy Young, as the mayor saying, 'I'm going to present your work and call the airlines so that you guys can go overseas and represent us in this "Other Americas" festival in Scandinavian countries for six weeks,' people are going to listen to that investment. That kind of capital wasn't happening anywhere else."[45] With the rise of black city and county leadership, African American arts and entertainment were cultivated through direct support to black theater companies such as Jomandi and Just Us, by showcasing black theater and other art forms at international venues such as the 1996 Olympic Games, by inviting black artists from outside of Atlanta to participate in the National Blacks Arts Festival, and by supporting the touring of black arts organizations both locally and internationally. While Atlanta has always had a vibrant music scene, the showcasing and promoting of other forms of black art such as theater, film, dance, and visual art started to be consciously cultivated and more robustly supported during the 1980s and 1990s.

Black theater production at this time also sought to connect with Atlanta's ever popular music scene.[46] For example, Jones created an original performance, *Bessie's Blues*, as a tribute to Atlanta blues singer Bernardine Mitchell. He explained the impetus for this production on the occasion of the play's twentieth anniversary remount.

> I was a huge fan of the woman who's actually the lead, named Bernardine Mitchell. When I got to Atlanta, she was this amazing club singer. She was, to me, the second coming of Nina Simone, in the way in which she phrased her voice, and she was also an actor. So, I decided at some point, you know, I approached her, and said, "I want to write a piece for you, just to showcase you, because I'm such a fan." And she said, "Well, I've always wanted to do a piece on Bessie Smith," and I was like, "Well, I'm not sure I'm totally interested in just doing a biography on Bessie Smith," but what if we were to look at it, in a certain sense, as looking at the black artists and the blues cycle through the twentieth century, through the lens of two women,

and parallel where blues as an art form comes from? I think particularly it also continued the idea . . . [Amiri] Baraka [makes in] *Blues People* . . . [that] people create an art form, a functional art form, in a certain sense to organize the chaos of what it is to be Negro and American and all of that.[47]

Bessie's Blues premiered in Washington, DC, where it won six Helen Hayes awards. It was created and inspired by Atlanta artists in the Jomandi style. Mitchell would go on to perform the roles of other musical legends such as Mahalia Jackson in the gospel musical *Mahalia*, which was directed by fellow Atlanta artist Carol Mitchell Leon in 2004.[48] Other Jomandi productions about famous singers included *Josephine Live!* by Marsha Jackson (1983) and *Queen of the Blues*, by Thomas W. Jones II (1991).[49] Jomandi also produced Sonia Sanchez's play *I'm Black When I'm Singing, I'm Blue When I Ain't* (1982), which tells the stories of three different women in the music business and shows how each of them were exploited in different ways. Sanchez wrote the piece specifically for Jomandi and gave it to them royalty free in an effort to help financially sustain the company.[50]

It would be impossible to gloss the prolific production history of Jomandi, which, by Jones's account, exceeded 250 plays in twenty-four years. Considering this, I asked Jones as the former artistic director to identify what he felt were some of the company's major production highlights and how the company thought these productions contributed to the development of black theater in America. Jones replied:

> The work that we did with Jeff Stetson [was significant]. We did a world premiere of *Keep the Faith*, the Adam Clayton Powell musical. We did *The Meeting* very often. That was actually a coproduction with Chuck Smith [resident director of the Goodman Theatre] in Chicago. We did a lot of work with New Federal [Theatre in New York] in terms of coproductions. . . . *That Serious He-Man Ball* [by Alonzo Lamont] was one piece that we launched that went on to the American Place Theatre and a couple of other places. *Sisters*, which was by my co–artistic director, Marsha Jackson, went on to do a lot of work. *The Wizard of Hip*. . . . Those were some of the works that went on to other places. We also did *And the Men Shall Also Gather*, which was a Jeff Stetson piece. We did *Fraternity*, which was a Jeff Stetson piece. We did a bunch of Alonzo Lamont pieces. In fact, it was the piece that we did for him that landed him a job on *A Different World*, the Cosby spinoff. The first production we did of *The Meeting* was with Harry Lennix and Greg Alan Williams.[51]

In addition to *Keep the Faith*, Jomandi produced several important plays having to do with black politicians and political activists.

> We did a piece, *El Haj Malik* [about Malcolm X], that featured Cassi
> Davis, who was one of Tyler [Perry]'s actors. Another piece we did
> was Robert Alexander's play *Servant of the People: The Rise and Fall
> of Huey Newton and the Black Panther Party*, which was kind of an
> amazing event, because all of the Panther leaders from Bobby Seale
> and Kathleen Cleaver on back to Afeni Shakur, Tupac's mom, all came
> to see it. They were sitting there having these mad, raging debates. In
> the piece we had this amazing group of folks including a young actor
> named Chuma, who was Charlayne Hunter-Gault's son, the woman
> who along with Hamilton Holmes desegregated the University of
> Georgia. We had Thomas Byrd, who went on to do a bunch of work
> with Spike Lee. We had Taurean Blacque, who had just come off of
> *Hill Street Blues*. We had Tony Vaughn, who got picked up to work for
> Tyler [Perry] in two of his series. It was an amazing array of people.[52]

The fact that these plays explored a rich array of political viewpoints and
practices in the hometown of Martin Luther King Jr. during a time when
black politicians were getting their first opportunity to shape and lead city
government must have been exhilarating. Offering a space to stage and
discuss the impacts of these political movements is one way that Jomandi
participated in the shaping of the politics of the city.

While Jomandi benefited from the patronage of the city's black leadership,
it also directly contributed to many of the political efforts of the city's black
population.

> One of the very first pieces we did was for the NAACP legal defense
> fund, with Julian Bond presiding. . . . We did a reading once with Andy
> Young, Julian Bond, Maynard Jackson, and Monica Kaufman, who
> was one of the first black anchorwomen in the South. She was part of
> an ABC affiliate here in the seventies. There was [former mayor] Shir-
> ley Franklin; it was just a who's who of black Atlanta leadership. We
> did it as a fundraiser, it was a reading of *God's Trombones* [by James
> Weldon Johnson]. . . . So, there was always a connection between art
> and recognizing that art and theater and performance had to be con-
> nected to the whole notion of community. . . . Nowhere else was that
> happening to the same degree, because you didn't have the kind of
> political capital and political gravitas going into it.[53]

Jones pointed out that in addition to domestic politics, Atlanta's black leadership was also deeply invested in international politics, particularly in the
international effort to support the end of Apartheid in South Africa.

> You had a black political world here. You had folks here that were
> moving and shaking the world. People forget that the reason why

Coca-Cola divested from South Africa was because of a woman named Ingrid Saunders Jones, who was brought on to negotiate that withdrawal from South Africa, and also helped to become one of the movers and shakers for getting Nelson Mandela out of jail. It was that kind of thing that was going on here that was part of [the legacy of] Andy Young and Maynard Jackson. I mean, they inherited the legacy of Martin Luther King. So, Julian Bond and John Lewis and Andy Young and Shirley Franklin and David Franklin and Michael Lomax and Pearl Cleage, all of them were part of the moving and shaking of this city. Part of what they recognized as a function of what they were doing was the support of black art and black theater specifically.[54]

Buoyed by the synergy between the political leadership and artistic community, Jomandi became one of the most influential African American theater companies in the nation. Jomandi Productions frequently toured to Washington, DC, and other cities with sizeable black populations. Productions created by Jomandi artists won many Helen Hayes awards in Washington, DC, and were nominated for several AUDELCO awards in New York.[55] In 1990, Jomandi was awarded the Georgia Governor's Award for the Arts. Toni Simmons Henson, cofounder of the Atlanta Black Theatre Festival, credited Jomandi for cultivating a "sophisticated" black theater audience interested in supporting and attending high-quality theater exploring black experiences.[56] Jomandi participated in many community-building local events, including its Community without Walls program, which "reached an audience of 100,000 people its second year."[57] This was one example of how the company also operated youth and educational programs in addition to presenting professional works onstage. The organization was, in myriad ways, deeply connected to the cultural and political development of the city.

Despite these successes, by the midnineties Jomandi's leadership started to feel frustrated by the changing funding prospects and philanthropic patronage of American theater. Like many African American theater companies, Jomandi was negatively impacted when the regional theaters began to produce African American work and hire African American artists.

It became apparent that given the traditional model we were handed, we weren't going to be able to move beyond a certain place. We were not going to get to the two or three million–dollar [operating budget] level. We were considered an important theater that had an important reputation that was doing good things in the field, so we were supported, but only to a certain degree. Again, once other theaters, the larger theaters started doing the same initiatives we were doing, you know, they would get three times the funding that we would get for the exact same initiative. So, it just became a glass ceiling. There was going to be a disproportionate amount of funding, even given the same thing. So, we were always going to hit a certain plateau and never go beyond that.[58]

An *Atlanta Constitution* article from 1994 supports Jones's articulation of this issue. In "Jomandi's Jam: Black Theater's in Fight for Its Life; It Lacks Funds, Audiences, and Must Compete with High-Profile Alliance," Dan Hulbert cites the differential between the NEA grants to the Alliance Theatre ($1.6 million in 1994) and Jomandi Productions ($70,000) as evidence of funding bias.[59] The still-common practice of funding agencies giving more to large-budget institutions and less to organizations equal in quality but not in operating budget perpetuates economic inequality in an arts ecology set up to aid those that have to the detriment of those that have not. For culturally specific organizations dedicated to producing works by artists of color, the issue was compounded by the fact that these companies, whose entire mission and production history had always been devoted to producing the work of artists of color, began to be chastised by funding organizations for their lack of cultural pluralism or, in the terms of the time, "commitment to multiculturalism." In the same 1994 *Atlanta Constitution* article, Marsha Jackson recounts how she was asked by a representative from the NEA, "What are you doing to diversify?"[60] This question reveals the fact that these funding institutions were preoccupied with initiatives geared toward integrating the large regional theaters and dismissive of the long-standing contributions of minority theaters to the diversity of the local arts ecology.

Frustrated by this reality and not seeing a clear way to increase financial support for the company, Jones left Jomandi in 2000 to work as a freelance director and performer. Jackson left in 2001. From 2001 to 2005, she served as the producing and artistic director of the acclaimed Ensemble Theatre in Houston, Texas, during which time she directed ten productions including August Wilson's *Fences* and Lynn Nottage's *Crumbs from the Table of Joy*.[61] Jomandi continued for a few years after Jones and Jackson left the company.[62] Jomandi's board of directors renamed the organization "New Jomandi" and hired Byron C. Saunders as artistic director in 2002. The company's scheduled 2003–4 season was cancelled, however, due to lack of funds.[63] The fate of Jomandi reveals the problematic nature of the implementation of the multicultural initiatives of the 1990s in American theater practice, which benefited larger, predominantly white arts institutions and disadvantaged the smaller, culturally specific arts institutions that had previously been doing this work. Woodie King Jr. writes eloquently about this travesty in his book *The Impact of Race: Theatre and Culture*.[64] The Helicon Collaborative's scathing report *Not Just Money: Equity Issues in Cultural Philanthropy* has recently quantified the extent to which inequality in American arts funding persists and has in fact worsened in recent years, favoring large, predominantly white arts organizations at the expense of smaller, culturally specific arts organizations.[65] As a nation and an arts community, we have yet to adequately address this issue.

Kenny Leon's True Colors Theatre Company

Luckily for the Atlanta theater community, another organization centered around African American cultural material, Kenny Leon's True Colors Theatre Company, was born the same year that Jomandi folded. True Colors is a unique example of black theater production in several respects, many of which have to do with the career path of its founder and namesake. In a telephone interview with me, the current artistic director of True Colors, Jamil Jude, expressed the opinion that "it would be impossible to overestimate the influence of Kenny Leon" in the Atlanta theater community.[66] Prior to the founding of True Colors, Leon had been the artistic director of Atlanta's Alliance Theatre, a major regional theater with a $15 million operating budget.[67] As such, he is one of only a handful of African Americans to lead the most well-funded nonprofit theaters in the country. In a 2015 study conducted by the Wellesley Centers for Women, researchers found that out of the seventy-four member theaters of the League of Resident Theatres, an organization that includes most of the country's largest nonprofit theaters, "there was only one female artistic director of color. For men of color, leadership representation was also bleak: there were five leaders on the artistic side . . . men and women of color were completely absent in top leadership on the executive and management side of theatres."[68] As artistic director of the Alliance Theatre from 1990 to 2001, Kenny Leon is part of a very small group of black artistic directors of nonprofit theaters with operating budgets over $6 million. That group includes Lloyd Richards (Canadian American), artistic director of Yale Repertory Theatre from 1979 to 1991; George C. Wolfe, artistic director of the Public Theater from 1993 to 2004; Sheldon Epps, artistic director or the Pasadena Playhouse from 1997 to 2007; Kwame Kwei-Armah (British), artistic director of Baltimore Stage from 2011 to 2018; and Nataki Garrett, artistic director of the Oregon Shakespeare Festival from 2019 to the present.

In his memoir *Take You Wherever You Go*, Leon chronicles his career path. After graduating from Clark College (now Clark Atlanta University), one of Atlanta's historically black colleges, Leon worked for ten years as a freelance actor and company member with the Academy Theatre, Jomandi, Just Us, and other theaters with small to midsized budgets in the Atlanta area. A career-changing directing fellowship funded by an NEA program designed to help diversify the regional theater system led to his appointment first as associate artistic director and then artistic director of the Alliance Theatre. Leon characterized this program and his subsequent hire as part of the effort of Alliance's board of directors and national funders to "integrate their theatre."[69] Leon writes, "When I first came to the Alliance Theatre, it was more than 90 percent white and more than 90 percent people who could easily afford theatre tickets."[70] At Alliance, Leon directed August Wilson's *Joe Turner's Come and Gone* in 1989 and *Fences* in 1990. He staged a world premiere of fellow Atlanta artist Pearl Cleage's *Flyin' West* in 1992 and also directed

Phylicia Rashad in Cleage's *Blues for an Alabama Sky* in 1995. He continued to act as well, appearing as Walter Lee opposite his first wife and artistic collaborator Carol Mitchell in a 1994 Alliance production of *A Raisin in the Sun* that was directed by Woodie King Jr. He clearly achieved his own artistic aims and those of the theater to broaden the cultural scope of the work being done on the Alliance stage during this time period.

As the first African American artistic director of the largest regional theater in the Southeast, Leon was in an enviable but also difficult position. While he felt supported by the Alliance board of directors and the majority of its audience base, he also mentions in his memoir that he received death threats and that the theater lost some subscribers who expressed "the idea that I was doing too many African American stories" and "trying to force something down their throats."[71] Leon was also implicitly criticized in the media for drawing funding away from Jomandi and other local black theaters. In Dan Hulbert's 1994 article regarding the philanthropic inequity between the resources dedicated to the Alliance and those dedicated to Jomandi, Hulbert quotes Leon as saying, "I am one of the biggest fans of Jomandi . . . grateful for my roots there," followed by Hulbert's assertion that "still, they are forced by a changing environment into the role of rivals."[72] These examples show the various pressures and dynamics Leon navigated during his eleven years at the Alliance from both advocates and disparagers of black theater.

Having accomplished his artistic and institutional goals, Leon left the Alliance in 2001, and in 2002 founded Kenny Leon's True Colors Theatre Company with Jane Bishop, who had worked with Leon for nine years at the Alliance Theatre as its general manager and who helped initiate "a team leadership approach to the earned and contributed revenue aspects of the theater, which resulted in a staff process of articulating values inherent in the Alliance."[73] The decision to found a theater with a midsized budget centered around African American cultural material allowed Leon more creative and personal freedom. Instead of defending seasons criticized for having too many African American plays to appeal to a predominantly white audience base, the season selection of True Colors would "flip the model. We would produce plays by African American writers while around the edges we would diversify. We would do plays from all cultures."[74] Leaving the Alliance also enabled Leon to continue to build his already substantial national reputation by directing work more frequently on Broadway and for television, something he felt he "never could have done if I was still running the Alliance."[75] In an era where Broadway shows frequently feature film and television celebrities in order to pull in audiences that might not otherwise attend live theater, Leon directed *A Raisin in the Sun* in 2004 with Sean Combs (aka Puff Daddy/P. Diddy) and Phylicia Rashad.[76] Rashad and Audra McDonald won Tony Awards for their respective portrayals of the characters of Lena and Ruth. Leon reprised the production as a made-for-television film featuring the same actors in 2008.[77] He directed the play again with actors

Denzel Washington and LaTanya Richardson Jackson in 2014, for which he won a Tony Award for best director.[78] In 2004 and 2007, he participated in two major moments in American theater history when he directed *Gem of the Ocean* and *Radio Golf*, the last two Broadway debuts of August Wilson's ten-play twentieth-century cycle.[79]

Kenny Leon has been able to leverage his national reputation and association with well-known television and film artists to help promote and fundraise for his local efforts with True Colors. One example of this was the annual celebrity golf and gala fundraiser organized by the theater in service of its primary education initiative, the August Wilson Monologue Competition National Finals. The August Wilson Monologue Competition is the company's highest-profile education initiative and an endeavor that Leon continued to lead after leaving his position as artistic director.[80] Designed by Leon and Todd Kreidler (August Wilson's longtime friend and dramaturg), the competition awards high school students cash prizes and college scholarships. The True Colors/Atlanta chapter of this competition is open to all Georgia high school students. On its education page, True Colors states, "All applicants are invited to attend free acting workshops. In-school August Wilson workshops are also provided at the request of any teacher who has more than 10 students apply."[81] The top three students from Georgia then have the opportunity to "compete against winners from other participating cities in the National Finals on Broadway at the August Wilson Theatre."[82] *Playbill* magazine listed the other 2018 participating cities as Boston, Buffalo, Chicago, Dallas, Los Angeles, New Haven, New York, Greensboro, Pittsburgh, Portland, and Seattle.[83] Students that reach the finals work closely with Leon and are given the opportunity to attend theater on Broadway. During the 2018 competition, students attended productions of the Lynn Ahrens musical *Once on This Island* and Mark Medoff's *Children of a Lesser God*, which Leon directed.[84] The August Wilson Monologue Competition thus exposes a new generation of young people to Wilson's work, provides professional coaching for students interested in participating, and provides the winners with professional development and support in pursuing a career in theater. To underwrite this endeavor, True Colors designed the golf and gala fundraiser, which was patronized for many years by local and national celebrities, such as Leon's friend, colleague, and fellow Atlanta resident Samuel L. Jackson.[85] The golf and gala event was discontinued in 2017 in favor of a major gifts campaign designed to maximize the impact of each gift. The new major giving society is called the Ovation Circle.[86] The funding and execution of this monologue competition is one example of how Leon has used his national reputation to support theatrical work in his local community.

Leon's decision to move from large regional theater production to commercial theater and film endeavors at the same time that he was creating a more intimate, nonprofit theater environment focused primarily on African American cultural material is unique. It has provided True Colors with a certain visibility and cultural cachet that has been difficult for black theaters in other cities and in other time periods to achieve. True Colors is also unique in terms of the dramatic material it produces. It has staged many classic African American plays (August Wilson's *Fences* was its first production), but it has also produced many original works and other lesser-known works focused on the experiences of middle-class and wealthy African Americans. For example, True Colors produced two of Lydia Diamond's plays, *Stick Fly* in 2007 (a play focusing on a wealthy African American family that takes place in their summer residence on Martha's Vineyard) and *Smart People* in 2016 (a play centered around the lives of four Harvard graduates and professors, two of whom are black). Each of these plays examines the relationship between wealth and race, a topic of interest to the black community of Atlanta, a community that includes sizeable middle-class and wealthy African American populations. As such, these productions are a means of speaking to and engaging with the socioeconomic conditions of Atlanta's black community. These productions operate not just as a reflection of these conditions but a means of examining and engaging in discussions around how the intersectionality of race and class is experienced in the Atlanta metro area by its residents.

The 2007 True Colors production of *Stick Fly* was directed by Derrick Sanders and featured Greg Alan Williams as the family patriarch.[87] After its production at True Colors, *Stick Fly* was directed by Kenny Leon and produced by Alicia Keys on Broadway in 2011.[88] Despite winning the 2006 Black Theater Alliance Award for best play, both the Atlanta production and the Broadway production of *Stick Fly* were criticized for being soap opera like. In his review of the Atlanta production, Wendell Brock called the script "a tedious, derivative, and virtually humorless train wreck of a play."[89] *New Yorker* theater critic Hilton Als panned the Broadway production for "pandering to black theatre-goers" by supposedly trashing one of the main character's white girlfriend and white people in general, an assessment of the plot I strongly disagree with.[90] Charles Isherwood's *New York Times* review of the Broadway production was more nuanced, stating the play "sometimes feels like a Tyler Perry melodrama (sans Madea), as it might be revised by a professor of African-American studies specializing in the complex signifiers of class in black society."[91] Isherwood's review acknowledged both the social issues of the play and the popularity of similar plots featuring domestic strife on television in soap operas and on stage in the works of Tyler Perry. These examples of critical distaste for and bemusement with the emotionally fraught content and significant twists and turns of *Stick Fly*'s plot (what Als called "trash" and Isherwood "melodrama") reveals a critical discomfort with the content and aesthetic of the play. I did not find the play soap opera like, despite the emotional highs and lows and behavior of its characters, because the plot goes beyond the mere expression of raw emotion and examines the social and political structures that have created the domestic realities of the play—something soap operas rarely do. Despite its romantic triangles and secret love child, *Stick Fly* is primarily about how African Americans relate to one another across class lines. In an interview with *Playbill*, Diamond explained how this play explored "my orientation to class as one who is often right on the margins or right on the peripheries of converging class realities."[92] Like its content, the play's style also operates on the peripheries of genre, blending elements from popular entertainment and intellectual drama. The critical distaste for the style of this production, the comparisons to Tyler Perry's work, and the popular reception of the play by a majority of black audiences reveal an interesting tension regarding the production of black theater both locally and nationally.

Leon's productions of *Stick Fly* provide an example of how Atlanta artists have challenged conventional critical judgment and aesthetics regarding black theater. Many black artists from Atlanta have navigated and ultimately profited from embracing a more populist sense of theatrical entertainment. Leon, for instance, has fully embraced the commercial aspect of theater by working on Broadway and in television and has consequently expanded employment opportunities for local African American actors. The other highest-profile example of this impulse is Tyler Perry.[93] While Perry's career has been largely self-made, for profit, and outside of the aesthetic and structural mode of nonprofit theater, Leon has managed to blend a variety of theatrical styles and means of production in his work and career. He has embraced the commercial without neglecting the intellectual depth for which nonprofit theater is cherished. His commitment to the founding and sustaining of True Colors Theatre is a testament to this. His role in producing Lydia Diamond's work in both nonprofit and for-profit theater venues is another example of this hybridity.

Lydia Diamond's plays work as popular entertainment, but unlike soap operas, they also offer a nuanced exploration of questions regarding culture, race, and class inside of their emotionally charged plots. In a less melodramatic way, *Smart People* continued Diamond's exploration of the intersection of race and class and the unique experiences and challenges facing middle- and upper-class African Americans. In her review of True Colors 2016 production of *Smart People*, Kelundra Smith writes, "Diamond has woven a web of witty one-liners from a definitely black, college-educated middle-class point of view, which is her lens," adding, "Everything that white people and people of color wish they could say to each other about their views on race is left on the stage. It is the type of show that forces people to look inward at their ideas of race and privilege and ask whether they are a part of the problem (and, hopefully, everyone answers yes)."[94] Set in the two years immediately preceding the election of Barack Obama to the American presidency, *Smart People* investigates changing notions of race, class, and gender in a way that sophisticatedly links the personal struggles, occupations, and worldviews of the four main characters to larger social and political forces. It juxtaposes hope for change with realistic depictions of racial bias, internalized racism, and other examinations of the legacy of America's deeply disturbing racial history. In the Atlanta production of *Smart People*, Danielle Deadwyler played Valerie Johnston, an African American Harvard-educated actor who volunteers for Obama's first campaign for presidency. At the beginning of her professional acting career, Johnston also participates in a Harvard psychology study dealing with racial bias as a means to pay her bills. Her interactions with the play's three other characters, all liberal, well-educated individuals of different races and occupations, complexly explores racial microaggressions, internalized racism, and socioeconomic bias and division among the Harvard elite. The penultimate scene enacts a brutally honest dinner party in which their fragile friendships with one another disintegrate. The play ends with all the characters separately watching Obama's inauguration with awe and hope. The juxtaposition of that hopeful moment with the characters' own disappointments (with each other and with themselves) is an example of how the play complexly and theatrically illustrates both the potentiality and limits of racial understanding in our contemporary moment.

Bert Osborne's review of the True Colors production modified W. E. B. Du Bois's famous assertion that black theater should be *by, about, for*, and *near* African Americans, fittingly revising the sentiments of the main proponent of the "talented tenth" by ending his review with "It's a terrific show—by and about and for smart people."[95] As this review indicates, *Smart People* was markedly better received than *Stick Fly*. Osborne called Deadwyler's portrayal of Johnston a "brilliant, career-defining performance."[96] Deadwyler had appeared in the True Colors 2009 production of Ntozake Shange's *for colored girls who have considered suicide when the rainbow is enuf* that was directed by Jasmine Guy and featured Deadwyler, Omelika Kuumba, Crystal Fox, Robin Givens, Nevaina Rhodes, Nicole Ari Parker, and Yakini Horn.[97] The acclaim she garnered from her role in *Smart People* helped her to further advance her career. Since then, she has worked extensively for theaters such as True Colors and the Alliance, on the Atlanta-based television series *Greenleaf*, and on Tyler Perry's television drama *The Haves and the Have Nots*.[98] Deadwyler was featured in a 2018 *New York Times* article about how the booming film and television industry in Atlanta has enabled black actors to make a living in the city.[99] Deadwyler's career provides an example of how True Colors participates in supporting and sustaining African American artists in this ecology.

In 2018, True Colors produced another play *Dot*, by Colman Domingo, with Denise Burse, a well-known television actor, best known for her role in the Tyler Perry sitcom *House of Payne*. The play tells the story of the matriarch of a black family who is slowly succumbing to Alzheimer's disease. Primarily focused on the interpersonal relationships between Dot and her three children, the play also touches upon the loss of the family's wealth. Over the course of her lifetime, Dot goes from being the wife of a prominent physician to the mother of children who cannot afford to pay for the medical care she needs. This depiction of a family that has slid from middle to working class was the most intriguing part of the play to me and illustrated a reality that is significantly more common for African Americans than for white Americans.[100]

In February 2019, Jamil Jude directed another play based on income instability and the schism between the black working and middle classes. *Skeleton Crew*, the third of Dominique Morisseau's Detroit cycle of plays, is set in an auto manufacturing plant during the 2008 recession. The plant is on the brink of closing down, and the play explores the choices and hardships facing three company workers (played by Tonia Jackson, Anthony Campbell, and Asia Howard) and their manager (played by Enoch King), all of whom are African American. In an interview with the director, Jude stated that he was intrigued by the choices facing all the characters, especially Reggie in his role as "middle management."[101] One of the central conflicts of the play is Reggie's desire to share the news that the plant is shutting down with his fellow workers so they can prepare themselves to find new jobs. The company's higher-ups have forbidden Reggie to share this information. Jude finds that the play expresses "the loneliness of climbing the corporate ladder as a black person and the reality of seeing fewer and fewer black faces the higher and higher you go."[102] The play's themes are salient to Atlanta's black community, which includes sizeable populations from all income levels and socioeconomic backgrounds. Seeking to engage this community and focusing on the experiences of the play's manager, Jude facilitated a panel presentation and audience discussion entitled "Coping in Corporate Cultures: Being a Minority in Corporate America" on January 26, 2019.[103] This discussion was part of the theater's Community Conversations programming series. In "Communication Is Key," the theater describes this series as providing "a safe space for discussion, and being a catalyst for conversations around race, diversity, inclusion, and cultural understanding."[104] These events are free and open to the public. As such, they deepen the civic engagement aspect of the production.

Taken together, the four plays I have just examined offer a deep and nuanced look at the experiences of those with various degrees of wealth within the black community. This is a topic few other theaters have explored as thoroughly as True Colors. I see the unique subject matter that True Colors presents as related to the distinctive nature of its audience and patronage. When I visited Atlanta in the spring of 2016, I noticed that the audience at the performance of *American Buffalo* that I attended was 99 percent black. When I attended the 2018 production of *Dot*, a play that featured three white characters (related in various ways to the African American family members at the heart of the drama), the audience was still over 80 percent black. Managing director Chandra Stephens-Albright shared the following demographic statistics with me. "Based on 393 responses to our last production survey for *Dot* . . . True Colors audience is 80% black, 9% white,

Fig. 5. Tonia Jackson and Enoch King performing a scene from Kenny Leon's True Colors Theatre Company's production of *Skelton Crew* in 2019. Photograph by Greg Mooney.

8% multi-racial or prefer not to answer."[105] These audience demographics are decidedly different from those of black theater companies in the North, which have more mixed audiences and rely more heavily on white patronage. Speaking with Jamil Jude about the benefits of being in the South and in Atlanta in particular, we both agreed that it was wonderful to see a theater like True Colors lovingly supported by a robust base of black patrons. Jude stated that True Colors proved wrong the "defeating narrative" he had heard in other theater communities regarding the difficulty of cultivating a black audience base.[106]

> It feels really good to be making theater in Atlanta, doing the shows that True Colors does. . . . Atlanta feels very unique. . . . Nothing feels like what it does when you're at a True Colors production. . . . In Atlanta, we have it all. There is a really strong cultural history here, and our mission is all about starting with the centrality of the African Diasporic tradition of storytelling, then using that to empower the voices of today to be as inclusive as possible.[107]

I felt the warmth and strength of this community each time I attended a production. The evening I attended *Dot* happened to be the birthday of Barack Obama, and Kenny Leon mentioned this fact during his curtain speech, wishing the former president a happy birthday and telling an audience of predominantly black people not to forget that "America is a great country."[108] This shout out to black political power was appropriate for the venue, the Fulton County Southwest Arts Center. On the previous occasion I had visited the theater, the lobby had contained the portraits of various Fulton County commissioners, all of whom were black. A mural by Louis Delsarte had replaced the lobby portraits since I had last been there. Delsarte's mural *New Hope Visions* (2008) was "an interpretation of the celebration of life in southwest Atlanta. Through a visual representation of figures in motion, the painting reflects the significance of family and community. Delsarte's imagery incorporates community icons including images of Turner Chapel AME Church, Niskey Lake and neighborhood homes."[109] The Niskey Lake area, which surrounds the art center, includes middle-class and wealthy suburbs. It is the home of former Atlanta mayor Kasim Reed and several other prominent members of the black community.[110] Both the mural and the portraits displayed in the lobby thus celebrated the black political power of Fulton County and implicitly linked this power to the cultivation and patronage of the art displayed and presented at the center. In his curtain speech Kenny Leon also gave a nod to this community, stating, "We love being here at Southwest and as long as you all keep showing up, we'll keep coming here."[111] From these visits, it was clear to me that the theater benefited from the size and might of Atlanta's black community. It was also clear that the theater served this community, not just in the content of the plays it produced but also through its youth programs and internships. At the conclusion of his curtain speech, for instance, Leon introduced one of the company's young interns, highlighting his career goals and the part he had played in the production.

The clearest example of Leon's mentorship of the next generation of theater artists came on September 24, 2018, when True Colors announced that Jamil Jude would succeed Kenny Leon as artistic director of True Colors Theatre at the start of the 2019–20 season. In the press release announcing this decision, Kenny Leon stated:

> It's time to engage a younger generation with fresh artistic leadership. . . . Since first meeting Jamil, I knew he was the right person to carry the torch for True Colors Theatre Company. Jamil is an inspiring artist and an empowering community leader who has the full support of our great board of directors. True Colors will continue to thrive locally under his leadership as a place where everyone's story is told.[112]

Leadership transitions for theater companies can be challenging, especially when the founder of a theater retires or moves on. In an interview with Sarah Bellamy on the theater commons site HowlRound, Jude and Bellamy spoke about their respective positions as successors in renowned black theater companies founded by charismatic and extremely accomplished leaders. Sarah Bellamy took over the leadership of Penumbra Theatre Company from her father, Lou Bellamy. Speaking about the challenges and opportunities afforded by these changes, Jude stated, "You and I both, as we move through the world, show up as leaders and present a different face than what people have known the companies to be. I think a lot about that, about what it means to show up as a different face for . . . Kenny Leon's True Colors Theatre Company. I'm not Kenny, right?"[113] Both leaders spoke about bringing their own talents and generational experience as well as honoring and learning from their theaters' founders and first generation of artists. Speaking about Kenny Leon, Jude stated, "It's been really nice to sit and talk to him more purposefully than we have before, passing ideas back and forth. . . . He's been a mentor to me the entirety of my theatre career . . . we also have Kenny in this emeritus position. So that's one of the ways we can work together. . . . I'm really excited about what that can look like."[114] In the case of both True Colors and Penumbra, long succession plans were in place, with Jude and the younger Bellamy working for years at their respective institutions before assuming their roles as leaders. This is one way that institutions can ease some of the strain of such a transition.

Given the financial challenges of running a successful black theater, and in order to get a better sense of True Colors' financial management and development efforts, I spoke to the company's managing director, Chandra Stephens-Albright, and to its development director, LaTeshia Ellerson. Chandra Stephens-Albright stated that the operating budget for the theater for the 2017–18 season was $1.88 million, making True Colors the "5th largest nonprofit theatre in the Atlanta area" according to available Guidestar data (an organization that provides nonprofit metrics).[115] This budget puts True Colors in comparable range with other prominent African American theaters in the nation such as Houston's Ensemble Theatre ($2.3 million), St. Paul's Penumbra Theatre Company ($2.2 million), and Cleveland's Karamu House ($1.83 million).[116] I asked Stephens-Albright about the greatest challenge involved in maintaining the financial stability of the theater and if there was any advice she might offer readers interested in building and sustaining black theater institutions. She replied:

> The greatest challenge is getting first time patrons to come back a second time. This is a pervasive issue in the arts around the country. If you haven't been exposed to live theatre, and you go for the first time without a sense of what goes into making the magic happen, you tend not to go back. One out of seven first-time patrons comes back a second time. What brought me back the second time? Twenty-five years ago, my little sister, who loves theatre, invited me to join Friends of Jomandi. We advocated for the art, brought our friends to shows, and volunteered as ushers. What got me personally hooked

was when Lisa Watson, who worked at Jomandi at the time, let me sit in the production booth for a performance. After that, it was over. Watching her say "go" [while cueing the lights and sound] and making the sun rise on stage literally blew me away. I think that giving people a glimpse of the magic that goes into the theatre will inspire them to come back, and the way to do that is to meet them where they are. We go out into the community to talk about themes in the work, and meet people that may not have been to a show before but are interested in that theme. We give them a taste of the work at these events. The challenge, and our goal, is to show them that what they are seeing on stage is not just entertainment, but a human story that resonates in a completely unique way, because you are there in the room as it is created anew, just for you. The subscribers and long-time patrons—and of course donors and sponsors that make financial gifts over and above tickets—are our life blood. The new patrons that come, and then come back and bring other new patrons, are our bones. They can make us not only live, but grow stronger.[117]

This response speaks to the strength of Atlanta's arts ecology and to the legacy of audience development undertaken by Jomandi and the other African American theaters of the 1970s and 1980s, building what Toni Simmons Henson described as Atlanta's "sophisticated" black audience.[118] This audience is now being further cultivated and expanded by True Colors and other Atlanta-based African American theater institutions.

Given this history of audience and patron cultivation, I asked LaTeshia Ellerson about the conception of Atlanta as the black mecca, if that image was accurate, and if it translated into greater financial support or stability for the theater. Ellerson's response was quite nuanced. First, she stated that the theater was well supported by municipal arts funding.

The city of Atlanta and Fulton County support the arts pretty well. I think they're both giving us about $40,000 for arts, which is huge for us with our budget size. So, having that government support is critical for us, and they are definitely behind us in that way because they see the value in what we are doing. The government can also push the corporations that are interested in being housed in the city limits or in specific areas in the metro to support the arts and the community. . . . There are a lot of corporate headquarters here, and there are still more that are moving here. We have huge global brands that are based here in this city or have a headquarters here. So, the corporations and the government can work together and make something larger.[119]

In terms of Atlanta's reputation as a magnet for black arts and entrepreneurship, she offered a more mixed view.

The arts ecology here is not as robust as I think it should be. Everyone from outside looks at Atlanta and sees opportunity whether it be the music industry, the film industry, all the way back to the eighties when they said this was the black mecca for businesses and whatnot. I don't see that we are living up to what people view us as. All-in-all, our arts scene is really grassroots. Right now, you have people that are looking for opportunities and there aren't as many as people would have possibly thought. I have friends who are coming from LA and Chicago because of the film industry and because Atlanta's so much more affordable. They're looking for opportunities and they're finding out, "Oh wow, there's not that many equity [union] houses [businesses] that are here." You know? Or, "my crew and I don't book on film." So, that's a thing. That's a real issue. Now that there's more film here, the theater actors do have more opportunity than they did before. Even though the parts that they may book aren't as large, they're still robust characters where they're having reoccurring roles on those shows. I have quite a few friends who are on *Greenleaf* quite often for example. So, there is a great opportunity here for our [theater] ecology to expand. It's just that we still have some more work to do to get the support that is needed to do that.[120]

Although Ellerson (and everyone else I spoke to) agreed that the Atlanta theater community had definite room to grow, she also pointed out that compared to other theaters in the area and nation, True Colors was doing quite well.

We know [theater season] subscriptions are declining across the country. At True Colors, we have actually maintained ours, which is interesting. We recently did a TRG [an arts consulting firm] study. Despite our lapsed donors and subscribers, we still had a high Net Promoter score. Out of the five organizations that TRG studied in Atlanta, we received an 80 over 80 in our scoring. So that tells you we still have a really strong core base of support. Of course, I think that is directly connected to Kenny's local celebrity in Atlanta and what he did when he went to Alliance Theatre and changed it, and made it a more inclusive environment for black folks to come and participate in. People fell in love with Kenny during that time, and they continue to follow him in his theater company. That is a core reason why we have such a high Net Promoter score and also why our subscriptions haven't declined. But just like everywhere, we do still need those individual givers and single stub ticket buyers. We're still pushing to make sure that we will be able to reach our [financial] goals.[121]

I asked Ellerson if she felt the image of Atlanta as a city hospitable to and supported by black wealth was accurate in her experience and if so, if that contributed to the financial stability of the theater.

> I want someone to do a study about it. I think it's such an interesting topic. . . . There is black wealth here. I can't say in comparison to other cities that it's not there, but it is here. The question is, how do we value the arts, and understand what that entails? To say that black folks don't give is ridiculous. And to say that they only give to the church is also ridiculous, I think. People give, intrinsically, to what they care about and what they understand. That is where their money is going. So, we need to help people with that understanding. One of our core values is abundance. We need to be able to reiterate that and market that and say, "Hey, it's important that out of your abundance, you're giving." Not just for wealthy individuals but for everyone. I get excited when I see a check for ten dollars from a patron because when someone gives they are saying, "Out of my abundance, I am giving to support a cause that I care about so this organization can continue to thrive." I'm discussing that individually, one-on-one, and I'm also creating verbiage for our promotional materials that are going out to the masses. For example, our end of the year campaign will say something like, "Please share out of your abundance with us, because we want to continue to do X, Y, and Z for you and for the community."[122]

These conversations indicate that True Colors was created, financially managed, and maintained through a carefully cultivated base of support and civic partnership. It continues to operate with close attention to its place in the Atlanta arts ecology and community. It has been able to succeed through the careful planning of Kenny Leon and Jane Bishop and the current efforts of Jamil Jude, Chandra Stephens-Albright, LaTeshia Ellerson, and the rest of the True Colors team.

The Atlanta Black Theatre Festival

While African American theater companies that offer a full season of dramatic work are instrumental to the development and sustenance of black theater practice, theater festivals provide another opportunity to invest, develop, and showcase the work of African American dramatists. Black theater festivals have proven to be particularly popular in the South, with the success of the National Black Theatre Festival in Winston-Salem being the most prominent. In 2007, the National Black Theatre Festival boasted an audience of 60,000 people.[123] In 2010, the first year of Atlanta's Black Theatre Festival, attendance topped 22,000 people.[124] To put these numbers in perspective, the Alliance Theatre's subscription audience at the beginning of Kenny Leon's tenure as that theater's artistic director was 20,000.[125] The Atlanta Black Theatre Festival boasts "40 plays in four days" and offers a menu of theater styles from "Tyler Perry to August Wilson."[126] The festival is a juried annual event that offers emerging, established, local, and out of town theater artists a chance to showcase their work. It thus contributes in a unique way to the diversity of black theater production in the city and to the image of Atlanta as a cosmopolitan city centered around black culture.

The cofounder of the festival, Toni Simmons Henson, describes herself as a "serial entrepreneur."[127] In a telephone interview with me, she explained what drew her to Atlanta and caused her to found the festival.

> Atlanta is truly unique. There's a strong sense of Afrocentric pride that exists here. I credit the music industry here, which is solid, and has been a very strong part of the identity of the city for a long time. You also have a large concentration of very well-educated people. Then, there was a doubling of the population in Atlanta from a half a million in the metro area to over a million people in a ten-year period from 2000 to 2010. . . . People moving here in droves, they still are, moving from Chicago, Los Angeles, Detroit, New York, Ohio, everywhere, coming to Atlanta. Because of the external myth that Atlanta is hot and black people are getting things done in Atlanta. . . . I was a part of that. I moved here in 2007. I was coming from New Jersey, the backyard of New York, and I was looking for great theater.[128]

Simmons Henson characterizes the theater work she does with the Atlanta Black Theatre Festival as directly inspired and enabled by a tradition and appreciation of black theater in Atlanta that began long before her arrival.

> Theater was very strong here in the 1990s. It was the home of one of the strongest, one of the top Afrocentric theater companies in the country, and that was Jomandi . . . then from 2000 to 2010 you had the Tyler Perry phenomenon. What I credit Tyler Perry with is taking the elitism out of theater. Tyler Perry came in and opened up the power of theater and live performance. . . . Then we had the influx of hip hop. . . . This perfect storm came together, and this is what put lightning in a bottle for us. Something happened to Atlanta from 2000 to 2010. You've got the Jomandi folks and the elite theater folks, you've got the Tyler Perry influx and then you've got all these folks moving here. I said, "Okay, how do I capture this?"[129]

Seeking to create a theater experience that was accessible and appealing to a wide swath of people, Simmons Henson and her sister, the playwright Wanda Simmons, began their research on festival production.

We engaged in several conversations. I interviewed Tom Jones from Jomandi. I took him to lunch. Tom and his sisters. I also talked to Taurean Blacque [the actor best known for his role on the television series *Hill Street Blues*] who was a part Jomandi back in the nineties and the people that were part of that theater movement back then. We did a lot of research. We went to DC and met Glenn Alan who headed up the DC Black Theatre Festival. We went to the National Black Theatre Festival [in Winston-Salem] and experienced that. So, what we did was, we made a gumbo. We took what we thought were the best parts of each experience from the patron's perspective and from a producing perspective, and we made it a component of our festival. When I say we, I mean my sister and I. It was strictly she and I from day one to year three.[130]

After two years of planning, Simmons Henson and Simmons launched the Atlanta Black Theatre Festival in October 2012. Much as True Colors Theatre benefits from frequently performing at the Southwest Arts Center, a performance space built and supported by Fulton County, the Atlanta Black Theatre Festival was able to make its operations sustainable by moving to the Sanford Porter III Performing Arts Center in Decatur. The $17 million facility was built through funding provided by De Kalb County and is named after the philanthropist and former De Kalb County commissioner who founded the county's first minority-owned real estate business.[131] By moving the festival to this location, the Atlanta Black Theatre Festival has benefited from civic investment in arts infrastructure and local support for black cultural offerings.

The business model of the Atlanta Black Theatre Festival is predicated on a system of production that makes it less expensive for individual artists to be a part of the festival than to produce a single work on their own. Simmons Henson stated that in the festival, "what we do is we pool our resources and we're able to put together this schedule and this wonderful product."[132] In order to make this business model work, there needs to be a high number of presentations and performances. When asked, "Why forty plays in four days?" Simmons Henson replied, "The truth is we needed that many plays to meet our budget. That's the truth. So, that's how we came up with, 'forty plays in four days.' That's very catchy and everybody likes it. We've scaled back a little bit since then. I think we have forty-four events, but there's only about thirty or thirty-two actual performances."[133] This large volume of production, while wonderful from an audience perspective, also indicates the difficulty of making such an artistic initiative financially sustainable, even with municipal support.

The initial financial challenges the festival faced also offer a sobering example of the reality of arts entrepreneurship in Atlanta. Like other Atlanta theater artists that I spoke with, Simmons Henson believes that Atlanta's reputation as a mecca for black business and innovation is a bit overstated.

She is very upfront and forthright about the financial challenges she has experienced as an entrepreneur and the financial setbacks she has overcome. For example, her first entrepreneurial endeavor after her arrival in Atlanta failed, and she was forced to declare bankruptcy. She and her sister financed the first year of the Atlanta Black Theatre Festival by maxing out their personal credit cards. The festival operated in the red for several years before they arrived at a business model that worked and kept production costs in the black. Given these challenges, I asked Simmons Henson to explain how she was able to correct for these past losses and arrive at a sustainable model.

> I think the strength of what I bring to the table is a very, very strong entrepreneurial spirit and a business background. I'm able to very comfortably look at a situation and streamline processes, and revamp and redirect resources so that we can get more bang for our buck. I'm also the mother of four. I don't think it is anything different from what a mother in a financial crisis would do to help her family. It was really just being able to create something out of nothing. In order to sustain ourselves, we knew we had to get rid of one part of it [the festival], and that was the hotel part. We could not do anything with any affiliation with a hotel because the commitment was too strong and we lost a lot. So, we focused on one venue, with multiple stages. That's when we looked at the Porter Sanford III Performing Arts Center where we are right now. It has two stages within one venue with forty-two thousand square feet. We put together the budget for the entire festival, and then we divided it by the number of presenters and plays that we wanted to perform. Once we divvyed that up, we divided the real estate [among the performers and the stages]. We also have a lobby; we chopped up the lobby for the vendors. Any kind of arts presenter is really purchasing real estate during the festival. All we had to do at that point was to make sure that we, at a minimum, broke even from our festival fees. When people pay their festival fee, that pays for their chunk of real estate in the festival during that four-day period.[134]

Simmons Henson's experience here shows the value of civic investment in the arts. The festival was not sustainable when it worked with a for-profit hotel. Working with a county-supported arts center allowed it to grow and thrive.

In addition to offering performance space at a discounted rate compared to what an individual artist would pay to self-produce his or her own work, the festival offers marketing and production coaching to its participating artists.

> We operate like a business incubator where the service is the production of live performances. We teach them the business side of production if they need it. Some of them don't need it, but some of

are just straight out of "hey, I wrote this play, what do you think about it?" We have everything from people who are totally new to experienced producers who have produced off Broadway or on Broadway. We even had Woodie King [Jr.] come down and produce a couple of plays.[135]

The variety of presenters, from well-known and lauded artists such as Woodie King Jr. to unknown and out-of-town artists producing their first work in Atlanta is one way in which the festival contributes to the presentation of a greater range of diverse works in the Atlanta area.

The content of the work presented at the festival is another way in which the festival contributes to a diverse array of stories and styles that speak to the varied tastes and experiences of Atlanta's black community. From the beginning, Simmons Henson has been committed to showcasing a variety of different voices.

In 2012 we were figuring out how to take the best of both worlds. How do we take the people whose palate is very sophisticated when it comes to their theater exposure because they're coming from high-culture cities, cities like Chicago and New York, how do you take those and how do you satisfy that palate, but also at the same time, satisfy the palate of people who have been Perry-ized? We figured that out, and I think that's really why we got so many people here in the first year and are continuing to grow in our market. It's because we offer both. We offer both traditional and popular performances, like our webpage says, "whether you're a fan of Tyler Perry or August Wilson, we've got something for you at the Atlanta Black Theatre Festival." What we did was, we acknowledged and we recognized that the urban contemporary theater can exist if it's high quality and not only can it exist, but it can also be enjoyed by people who are used to August Wilson and Lorraine Hansberry. . . . So what we do is help people raise the bar and expand their palates.[136]

Given this commitment, I asked Simmons Henson to explain her process for selecting work to present at the festival.

To be quite transparent, we really didn't have a system at first. We were just hoping people would submit the first year and we ended up picking some really good plays. And then after you start reading a lot of plays, you kind of get a sixth sense for what's good. Eventually, it got overwhelming to try to read them all. So, we then created a rubric. After the third or fourth year we said, "Okay, we can't possibly read all these plays," because it was overwhelming. And so, we put together a rubric and now we ask for volunteers to read the plays and score them based on this rubric. Once they score a play, they submit it to me; I'm the one who does the final cut. Anything that's scored a 90 or better, those are the ones I look at first. Then I can create a really nice program that I feel is diverse and that people will come to. . . . I'll look at the ones that score 90 or better first and say, "Okay, can we create a good program with this?" If there's too much of one thing or too much of another, like too much historical material or too much Black Lives Matter or too much "I've lost my man or my woman" or domestic drama or whatever, if it's too much of any one kind of material, we'll start looking into the 80s pile, the ones that scored 80 or better, because we want a great mix of voices. We want men's voices as well as women's voices. We want voices of people who have gone through something, and we want voices of people who just want to laugh. One of the things that I really, really appreciate from being in this position is that I get to experience people's stories in their own voice.[137]

This selection process inherently values diversity of style and content along with inclusion of a diverse range of experiences and identities. Combined with the sheer volume of work presented at the Atlanta Black Theatre Festival, this commitment ensures a rich and varied theater experience that is a gift to the theater community of Atlanta, as well as to those who travel to the area to participate in the festival.

Sardia Robinson's one-woman show *From a Yardie to a Yankee*, presented at the Atlanta Black Theatre Festival in 2013 and again in 2019, provides an example of how the festival has helped to create more opportunities for more artists and present a wider range of cultural experiences on the Atlanta stage. A Jamaican American trained in theater at Columbia College in Chicago, Robinson was frustrated by the lack of acting opportunities she found after graduating.

I wrote the show because I was at a place in my life where my creative juices were flowing but nothing was happening. No auditions were happening. I couldn't get a job, and I wasn't sure where I wanted to go next. I wasn't sure I was even a writer or that I could write. I decided to go through my diary. I would write stories of what was happening with me, and I took those and started to form them into essays. And then it just took on a life of its own.[138]

Robinson wrote her one-woman show both to provide an acting opportunity for herself and to create a broader range of black cultural material on the American stage.

Almost all of the black plays that I've seen or that I've been in are usually based on African American stories. What I would like to see

Fig. 6. Sardia Robinson performing her one-woman show *From a Yardie to a Yankee*, which was presented at the Atlanta Black Theatre Festival in 2013 and 2019. Photograph courtesy of Sardia Robinson.

moving forward as a theater performer is a wider exploration of black theater stories, not just African Americans, but Caribbean and African stories. Also, our stories don't always have to be about serious topics. We can do a whole comedy show and tell our stories. That goes back to my show, even though it has moments when you're crying, there are also moments when you're laughing. Because you want the audience to feel comfortable and let them know, it's okay to laugh with me. It's okay to cry with me. I'm okay.[139]

As is the case with many solo performers, Robinson's work is deeply personal. She described her show as:

Based on my life journey as an immigrant from Jamaica to America, and the struggle that I went through in Jamaica to get to America. Then, when I finally get here, what I've experienced. Because the vision that you have as an immigrant in another country coming here, when you get here, it's totally different. That's what the show is based on. It's called *From a Yardie to a Yankee* because the word "yardie" just associates with Jamaicans. When we run into each other and we detect an accent, we usually stop and ask each other, "Hey, are you from the yard, are you from backa yard? Are you a yardie?" So, it's like a way of giving the thumbs up and saying, "Yeah, I'm one of you or you're one of us," so to speak. So that's why I use the word "yardie." When we go back home, Jamaicans associate us with Americans, calling us Yankee, "Oh, you're a Yankee girl now," that kind of thing. So that's where the name of the show came from.[140]

In the show, Robinson mixes humorous family anecdotes and cultural misunderstandings with poignant portrayals of being raised by her extended family and their experience of violence and poverty in Kingston, Jamaica.

At first, I was really just being funny with it, because I also do stand-up comedy. And then, when I realized that it had an impact on me—the more I talked out what was going on inside me personally, it become my therapy. So, I started to get deeper into the writing. . . . I decided if I was going to write a one-person show, I should write my truth. That's how that came together.[141]

Robinson first started producing her show in 2009. She performed segments of the show at open mics in coffee shops in the LA area where she lives and works as a comedian and screen actor. She then rented a small ninety-nine-seat black box theater to present the work. After positive reviews, she moved to a larger space and started applying to festivals. In addition to the Atlanta Black Theatre Festival, she has performed the work at the Hollywood Fringe Festival in 2014, where she won the Innovative Women in Theatre Award; the United Solo theater festival in New York in 2015; the Edna Manley College for Visual and Performing Arts in Kingston, Jamaica, in 2016; the Bahamian theater company Shakespeare in Paradise in 2017; and the Whitefire Theatre's SoloFest in Sherman Oaks, California, in 2018. Often a featured performer or award winner at these festivals, Robinson's career shows how festival organizations can support artists with great work that do not necessarily have strong professional affiliations with traditional theater companies.

Professional theater companies with a year-long season of production often work with the same pool of actors and only accept script submissions from literary agents (if at all). They typically do very little new work because of the costs associated with new play development and because of the greater audience draw for well-known, previously produced plays. For these reasons it is hard for people that are not already associated with these theater companies to break in or show their work there. When I asked if Robinson had tried to get her work shown as part of the regular season of any traditional theater companies, she replied,

> When I started my solo show, I ran up against a lot of what you were just talking about, when I tried to reach out to certain theaters, they only do their own. They have no room for newcomers. A lot of theaters, especially the bigger theaters, the only way I could get my show up in there would be for someone who is a resident artist there to say, "I want to bring this show in." That's how I ended up going to the Atlanta Black Theatre Festival and the Hollywood Fringe, and Shakespeare in Paradise, because they're open. . . . They don't care who you are. You can come in and you tell your story.[142]

Organizations like the Atlanta Black Theatre Festival offer more opportunities for early and midcareer theater professionals because their production model uses an open submission process and is predicated on presenting a large volume of work by a wide variety of artists at various stages of their careers.

As Robinson has presented her show in many different venues both domestically and internationally, I asked her to talk about her experience at the Atlanta Black Theatre Festival and to explain what was unique about presenting her work in that particular ecology.

> Well, in addition to getting my show seen by a wider audience, performing my show at the Atlanta Black Theatre Festival allowed me to drill down and explore how a predominantly black audience experienced and authenticated my show. It's a tougher audience when you're doing it for your own people, in my opinion. The audience expects the stories that are told to be authentic and reflect realistic experiences that they can closely identify with. If you aren't authentic, you will hear it from this audience. These are the grandmothers and great grandmothers, you know? One of my artistic goals is to make sure that my truth is reflective and relatable to a wider black audience than just the Jamaican or the Caribbean audience. The Atlanta Black Theatre Festival allowed me to perform my show in a safe and supportive space where I really felt the love of the audience and the organizers. I did my show there twice, once in 2013 and once in 2019. That's how much I enjoy the Atlanta Black Theatre Festival because they're so supportive. The audience, they come out, they support, and they really engage and encourage you. That's so valuable because, in order for you to get to where you need to get to as an artist, you have to be not just good, but great. We have to work harder than the other person who is not our color.[143]

Robinson was also surprised by the number of audience members at the Atlanta Black Theatre Festival that had Caribbean heritage. "When I was in Atlanta, almost every person that I talked to had some Caribbean roots. They said to me, 'You took me back home,' and they meant that either they themselves were raised in the Caribbean or their grandmother was from the Caribbean, and they were hearing their grandma's story through my show. In Atlanta, there were the most people that said, 'You took me back home.' "[144] Performing as part of the Atlanta Black Theatre Festival also helped Robinson confirm that her story had universal appeal.

> It's also a universal story that I'm telling, it just so happened that I'm from Jamaica. I could've been from Compton, I could have been from Minneapolis. The whole story is based on being a single mom, missing a parent, your grandmother raising you and the lessons you learned from your grandmother. People can relate to that. Some audience members asked questions like, "How do you survive all of that and still stay so positive" or "how are you not on drugs after all that?" I always say it goes back to your ancestors, it goes back to the grandmothers. I was lucky enough to be raised by strong black Caribbean women. Most of them had no formal education. I just learned this last year when she died that my aunt left school when she was fifteen. And yet, she was the one who taught me how to read. So, these were women that paved the path for me, and because they're so well developed in my show, people can relate to them. Someone came to me and said, "I have an auntie like that." Another person said, "Boy, I don't want to be around your mama." Everybody can relate somehow. Many people have said, "You inspired me. I always wanted to write a one-person show. I saw your show and now I'm inspired to write one myself." So, when you hear those things, you know that you've done well.[145]

Robinson's appreciation for the Atlanta Black Theatre Festival and the community it creates speaks to the collective power and cultural import of the Atlanta theater community. It speaks to the inclusiveness of the festival and to the festival's exploration of a variety of black experiences, histories, and perspectives.

Toni Simmons Henson and Wanda Simmons's journey with the Atlanta Black Theatre Festival over the years of its existence reveals a tenacity of spirit and creative approach to arts production particularly well suited to Atlanta and its history and culture of entrepreneurship. All three of the theater institutions discussed in this chapter have resulted from the bold leadership, unique vision, and persistent determination of their founders. While these three institutions are not the only African American theater companies in Atlanta, their stories serve as an illustration of a commitment to supporting

African American art and artists by supporting African American *institutions* that is quite strong in Atlanta. The history of Atlanta and the achievements of black politicians and business leaders in making African American art and identity central to the identity of the metro area has been a key part of the success of each of these institutions.

Chapter 5

Finding Joy, Creating Justice

As I was finishing this manuscript, George Floyd was killed by four police-men in Minneapolis, my hometown. From my current home in California, I watched the city I was born in, my country, and then the entire world erupt in defiance of racial violence and white supremacy. The wave of conscience that swept America also swept American theater. Black, indigenous, and other artists of color called out racism and white supremacy in many ways includ-ing the collective open letter "Dear White American Theater" and a Google doc created by Marie Cisco tracking whether or not theater institutions had made antiracist public statements in solidarity with the Black Lives Matter movement and notating their track record working with and producing work by black artists in their organizations.[1] After these public condemnations of racism in the theater, company after company rushed to issue solidarity state-ments with the Black Lives Matter movement. Black artists then called out many of these white-run institutions again, reacting to their statements as opportunistic, disingenuous, and not enough in publications and editorials such as "We Don't Want Your Statements American Theatre, or, the Soli-darity We Actually Needed."[2] The dynamic of this exchange struck me as another way in which white-led institutions seek to profit off of discussions of diversity and virtue signal rather than actually doing the work of disman-tling their own racism. If white theaters really cared about racial equity, they would financially support black institutions and artists without trumpeting their intention to do so. They would have stepped out of and not into the limelight. Black theaters have been condemning racial violence and other forms of racism and racial trauma for decades, doing the work to support and heal black artists and black communities. They continue to do so, with or without performative statements. Karamu House, for example, under the direction of Tony Sias, accomplished the Herculean task of producing an original one-hour production in a little over a week during a global pandemic entitled *Freedom on Juneteenth*, as a "way to channel some of that rage and sadness and disbelief" and bring the historical observance of Juneteenth "into the current moment."[3] The production was livestreamed on several digital platforms for free on June 19, 2020. *Freedom on Juneteenth* featured a large

Fig. 7. Mariama Whyte performing a scene from Karamu House's 2020 production of *Freedom on Juneteenth*. Photograph by Kayla Lupean.

cast performing original and curated poetry, spoken word, music, and dance designed to help black individuals process our rage and grief, inspire us, and sustain our fight for freedom. As one of the lines of dialogue in the performance put it, "We push along our creative hopes, this must be the medicine that melds our madness into memorial."[4] Encompassing expressions of grief, pain, rage, hope, survival, and resistance, this incredibly powerful production was another example of the vital and productive work that black theater companies regularly do and how they serve and shape the social, cultural, and political landscapes of the cities of which they are a part.

The public reckoning precipitated by the murder of George Floyd revealed a truth about American theater practice, a truth that has never been very deeply hidden. American theater communities, from the Progressive Era to the present, have liked to imagine themselves as cosmopolitan, culturally sophisticated contributors to the public good. The truth is that American theater practice, like America itself, has always been and continues to be shaped by white supremacy. In a speech given at the 2020 Theatre Communications Group virtual conference and later published in *American Theatre* magazine, Kenny Leon's True Colors Theatre Company artistic director Jamil Jude used this moment of national clarity to call attention to the lie of racial equity in American theater. In a roundtable discussion titled after his directive to "find joy in the destruction of the lie," Jude laid bare the lack of progress on racial justice, inclusion, and equity in American theater. He concluded his remarks by refocusing on the productive work he was doing with True Colors, pointing out the fact that calling out the racist superstructure of the larger system of America theater production—something he felt compelled to do in that moment—nevertheless took him away from doing more productive work with True Colors.

> Honestly, saying these things shouldn't be on me. It shouldn't be up to a first-year Black AD [artistic director] to stand up and say enough is enough. I should be focused on ensuring True Colors is living up to the values we state and be a home for Black artists and community. I shouldn't have to feel nervous about the effect of sharing these truths and the negative repercussions that may befall me or my organization or my Black colleagues.[5]

African American theater history exposes the racism that is pandemic to American theatrical practice. Whether through explicitly racist acts of exclusion (Karamu actors' exclusion from the consolidated Cleveland FTP unit during the 1930s or attempts by the neighbors of BRG to displace them from their Berkeley home during the early 2000s) or from not-so-benign neglect (racially based funding inequities that have specifically disadvantaged arts organizations of color like Jomandi in Atlanta), black theater production has always held the mirror up to the true nature of American theater practice. An examination of this truth is a necessary but insufficient exploration of the aims and accomplishments of black theater organizations. It is ultimately more important to amplify the productive work that black theater companies do. By looking at the history of black theater institutions in four American cities, I have shown how these companies have withstood acts of racism, evictions, and attempts to silence them, and flourished by telling the stories of their cities' black residents. They have strengthened black performing arts communities and served their cities by finding and spreading joy in expressions of black artistic practice rooted in a multiplicity of black experiences and cultures.

By looking at black theater institutions as part of dynamic arts ecologies I have shown how theater making is a product of its time, place, and culture, what naturalist forbearer Hippolyte Taine referred to as "race, moment, and milieu."[6] The operations of the black theater companies studied here reveal a struggle against the persistence of white supremacist attitudes in communities that in many cases profess to value equity and inclusion. Despite the inherently unequal distribution of resources in each of these ecologies, the black theater institutions in this book have found ways to create art that asserts and *enacts* the importance of black culture as a core component of the identity of the cities in which these institutions operate. My stated aim in the introduction to this book was to articulate the important cultural, artistic, and civic work done by these institutions. In each substantive chapter I have accomplished this, showing how the history of each company is intertwined with the unique history and sociocultural racial politics of its city. Looking at these urban arts ecologies comparatively also reveals several commonalties.

First, by necessity and by ideology, the founding and nourishment of black theater institutions have in most cases operated from a local, grassroots, neighborhood-based model which differs dramatically from other models of theater production (such as the regional theater or Broadway system of theatrical production). Black theater's unique approach to institution building and community engagement deserves further scholarly inquiry and recognition. I have illustrated some of the distinctive strengths and challenges of this approach in this book. The grassroots approach is the most democratic and accessible but also the most difficult to sustain, and the successful theaters using this model have often partnered with other institutions such as community centers, arts boards, and universities in order to survive and grow beyond the personal resources of their founding members. Using different tactics, these grassroots companies have each contributed to an American theatrical practice that is more inclusive than the flagship magnet-style arts institutions that often receive a majority of a city's arts funding. It is also important to note that the majority of the black theater institutions covered in this book predate the diversity initiatives of major foundations and civic arts funding organs. It is not a coincidence that the black theater institutions in this book that have arisen organically out of black communities remain the most dedicated organizations in service of those communities.

Next, every African American theater institution covered in this book has helped articulate the unique character of black cultural life in its city. Whether the dramatic material is historical or contemporary, serious or comedic, political or domestic, realistic or avant-garde, black theater is place based and expresses the specificity of particular black cultural experiences speaking to unique, heterogenous black audiences. As D. Soyini Madison writes in *Black Performance Theory*, "Race is a fact of blackness within racially boundless articulations and performatives that rise from this fact."[7] LHT's production of Robert Alexander's play *Air Guitar* spoke to a black audience that had been a part of San Francisco's counterculture and music scene, while Karamu House's production of Langston Hughes's play *Joy to My Soul* offered a humorous portrait and good-natured roast of Cleveland's biggest and most influential African American hotel, a place familiar to and frequented by many Karamu audience members. To quote Harvey Young and Queen Meccasia Zabriskie's title of their oral history of black theater in Chicago, "Black theatre is black life."[8] It contains multitudes, but it is also site specific. A look at the content of the work presented in each of the cities that operate as my chapter case studies reveals black theater's cultural and geographic specificity; the book as a whole reveals some of black theater's scope and multiplicity.

Each of the African American theater institutions studied in this book is also and importantly the result of the civic and political legacies of previous generations. Beginning with Karamu, I have tried to show some of the thread that connects the present to the past. The settlement house, civil rights, Black Power, black arts, and feminist/womanist movements are still very much alive in the black theaters of today. These earlier sociopolitical struggles are as present in the artistic practice of these theaters as the contemporary moment and political struggle embodied by the Black Lives Matter movement. The historical and contemporary practice of the black theaters studied here are intertwined with these political movements, and the production choices of these theaters often reflect this fact. Twenty-first-century productions such as Pittsburgh's Playwrights Theatre Company's presentation of Rob Penny's *Boppin' with the Ancestors*, True Colors productions of Dominque Morisseau's *Detroit 67*, AASC's production of Ntozake Shange's *for colored girls*, and Karamu's production of *Simply Simone* relate the histories and struggles of past movements in ways that speak to the current sociopolitical realities of contemporary black audiences. These institutions are not just presenters of black history; they are makers and shapers of that history. They have participated directly in civic and political movements, from Karamu's participation in the March on Washington, to Jomandi's association with the first and second waves of black civic leadership in Atlanta, to the founding and maintenance of BHT as an arm of the black liberation movement in Pittsburgh, to the use of Berkeley's BRG's stage for town hall meetings featuring Congresswoman Barbara Lee. These institutions have all been part of the political movements and operations of their cities.

In addition to participating in political movements, another commonality between all of the institutions studied here is their focus on youth education. This focus is likely a result of their community-based origins. Each institution has mentorship programs or youth education programs that nurture the artists and audiences of the future. For example, Karamu welcomed black children who were barred from the recreational activities of all of Cleveland's other settlement houses as well as the YMCA. True Colors hosts the nationally acclaimed August Wilson Monologue Competition for high school students and has a robust internship program. The San Francisco–based AATAIN's youth-lead audience engagement program takes seriously the development of the next generation of African American artists and audiences, investing in youth programs and paying youth to help craft an engagement plan that will bring in and develop younger audiences. This is another way of shaping the city.

The black theaters covered here have also cultivated African American dramatic literature by developing and presenting world premieres by such literary giants as Langston Hughes (Karamu), August Wilson (BHT), Ishmael Reed and Ntozake Shange (BRG and LHT), and Lydia Diamond (True Colors). Hundreds of productions and initiatives created by these theaters have helped to train, nurture, and support a thriving African American performing arts community closely connected to the black communities in the each of their resident cities. It is clear that a network of mostly small to mid-sized black theaters sustains African American artists in a unique way from the star system of the larger regional theaters and Broadway, which offer greater financial rewards to a much smaller pool of black artists.

From an administrative perspective, looking comparatively at these institutions makes clear that the most successful and enduring black theaters in this study have understood that the financial management of their organization is equally as important as its artistic leadership. This does not mean focusing exclusively on fundraising, but it does mean expending considerable resources and innovative thought on how to sustain an organization by finding ways to take advantage of the unique resources of the city in which an organization resides. In San Francisco, this means working with the city and the arts commission and pooling resources with other organizations to build critical mass and gain access to what is some of the most expensive real estate in the nation. In Atlanta, it means partnering with the city's black leadership and speaking directly to that city's enormous and diverse African American population. In Pittsburgh, it means leveraging the international reputation of August Wilson and the artistic legacy he left to his hometown. In Cleveland, it means building upon a hundred years of philanthropy and service and demonstrating the continued relevance of a cherished and beloved institution.

When looking at the production histories and accomplishments of the institutions included in this book, it is astounding how much has been achieved, often with very modest financial investment, and against incredible odds. By studying Karamu decade by decade, it is clear that the organization continuously pushed for more equitable forms of participation for African Americans in the arts ecology of Cleveland. Its history spans a time when African Americans were completely shut out of the arts and recreational outlets of the city, and its efforts have contributed to the contemporary moment when African Americans lead some the city's major educational and artistic enterprises. Karamu's production of *Freedom on Juneteenth* is an example of the organization's current strength, depth of community involvement, and vision.

In Pittsburgh, black theater companies had to perform in buildings literally built to memorialize architects of white supremacy, but that did not stop them from transforming their city through their artistic and political acts. BHT, Kuntu Repertory Theatre, New Horizon Theater, Pittsburgh Playwrights Theatre Company, and the August Wilson Center each took part in the struggle to tell the story of Pittsburgh's black residents with resources concomitant with the vast wealth generated by the industrial labor of Pittsburgh's black residents, a wealth that until very recently was never invested in black individuals or black communities. The world would not have the twentieth-century cycle of August Wilson's plays without the black theaters of Pittsburgh, nor would the city have been able to marshal the substantial financial investment needed to build and operate the state-of-the-art August Wilson Center without the tireless efforts of the many individuals that were part of Pittsburgh's black theater companies.

Even as the black population of the San Francisco Bay Area has been decimated, black theaters have found a way to remain and continue their important work. As participants in the black power, womanist, and countercultural activities and movements of the Bay Area from the 1960s to the present, BRG, LHT, and AASC have all shaped their respective cities, serving and reflecting the unique experiences of black Californians. These companies have helped produce and support the world-renowned womanist dance theater practices of Ntozake Shange, tell the stories of black residents of the area, such as the tragedy of the Port Chicago 50, and challenge the exclusion of African Americans from European classical work, which is still the most produced and financially remunerative theater work in America, providing needed economic opportunities for the Bay Area's black theater artists.

In Atlanta, the city's political leaders collaborated with black theaters like Jomandi to help craft an image of a city steeped in black culture and known for its entrepreneurial artistic spirit. The Atlanta Black Theatre Festival continues this tradition, drawing performers from around the country to explore black artistic practice and further their careers in the city of dreams. Unable to completely transform the racial politics of the regional theater system of which he has a part, Kenny Leon flipped the script and used the career capital he had gained from participating in that system to create an Atlanta-based black theater institution, Kenny Leon's True Colors Theatre Company, that is well supported, currently thriving, and nurturing the next generation of African American theater artists.

In one of the more powerful moments of Karamu's production of *Freedom on Juneteenth*, the cast speaks in unison, proclaiming, "The system was never made for us. If we want justice, we will have to make it ourselves."[9] Although referring to America's legal system, this sentiment is equally true for America's theater system. African Americans have had to create autonomous institutions in order to enact equitable practices of theater production. Black theater companies have shaped the cities in which they operate, making them more just and more inclusive while enriching the lives of their citizens by producing a sophisticated and varied expression of black artistic material. By chronicling some of the achievements of these theaters, I hope in some small way to increase their circle of influence, honor their legacies, and inspire others to support and advance the work that they have so carefully wrought.

NOTES

Introduction

1. Bridge and Watson, "Reflections on Publics and Cultures," 380.
2. United States Census Bureau, "U.S. Census Bureau Projections."
3. Helicon Collaborative, *Not Just Money*, full report.
4. Theodore, Peck, and Brenner, "Neoliberal Urbanism," 22–23.
5. Howkins, *The Creative Economy*; Clark, *The City as an Entertainment Machine*.
6. For recent monographs on important African American theater institutions, see Shandell, *The American Negro Theatre*; Mayo and Holt, *Stages of Struggle and Celebration*; Young and Zabriskie, *Black Theater Is Black Life*.
7. Miller, *Drop Dead*, 192.
8. Atlanta Black Theatre Festival, "What Is the Atlanta Black Theatre Festival?"

Chapter 1

1. Grabowski, "Settlement Houses."
2. Alta House did sponsor the city's only black basketball team in 1903 and 1904 but remained otherwise dedicated to Italian and Italian American communities. Davis, *Black Americans in Cleveland*, 218.
3. Lasch-Quinn, *Black Neighbors*, 1.
4. Lasch-Quinn, *Black Neighbors*, 3.
5. Silver, "A History of the Karamu Theatre," 105.
6. Davis, *Black Americans in Cleveland*, 260.
7. Davis, *Black Americans in Cleveland*, 194.
8. Davis, *Black Americans in Cleveland*, 196–97.
9. Silver, "A History of the Karamu Theatre," 104.
10. Bradshaw, "The Sutphen School of Music."
11. Silver, "A History of the Karamu Theatre," 13.
12. Jackson, *Lines of Activity*.
13. Silver, "A History of the Karamu Theatre," 17–19.
14. Blood, "Theatre in Settlement Houses," 45.
15. Silver, "A History of the Karamu Theatre," 28.
16. Newman, *Karamu House Inc. 75th Anniversary*, 5.
17. Silver, "A History of the Karamu Theatre," 42.
18. Silver, "A History of the Karamu Theatre," 42.
19. Silver, "A History of the Karamu Theatre," 28.
20. In a 1930 essay entitled "The Negro in Cleveland," Charles W. Chesnutt wrote, "Other residential districts are resistant to their [persons of African descent] advent, sometimes by intimidation or violence. . . . This exclusiveness is maintained by care in sales, and by restrictive clauses in deeds, the legality of

which is doubtful and has never thoroughly been tested." *Charles W. Chesnutt: Essays and Speeches*, 535.

21. Silver, "A History of the Karamu Theatre," 31–32.

22. Silver, "A History of the Karamu Theatre," 32.

23. *The Progressive Era.*

24. Silver, "A History of the Karamu Theatre," 35.

25. Silver, "A History of the Karamu Theatre," 43–44.

26. Newman, *Karamu House Inc. 75th Anniversary*, 7.

27. Silver, "A History of the Karamu Theatre," 53–54.

28. Silver, "A History of the Karamu Theatre," 55–56.

29. Newman, *Karamu House Inc. 75th Anniversary*, 8; Silver, "A History of the Karamu Theatre," 103.

30. Hemmings, *Alexandre Dumas*; Reiss, *The Black Count.*

31. Silver, "A History of the Karamu Theatre," 132–37.

32. Shultz, *Karamu: 100 Years in the House.*

33. Silver, "A History of the Karamu Theatre," 112.

34. For an excellent overview of the aims and impacts of the little theater movement see Chansky, *Composing Ourselves.* For an examination of the racial and ethnic tensions involved in the little theater movement in Cleveland, see Hunter, "Art in Democracy," 106–21.

35. Silver, "A History of the Karamu Theatre," 65, 69.

36. Silver, "A History of the Karamu Theatre," 68.

37. Eric Rauchway, quoted in the documentary *The Progressive Era.*

38. Silver, "A History of the Karamu Theatre," 65–66.

39. Silver, "A History of the Karamu Theatre," 68–69.

40. Silver, "A History of the Karamu Theatre," 102.

41. Blood, "Theatre in Settlement Houses," 45–69.

42. Hatch and Shine, *Black Theatre USA*, 214.

43. Ritschel, "Synge and the Irish Influence," 129–50; Harrington, "New World Drama," 306–26.

44. Mishkin, *The Harlem and Irish Renaissances*, x1.

45. Silver, "A History of the Karamu Theatre," 75–76.

46. Hatch and Shine, *Black Theatre USA*, 214.

47. Rena Fraden writes about this phenomenon, stating, "One of the distinctive cultural features of the twenties and thirties is this outpouring of white authored books depicting black subjects: from Edna Ferber's novel *Showboat*, to DuBose Heywards' novel and George Gershwin's opera based on it, *Porgy and Bess*." *Blueprints for a Black Federal Theatre*, 59.

48. Silver, "A History of the Karamu Theatre," 107.

49. Silver, "A History of the Karamu Theatre," 129.

50. Newman, *Karamu House Inc. 75th Anniversary*, 8.

51. Hatch and Shine, *Black Theatre USA*, 214.

52. Mishkin, *The Harlem and Irish Renaissances*, xl.

53. Howey, "*God's Trombones* Captivates, Electrifies at Karamu House."

54. Karamu House Records.

55. Silver, "A History of the Karamu Theatre," 99–101.

56. Silver, "A History of the Karamu Theatre," 495.

57. Kelly, "Gilpin Players' Final Program," 21; Kelly, "Gilpin Players," 3.

58. *Stevedore* Becomes 100th Play," 12.

59. Kelly, "Gilpin Players' Final Program," 21.

60. Smith, "The Rounder on What's Doing," 1.

61. *The Gazette* was founded in 1883 and operated by its owner and chief editor Harry C. Smith until 1945. As such, it was the longest continuously publishing African American newspaper in the United States during its existence. It was supported by the Republican Party, of which Smith was a dedicated member. The Encyclopedia of Cleveland History states that "Smith's causes became the *Gazette*'s causes, as he mobilized it against segregated schools, minstrel shows, and the last of Ohio's Black Laws," "Cleveland Gazette," *Encyclopedia of Cleveland History*.

The *Call & Post* was founded in 1927 when two struggling papers merged. It did not achieve major popular success until the 1930s when William Otis Walker became its owner and chief editor. The *Call & Post* supported local African American democratic candidates and was less socially conservative than the *Gazette*. After filing for bankruptcy in the 1990s, the *Call & Post* was purchased and is now operated by the boxing promoter Don King. "Cleveland *Call & Post*," *Encyclopedia of Cleveland History*.

62. Silver, A History of the Karamu Theatre," 267.

63. Smith, "The Rounder on What's Doing," December 11, 1937: 1.

64. Silver, "A History of the Karamu Theatre," 213–28.

65. Silver, "A History of the Karamu Theatre," 230.

66. Dolinar, *The Black Cultural Front*, 81.

67. Williams and Tidwell, eds., *My Dear Boy*, 18.

68. Vacha, *Showtime in Cleveland*, 160.

69. Dolinar, *The Black Cultural Front*, 82.

70. Hughes, *The Big Sea*, 335.

71. Dolinar, *The Black Cultural Front*, 116; Harper, *Not So Simple*.

72. McLaren, *Langston Hughes*, 10–11.

73. Rampersad, *The Life of Langston Hughes*, 190–92.

74. Dolinar, *The Black Cultural Front*, 72.

75. Dolinar, *The Black Cultural Front*, 76. McLaren, *Langston Hughes*, 40–41.

76. Rampersad, *The Life of Langston Hughes*, 184–85, 194–98; Hughes, *The Big Sea*, 131–34.

77. Silver, "A History of the Karamu Theatre," 506, 508.

78. Hughes, *Five Plays by Langston Hughes*, 43–112.

79. Rampersad, *The Life of Langston Hughes*, 317.

80. Hughes, *Five Plays*, 43–112.

81. Silver, "A History of the Karamu Theatre," 233; McLaren, *Langston Hughes*, 85.

82. Silver, "A History of the Karamu Theatre," 234; Dolinar, *The Black Cultural Front*, 83.

83. Rampersad, *The Life of Langston Hughes*, 323.

84. Dolinar, *The Black Cultural Front*, 85.

85. Dolinar, *The Black Cultural Front*, 83.

86. McLaren, *Langston Hughes*, 88.

87. Silver, "A History of the Karamu Theatre," 50.

88. Dolinar, *The Black Cultural Front*, 83.

89. McLaren, *Langston Hughes*, 91.

90. Rampersad, *The Life of Langston Hughes*, 327.

91. McLaren, *Langston Hughes*, 92.

92. Nichols, *Arna Bontemps-Langston Hughes Letters*, 25–26.

93. Hughes, *I Wonder as I Wander*, 3–37.

94. McLaren, *Langston Hughes*, 82, 101.

95. Silver, "A History of the Karamu Theatre," 236–37.

96. Silver, "A History of the Karamu Theatre," 270–71.

97. Rampersad, *The Life of Langston Hughes*, 330–31.

98. Kernodle, "Arias, Communists, and Conspiracies," 487.

99. For more about racial representations in opera, see Ingraham, So, and Moodlet, *Opera in a Multicultural World*.

100. McLaren, *Langston Hughes*, 99–100.

101. Hughes, *The Plays to 1942*, 410.

102. Rampersad, *The Life of Langston Hughes*, 336.

103. Rampersad, *The Life of Langston Hughes*, 330.

104. Morris, "Majestic Hotel."

105. Rampersad, *The Life of Langston Hughes*, 326, 355.

106. See the introduction and editorial commentary in Williams and Tidwell, *My Dear Boy*.

107. Rampersad, *The Life of Langston Hughes*, 319.

108. Hughes, *Five Plays*, 40–41.

109. Hughes, *The Plays to 1942*, 266.

110. Hughes, *Five Plays*, 42.

111. Hughes, *Five Plays*, 42.

112. Rampersad, *The Life of Langston Hughes*, 364; Kinzer, "From Oblivion to Ovation."

113. Rampersad, *The Life of Langston Hughes*, 364.

114. Hughes, *The Plays to 1942*, 481.

115. Hughes, *The Plays to 1942v* 513.

116. Hughes, *The Plays to 1942*, 184.

117. Hughes, *The Plays to 1942*, 537.

118. Hughes, *The Plays to 1942*, 528.

119. Silver, "A History of the Karamu Theatre," 239.

120. Hatch and Shine, *Black Theatre U.S.A*, 5.

121. Rampersad, *The Life of Langston Hughes*, 315.

122. Rampersad, *The Life of Langston Hughes*, 311–15, 317–20.

123. Silver, "A History of the Karamu Theatre," 251.

124. Silver, "A History of the Karamu Theatre," 242.

125. Silver, "A History of the Karamu Theatre," 243.

126. Silver, "A History of the Karamu Theatre," 243.

127. Silver, "A History of the Karamu Theatre," 246.

128. Fearnley, "Writing the History of Karamu House," 80–100.

129. Reuben Silver asked Rowena Jelliffe if she thought the fire was caused by arson and she replied, "It probably was." Silver, "A History of the Karamu Theatre," 293.

130. Fearnley, "Writing the History of Karamu House," 92.

131. Fearnley, "Writing the History of Karamu House," 90.

132. Silver, "Writing the History of Karamu House," 252–53.

133. Hughes, "For Russell and Rowena Jelliffe," 356.

134. O'Connor and Brown, *The Federal Theatre Project*, 18.

135. O'Connor and Brown, *The Federal Theatre Project*, 8.

136. Vacha, *Showtime in Cleveland*, 165.

137. Silver, "A History of the Karamu Theatre," 270.

138. Christy, "The Contributions of the Gilpin Players," 52–53.

139. Christy, "The Contributions of the Gilpin Players," 52.

140. Silver, "A History of the Karamu Theatre," 270–71.

141. Silver, "A History of the Karamu Theatre," 533.

142. Vacha, *Showtime in Cleveland*, 166.

143. Vacha, *Showtime in Cleveland*, 166–67.

144. Vacha, *Showtime in Cleveland*, 167.

145. Selby, *Beyond Civil Rights*, 98.

146. "Minnie Gentry, 77, An Actress on Stage and *Cosby Show*."

147. Minnie Gentry, personal letter to Denise R. Christy, quoted in Christy, "The Contributions of the Gilpin Players," 53.

148. Silver, "A History of the Karamu Theatre," 271.

149. Silver, "A History of the Karamu Theatre," 272.

150. Fearnley, "Writing the History of Karamu House," 85.

151. Fearnley, "Writing the History of Karamu House," 86.

152. K. Elmo Lowe was not a part of the repertory unit's refusal to work with the integrated unit. Lowe quit the FTP prior to the budget cuts that necessitated the merging of the two groups. Vacha, *Showtime in Cleveland*, 165.

153. Silver, "Writing the History of Karamu House," 271–72.

154. Bernard, *Remember Me to Harlem*, 139.

155. Silver, "A History of the Karamu Theatre," 273.

156. Silver, "A History of the Karamu Theatre," 507.

157. Horne, *Race Woman*, 72–80.

158. Horne, *Race Woman*, 85.

159. Schmalenberger, "Debuting Her Political Voice," 40, 41.

160. Livingstone, "African Rhythms Prevail," 4.

161. Silver, "A History of the Karamu Theatre," 508–9.

162. Selby, *Beyond Civil Rights*, 113.

163. Horne, *Race Woman*, 86.

164. McFadden, "The Artistry and Activism of Shirley Graham Du Bois," 210.

165. Silver, "A History of the Karamu Theatre," 298.

166. Horne, *Race Woman*, 84.

167. Vacha, *Showtime in Cleveland*, 169; Fearnley, "Writing the History of Karamu House," 86.

168. Fearnley, "Writing the History of Karamu House," 86.

169. Fearnley, "Writing the History of Karamu House," 85.

170. Silver, "A History of the Karamu Theatre," 300.

171. Vials, *Realism for the Masses*, 71.

172. "Scene from Shirley Graham's *I Gotta Home at Karamu*," archival photograph, February 1940, Cleveland Press Repository, https://clevelandmemory .contentdm.oclc.org/digital/collection/press/id/9927/rec/1.

173. Silver, "A History of the Karamu Theatre," 301–2.

174. Fearnley, "Writing the History of Karamu House," 92.

175. Silver, "A History of the Karamu Theatre," 509.

176. Inflation calculator, accessed February 15, 2022, https://www.saving.org /inflation/inflation.php?amount=500,000&year=1947.

177. Fearnley, "Writing the History of Karamu House," 95.

178. Fearnley, "Writing the History of Karamu House," 98.

179. Silver, "A History of the Karamu Theatre," 333; Zeigler, *Regional Theatre: The Revolutionary Stage*, 38.

180. Silver, "A History of the Karamu Theatre," 303.

181. Silver, "A History of the Karamu Theatre," 166, 173.

182. Karamu House, "Home."

183. Silver, "A History of the Karamu Theatre," 306.

184. "Interracial House Gets $100,000 Grant," 2.

185. Selby, *Beyond Civil Rights*, 129.

186. Silver, "A History of the Karamu Theatre," 329–30.

187. "Biography of Benno Frank."

188. Gassner and Quinn, *The Reader's Encyclopedia of World Drama*, 81.

189. Cole, "I, Too Am America," 146; Calkins, Woodham Jelliffe, and Jelliffe, *Correspondence: With Marian Anderson*.

190. Selby, *Beyond Civil Rights*, 152.

191. Saxon, "Zelma George, 90."

192. Selby, *Beyond Civil Rights*, 152.

193. Siegel, "Amahl and the Night Visitors."

194. "Boy Visits the Set of Karamu's Amahl and the Night Visitors courtesy of Easter Seals," archival photograph, April 9, 1952, Cleveland Press Repository, https://clevelandmemory.contentdm.oclc.org/digital/collection/press/id/9882 /rec/1.

195. "Boy Visits the Set of Karamu's 'Amahl and the Night Visitors.' "

196. Silver, "A History of the Karamu Theatre," 513–23.

197. Silver, "A History of the Karamu Theatre," 457, 464.

198. Silver, "A History of the Karamu Theatre," 464.

199. Silver, "A History of the Karamu Theatre," 466.

200. Slotnik "Robert Guillaume."

201. Slotnik, "Robert Guillaume."

202. Bergan, "Ron O'Neal."

203. Silver, "A History of the Karamu Theatre," 513–23.

204. Silver, "A History of the Karamu Theatre," 513–23.

205. Silver, "A History of the Karamu Theatre," 512–23; "Cleveland to Host Meeting of African Culture Society."

206. Gibbs and Lindfors, *Research on Wole Soyinka*, 52.

207. "Karamu Actors Preparing to Leave on a Trip to Denver," archival photograph, May 4, 1964, Cleveland Press Repository, https://clevelandmemory .contentdm.oclc.org/digital/collection/press/id/9795/rec/1.

208. Silver, "A History of the Karamu Theatre," 467–68.

209. Newman, *Karamu House Inc. 75th Anniversary*, 17.

210. Silver, "A History of the Karamu Theatre," 469–70.

211. For more about the politics of arts diplomacy during the Cold War see Prevot's *Dance for Export*, Croft's *Dancers as Diplomats*, Davenport's *Jazz Diplomacy*, and Wulf's *U.S. International Exhibitions during the Cold War*.

212. "Karamu Goes to Washington," archival photograph, August 27, 1963, Cleveland Press Repository, https://clevelandmemory.contentdm.oclc.org/digital /collection/press/id/9714/rec/1.

213. "Martin Luther King Jr., Signature Found in Karamu House Guestbook."

214. Clark, "Antioch College Opened Its Arms to Coretta Scott," 5A.

215. O'Leary, "Co-Existence without Condescension," B14.

216. Abookire and McNair, "Children's Theatre Activities at Karamu House," 78.

217. "Actors from Karamu Theatre," archival photograph, January 19, 1960, Cleveland Press Repository, https://clevelandmemory.contentdm.oclc.org/digital /collection/press/id/9946/rec/1.

218. Dent, Schechner, and Moses, *The Free Southern Theater*.

219. Dent, Schechner, and Moses, *The Free Southern Theater*, front matter, n.p.

220. "Karamu Play Will Open Tomorrow," 7.

221. Archival records show that the Jelliffes began the search for their replacement a full six years before they eventually retired in 1963. Russell and Rowena Jelliffe Papers.

222. Karamu Theatre Golden Anniversary Program, "Three One Act Operas," November 30–December 8, 42 season, 1965–1966, Karamu Theatre Programs 1927–1972, Karamu Programs, Cleveland Public Library Repository.

223. Bernie Noble, archival photograph and accompanying description, "J. Newton Hill 1966," August 17, 1966, Notable Blacks of Cleveland, Cleveland Press Repository, http://images.ulib.csuohio.edu/cdm/singleitem/collection/afro /id/1153/rec/4.

224. Peterson Jr., *The African American Theatre Directory*, 127.

225. Morton, *Cleveland Heights*, 126.

226. "J. Newton Hill, Educator, 88."

227. In April 1966, the United States Commission on Civil Rights held public hearings in Cleveland, where it presented extensive evidence of economic and housing discrimination, police brutality, continued school segregation, and other examples of racism. Moore, "Carl Stokes: Mayor of Cleveland," 83.

228. Moore, *Carl B. Stokes and the Rise of Black Political Power*, 1.

229. Shultz, *Karamu: 100 Years in the House*.

230. Delaney, "Black Culture Seeks Strength."

231. Karamu Theatre Golden Anniversary Program, "Three One Act Operas."

232. "Karamu House," 20.

233. "Karamu Executive Director Change," 66.

234. Shultz, *Karamu: 100 Years in the House*.

235. Shultz, *Karamu: 100 Years in the House*.

236. Shultz, *Karamu: 100 Years in the House*.

237. Newman, *Karamu House Inc. 75th Anniversary*, 22.

238. Newman, *Karamu House Inc. 75th Anniversary*, 24.

239. Hill and Hatch, *A History of African American Theatre*, 399–400, 406; Mahala, *Penumbra*, 4–7.

240. Jackson et al., "Investing in Creativity," 33.

241. "Mike Malone Named Theatre Director of Karamu House," 17.

242. Simonson, "Mike Malone, Director and Choreographer."

243. For an examination of the importance of *Black Nativity* as an annual production for black theater companies, see Mahala, *Penumbra*, 43–58; Evett, "Vinnette Carroll Back with Black Nativity," N1.

244. Lamb, "Director and Teacher Mike Malone."

245. Cardwell, "Black Center Nurtures Solid Cultural Climate," 22.

246. "Karamu Celebrates Black History Month," G6.

247. Cleveland Foundation, Annual Report, 44.

248. Andrea Simakis, "Planet Silver."

249. Vacha, *Showtime in Cleveland*, 188; "The Night Beat," 14; O'Connor, "Powerful Play for Karamu's New Company," D3.

250. O'Connor, "Audience Confused by Karamu's *Eyes*," B12.

251. Newman, *Karamu House Inc. 75th Anniversary*, 23–24.

252. *American Theatre* excludes Shakespeare productions from their annual list of top ten and top twenty most produced playwrights because Shakespeare "would top both lists every year, making them much less inclusive. . . . Shakespeare remains the most-produced playwright in the country, with 108 productions." Tran, "The Top 20 Most-Produced Playwrights."

253. Malovany, "Karamu Artist's View of Stardom Matures," 3.

254. Newman, "Holding Back: The Theatre's Resistance to Non-Traditional Casting," 23.

255. Malovany, "Karamu Artist's View of Stardom Matures," 3.

256. Malovany, "Karamu Artist's View of Stardom Matures," 3.

257. Johnston, "Lucia Colombi."

258. Johnston, "Lucia Colombi."

259. Burnham, "Theater: The Clown Prints of Autumn," 58–60.

260. Mastroianni, "Going Back to Basics," 18, 22.

261. Spivey, "Midwest Theatre Collaboration."

262. Shola Adenekan, "Don Evans."

263. "Ricardo Khan biography."

264. Adenekan, "Don Evans."

265. The Ensemble Theatre, "The Ensemble Theatre Presents *One Monkey Don't Stop No Show*."

266. Mastroianni, "Showcase for Playwrights," F1.

267. Mastroianni, "Showcase for Playwrights," F1.

268. Mastroianni, "Sharper Focus Needed in Play's Two Stories," C5; Mastroianni, "Karamu's H.M.S. Pinafore Shows Few Sparks," B3; Mastroianni, "Laughs Just Don't Stop in *Monkey*," A8; Mastroianni, "Karamu's Showdown a Zestful Fable," B3.

269. Seiler, "Playwright Evans Not Quite Sure of What He's Got," 14.

270. Evett, "A Karamu Creation," P1.

271. Evett, "A Karamu Creation," P2.

272. Evett, "A Karamu Creation," P2.

273. Evett, "A Karamu Creation," P1.

274. Margaret Ford Taylor is listed as "Interim Director of Karamu" in a television interview program in October 1987. "Channels Update," D2.

275. August Wilson, *The Ground on Which I Stand*.

276. Newman, *Karamu House Inc. 75th Anniversary*, 24; Perry, "Keeping Karamu Legacy Alive," 30.

277. "Karamu Names Ford-Taylor Permanent Executive Director," E11.

278. Evett, "Singing, Dancing the Blues and Mighty Proud of It," H2.

279. Newman, *Karamu House Inc. 75th Anniversary*, 25–26.

280. Chatman, "If Bricks Could Speak," 6.

281. "Bank One Aims for Minority Business," C1.

282. Chancellor, "Karamu Is Too Special to Let It Die," B3.

283. Simmons, "Hard Times for Karamu," 1A.

284. Evett, "Ensemble Sizzles in Play," 13.

285. "For Colored Girls Top 50% Ticket Mark," 12A.

286. Evett, "2 Plays End Karamu Season," 16.

287. Evett, "2 Plays End Karamu Season," 16.

288. Case, *Feminism and Theatre*, 128.

289. Case, *Feminism and Theatre*, 129.

290. Johnston, "Dream on East 89th Street."

291. Mastroianni, "Women of Plums," C1.

292. Mastroianni, "Women of Plums," C1.

293. Mastroianni, "Women of Plums," C1.

294. Mastroianni, "Unfocused *Grapes of Wrath*," D2.

295. Mastroianni, "Imagine Macbeth in Haiti," C6.

296. Perry, "Karamu House Revives Art, Theater from WPA Era," 24; Evett, "A Winner from Any Point in Time," 5E.

297. Evett, "Hopeful Message Weighted Down" 10E; Evett, "Women Cast into Fires," 5E; Brown, "Theater Review: Karamu and Dobama Collaborate."

298. Rampersad, *The Life of Langston Hughes*, 184–85, 194–98; Hughes, *Big Sea*, 131–34.

299. Gates Jr., "Theatre: Why the Mule Bone Debate Goes On."

300. Eisenstein, "Lost Play a Delight to See and Hear," 7E.

301. Eisenstein, "Lost Play a Delight to See and Hear," 7E.

302. Sadoff, "Black Matrilineage," 4–26.

303. Mastroianni, "Bolder Work from Author of *Fences*," C8; "Karamu Presents the Premiere of August Wilson's *Jitney*" SH2.

304. Mastroianni, "Drama of Power at Karamu," C5.

305. Mastroianni, "*The Piano Lesson* Resonates at Karamu," C7.

306. Evett, "Karamu Cast Sparkles in Wilson Play," 7E.

307. Howey, "King Me: Sensational Performances."

308. Simakis, "Pacing Slow in Wilson's Layered *Gem*"; Wade, "Joe Turner Comes to Karamu House Theater," C1.

309. Johnston, "Dream on East 89th Street."

310. Pantsios, "Terrence Spivey Shakes Up Our Theater Scene."

311. Jones, "5 Responses to Terrence Spivey."

312. Jones, Theatrical resume.

313. Spivey, telephone interview with author, May 25, 2018.

314. Kurahashi, "Terrence Spivey Energy Source," 42–45.

315. "Best Theatre Honcho: Terrence Spivey."

316. Kurahashi, "Terrence Spivey Energy Source," 42–45.

317. Spivey, *Objectively/Reasonable*.

318. Gramza, "Karamu House's Terrence Spivey to Deliver Keynote."

319. Spivey, telephone interview.

320. Spivey, telephone interview.

321. Spivey, telephone interview.

322. Heller, "Play at Karamu Recalls Dark Chapter of American History"; Brown, "Haunting *Ruined* at Karamu."

323. Rosenberg, "Karamu House Playwright in Residence Michael Oatman."

324. Cleveland Arts Prize, "Michael Oatman."

325. Piepenburg, "Tupac Shakur, Immortalized Again."

326. Cleveland Arts Prize, "Michael Oatman."

327. Simakis, "Pacing Slow in Wilson's Layered *Gem*"; Simakis, "Director and Playwright."

328. Simakis, "Director and Playwright."

329. Gallucci, "About a Boy."

330. Kearney, "About the Author."

331. Gill, "Halleluja. Yo Da Lay Hee."

332. Kearney, "5 Responses to Terrence Spivey Shakes Up Our Theater Scene."

333. Kurahashi, "Terrence Spivey, Energy Source," 42.

334. Pantsios, "Dark Days for the Black Arts."

335. Crump, "Karamu House Inspires Executive Director."

336. Terrence Spivey, quoted in Kurahashi, "Terrence Spivey Energy Source," 45.

337. Gregory Ashe, quoted in Pantsios, "Dark Days for the Black Arts."

338. Cleveland Foundation, Grant Search, Karamu House 1988–2013.

339. "National Endowment for the Arts Funds Organizations throughout Ohio."

340. "National Endowment for the Arts Funds Organizations throughout Ohio."

341. Helicon Collaborative, *Not Just Money*, full report, 4, 5.

342. Helicon Collaborative, "Not Just Money: Where Is the Money Going?".

343. Helicon Collaborative, *Not Just Money*, full report, 5.

344. Cleveland Foundation, Grant Search, Karamu House 1988–2013.

345. Cleveland Playhouse, GuideStar Profile.

346. Pantsios, "Dark Days for the Black Arts."

347. Wilson, "Re: Dark Days for the Black Arts."

348. Scruggs, "Curtain Stall?"

349. Scruggs, "Curtain Stall?"

350. Sias, interview with author, Karamu House, November 20, 2017.

351. Simakis, "Cleveland Schools' Arts Guru Tony Sias."

352. Sias, interview with author.

353. King, "Alumnus Takes Helm of Cleveland's Karamu House."

354. Simakis, "Karamu House Axes 15."

355. Simakis, "Karamu House Axes 15."

356. Johnston, "Shakeup Aims to Put Karamu House Together."

357. Sias, interview with author.

358. Selby, *Beyond Civil Rights*, 129.

359. Selby, *Beyond Civil Rights*, 129.

360. Tony Sias, quoted in Scruggs, "Curtain Stall?"

361. Johnston, "Shakeup Aims to Put Karamu House Together."

362. Spivey, telephone interview.

363. Lisa Langford, *Rastus and Hattie.*

364. Spivey, telephone interview.

365. Simakis, "Historic Karamu House Loses Its Tax-Exempt Status."

366. Scruggs, "Karamu House Regains Nonprofit Status."

367. Scruggs, "Karamu House Regains Nonprofit Status."

368. Sias, interview with author.

369. Kelly, "Dynamic Musical."

370. Howey, "Great Singing Perfectly Complements a Lush Production."

371. "Cleveland Critics Circle 2016 Theater Awards."

372. Sias, interview with author.

373. Burnett, "Actress Returns to Karamu."

374. Roller, interview with author, Karamu House, November 20, 2017.

375. Abelman, "When Northeast Ohio's Theaters Collaborate."

376. Bolton Elementary School, "Community Partners."

377. O'Donnell, "New Tremont Montessori school, Karamu House Partnership Preferred"; Sias, interview with author.

378. A study of art programs from 1999 to 2009 by the Department of Education found an overall decline in the offering of arts curriculum for urban public schools. The study also reported a drop in drama offerings, with 20 percent of elementary schools offering drama classes in 1999 to just 4 percent of elementary schools offering drama classes in 2009. Freeze, "Report: Art Education Programs on the Decline."

379. Roller, interview with author.

380. Sias, interview with author.

381. Litt, "Cleveland Foundation Announces $2M grant to Karamu House."

382. Sias, interview with author.

383. Litt, "Opportunity Corridor Is Back on Track."

384. Diamond, "How the Cleveland Clinic Grows Healthy While Its Neighbors Stay Sick."

385. Sias, interview with author.

386. Spivey, telephone interview.

387. Breckenridge, "Opportunity Corridor's Latest Alignment Would Uproot More Than 90 Families, A Dozen Businesses."

388. Litt, "Cleveland Foundation Announces."

389. Tony Sias, quoted in Litt, "Cleveland Foundation Announces."

390. King, Jr. *The Impact of Race,* 95–96.

Chapter 2

1. Wilson, Knox, and Bragg, *August Wilson.*

2. Wilson, *The Ground on Which I Stand.*

3. Helicon Collaborative, *Not Just Money,* Pittsburgh PA Data Profile.

4. See, e.g., the public comments in response to Belko, "Dollar Bank Sells August Wilson Center to Three Pittsburgh Foundations."

5. Helicon Collaborative, *Not Just Money,* Pittsburgh PA Data Profile; Connor, *Pittsburgh in Stages,* 119–20.

6. Trotter and Day, *Race and Renaissance.*

7. Bodnar, Simon, and Weber, *Lives of Their Own.*

8. For example, Patricia Prattis Jennings broke the color barrier in 1956 by becoming the first African American musician to perform with the Pittsburgh Symphony. Pitz, "Former PSO Keyboardist to Read from Essays"; Lynne Conner also details several examples of "the racism that had long characterized Pittsburgh's cultural sector," in *Pittsburgh in Stages*, 117.

9. Conner, *Pittsburgh in Stages*, 111–22.

10. Conner, *Pittsburgh in Stages*, 119–21.

11. Glasco, telephone interview with author, June 13, 2017.

12. Conner, *Pittsburgh in Stages*, 144; Glasco, telephone interview.

13. Conner, *Pittsburgh in Stages*, 168.

14. Glasco, telephone interview.

15. Glasco, telephone interview.

16. Glasco, telephone interview.

17. Both the singular and plural versions of the company name were used at different time periods by different members of the original company. I use the plural form as original company members Curtiss Porter and Sala Udin refer to the company as Black Horizons in their interviews. There is also some disagreement about the exact starting date of the company. Lynne Connor cites Rob Penny's 1974 resume, which lists the first production of "Black Horizon Theater" as 1967. Conner, *Pittsburgh in Stages*, 245. Udin and Glasco reference the starting point of Black Horizons as 1968, the date I use here.

18. Udin, telephone interview with author, July 17, 2017.

19. Udin, telephone interview.

20. Branson, email correspondence with author, July 25, 2017.

21. Penny, *Good Black Don't Crack*, 332–92.

22. Udin, telephone interview.

23. Porter, email correspondence, September 7, 2017.

24. Porter, email correspondence, September 7, 2017.

25. There is correspondence between Wilson and Johnson regarding the 1982/1983 productions of *Jitney* in Johnson's archives, including an early, unpublished version of the play, in the Bob Johnson Papers.

26. Glasco, telephone interview.

27. Neal, "The Black Arts Movement."

28. Baron, "Etta Cox Stars in *King Hedley*."

29. Branson, email correspondence.

30. Glasco, telephone interview.

31. "Celebrating Theatre Icon, Bayo Oduneye"; Alakam, "Theatre Is Dead in Nigeria—Prof Bayo Oduneye."

32. Porter, email correspondence with author, October 3, 2017.

33. Glasco, telephone interview.

34. Glasco, telephone interview.

35. Neal, "The Black Arts Movement," 32.

36. Udin, telephone interview.

37. Susan Ressler, "In Tune to the Rhythm of Our Time," *Point*, June 4, 1970, 6, press clipping, Bob Johnson Papers.

38. Glasco, telephone interview.

39. Udin, telephone interview.

40. Branson, email correspondence.

41. Porter, email correspondence, September 7, 2017.

42. Branson, email correspondence.

43. Branson, email correspondence.

44. Jones, "Obituary: Maisha Baton, Nurturing Poet, Playwright, Therapist and Teacher."

45. Rawson, "Purdy Lends his Energy to Iguana," 2.

46. Purdy and Wilson continued to collaborate on work at Penumbra Theatre Company in St. Paul, where the two lived and worked in the late 1970s and early 1980s. Mahala, *Penumbra*, 59–80.

47. Ujima Theatre Company, "About the Ujima Theatre Company."

48. Ujima Theatre Company, "About the Ujima Theatre Company."

49. Mayes, *Kwanzaa*, 226.

50. Glasco, telephone interview.

51. Ujima Theatre Company, "About the Ujima Theatre Company."

52. Southers, telephone interview with author, June 1, 2017.

53. Glasco, telephone interview.

54. Glasco, telephone interview.

55. Glasco, telephone interview; Wilson, *Two Trains Running*, 40, 41–42.

56. Branson, email correspondence.

57. Udin, telephone interview.

58. Vernell A. Lillie, "Message from the Founder/Artistic Director," 2000–2001 Season Brochure, Kuntu Repertory Theatre Archives.

59. Suber, "*Little Willie Armstrong Jones*," 21.

60. Saxton, "Blackface Minstrelsy and Jacksonian Ideology," 5.

61. Byrd, "Whitewashing Blackface Minstrelsy," 80.

62. Foster, "Oh! Susanna."

63. Smeltz, "Pittsburgh Workers Remove Controversial Stephen Foster Statue."

64. Suber, "*Little Willie Armstrong Jones*," 21.

65. Ethel M. Parris, "Bringing Back *Little Willie*" *Pitt News*, February 9, 1977, press clipping, Kuntu Theatre Archives.

66. Penny, *Little Willie Armstrong Jones*.

67. Hart, "Obituary: Robert Lee 'Rob' Penny."

68. Alker et al. "A Collective Call against Critical Bias."

69. Jackson, preface to *Kuntu Drama*, xi.

70. Vernell Lillie, quoted in Parris, "Bringing Back *Little Willie*."

71. Vernell A. Lillie, "Kuntu: An African Aesthetic," *Kuntu Magazine*, November 1979, 43, Kuntu Repertory Theatre Archive.

72. Harrison, *Kuntu Drama*, 29.

73. Kuntu Repertory Theatre, "About."

74. Vernell A. Lillie, "Message from the Founder/Artistic Director," 2000–2001 Season Brochure, Kuntu Repertory Theatre Archives.

75. Kuntu Repertory Theatre, "About."

76. Aristotle, *Poetics*, 32–33.

77. Campbell, *The Hero with a Thousand Faces*.

78. Kuntu Repertory Theatre, "About."

79. Kuntu Repertory Theatre, "About."

80. Udin, quoted in Carpenter, "Curtain Falls on Pittsburgh's Kuntu."

81. Kuntu Repertory Theatre, "About."

82. Carpenter, "Curtain Falls on Pittsburgh's Kuntu."

83. Kuntu Repertory Theatre, "About."

84. Kuntu Repertory Theatre, "About."

85. Lillie, "Dr. Vernell A. Lillie."

86. Mahala, *Penumbra*, 86–87.

87. *Black Happening* playbill, Bob Johnson Papers.

88. Wilkinsburg Art Theatre Papers.

89. Christopher Applegate, "Allegheny Rep's Latest Gamble Pays Off," press clipping, Bob Johnson Papers.

90. Christopher Applegate, "Allegheny Rep's Latest Gamble Pays Off," press clipping, Bob Johnson Papers.

91. Powell, "*Jitney* Captures Drama," B2.

92. *Jitney* promotional flyer, Bob Johnson Papers.

93. Timothy Cox, "Jitney—Representing a Realistic Portrayal," *Pittsburgh Courier*, September 3, 1983, press clipping, Bob Johnson Papers.

94. Gussow, "Stage: At New Federal," C3.

95. *Who Loves the Dancer?*, press release, April 1985, Kuntu Repertory Theatre Papers.

96. Penny, *Good Black Don't Crack*, 389.

97. Hampton, "Perils of Dalejean in *Good Black*," C16.

98. Blake, "Pitt's Kuntu Repertory Theatre Kicks Off 2007 Season."

99. Blake, "Pitt's Kuntu Repertory Theatre Kicks Off 2007 Season."

100. Frank DiGiacomo, "Big Pay Cut: Salary Bows to Quality TV Star Says of Role Here," *Pittsburgh Press*, n.d., C11, press clipping, Kuntu Repertory Theatre Papers.

101. DiGiacomo, "Big Pay Cut." Kuntu Repertory Theatre Papers.

102. "TV's Esther Rolle Joining Kuntu Play," *Pittsburgh Press*, March 13, 1984: B7, press clipping, Kuntu Repertory Theatre Papers.

103. Phyllis Fields, "Kuntu Struts Its Stuff in Edinburgh" *Pittsburgh Post-Gazette*, August 23, 1989, press clipping, Kuntu Repertory Theatre Papers.

104. Sandra Mayo and Elvin Holt cite this folk idiom in reference to the efforts and accomplishments of the African American theater practitioners they chronicle in their comprehensive look at black theater organizations in Texas. Mayo and Holt, *Stages of Struggle and Celebration*, 3.

105. Smith, "Kuntu's *Ma Rainey* Fine Tribute to Wilson," D2.

106. Smith, "Kuntu's *Ma Rainey* Fine Tribute to Wilson," D2.

107. *Ma Rainey's Black Bottom* autographed playbill and notes, September 1987, Kuntu Repertory Theatre Papers.

108. Edward L. Blank, "Black Drama Keys on Love Expression," *Pittsburgh Press*, June 23, 1977, D7, press clipping, Kuntu Repertory Theatre Papers.

109. Jim Davidson, "Theater: *Strong Breed* Slice of Nigerian Life," *Pittsburgh Press*, May 5, 1983, D4, press clipping, Kuntu Repertory Theatre Papers.

110. Christopher Rawson, "Nigerian Play Is Work of a Master," *Pittsburgh Post-Gazette*, May 6, 1983, press clipping, Kuntu Repertory Theatre Papers.

111. "Kuntu Theatre Stages *Dilemma of a Ghost*," *Pittsburgh Press*, March 17, 1988, D3, press clipping, Kuntu Repertory Theatre Papers.

112. "Kuntu Theatre Stages *Dilemma of a Ghost*," Kuntu Repertory Theatre Papers.

113. Aidoo, *"The Dilemma of a Ghost" and "Anowa"*; *The Girl Who Can and Other Stories*.

114. Badoe, Mama, Busia, and Aidoo, *The Art of Ama Ata Aidoo*.

115. *Two Can Play* postcard mailing, Kuntu Repertory Theatre Papers.

116. Winks, "Jamaican Culture Meets American," D3.

117. Winks, "Jamaican Culture Meets American."

118. Winks, "Jamaican Culture Meets American."

119. Adrian McCoy, "Three Day Conference Honors Black Writers and Poets," *Pittsburgh Press*, June 6, 1991, D3, press clipping, Kuntu Repertory Theatre Papers.

120. McCoy, "Three Day Conference," Kuntu Repertory Theatre Papers.

121. Eberson, "Weekend Hotlist."

122. Frank Hightower, in *Lifting* production program, Kuntu Repertory Theatre Papers.

123. "Pitt's Kuntu Repertory Theatre's Production of Lifting Opens Jan. 28th," January 5, 1999, Kuntu Repertory Theatre Papers.

124. Mayo and Holt, *Stages of Struggle and Celebration*, 249.

125. Eileen J. Morris, "Director's Notes," *Lifting* playbill, January 1999, Kuntu Repertory Theatre Papers.

126. Smith, *Best Black Plays*, 221.

127. Hayes, "Kuntu's *Sing Black Hammer*," D6.

128. James, artist's website.

129. Season programs, Kuntu Repertory Theatre Papers.

130. Carpenter, "Curtain Falls on Pittsburgh's Kuntu Repertory Theatre."

131. Southers, telephone interview.

132. Carpenter, "Curtain Falls on Pittsburgh's Kuntu Repertory Theatre."

133. Southers, telephone interview.

134. Southers, telephone interview.

135. Southers, telephone interview.

136. Rawson, "On Stage: Politics Hard on Stage."

137. Pittsburgh Playwrights Theatre, "2003 Productions."

138. Southers, telephone interview.

139. Robertson, "Lloyd Richards"; Pogrebin, "Wolfe Is Leaving Public Theater"; Gelt, "Sheldon Epps to Step Down."

140. Southers, telephone interview.

141. Southers, telephone interview.

142. Southers, telephone interview.

143. August Wilson House, "Transformation."

144. Pittsburgh Playwrights Theatre Company, *Seven Guitars*.

145. Arons, "*Seven Guitars* at the Pittsburgh Playwrights."

146. Clearfield, "*King Hedley II*."

147. Klein, "The Hill District, a Community Holding On."

148. Southers, television interview by Mickey Hood on *Pittsburgh Live Today*.

149. Pittsburgh Playwrights Theatre Company, "*Gem of the Ocean*."

150. Gordon, "Aunt Ester, the Hill District and the Surreal World of August Wilson's *Gem*."

151. Kapp and Armstrong, *SynergiCity*, 7.

152. Kapp and Armstrong, *SynergiCity*, 5–6.

153. Trotter and Day, *Race and Renaissance*, 69.

154. Pittsburg Cultural Trust, "Background and History."

155. Pittsburg Cultural Trust, "Background and History."

156. Pittsburg Cultural Trust, "Background and History."

157. The building and nonprofit organization that programs arts activities within it have had several name changes prompted by legal proceedings and rebranding campaigns, which are detailed in this chapter. Here I refer to the organization by its original name.

158. Bloom, "The Rise and Fall of the August Wilson Center."

159. Wilson, *The Ground on Which I Stand*, 17.

160. Wilson, *The Ground on Which I Stand*, 17.

161. Weinert-Kendt, "The Ground on Which He Stood."

162. For more on Wilson's association with Penumbra Theatre Company, see Mahala, *Penumbra*, 59–80.

163. Ferola, Ginsberg, and Sutton, "Saving the August Wilson Center."

164. Bloom, "The Rise and Fall of the August Wilson Center."

165. For a detailed analysis of the history and development of the regional theater system, including a discussion of the paucity of diversity in the early history of most regional theaters, see Berkowitz, *New Broadways*.

166. Neal, "The Black Arts Movement," 29.

167. Udin, telephone interview.

168. Udin, telephone interview.

169. Ferola, Ginsberg, and Sutton, "Saving the August Wilson Center."

170. Trotter and Day, *Race and Renaissance*, 186.

171. Perkins + Will, "The August Wilson Center for African American Culture."

172. Perkins + Will, "The August Wilson Center for African American Culture."

173. "August Wilson Center Adds Feather in Cap of Cultural District."

174. "August Wilson Center Adds Feather in Cap of Cultural District."

175. Perkins + Will, "The August Wilson Center for African American Culture."

176. Erdley and Smeltz, "Pittsburgh's August Wilson Center: Classic Mistake."

177. Udin, telephone interview.

178. Bloom, "The Rise and Fall of the August Wilson Center."

179. Ping Chong and Company, "The Women of the Hill, 2009."

180. Rawson, "August Wilson's Mythic Character Explored in Theater Festival."

181. O'Driscoll, "A Unique Theatrical Project."

182. Harris's photography work for the *Pittsburgh Courier* is one of the most extensive visual records of African Americans neighborhoods and people of the twentieth century. The Carnegie Museum of Art has a collection of eighty thousand of his photographs. As the daughter of the celebrated minister and civil rights leader Charles Foggie, Charlene Foggie Barnett was photographed by Harris as a young child many times as part of Harris's documentation of black life in Pittsburgh. "New Teenie Harris Exhibit Opens at Carnegie Museum of Art."

183. Kurahashi, "Celebrating the 'Historical' Community through Different Voices," 13.

184. Kurahashi, "Celebrating the 'Historical' Community through Different Voices," 14.

185. Kalson, "Wilson Center's New Leader Has Lofty Vision."

186. Pitz, "August Wilson Center Struggles to Reduce $9 million debt."

187. Guess, email correspondence with author, June 13, 2017.

188. Southers, telephone interview.

189. Guess, email correspondence.

190. *Every Tongue Confess* playbill, August Wilson Center Archives, Curtis Theatre Collection, University of Pittsburgh.

191. Southers, telephone interview.

192. Ferola, Ginsberg, and Sutton, "Saving the August Wilson Center."

193. Udin, telephone interview.

194. Ferola, Ginsberg, and Sutton, "Saving the August Wilson Center."

195. Eberson, "Cultural Trust Vice President Tapped to Head August Wilson Center."

196. Dollar Bank, "Dollar Bank Sells August Wilson Center Building to Foundation."

197. Ferola, Ginsberg, and Sutton, "Saving the August Wilson Center."

198. Dass, "Humanae/I Am August."

199. Carter, "Review: Strong 'Piano Lesson' Ignites August Wilson Center."

200. Eberson, "Cultural Trust Vice President Tapped to Head August Wilson Center."

201. August Wilson African American Cultural Center, "Anna Deavere Smith" and "Harlem to Hollywood."

202. Wilson, radio interview in "The Confluence."

203. O'Driscoll, "August Wilson Center Stabilizes."

Chapter 3

1. O'Connor, "America's Most Expensive City"; Stone, "Rent for a 1 Bedroom Apartment."

2. Barnes, "Why We Protest the 'Google' Buses"; Gumbel, "San Francisco's Guerilla Protest at Google Buses"; Hollister, "Activists Sue San Francisco for Letting 'Google Bus' Use Public Bus Stops."

3. Anti-Eviction Mapping Project, "Ellis Act Evictions."

4. Using the Asian American arts organization Kearney Street Workshop as a case study, the Yerba Buena Center for the Arts Equity cohort group published an article designed to help other arts organizations gather tools to "survive a major eviction" and "continue to thrive through precarious economic cycles and waves of displacement and gentrification." YBCA Equity Cohort, "What Is the Role of Art in Gentrification and Displacement?"

5. For one of the seminal examinations of twentieth-century urban development and displacement in San Francisco, see Hartman, *City for Sale.*

6. Lai, "The Racial Triangulation of Space," 156.

7. Lai, "The Racial Triangulation of Space," 160.

8. Lai, "The Racial Triangulation of Space," 152.

9. The Anti-Eviction Mapping Project is a "a data-visualization, data analysis, and storytelling collective documenting the dispossession of San Francisco Bay

Area residents in the wake of the Tech Boom 2.0." Anti-Eviction Mapping Project, "About A(E)MP."

10. Talbot, *The Last Black Man in San Francisco*.
11. Haber, "Oakland: Brooklyn by the Bay."
12. Cagle, "Oakland Wants You to Stop Calling It 'The New Brooklyn.'"
13. Robertson, "A Six-Figure Salary Is Considered 'Low Income.'"
14. Black Repertory Group, "Our Story."
15. Black Repertory Group, "About Us."
16. Black Repertory Group, "About Us."
17. Nancy Scott, quoted in "Nora Vaughn, Founded Black Repertory," A17.
18. Black Repertory Group, Facebook page, listings from 2017–19, https://www.facebook.com/BRGNation/.
19. Bloom and Martin Jr., *Black against Empire*, 181–82.
20. "Black Arts West."
21. "Black Theatre Groups: A Directory," 173.
22. Bullins, "Black Theatre," special issue, *Tulane Drama Review*.
23. In addition to his editorial work, Ed Bullins's contributions to this volume included two essays and one play: a commentary on Martin Luther King's assassination, instructions for conducting street theater performances, and the play *Clara's Old Man*. Henrietta Harris contributed the essay "Building a Black Theatre," and Marvin X contributed the play, *Take Care of Business*. Bullins, "Black Theatre," 23–25, 85–92, 93, 157–58, 159–71.
24. Black Repertory Group, "Our Story."
25. 94.1 KPFA, "Events: Marvin X in Concert."
26. Black Repertory Group, "Our Story."
27. "Community Stage," Datebook 3.
28. Davis, *Purlie Victorius*.
29. "*Purlie* Benefit," 35.
30. Nora Vaughn, quoted in Payton, "Black Repertory Theater Has a Dream," F1.
31. "A Conference on Black Theater," 26.
32. "Theater," *San Francisco Examiner*, September 5, 1982, 7.
33. "Buriel Clay."
34. Payton, "Black Repertory Theater Has a Dream," F1.
35. Black Repertory Group, "Our Story"; Scott, "Good News for Black Theater."
36. Black Repertory Group, "Our Story."
37. Scott, "Good News for Black Theater," E3.
38. "Theater," Datebook 7.
39. "Black Repertory Marks 20th Year," E11.
40. Morse, "Is This Police Oppression?," A3.
41. Reed, "Curtain for Black Rep?"
42. Hurwitt, "Claude Purdy's Perfect Play," E3.
43. "Beat Checks: Black Repertory Group," E2.
44. "30th Summer of Love," D10.
45. Armstrong, "Reed Wins a MacArthur Grant," B1, B6.
46. Hurwitt, "Gethsemane Park Struggles to Tell Story," C9.
47. Ishmael Reed is listed as a board member of LHT on its 2015 public tax records and as a board member of BRG on its 2013 public tax records. "2016

Form 990," Lorraine Hansberry Theatre; "2014 Form 990," Black Repertory Group.

48. Reed, "Curtain for Black Rep?"

49. Reed, "Black Repertory Theater and the Creation of Opportunity for Kids."

50. Reed, "Black Repertory Theater and the Creation of Opportunity for Kids."

51. Holtz, "Black Theater Group Faces Criticism."

52. Holtz, "Berkeley Should Stop Funding Theater."

53. Black Repertory Group, Event Calendar.

54. Curtis, "Reenactment Will Mark One Year Anniversary of Execution," B3.

55. Black Repertory Group, "Courage under Fire: The Story of Elroy."

56. Black Repertory Group, "The 2017 Nora B. Vaughn Essay Writing Contest."

57. Allen, *The Port Chicago Mutiny.*

58. King, "Black Repertory to Present *Port Chicago 50* Play."

59. Sabir, "*Port Chicago 50* at Black Rep This Weekend."

60. Winn, "Black Bay Stage," Datebook 28.

61. Winn, "Black Bay Stage."

62. For more about the arts colony at the Goodman Building, see Caldararo, *An Ethnography of the Goodman Building.*

63. Winn, "A Bay Area Success for the Black Stage," Datebook 28.

64. "Two One-Act Plays," A8; Wadud, *Companions of the Fire.*

65. Lorraine Hansberry Theatre, "Production History."

66. All American Speakers, "Danny Glover and Felix Justice."

67. Whitney LeBlanc Papers; Kolin, "An Interview with Whitney J. LeBlanc," 307–17.

68. "Air Guitar: A Musical Fantasy," E7.

69. Steidtmann, "A Tragic Escape into Drugs and MTV," Datebook 40.

70. Lorraine Hansberry Theatre, "Production History."

71. Hurwitt, "Black History Month."

72. Hurwitt, "Black History Month."

73. Hurwitt, "Black History Month."

74. San Francisco Mime Troupe Archives.

75. Mason, *The San Francisco Mime Troupe Reader.*

76. Sullivan, *The Plays of the San Francisco Mime Troupe: 2000–2016,* 5.

77. Alexander, *I Ain't Yo Uncle.*

78. Alexander, *Servant of the People.*

79. Hurwitt, "Life as Huey's Doppleganger," C15.

80. Collins, "Activists Who Yearn for Art That Transforms," 744; Wilmeth and Miller, *The Cambridge Guide to American Theatre,* 157; Hurwitt, "'rainbow' Still 'enuf' 20 Years Later," B3.

81. Wilmeth and Miller, *The Cambridge Guide to American Theatre,* 157; Vine, "Look Back at Ntozake Shange's For Colored Girls."

82. Collins, "Activists Who Yearn for Art That Transforms," 744.

83. Collins, "Activists Who Yearn for Art That Transforms," 744.

84. Collins, "Activists Who Yearn for Art That Transforms," 744.

85. Berson, "*Boogie Woogie Landscapes,*" Datebook 32–33.

86. Scott, "SEW Threads Jazz, Dance, and Poetry," B14.

87. "*Spell #7,*" E2.

88. "Ntozake Shange, Ishmael Reed Benefit," D9.

89. Hurwitt, "*Three Views of Mt. Fuji*," image 30.

90. Hurwitt, "*Three Views of Mt. Fuji*," image 30.

91. Hurwitt, "*Three Views of Mt. Fuji*," image 30.

92. Hurwitt, "*Three Views of Mt. Fuji*," image 30.

93. Power, "Catching Up with Ntozake Shange," 30–33.

94. "Lorraine Hansberry Theatre," Datebook 20; Peterson and Bennett, "Ntozake Shange," 305. Lorraine Hansberry Theatre, "Production History."

95. Hamlin, "Ntozake Shange Weaves Tapestries of Poetry."

96. Jones, telephone interview with the author, February 29, 2016.

97. Hurwitt, "'rainbow' Still 'enuf' 20 Years Later," B3.

98. Janiak, "African-American Shakes' *for colored girls*."

99. Scott, "The City's Homeless Ethnic Theatres."

100. Scott, "The City's Homeless Ethnic Theatres."

101. Helicon Collaborative, *Not Just Money*, full report, 9–10.

102. Scott, "Good News for Black Theatre," E3.

103. Hurwitt, "Gene Angell—Innovative Bay Area Theater Designer."

104. Lorraine Hansberry Theatre, "Production History."

105. "*The Resurrection of Lady Lester*," C10.

106. "The Colored Museum," C11.

107. Rosenberg, "Joe Turner's Here to Stay," D1, D7.

108. Mahala, *Penumbra*, 74–80.

109. Mahala, *Penumbra*, 74–80.

110. Jones, telephone interview.

111. Shinoff, "Cash Crunch Forces Bay Area Arts to the Wall," A13; Scott, "The City's Homeless Ethnic Theatres."

112. American Conservatory Theatre Foundation, aka A.C.T., "2016 990 tax form," Guidestar profile; Lorraine Hansberry Theatre, "2017 990 tax form," Guidestar profile.

113. Hurwitt, "Claude Purdy's Perfect Play," E3; Rosenberg, "Joe Turner's Here to Stay," D1, D7.

114. Lorraine Hansberry Theatre, "Production History."

115. Chastang, "If You Thought Yoshi's Situation Was Bad."

116. Hamlin, "San Francisco Art Academy.."

117. Hamlin, "San Francisco Art Academy.."

118. Matier and Ross, "SF Suing Academy of Art over Real Estate Empire."

119. Hurwitt, "Lorraine Hansberry Theatre to Close for Season."

120. Lorraine Hansberry Theatre, "Our History."

121. San Francisco Playhouse, "2016 990 tax form," Guidestar profile.

122. Jones, telephone interview.

123. Ronson, "San Francisco Is Burning."

124. Jones, telephone interview.

125. Janiak, "*Home*: A Too Rare Show from Lorraine Hansberry Theatre."

126. Jones, telephone interview.

127. San Francisco Arts Commission, "San Francisco Arts Commission Strategic Plan: 2014–2019," 10.

128. Jones, telephone interview.

129. Woodie King Jr., *The Impact of Race*.

130. Jones, telephone interview.

131. Jones, telephone interview.

132. Berkowitz's *New Broadways*, 221–23.

133. The statistics included in this paragraph were generated by analyzing the 2015–16 season profiles, cast lists, and press reviews of the Theatre Communications Group's budget 5 and 6 category Bay Area theaters.

134. Jones, telephone interview.

135. See, for example, the controversy surrounding the removal of the homeless in preparation of the city's hosting of Super Bowl 50. Matier and Ross, "S.F. Mayor: Homeless 'Have to Leave the Street'"; Waldron, "How Super Bowl 50 Became Ground Zero for the Fight over Homelessness."

136. Janiak, "Jones to Step Down from Lorraine Hansberry Theatre."

137. Ubuntu Theater Project, "Past Productions—How I Learned What I Learned."

138. Janiak, "New Leader, New Ethos."

139. Janiak, "New Leader, New Ethos."

140. Janiak, "New Leader, New Ethos."

141. Irene Nelson, "Home Sweet Home at Lorraine Hansberry Theatre, S.F."

142. Lorraine Hansberry Theatre, "2017 990 tax form," Guidestar profile; Scott, "Good News for Black Theater," E3.

143. Lorraine Hansberry Theatre, "Our Staff."

144. Janiak, "Lorraine Hansberry Theatre's New Leader."

145. Shotgun Players, "Shotgun Players, in Association with Lorraine Hansberry Theatre, presents Kill, Move Paradise."

146. Janiak, "Lorraine Hansberry Theatre's New Leader."

147. Janiak, "Lorraine Hansberry Theatre's New Leader."

148. Hurwitt, "Has Hip-Hop Lost Its Way?"

149. Oldenburg, "Jack Kerouac"; Herzog, "The Beat Generation's Hidden Refuge."

150. Hurwitt, "Has Hip-Hop Lost Its Way?"

151. Hurwitt, "Has Hip-Hop Lost Its Way?"

152. Sabir, "*The Urban Retreat*, a Play."

153. Krigwa Players, "Krigwa Players Little Negro Theatre."

154. Neal, "The Black Arts Movement," 29–30.

155. Wilson, "The Ground on Which I Stand," 33.

156. Catanese, *The Problem of the Color[blind]*, 67–68.

157. Hill and Hatch, *A History of African American Theatre*, 25.

158. African American Shakespeare Company, "Mission."

159. Dewberry, "The African Grove Theatre and Company," 128–31.

160. Lindfors, *Ira Aldridge: The African Roscius*.

161. Locke, *The New Negro: An Interpretation*.

162. Howard University Department of Theatre Arts, "About the Department: History."

163. Hill, *Shakespeare in Sable*, 111–14.

164. Fraden, *Blueprints for a Black Federal Theatre*, 97.

165. Pao, *No Safe Spaces*, 68.

166. Perucci, *Paul Robeson*.

167. African American Shakespeare Company, "Mission."

168. Appiah, *Cosmopolitanism: Ethics in a World of Strangers*.

169. Young, telephone interview with author, May 2, 2015.

170. Beete, "Art Talk with Sherri Young of the African-American Shakespeare Company."

171. Young, telephone interview.

172. Young, telephone interview.

173. Shakespeare, *As You Like It*, 3.2.7.

174. Catanese, *The Problem of the Color[blind]*, 9.

175. Wetmore Jr., "Big Willie Style," 158–59.

176. Pepin and Watts, *Harlem of the West*.

177. "African-American Shakespeare Company Closes Season with TWELFTH NIGHT."

178. Pao, *No Safe Spaces*, 37.

179. Pao, *No Safe Spaces*, 79.

180. Pao, *No Safe Spaces*, 38.

181. Catanese, *The Problem of the Color[blind]*, 12; Pao, *No Safe Spaces*, 4.

182. Wilkins, "Actors' Performances Reveal Fraught Politics of Black Bodies on Stage."

183. For seminal theoretical examinations of racial double consciousness see Fanon, *Black Skins, White Masks*; Du Bois, *The Souls of Black Folk*.

184. Jonathan Gil Harris provides a succinct survey of the ways various scholars have interpreted the opposing characteristics of Cleopatra and Antony as racialized and gendered. Harris, "Narcissus in Thy Face: Roman Desire and the Difference It Fakes," 408–25.

185. Shakespeare, *The Arden Edition of the Works of William Shakespeare: Antony and Cleopatra*, 137.

186. Pao, *No Safe Spaces*, 79.

187. Pao, *No Safe Spaces*, 80.

188. Tracy, "Director's Note."

189. Barach, "*A Streetcar Named Desire* Spellbinds, Chills, at African American Shakespeare."

190. Janiak, "African American Shakespeare's Lusty, Furious *Streetcar* Belongs to All of Us."

191. Williams, *A Streetcar Named Desire*, 36.

192. Gates Jr., "Did Black People Own Slaves?"

193. Golden Thread Productions, "About Golden Thread Productions."

194. "Duke Ellington's Spirit Electrifies *Isfahana Blues*."

195. Cachapero, "TCG Awards Over $900,000 for Audience (R)Evolution Cohort Grants."

196. California Shakespeare Theater, "2018 990 Tax Form," Guidestar profile.

197. Afro Solo Theatre Company, "African American Theatre for Independence Collaboration (AATAIN)."

198. African American Shakespeare Company, "2019 Financials," Guidestar profile.

Chapter 4
1. Corson, "Atlanta's Population in Black and White"; United States Census Bureau, "Quick Facts: Atlanta City, Georgia."

2. Hornsby, *Black Power in Dixie*.

3. For a critique of the city's neoliberal politics, see Rutheiser, *Imagineering Atlanta*, 288.

4. Dingle, "Maynard Jackson," 32.

5. Dingle, "Maynard Jackson," 32.

6. Scott, "Yes, Atlanta Is the Black Mecca," 50.

7. Simmons Henson, telephone interview with author, July 17, 2018.

8. Cain and Cleage, "Hotlanta! An Inside Look," 78.

9. Abrams is a graduate of Spelman, one member of the Atlanta University Center Consortium of historically black colleges that have helped to build the black power base of the city. For more on Atlanta's historically black colleges and universities, see Brooks and Starks, *Historically Black Colleges and Universities*. For more on Stacey Abrams, see Smith, "Why Stacey Abrams Is the Future for Democrats."

10. Jackson and Karimah, *Black Comedy*, 372; Jones, "Thomas W. Jones, founding member of Jomandi Theater."

11. Brooks and Starks, *Historically Black Colleges and Universities*.

12. Jones II, telephone interview, September 5, 2018.

13. Molette and Molette, "About the Authors."

14. Molette and Molette, *Black Theatre*, iv.

15. Molette and Molette, "About the Authors."

16. Jones II, telephone interview.

17. Forsgren, *In Search of Our Warrior Mothers*; Sanchez, *I'm Black When I'm Singing*.

18. Jackson and Karimah, *Black Comedy*, 372.

19. Jones II, *Art Works* podcast.

20. Marsha Jackson, quoted in "Black Theater Stages a Comeback," 58.

21. Jones II, telephone interview.

22. Jones II, telephone interview.

23. Jones II, "Thomas W. Jones, founding member of Jomandi Theater."

24. Jones II, telephone interview.

25. Leon with Hassan, *Take You Wherever You Go*, 24.

26. Leon, *Take You Wherever You Go*, 24.

27. Jones II, *The Wizard of Hip*, in Jackson and Karimah, *Black Comedy*, 374.

28. Hulbert, "Tom Jones Stands Alone in 'Hip,'" F4.

29. Hulbert, "Dizzying Array of Dramatics," 35.

30. Hulbert, "Dizzying Array of Dramatics," 35.

31. Bruckner, "A Solo Turn That Aims at Women," 60.

32. Jackson, "*The Wizard of Hip*."

33. Peterson and Bennett. *Women Playwrights of Diversity*, 179.

34. Hulbert, "Lively Performances Make Jomandi's *Sisters*," 3E.

35. Rich, "Review/Theater; Milner's Checkmates."

36. Gussow, "Two Disparate Women Who Find a Sisterly Tie," C19.

37. Jackson, *Sisters*, 145.

38. Hulbert, "Black Playwrights Listening to the Past," N4.

39. Cain and Cleage, "Hotlanta! An Inside Look," 78.

40. Hulbert, "Atlanta's Olympic Moment," 51.

41. Hulbert, "Atlanta's Olympic Moment," 51.

42. Jones II, telephone interview.

43. Jones II, telephone interview.

44. Jones II, telephone interview.

45. Jones II, telephone interview.

46. Mason Jr., *African American Entertainment in Atlanta.*

47. Jones II, *Art Works* podcast.

48. Holman, "Theatre in the Square Racks up Suzies."

49. Peterson and Bennett, *Women Playwrights of Diversity*, 179; Johnson, "Jomandi Productions' *Queen of the Blues* Comes to Town," A8.

50. Sanchez, *I'm Black When I'm Singing*, 12.

51. Jones II, telephone interview.

52. Jones II, telephone interview.

53. Jones II, telephone interview.

54. Jones II, telephone interview.

55. Jones II, telephone interview.

56. Simmons Henson, telephone interview.

57. King Jr., ed., *The National Black Drama Anthology*, 102.

58. Jones II, telephone interview.

59. Hulbert, "Jomandi's Jam," N1.

60. Hulbert, "Jomandi's Jam," N1.

61. Mayo and Holt, *Stages of Struggle and Celebration*, 247–49.

62. The last 990 tax form filed on behalf of Jomandi Productions was for the fiscal year 2000, which was not filed until 2002. No subsequent 990 forms were filed on behalf of the company, whose nonprofit status was subsequently "automatically revoked by the IRS for failure to file a Form 990, 990-EZ, 990-N, or 990-PF for 3 consecutive years." Jomandi Productions Inc, Guidestar profile.

63. Brock, "Jomandi: No Money to Fund Season," D1–D2.

64. King Jr., *The Impact of Race.*

65. Helicon Collaborative, *Not Just Money,* full report, 5.

66. Jude, telephone interview with author, September 12, 2018.

67. Leon, *Take You Wherever You Go*, 112.

68. Erkut and Ceder, "Women's Leadership in Resident Theatres, 2013–2018."

69. Leon, *Take You Wherever You Go*, 102.

70. Leon, *Take You Wherever You Go*, 117.

71. Leon, *Take You Wherever You Go*, 120.

72. Hulbert, "Jomandi's Jam," N1.

73. Kenny Leon's True Colors Theatre Company, "About Jane Bishop."

74. Leon, *Take You Wherever You Go*, 158.

75. Leon, *Take You Wherever You Go*, 160.

76. Brantley, "Theater Review: A Breakthrough 50's Drama Revived."

77. Lee, "Deferred Dreams That Resonate across Decades."

78. Healy, "Broadway *Raisin* Recoups."

79. Brantley, "In the Rush to Progress"; Brock, "Kenny Leon Directs His Many Energies," K1, K5.

80. Emerson, "Kenny Leon Stepping Away."

81. Kenny Leon's True Colors Theatre Company, "Education Programs."

82. Kenny Leon's True Colors Theatre Company, "Education Programs."

83. Clement, "10th Annual August Wilson Monologue."

84. Clement, "10th Annual August Wilson Monologue."

85. Brett, "Watch Samuel L. Jackson's Powerful Monologue at True Colors Gala."

86. Stephens-Albright, email correspondence with author, April 5, 2019.

87. Brock, "Sticky Issues Spoil the Soap Opera," H10.

88. Isherwood, "So Many Secrets, Soon to See the Light."

89. Brock, "Sticky Issues Spoil the Soap Opera," H10.

90. Als, "How *Stick Fly* Panders to Black Theatre-Goers."

91. Isherwood, "So Many Secrets."

92. Lydia Diamond, quoted in Ganz and Hetrick, "*Stick Fly* Announces Closing Date on Broadway."

93. Bell and Jackson II, *Interpreting Tyler Perry*.

94. Smith, "Review: True Colors' Smart People."

95. Osborne, "Razor Sharp Dialogue Makes Smart People Terrific," D2.

96. Osborne, "Razor Sharp Dialogue Makes Smart People Terrific," D2.

97. Hernandez, "Photo Call: Guy-Directed *for colored girls*."

98. Smith, "A Boom in Filming."

99. Smith, "A Boom in Filming."

100. Badger, Miller, Pearce, and Quealy, "Extensive Data Shows Punishing Reach of Racism."

101. Jude, telephone interview.

102. Jude, telephone interview.

103. Kenny Leon's True Colors Theatre Company, "Coping in Corporate Cultures."

104. Kenny Leon's True Colors Theatre Company, "Communication Is Key."

105. Stephens-Albright, email correspondence.

106. Jude, telephone interview.

107. Jude, telephone interview.

108. Leon, curtain speech.

109. Delsarte, *New Hope Visions* artwork label.

110. Lake, "Fixer, Charmer, Builder, Mayor."

111. Leon, curtain speech.

112. Kenny Leon's True Colors Theatre Company, "Jamil Jude to Succeed Kenny Leon."

113. HowlRound Theater Commons, "Standing in Our Grandfathers' Shoes."

114. HowlRound Theater Commons, "Standing in Our Grandfathers' Shoes."

115. Stephens-Albright, email correspondence.

116. These figures are based on the listed African American theaters' gross receipts reported on Guidestar nonprofit profiles as of December 1, 2018.

117. Stephens-Albright, email correspondence.

118. Simmons Henson, telephone interview.

119. LaTeshia Ellerson, telephone interview with author, September 4, 2018.

120. Ellerson, telephone interview.

121. Ellerson, telephone interview.

122. Ellerson, telephone interview.

123. National Black Theatre Festival, "The National Black Theatre Festival History."

124. Toni Simmons Henson, telephone interview.

125. Leon, *Take You Wherever You Go*, 119.

126. Atlanta Black Theatre Festival, "What Is the Atlanta Black Theatre Festival?"

127. Simmons Henson, telephone interview.

128. Simmons Henson, telephone interview.

129. Simmons Henson, telephone interview.

130. Simmons Henson, telephone interview.

131. Porter Sanford Arts Center, "Our History: Porter Sanford III."

132. Simmons Henson, telephone interview.

133. Simmons Henson, telephone interview.

134. Simmons Henson, telephone interview.

135. Simmons Henson, telephone interview.

136. Simmons Henson, telephone interview.

137. Simmons Henson, telephone interview.

138. Robinson, telephone interview with author, June 9, 2020.

139. Robinson, telephone interview.

140. Robinson, telephone interview.

141. Robinson, telephone interview.

142. Robinson, telephone interview.

143. Robinson, telephone interview.

144. Robinson, telephone interview.

145. Robinson, telephone interview.

Chapter 5

1. "We See You, White American Theater"; Marie Cisco, "Theatres Not Speaking Out."

2. Dinkins Jr. and Heartley, "We Don't Want Your Statements American Theatre."

3. Barnett, "Karamu Speaks to Unrest."

4. Karamu House, *Freedom on Juneteenth*.

5. Jude, "What We Are Fighting For," in "Find Joy in the Destruction of the Lie."

6. Wellek, "Hippolyte Taine's Literary Theory and Criticism," 1–18.

7. Madison, *Black Performance Theory*, ix.

8. Young and Zabriskie, *Black Theater Is Black Life*.

9. Karamu House, *Freedom on Juneteenth*.

Abelman, Bob. "When Northeast Ohio's Theaters Collaborate Audiences Benefit." *Canvas*, August 16, 2017. http://canvascle.com/strange-bedfellows/.

Abookire, Noerena, and Jennifer Scott McNair. "Children's Theatre Activities at Karamu House, 1915–1975." In *Spotlight on the Child: Studies in the History of American Children's Theatre*, edited by Roger L. Bedard and C. John Tolch, 69–84. Westport, CT: Greenwood Press, 1989.

Adenekan, Shola. "Don Evans." *Guardian*, January 15, 2014. https://www.theguardian.com/news/2004/jan/16/guardianobituaries.artsobituaries.

African-American Shakespeare Company. "Mission." Accessed May 5, 2016. http://www.african-americanshakes.org/about/.

———. "2019 Financials." Guidestar profile. https://www.guidestar.org/profile/94–3192980#financials.

"African-American Shakespeare Company Closes Season with TWELFTH NIGHT." *Broadway World San Francisco*, March 3, 2011. https://www.broadwayworld.com/san-francisco/article/AfricanAmerican-Shakespeare-Company-Closes-Season-with-TWELFTH-NIGHT-20110303-page2.

Afro Solo Theatre Company. "African American Theatre for Independence Collaboration (AATAIN)." Accessed July 3, 2019. http://events.afrosolo.org.

Aidoo, Ama Ata. *"The Dilemma of a Ghost" and "Anowa."* Harlow: Longman, 1995.

———. *The Girl Who Can and Other Stories*. Oxford: Heinemann, 2000.

"Air Guitar: A Musical Fantasy." *San Francisco Examiner*, July 11, 1985.

Alakam, Japhet. "Theatre Is Dead in Nigeria—Prof Bayo Oduneye," *Vanguard*, March 22, 2015. https://www.vanguardngr.com/2015/03/theatre-is-dead-in-nigeria-prof-bayo-oduneye/.

Alexander, Robert. *I Ain't Yo Uncle: The New Jack Revisionist Uncle Tom's Cabin*. Woodstock, IL: Dramatic Publishing, 1996.

———. *Servant of the People: The Rise and Fall of Huey Newton and the Black Panther Party*. New York: Playscripts, 2005. https://www.playscripts.com/play/243.

Alker, Gwendolyn, et al. "A Collective Call against Critical Bias." HowlRound, June 16, 2017. http://howlround.com/a-collective-call-against-critical-bias.

All American Speakers. "Danny Glover and Felix Justice." Accessed May 4, 2019. https://www.allamericanspeakers.com/celebritytalentbios/Danny+Glover+%26+Felix+Justice/402739.

Allen, Robert. *The Port Chicago Mutiny: The Story of the Largest Mass Mutiny Trial in U.S. Naval History*. Berkeley, CA: Heyday Books, 1993.

Als, Hilton. "How *Stick Fly* Panders to Black Theatre-Goers." *New Yorker*, January 10, 2012. https://www.newyorker.com/culture/culture-desk/how-stick-fly-panders-to-black-theatre-goers.

American Conservatory Theatre Foundation, aka A.C.T., "2016 Form 990." Guidestar profile. https://pdf.guidestar.org/PDF_Images/2017/946/135/2017 –946135772–0faa28f4–9.pdf.

Anti-Eviction Mapping Project. "About A(E)MP." Accessed June 1, 2016. https:// www.antievictionmap.com/about/.

———. "Ellis Act Evictions." Accessed June 1, 2016. http://www.antieviction mappingproject.net/ellis.html.

Appiah, Kwame Anthony. *Cosmopolitanism: Ethics in a World of Strangers.* New York: W. W. Norton, 2007.

Aristotle, *Poetics.* Translated by S. H. Butcher. In *Dramatic Theory and Criticism: From Greeks to Growtowski,* edited by Bernard F. Dukore, 32–33. Fort Worth: Harcourt Brace Jovanovich College Publishers, 1974.

Armstrong, David. "Reed Wins a MacArthur Grant." *San Francisco Examiner,* June 2, 1998.

Arons, Wendy. "*Seven Guitars* at the Pittsburgh Playwrights Theatre." *Pittsburgh Tattler,* August 25, 2016. https://wendyarons.wordpress.com/2016/08/25 /seven-guitars-at-the-pittsburgh-playwrights-theatre/.

Atlanta Black Theatre Festival. "What Is the Atlanta Black Theatre Festival?" Accessed July 6, 2018. https://atlantabtf.org/black-theatre.

August Wilson African American Cultural Center. "Anna Deavere Smith." April 27, 2018. https://aacc-awc.org/event/anna-deveare-smith/.

———. "Harlem to Hollywood." December 8, 2018. https://aacc-awc.org/event /harlem-to-hollywood/.

"August Wilson Center Adds Feather in Cap of Cultural District." *New Pittsburgh Courier,* September 24, 2009. https://newpittsburghcourieronline.com /2009/09/24/august-wilson-center-adds-feather-to-cap-of-cultural-district/.

August Wilson Center Papers. Curtis Theatre Collection, Archives and Special Collections, University of Pittsburgh Library System, Pittsburgh, PA.

August Wilson House. "Transformation." Accessed May 5, 2019. http:// augustwilsonhouse.org.

Badger, Emily, Claire Cain Miller, Adam Pearce, and Kevin Quealy. "Extensive Data Shows Punishing Reach of Racism for Black Boys." *New York Times,* March 19, 2018. https://www.nytimes.com/interactive/2018/03/19/upshot /race-class-white-and-black-men.html.

Badoe, Yaba, Amina Mama, Abena P. A. Busia, and Ama A. Aidoo. *The Art of Ama Ata Aidoo.* Fadoe Films, 2014.

"Bank One Aims for Minority Business." *Newark Advocate,* December 1, 1993.

Baron, Jennifer. "Etta Cox Stars in *King Hedley,* Presented at Historic August Wilson House." *Next Pittsburgh,* May 14, 2018. https://www.nextpittsburgh .com/events/pittsburgh-playwrights-theatre-company-presents-king-hedley-ii -historic-august-wilson-house/.

Barnes, Michael. "Why We Protest the 'Google' Buses." SF Gate, February 17, 2014. http://www.sfgate.com/opinion/openforum/article/Why-we-protest-the -Google-buses-5242948.php.

Barnett, David C. "Karamu Speaks to Unrest Sparked by George Floyd's Killing." Ideastream, June 17, 2020. https://www.ideastream.org/news/karamu-speaks -to-unrest-sparked-by-george-floyds-killing.

Barach, Gilad. "*A Streetcar Named Desire* Spellbinds, Chills, at African American Shakespeare. S.F." *Theatrius*, March 8, 2018. https://www.theatrius.com /2018/03/08/a-streetcar-named-desire-spellbinds-chills-at-african-american -shakespeare-s-f/.

"Beat Checks: Black Repertory Group." *San Francisco Examiner*, October 23, 1990.

Beete, Paulette. "Art Talk with Sherri Young of the African-American Shakespeare Company." National Endowment for the Arts, February 25, 2015. https://www .arts.gov/art-works/2015/art-talk-sherri-young-african-american-shakespeare -company.

Belko, Mark. "Dollar Bank Sells August Wilson Center to Three Pittsburgh Foundations." *Pittsburgh Post-Gazette*, November 5, 2014. http://www.post-gazette .com/business/2014/11/05/Dollar-Bank-sells-August-Wilson-Center-to-three -Pittsburgh-foundations/stories/201411050250.

Bell, Jamel Santa Cruze, and Ronald L. Jackson II, eds. *Interpreting Tyler Perry: Perspectives on Race, Class, Gender, and Sexuality.* New York: Routledge, 2014.

Bergan, Ronald. "Ron O'Neal: Actor Whose Career Was Limited by the Success of His Blaxploitation Image." *Guardian*, February 18, 2004. https://www .theguardian.com/news/2004/feb/18/guardianobituaries.film.

Berkowitz, Gerlad M. *New Broadways: Theatre across America: Approaching a New Millennium.* New York: Applause, 1997.

Bernard, Emily, ed. *Remember Me to Harlem: The Letters of Langston Hughes and Carl Van Vechten, 1925–1937.* New York: Vintage, 2002.

Berson, Misha. "*Boogie Woogie Landscapes*: Dancing through Drama." *San Francisco Examiner and Chronicle*, January 8, 1984.

"Best Theatre Honcho: Terrence Spivey, Karamu Performing Arts Theatre." Best of Cleveland 2005. Cleveland Scene. https://www.clevescene.com/cleveland /best-theater-honcho/BestOf?oid=1536048.

"Biography of Benno Frank." Benno Frank Papers. Western Reserve Historical Society. Cleveland, Ohio. Accessed May 27, 2017. http://ead.ohiolink.edu/xtf -ead/view?docId=ead/OCLWHi0285.xml;chunk.id=bioghist_1;brand=default.

"Black Arts West: The Black Arts Movement and Its Influences." *Blackbird Press News and Review*, January 25, 2014. https://blackbirdpressnews.blogspot .com/2014/01/black-arts-west-black-arts-movement-and.html.

Black Repertory Group. "About Us." Accessed May 3, 2019. http://www .blackrepertorygroup.com/about-us.html.

———. "Courage under Fire: The Story of Elroy." August 25, 2018. http://www .blackrepertorygroup.com/courage-under-fire---the-story-of-elroy.html.

———. Event calendar. Accessed May 3, 2019. http://www.blackrepertorygroup .com/event-calendar.html.

———. Facebook page, listings from 2017–19. https://www.facebook.com /BRGNation/.

———. "Our Story." Accessed May 3, 2019. http://www.blackrepertorygroup .com/our-story.html.

———. "2014 Form 990." Guidestar profile. https://pdf.guidestar.org/PDF _Images/2014/237/169/2014–237169863–0ad51cc5-Z.pdf

———. "The 2017 Nora B. Vaughn Essay Writing Contest. In Honor of Humanitarian Catherine Prater." Press release, May 12, 2017. https://www.prlog .org/12639481-the-2017-nora-vaughn-essay-writing-contest-in-honor-of -humanitarian-catherine-prater.html.

"Black Repertory Marks 20th Year." *San Francisco Examiner*, June 14, 1985.

"Black Theater Stages a Comeback." Ebony, November 1986.

Blake, Sharon. "Pitt's Kuntu Repertory Theatre Kicks Off 2007 Season with *Good Black Don't Crack* Oct. 18–Nov. 3." University of Pittsburgh News Services, October 11, 2007. http://www.news.pitt.edu/news/pitts-kuntu -repertory-theatre-kicks-2007-season-rob-pennys-good-black-dont-crack-oct -18-through.

Blood, Melanie N. "Theatre in Settlement Houses: Hull-House Players, Neighborhood Playhouse, and Karamu Theatre." *Theatre History Studies* 16 (June 1996): 45–69.

Bloom, Elizabeth. "The Rise and Fall of the August Wilson Center." *Pittsburgh Post-Gazette*, February 9, 2014. http://www.post-gazette.com/ae/theater-dance /2014/02/09/Rise-and-fall-of-August-Wilson-Center/stories/201402090045.

Bloom, Joshua, and Waldo E. Martin Jr. *Black against Empire: The History and Politics of the Black Panther Party*. Oakland: University of California Press, 2013.

Bob Johnson Papers, 1949–2003. Curtis Theatre Collection, Archives and Special Collections, University of Pittsburgh Library System, Pittsburgh, PA.

Bodnar, John, Roger Simon, and Michael P. Weber. *Lives of Their Own: Blacks, Italians, and Poles in Pittsburgh, 1900–1960*. Urbana: University of Illinois Press, 1982.

Bolton Elementary School. "Community Partners." Accessed May 15, 2018. https://www.clevelandmetroschools.org/domain/3055.

Bradshaw, Jacqueline. "The Sutphen School of Music." Cleveland Historical, Center for Public History and Digital Humanities. Accessed May 15, 2018. https://clevelandhistorical.org/index.php/files/show/176.

Brantley, Ben. "In the Rush to Progress, the Past Is Never Too Far Behind." *New York Times*, May 9, 2007. https://www.nytimes.com/2007/05/09/theater /reviews/09radio.html.

———. "Theater Review: A Breakthrough 50's Drama Revived in a Suspenseful Mood." *New York Times*, April 27, 2004. https://www.nytimes.com /2004/04/27/theater/theater-review-a-breakthrough-50-s-drama-revived-in -a-suspenseful-mood.html.

Breckenridge, Tom. "Opportunity Corridor's Latest Alignment Would Uproot More Than 90 Families, a Dozen Businesses." *Cleveland Plain Dealer*, July 17, 2011. http://blog.cleveland.com/metro/2011/07/post_498.html.

Brett, Jennifer. "Watch Samuel L. Jackson's Powerful Monologue at True Colors Gala." *Atlanta Journal-Constitution*, May 22, 2017. https://www.ajc .com/blog/buzz/watch-samuel-jackson-powerful-monologue-true-colors-gala /u9XLPSuWnBrPcKyRI0Gp0O/.

Bridge, Gary, and Sophie Watson. "Reflections on Publics and Cultures." In *The New Blackwell Companion to the City*, edited by Gary Bridge and Sophie Watson, 379–89. Malden, MA: Blackwell, 2011.

Brock, Wendell. "Jomandi: No Money to Fund Season." *Atlanta Journal-Constitution*, August 30, 2003.

———. "Kenny Leon Directs His Many Energies." *Atlanta Journal-Constitution*, December 12, 2004.

———. "Sticky Issues Spoil the Soap Opera." *Atlanta Journal-Constitution*, May 25, 2007.

Brooks, F. Erik, and Glenn L. Starks. *Historically Black Colleges and Universities: An Encyclopedia*. Santa Barbara, CA: ABC-CLIO, 2011.

Brown, Tony. "Haunting *Ruined* at Karamu Shows Effects of War on Traumatized Women." Cleveland.com, May 13, 2011. https://www.cleveland.com/onstage/index.ssf/2011/05/haunting_ruined_at_karamu_show.html.

———. "Theater Review: Karamu and Dobama Collaborate on a Gorgeous *Caroline, or Change*." Cleveland.com, September 24, 2008. https://www.cleveland.com/onstage/index.ssf/2008/09/theater_review_karamu_and_doba.html.

Bruckner, D. J. R. "A Solo Turn That Aims at Women." *New York Times*, October 28, 1990.

Bullins, Ed, ed. "Black Theatre Groups: A Directory." "Black Theatre," edited by Ed Bullins. Special issue, *Tulane Drama Review*, 12, no. 4 (1968): 172–75.

———. "Black Theatre." Special issue, *Tulane Drama Review* 12, no. 4 (1968).

"Buriel Clay." Woodie King Jr's New Federal Theatre. Accessed March 1, 2022. https://newfederaltheatre.com/nft-artist/buriel-clay/.

Burnett, Greg. "Actress Returns to Karamu: *Letters from Zora* Is Onstage at the Newly Renovated Jelliffe Theatre." Cleveland.com, June 15, 2018. https://www.cleveland.com/friday/index.ssf/2018/06/actress_returns_to_karamu_lett.html.

Burnham, Michael. "Theater: The Clown Prints of Autumn." *Cincinnati Magazine*, January 1978.

Byrd, Joseph. "Whitewashing Blackface Minstrelsy in American College Textbooks." *Popular Music and Society* 32, no. 1 (February 2009): 77–86.

Cachapero, Emily. "TCG Awards Over $900,000 for Audience (R)Evolution Cohort Grants." Theatre Communications Group, May 1, 2019. https://circle.tcg.org/blogs/emilya-cachapero/2019/05/01/tcg-awards-over-900000-for-audience-revolution-coh.

Cagle, Susie. "Oakland Wants You to Stop Calling It 'The New Brooklyn:' Can the Birthplace of the Black Panthers Gentrify without Displacement." Next City. December 15, 2014. https://nextcity.org/features/view/oakland-gentrification-libby-schaaf-tech-industry-inequality-foreclosures.

Cain, Joy Duckett, and Pearl Cleage. "Hotlanta! An Inside Look at This Olympic City and the Sisters Who Make It Tick." *Essence*, June 1996.

Caldararo, Niccolo. *An Ethnography of the Goodman Building: The Longest Rent Strike*. Cham, Switzerland: Palgrave Macmillan, 2019.

California Shakespeare Theater. "2018 990 Tax Form." Guidestar profile. https://www.guidestar.org/profile/51-0169452.

Calkins, Hugh, Rowena Woodham Jelliffe, and Russell W. Jelliffe. *Correspondence: With Marian Anderson: 1940–1968*. Marian Anderson Papers. Folder 2974. University of Pennsylvania Special Collections, Philadelphia, PA.

Campbell, Joseph. *The Hero with a Thousand Faces*. New York: Pantheon Books, 1949.

Cardwell, Jewell. "Black Center Nurtures Solid Cultural Climate." *Dayton Daily News*, January 3, 1981.

Carpenter, Mackenzie. "Curtain Falls on Pittsburgh's Kuntu Repertory Theatre." *Pittsburgh Post-Gazette,* April 24, 2013. http://www.post-gazette.com/ae/theater-dance/2013/04/24/Curtain-falls-on-Pittsburgh-s-Kuntu-Repertory-Theatre/stories/201304240163.

Carter, Alice. "Review: Strong 'Piano Lesson' Ignites August Wilson Center." *Trib Live,* November 17, 2015. http://triblive.com/aande/theaterarts/9451389-74/piano-wilson-berniece.

Case, Sue Ellen. *Feminism and Theatre*. New York: Methuen, 1988.

Catanese, Brandi Wilkins. *The Problem of the Color[blind]: Racial Transgression and Black Performance*. Ann Arbor: University of Michigan Press, 2011.

"Celebrating Theatre Icon, Bayo Oduneye." *New Telegraph*, August 23, 2017. https://newtelegraphonline.com/2017/08/celebrating-theatre-icon-bayo-oduneye/.

Chancellor, Carl. "Karamu Is Too Special to Let It Die." *Akron Beacon Journal*, August 16, 1994.

"Channels Update." *Akron Beacon Journal*, October 25, 1987, D2.

Chansky, Dorothy. *Composing Ourselves: The Little Theatre Movement and the American Audience*. Carbondale: Southern Illinois University Press, 2005.

Chastang, Harrison. "If You Thought Yoshi's Situation Was Bad . . . Act to Save the Lorraine Hansberry Theatre." *Freedom Archives*, June 25, 2007. http://freedomarchives.org/pipermail/news_freedomarchives.org/2007-June/002179.html.

Chatman, Angela D. "If Bricks Could Speak." *Plain Dealer*, October 28, 1989.

Chestnutt, Charles W. "The Negro in Cleveland." In *Charles W. Chesnutt: Essays and Speeches,* edited by Joseph R. McElrath, Jr., Robert C. Leitz III, and Jesse S. Crisler, 535. Stanford, CA: Stanford University Press, 1999.

Christy, Denise R. "The Contributions of the Gilpin Players of Karamu Theatre to Cleveland's Interracial Unit of the Federal Theatre Project." Master's thesis, Kent State University, 1976.

Cisco, Marie. "Theatres Not Speaking Out." Accessed June 15, 2020. https://docs.google.com/spreadsheets/d/1vbTjlhaBY-MefEdh3N9sJqtT5ie-6zfHJ90FOUhmTNs/edit?fbclid=IwAR0NZS-VFrCT-y8UQFIwV88Nm253IcZbFku-0ADFASRw9kx8rY8y-zyuTRw#gid=0.

Clark, Edwina Blackwell. "Antioch College Opened Its Arms to Coretta Scott." *Dayton Daily News*, January 15, 1994.

Clark, Terry Nichols. *The City as an Entertainment Machine*. New York: Lexington, 2011.

Clearfield, Jason. *"King Hedley II." Pittsburgh in the Round,* May 15, 2018. http://www.pghintheround.com/king-hedley-ii/.

Cleveland Foundation. Annual Report. 1977. https://issuu.com/clevelandfoundation/docs/cleveland-foundation-1977-annual-re.

———. Grant Search, Karamu House 1988–2013. https://www.clevelandfoundation100.org/foundation-of-change/impact/grant-search/?year_start=1988&year_end=2013&low_amount=0&high_amount=10000000&program_area=&organization=Karamu&sort_order=ASC&display_sort=Year&search=Search.

"Cleveland Call & Post." *Encyclopedia of Cleveland History*. Case Western Reserve University. Accessed February 5, 2018. https://case.edu/ech/articles /c/cleveland-call-post.

"Cleveland Critics Circle 2016 Theater Awards." Cleveland Theater Reviews, December 19, 2016. http://clevelandtheaterreviews.blogspot.com/2016/12 /cleveland-critics-circle-2016-theater.html.

"Cleveland Gazette." *Encyclopedia of Cleveland History*. Case Western Reserve University. Accessed February 5, 2018. https://case.edu/ech/articles/c/cleveland -gazette.

Cleveland Playhouse. GuideStar profile. Accessed June 4, 2019. https://www .guidestar.org/profile/7414349.

Cleveland Press Repository. Michael Schwartz Library Special Collections, Cleveland State University, Cleveland, OH.

"Cleveland to Host Meeting of African Culture Society." *Jet*, May 28, 1964.

Clement, Olivia. "10th Annual August Wilson Monologue Competition Held May 7." *Playbill*, April 3, 2018. http://www.playbill.com/article/10th-annual -august-wilson-monologue-competition-will-be-held-may-7.

Cole, Mark. "I, Too Am America: Karamu House and African American Artists in Cleveland." In *Transformations in Cleveland Art: 1796–1946*, edited by William Robinson, 146–61. Cleveland: Ohio University Press, 1996.

Collins, Lisa Gail. "Activists Who Yearn for Art That Transforms: Parallels in the Black Arts Movement and Feminist Art Movements in the United States." *Signs: Journal of Women in Culture and Society* 31, no. 3 (2006): 717–52.

"The Colored Museum." *San Francisco Examiner*, June 10, 1988.

"Community Stage." *San Francisco Examiner*, January 18, 1976.

"A Conference on Black Theater." *San Francisco Examiner*, October 15, 1974.

Connor, Lynne. *Pittsburgh in Stages: Two Hundred Years of Theater*. Pittsburgh: University of Pittsburgh Press, 2007.

Corson, Pete. "Atlanta's Population in Black and White." *Atlanta Journal-Constitution*, July 24, 2014. https://www.myajc.com/news/local/atlanta -population-black-and-white/7VKqmI0GM4Ln7GV50atvKL/.

Croft, Clare. *Dancers as Diplomats: American Choreography in Cultural Exchange*. Oxford: Oxford University Press, 2015.

Crump, Sarah. "Karamu House Inspires Executive Director Gregory Ashe: My Cleveland." Cleveland.com, August 2, 2010. https://www.cleveland.com /mycleveland/index.ssf/2010/08/clevelands_karamu_house_inspir.html.

Curtis, Kim. "Reenactment Will Mark One Year Anniversary of Execution." *Santa Maria Times*, November 29, 2006.

Dass, Angélica. "Humanae/I Am August." Artist's website. Accessed May 27, 2017. http://www.angelicadass.com/events/2015/9/25/humanaei-am-august -august-wilson-center-awc-pittsburgh-pa.

Davenport, Lisa E. *Jazz Diplomacy: Promoting America in the Cold War Era*. Jackson: University of Mississippi, 2009.

Davis, Russell H. *Black Americans in Cleveland: From George Peake to Carl B. Stokes*. Cleveland: Associated Publishers, 1972.

Davis, Ossie. *Purlie Victorius: A Comedy in Three Acts*. New York: Samuel French, 1961.

Delaney, Paul. "Black Culture Seeks Strength at the Community Level." *New York Times,* February 22, 1975. https://www.nytimes.com/1975/02/22/archives /black-culture-seeks-strength-at-the-community-level.html.

Delsarte, Louis. *New Hope Visions,* artwork label. Fulton County Southwest Arts Center, 2008.

Dent, Thomas, Richard Schechner, and Gilbert Moses, eds. *The Free Southern Theater by the Free Southern Theater: A Documentary of the South's Radical Black Theater, with Journals, Letters, Poetry, Essays and a Play Written by Those Who Built It.* Indianapolis: Bobbs-Merrill, 1969.

Dewberry, Jonathan. "The African Grove Theatre and Company." "Black Theatre," edited by Andrzej Ceynowa and James V. Hatch. Special issue, *Black American Literature Forum* 16. no. 4 (Winter 1982): 128–31.

Diamond, Dan. "How the Cleveland Clinic Grows Healthy While Its Neighbors Stay Sick." Politico, July 17, 2017. https://www.politico.com/interactives/2017 /obamacare-cleveland-clinic-non-profit-hospital-taxes/.

Dingle, Derek. "Maynard Jackson: Creating a Bully Pulpit for Black Business." *Black Enterprise,* May 10, 2005.

Dinkins, Calvin, Jr., and Al Heartley. "We Don't Want Your Statements American Theatre, or, the Solidarity We Actually Needed." Howlround Theatre Commons, June 11, 2020. https://howlround.com/we-dont-want-your-statements -american-theatre.

Dolinar, Brian. *The Black Cultural Front: Black Writers and Artists of the Depression Generation.* Jackson: University Press of Mississippi, 2012.

Dollar Bank. "Dollar Bank Sells August Wilson Center Building to Foundation." November 4, 2014. https://www.dollar.bank/Company/About/In-The-News /Dollar-Bank-Sells-August-Wilson-Center-Building-to.aspx.

Du Bois, W. E. B. *The Souls of Black Folk.* Edited by Brent Hayes Edward. Oxford: Oxford University Press, 2007.

"Duke Ellington's Spirit Electrifies *Isfahana Blues.*" *SF Examiner,* April 30, 2015. https://www.sfexaminer.com/entertainment/duke-ellingtons-spirit-electrifies -isfahan-blues/.

Eberson, Sharon. "Cultural Trust Vice President Tapped to Head August Wilson Center." *Pittsburgh Post-Gazette,* July 20, 2017. http://www.post-gazette.com /ae/theater-dance/2017/07/20/August-Wilson-Center-Pittsburgh-Janis-Burley -Wilson-new-CEO-President/stories/201707190146.

———. "Weekend Hotlist." *Pittsburgh Post-Gazette,* May 27, 2009. https:// www.post-gazette.com/ae/music/2009/05/28/Weekend-Hotlist-100/stories /200905280384+&cd=1&hl=en&ct=clnk&gl=us&client=safari.

Eisenstein, Linda. "Lost Play a Delight to See and Hear." *Plain Dealer,* May 14, 1996.

Emerson, Bo. "Kenny Leon Stepping Away from True Colors Theatre Company." *Atlanta Journal-Constitution,* September 24, 2018. https://www.ajc .com/entertainment/arts--theater/kenny-leon-stepping-away-from-true-colors -theatre-company/u4ZYBSoF6QbMUcjYPrCiSK/.

Ensemble Theatre. "The Ensemble Theatre Presents *One Monkey Don't Stop No Show,*" June 19, 2007. http://www.globenewswire.com/news-release/2007/06 /19/361484/121600/en/The-Ensemble-Theatre-Presents-One-Monkey-Don -t-Stop-No-Show.html.

Erdley, Debra, and Adam Smeltz. "Pittsburgh's August Wilson Center: Classic Mistake." *Trib Live*, January 26, 2014. http://triblive.com/news/allegheny /5463483–74/center-million-august.

Erkut, Sumru, and Ineke Ceder. "Women's Leadership in Resident Theatres, 2013–2018." Accessed June 3, 2020. Wellesley Centers for Women. https:// www.wcwonline.org/Active-Projects/womens-leadership-in-resident-theaters.

Evett, Marianne. "Ensemble Sizzles in Play." *Plain Dealer*, October 20, 1989.

———. "Hopeful Message Weighted Down." *Plain Dealer*, October 27, 1994.

———. "Karamu Cast Sparkles in Wilson Play." *Plain Dealer*, October 12, 1995.

———. "A Karamu Creation." *Plain Dealer*, February 3, 1985.

———. "Singing, Dancing the Blues and Mighty Proud of It." *Plain Dealer*, February 1, 1987.

———. "2 Plays End Karamu Season." *Plain Dealer*, June 14, 1991.

———. "Vinnette Carroll Back with Black Nativity: A Living Legend with a Legendary Show." *Plain Dealer*, November 28, 1991.

———. "A Winner from Any Point in Time." *Plain Dealer*, June 6, 1992.

———. "Women Cast into Fires Documentary Play on Crown Heights Incident." *Plain Dealer*, October 26, 1995.

Fanon, Frantz. *Black Skins, White Masks*. New York: Grove Press, 1967.

Fearnley, Andrew. "Writing the History of Karamu House: Philanthropy, Welfare, and Race in Wartime Cleveland." *Ohio History* 115 (2008): 80–100.

Ferola, Anne, Jennifer Ginsberg, and Martice Sutton, "Saving the August Wilson Center." *Nonprofit Quarterly*, January 20, 2016. https://nonprofitquarterly.org /2016/01/20/saving-the-august-wilson-center/.

Fisher, Pamela. "Classics with Color Are African-American Shakespeare's Specialty." *San Francisco Examiner*, January 4, 2001.

"For Colored Girls Top 50% Ticket Mark." *Call & Post*, March 8, 1980.

Forsgren, La Donna. *In Search of Our Warrior Mothers: Women Dramatists of the Black Arts Movement*. Evanston, IL: Northwestern University Press, 2018.

Foster, Stephen. "Oh! Susanna." Notated music, 1858–1876. Stephen Foster Collection, University of Pittsburgh. Accessed May 27, 2017. https://digital.library .pitt.edu/islandora/object/pitt%3A31735061833509/viewer#page/4/mode/2up.

Fraden, Rena. *Blueprints for a Black Federal Theatre 1935–1939*. Cambridge: Cambridge University Press, 1994.

Freeze, Alix. "Report: Art Education Programs on the Decline." Association of American Educators, April 3, 2012. https://www.aaeteachers.org/index.php /blog/700-report-art-education-programs-on-the-decline.

Gallucci, Michael. "About a Boy: In Karamu's Latest Production, a Tragic Death Brings History to Life." Cleveland Scene, February 2, 2005. https://www .clevescene.com/cleveland/about-a-boy/Content?oid=1489504.

Ganz, Andrew, and Adam Hetrick. "*Stick Fly* Announces Closing Date on Broadway." *Playbill*, February 9, 2012. http://www.playbill.com/article/stick-fly -announces-closing-date-on-broadway-com-187338.

Gassner, John, and Edward Quinn. *The Reader's Encyclopedia of World Drama*. Mineola, NY: Dover, 1969.

Gates, Henry Louis, Jr. "Theatre: Why the Mule Bone Debate Goes On." *New York Times*, February 10,1991. https://www.nytimes.com/1991/02/10/theater /theater-why-the-mule-bone-debate-goes-on.html.

———. "Did Black People Own Slaves?" *Root*, March 4, 2013. https://www
.theroot.com/did-black-people-own-slaves-1790895436.

Gelt, Jessica. "Sheldon Epps to Step Down as Artistic Director of Pasadena
Playhouse." *Los Angeles Times*, January 7, 2016. http://www.latimes.com
/entertainment/arts/culture/la-et-cm-sheldon-epps-steps-down-pasadena
-playhouse-20160106-story.html.

Gibbs, James, and Bernth Lindfors. *Research on Wole Soyinka*. Trenton, NJ:
Africa World Press, 1993.

Gill, Michael. "Halleluja. Yo Da Lay Hee: Laurie Anderson Visits the Ohio Theatre Saturday February 7 and Leads This Week's Art Picks." Cleveland Scene,
February 4, 2009. https://www.clevescene.com/cleveland/hallelujah-yo-da-lay
-hee-hoo/Content?oid=1534699.

Golden Thread Productions. "About Golden Thread Productions." Accessed May
3, 2019. https://www.goldenthread.org/about/.

Gordon, Alex. "Aunt Ester, the Hill District and the Surreal World of August
Wilson's *Gem of the Ocean*." *Pittsburgh City Paper*, August 27, 2019. https://
www.pghcitypaper.com/pittsburgh/the-hill-district-of-the-1900s-comes-alive
-in-august-wilsons-gem-of-the-ocean/Content?oid=15720946.

Grabowski, John J. "Settlement Houses." *Encyclopedia of Cleveland History*.
Case Western Reserve University. Accessed January 10, 2018. http://case.edu
/ech/articles/s/settlement-houses/.

Gramza, Janet. "Karamu House's Terrence Spivey to Deliver Keynote." *Sightlines:
The Monthly Newsletter for USITT Members*, October 2014. http://sightlines
.usitt.org/archive/2014/10/SpiveyToGiveKeynote.asp.

Gumbel, Andrew. "San Francisco's Guerilla Protest at Google Buses Swells into
a Revolt." *Guardian*, January 25, 2014. http://www.theguardian.com/world
/2014/jan/25/google-bus-protest-swells-to-revolt-san-francisco.

Gussow, Mel. "Stage: At New Federal 'Who Loves the Dancer.'" *New York
Times*, March 5, 1982.

———. "Two Disparate Women Who Find a Sisterly Tie." *New York Times*, June
7, 1990.

Haber, Matt. "Oakland: Brooklyn by the Bay." *New York Times*, May 2, 2014.
http://www.nytimes.com/2014/05/04/fashion/oakland-california-brooklyn-by
-the-bay.html?_r=0.

Hamlin, Jesse. "Ntozake Shange Weaves Tapestries of Poetry, Music, Dance, in
Her Search for Love's Meaning." SF Gate, February 17, 2006. https://www
.sfgate.com/entertainment/article/Ntozake-Shange-weaves-tapestries-of-poetry
-2504282.php?utm_campaign=premiumsfgate&utm_source=sitesearch&utm
_medium=result#photo-2675653.

———. "San Francisco Art Academy Offers to Help Pay Theater to Relocate,
Lorraine Hansberry Signed Away Lease Options for Free Rent." SF Gate, June
27, 2007. https://www.sfgate.com/bayarea/article/SAN-FRANCISCO-Art
-academy-offers-to-help-pay-2554660.php.

Hampton, Wilborn. "Perils of Dalejean in *Good Black*." *New York Times*, October 31, 1988.

Hansberry, Lorraine, *A Raisin in the Sun*. New York: Modern Library Editions,
1995.

Harper, Donna Akiba Sullivan. *Not So Simple: The "Simple" Stories by Langston Hughes*. Columbia: University of Missouri Press, 1995.

Harrington, John P. "New World Drama: Fashioning Irish Theater in Lower Manhattan." *Princeton University Library Chronicle* 68, nos. 1–2 (2007): 306–26.

Harris, Jonathan Gil. "Narcissus in Thy Face: Roman Desire and the Difference It Fakes in *Antony and Cleopatra*." *Shakespeare Quarterly* 45, no. 4 (Winter 1994): 408–25.

Harrison, Paul Carter, ed. *Kuntu Drama: Plays of the African Continuum*. New York: Grove Press, 1974.

Hart, Peter. "Obituary: Robert Lee "Rob" Penny." *University Times*. University of Pittsburgh, March 20, 2003. http://www.utimes.pitt.edu/?p=1226.

Hartman, Chester. *City for Sale: The Transformation of San Francisco*. Berkeley: University of California Press, 2002.

Hatch, James V., and Ted Shine, eds. *Black Theatre USA: Plays by African Americans, The Early Period 1847–1938*. New York: Free Press, 1996.

———. *Black Theatre U.S.A.: The Recent Period 1935–Today*. New York: Free Press, 1996.

Hayes, John. "Kuntu's *Sing Black Hammer* Has Rough Edges and the Ring of Truth." *Pittsburgh Post-Gazette*, June 28, 1999.

Healy, Patrick. "Broadway *Raisin* Recoups." *New York Times*, June 11, 2014. https://artsbeat.blogs.nytimes.com/2014/06/11/broadway-raisin-recoups/.

Hernandez, Ernio. "Photo Call: Guy-Directed *for colored girls . . .* , with Givens and Parker, Plays Atlanta." *Playbill*, July 20, 2009. http://www.playbill.com/article/photo-call-guy-directed-for-colored-girls-with-givens-and-parker-plays-atlanta-com-162907.

Helicon Collaborative. *Not Just Money: Equity Issues in Cultural Philanthropy*. Full report. July 2017. http://heliconcollab.net/wp-content/uploads/2017/08/NotJustMoney_Full_Report_July2017.pdf.

———. *Not Just Money: Equity Issues in Cultural Philanthropy*. Pittsburgh PA Data Profile. July 17, 2017. http://www.notjustmoney.us/docs/NotJustMoney_data_profile_PittsburghPA.pdf.

———. "Not Just Money: Where Is the Money Going?" *Medium*, July 10, 2017. https://medium.com/helicon-collaborative/not-just-money-part-1-abd18e277703.

Heller, Fran. "Play at Karamu Recalls Dark Chapter of American History." *Cleveland Jewish News*, February 5, 2004. https://www.clevelandjewishnews.com/archives/play-at-karamu-recalls-dark-chapter-of-american-history/article_3e446169-9598-5612-8567-9ae0de325284.html.

Hemmings, F. W. J. *Alexandre Dumas: Bloomsbury Reader*. London: Bloomsbury, 2012.

Herzog, Kira. "The Beat Generation's Hidden Refuge: Retracing Jack Kerouac's Literary Legacy Beneath Mount Tamalpais." *Marin Magazine*, June 30, 2017. https://www.marinmagazine.com/the-beat-generations-hidden-refuge/.

Hill, Errol. *Shakespeare in Sable: A History of Black Shakespearean Actors*. Amherst: University of Massachusetts Press, 1984.

Hill, Errol G., and James V. Hatch. *A History of African American Theatre*. Cambridge: Cambridge University Press, 2003.

Hollister, Sean. "Activists Sue San Francisco for Letting 'Google Bus' Use Public Bus Stops." The Verge, May 1, 2014. http://www.theverge.com/2014 /5/1/5673742/activists-sue-san-francisco-for-letting-google-bus-use-public -bus.

Holtz, Debra Levi. "Black Theater Group Faces Criticism." *San Francisco Chronicle*, November 11, 1999. https://www.sfchronicle.com/bayarea/article/Black -Theater-Group-Faces-Criticism-2896496.php.

———. "Berkeley Should Stop Funding Theater, Audit Says/Black Repertory Group Accused of Nepotism." *San Francisco Chronicle*, September 15, 1999. https://www.sfchronicle.com/performance/article/Berkeley-Should-Stop -Funding-Theater-Audit-Says-2907337.php?psid=8FN95.

Holman, Curt. "Theatre in the Square Racks Up Suzies." Creative Loafing, November 2, 2005. https://creativeloafing.com/content-193643-Theatre-in-the -Square-racks-up-Suzis.

Horne, Gerald. *Race Woman: The Lives of Shirley Graham Du Bois*. New York: New York University Press, 2000.

Hornsby, Alton. *Black Power in Dixie: A Political History of African Americans in Atlanta*. Gainesville: University Press of Florida, 2009.

Howard University Department of Theatre Arts. "About the Department: History." Accessed May 3, 2016. http://coas.howard.edu/theatrearts/history.html.

Howey, Christine. "*God's Trombones* Captivates, Electrifies at Karamu House." Cleveland.com, April 1, 2011. https://www.cleveland.com/arts/2011/04/gods _trombones_captivates_elec.html.

———. "Great Singing Perfectly Complements a Lush Production in *Blues in the Night* at Karamu." Cleveland Scene, September 14, 2016. https:// www.clevescene.com/cleveland/great-singing-perfectly-complements-a-lush -production-in-blues-in-the-night-at-karamu/Content?oid=4959265.

———. "King Me: Sensational Performances and Superb Direction Make *King Hedley II* at Karamu Must-See Theater." Cleveland Scene, May 30, 2007. https://www.clevescene.com/cleveland/king-me/Content?oid=1498765.

Howkins, John. *The Creative Economy: How People Make Money from Ideas*. London: Penguin, 2002.

HowlRound Theatre Commons. "Standing in Our Grandfathers' Shoes: Sarah Bellamy and Jamil Jude in Conversation." The Changeover: Leadership in Transition Series, curated by David Dower. December 9, 2018. https://howlround .com/standing-our-grandfathers-shoes.

Hughes, Langston. *The Big Sea*. New York: Hill and Hwang, 1940.

———. *The Plays to 1942: Mulatto to The Sun Do Move*. Edited by Leslie Catherine Sanders with Nancy Johnston. Vol. 5 of *The Collected Works of Langston Hughes*. Columbia: University of Missouri Press, 2002.

———. "For Russell and Rowena Jelliffe." In *The Oxford Anthology of African American Poetry*. Edited by Arnold Rampersad. Oxford: Oxford University Press, 2006.

———. *Five Plays by Langston Hughes*. Edited by Webster Smalley. Bloomington: Indiana University Press, 1963.

———. *I Wonder as I Wander: An Autobiographical Journey*. New York: Rinehart, 1956.

Hulbert, Dan. "Atlanta's Olympic Moment." *American Theatre*, July/August 1996.

———. "Black Playwrights Listening to the Past," *Atlanta Constitution*, February 17, 1991.

———. "Dizzying Array of Dramatics Waits in Wings." *Atlanta Constitution*, weekend ed., September 10, 1988.

———. "Jomandi's Jam: Black Theater's in Fight for Its Life; It Lacks Funds, Audiences, and Must Compete with High-Profile Alliance." *Atlanta Constitution*, November 13, 1994.

———. "Lively Performances Make Jomandi's *Sisters* a Funny Fail-Safe Crowd Pleaser." *Atlanta Constitution*, August 2, 1988.

———. "Tom Jones Stands Alone in 'Hip' Autobiographical Odyssey." *Atlanta Constitution,* June 14, 1990.

Hunter, Les. "Art in Democracy: Early Houses of the Cleveland Playhouse." In *Performing the Progressive Era: Immigration, Urban Life, and Nationalism on Stage*, edited by Max Shulman and J. Chris Westgate, 106–21. Iowa City: University of Iowa Press, 2019.

Hurwitt, Robert. "Black History Month/Setting the Stage for Social Change." SF Gate, February 21, 2007. https://www.sfgate.com/entertainment/article /BLACK-HISTORY-MONTH-Setting-the-stage-for-2647282.php.

———. "Claude Purdy's Perfect Play." *San Francisco Examiner*, June 8, 1989.

———. "Gene Angell—Innovative Bay Area Theater Designer Dies at 80." SF Gate, October 4, 2007. https://www.sfgate.com/bayarea/article/Gene-Angell -innovative-Bay-Area-theater-2498952.php.

———. "Gethsemane Park Struggles to Tell Story without Its Center." *San Francisco Examiner*, May 7, 1999.

———. "Has Hip-Hop Lost Its Way? New Play in SF Explores the Music and Its Meaning." *Mercury News*, March 30, 2019. https://www.mercurynews.com /2019/03/30/has-hip-hop-lost-its-way-new-play-in-sf-explores-the-music-and -its-meanings/.

———. "Life as Huey's Doppleganger." *San Francisco Examiner*, March 17, 2000.

———. "Lorraine Hansberry Theatre to Close for Season." SF Gate, April 9, 2010. http://www.sfgate.com/bayarea/article/Lorraine-Hansberry-Theatre-to -close-for-season-3267916.php.

———. "'rainbow' Still 'enuf' 20 Years Later: Ntozake Shange's Choreopoem Keeps Its Strong Message." *San Francisco Examiner*, March 27, 1995.

———. "*Three Views of Mt. Fuji*: Ntozake Shange's Latest Work." *San Francisco Examiner*, May 31, 1987.

Ingraham, Mary I., Joseph K. So, and Roy Moodlet, eds. *Opera in a Multicultural World: Coloniality, Culture, Performance*. London: Routledge, 2016.

"Interracial House Gets $100,000 Grant." *Kansas American*, October 8, 1954.

Isherwood, Charles. "So Many Secrets, Soon to See the Light." *New York Times*, December 8, 2011. https://www.nytimes.com/2011/12/09/theater/reviews/stick -fly-at-the-cort-theater-review.html.

"J. Newton Hill, Educator, 88." *New York Times*, February 15, 1989. https://www .nytimes.com/1989/02/15/obituaries/j-newton-hill-educator-88.html.

Jackson, Debbie Minter. "*The Wizard of Hip (or When in Doubt, Slam Dunk)* at MetroStage (review)." DC Theatre Scene, August 22, 2017. https:// dctheatrescene.com/2017/08/22/wizard-hip-doubt-slam-dunk-metrostage -review/.

Jackson, Maria-Rosario, Florence Kabwasa-Green, Daniel Sewnson, Joaquin Herranz, Jr., Kadija Ferryman, Caron Atlas, Eric Wallner, and Carole Rosen- stein, eds. "Investing in Creativity: A Study of the Support Structure for U.S. Artists." Culture, Creativity and Communities Program. Urban Institute. Accessed May 4, 2019. http://webarchive.urban.org/UploadedPDF/411311 _investing_in_creativity.pdf.

Jackson, Marsha A. *Sisters*. In *The National Black Drama Anthology: Eleven Plays from America's Leading African-American Theaters*, edited by Woodie King Jr., 99–148. New York: Applause, 1995.

Jackson, Oliver. Preface to *Kuntu Drama: Plays of the African Continuum*. Edited by Paul Carter Harrison, xi–xiii. New York: Grove Press, 1974.

Jackson, Pamela Faith, and Karimah. *Black Comedy: Nine Plays: A Critical Anthology with Interviews and Essays*. New York: Applause, 1997.

Jackson, Shannon. *Lines of Activity: Performance, Historiography, Hull-House Domesticity*. Ann Arbor: University of Michigan Press, 2001.

James, Nathan. Artist's website. Accessed May 27, 2017. http://nathanjamespoet .wixsite.com/nathanjjames/about-nathan.

Janiak, Lily. "African-American Shakes' *for colored girls* Offers a Rainbow of Pain, Hope." *San Francisco Chronicle*, September 17, 2018. https://datebook .sfchronicle.com/theater/african-american-shakes-for-colored-girls-offers -a-rainbow-of-pain-hope.

———. "African American Shakespeare's Lusty, Furious *Streetcar* Belongs to All of Us." *San Francisco Chronicle*, March 5, 2018. https://www.sfchronicle .com/performance/article/African-American-Shakespeare-s-lusty-furious -12729391.php.

———. "*Home*: A Too Rare Show from Lorraine Hansberry Theatre." SF Gate, May 9, 2017. https://www.sfgate.com/performance/article/Home-a-too-rare -show-from-Lorraine-11134198.php.

———. "Jones to Step Down from Lorraine Hansberry Theatre." *San Francisco Chronicle*, June 14, 2017. https://www.sfchronicle.com/performance/article /Jones-to-step-down-from-Lorraine-Hansberry-Theatre-11217882.php.

———. "Lorraine Hansberry Theatre's New Leader Envisions Another Chap- ter of Liberation." *San Francisco Chronicle*, May 18, 2019. https://datebook .sfchronicle.com/theater/lorraine-hansberry-theatres-new-leader-envisions -another-chapter-of-liberation.

———. "New Leader, New Ethos at Lorraine Hansberry Theatre." *San Francisco Chronicle*, December 15, 2017. https://www.sfchronicle.com/entertainment /article/New-leader-new-ethos-at-Lorraine-Hansberry-12432449.php?psid= 9yxa1#photo-12884122.

Johnson, James Weldon. *God's Trombones: Seven Negro Sermons in Verse*. New York: Viking, 1927.

Johnson, Reggie. "Jomandi Productions' *Queen of the Blues* Comes to Town." *Winston-Salem Chronicle*, January 31, 1991.

Johnston, Christopher. "Dream on East 89th Street." *Cleveland Magazine*, September 28, 2005. https://clevelandmagazine.com/entertainment/articles/dream-on-east-89th-street.

———. "Shakeup Aims to Put Karamu House Together." *American Theatre*, March 14, 2016. https://www.americantheatre.org/2016/03/14/shakeup-aims-to-put-karamu-house-in-order/.

Johnston, Laura. "Lucia Colombi, Founder of Ensemble Theatre: Obituary." Cleveland.com, January 9, 2009. https://www.cleveland.com/onstage/index.ssf/2009/01/lucia_colombi_founder_of_ensem.html.

Jomandi Productions Inc. Guidestar profile. Accessed August 3, 2018. https://www.guidestar.org/profile/58-1348329.

Jones, Peter Lawson. Theatrical resume. Artist's website. Accessed August 3, 2018. http://www.peterlawsonjones.com/theatrical-resume.html.

———. "5 Responses to Terrence Spivey Shakes Up Our Theater Scene." Cool Cleveland, November 9, 2016. https://coolcleveland.com/2016/11/ex-karamu-artistic-director-terrence-spivey-continues-shake-area-theater-scene/.

Jones, Thomas W., II. *Art Works*. National Endowment for the Arts podcast, February 12, 2015. https://www.arts.gov/audio/thomas-w-jones-ii.

———. "Thomas W. Jones, Founding Member of Jomandi Theater Shares the Beginnings of the Atlanta Based Company." Filmed interview. African American Registry. Accessed July 10, 2018. https://aaregistry.org/story/jomandi-productions-debuts/.

Jude, Jamil. "What We Are Fighting For." In "Find Joy in the Destruction of the Lie." *American Theatre*, June 10, 2020. https://www.americantheatre.org/2020/06/10/find-joy-in-the-destruction-of-the-lie/.

Kalson, Sally. "Wilson Center's New Leader Has Lofty Vision." *Pittsburgh Post-Gazette*, July 25, 2010. http://www.post-gazette.com/local/region/2010/07/25/Wilson-Center-s-new-leader-has-lofty-vision/stories/201007250261.

Kapp, Paul Hardin, and Paul J. Armstrong. *SynergiCity: Reinventing the Postindustrial City*. Urbana: University of Illinois Press, 2012.

"Karamu Celebrates Black History Month." *Akron Beacon Journal*, February 22, 1981.

"Karamu Executive Director Change." *Black World*, April 1976.

"Karamu House." *Black World*, April 1973.

Karamu House Records. Western Reserve Historical Society. Sub series I: correspondence, 1919–1974. Box 8, folders 150–157. http://ead.ohiolink.edu/xtf-ead/view?docId=ead/OCLWHi0331.xml;chunk.id=c02_1CJ;brand=default.

Karamu House. *Freedom on Juneteenth*. Written by Latecia D. Wilson and contributing writers. Directed by Tony Sias with musical arrangements by Dr. David M. Thomas. Livestreamed production, June 19, 2020. https://karamuhouse.org/events/freedom-on-juneteenth.

———. "Home." Accessed May 5, 2018. https://www.karamuhouse.org.

"Karamu Names Ford-Taylor Permanent Executive Director." *Plain Dealer*, July 28, 1988.

"Karamu Play Will Open Tomorrow." *Medina County Gazette*, February 21, 1966.

"Karamu Presents the Premiere of August Wilson's Jitney." *Call & Post*, February 4, 1999.

Karamu Theatre Programs 1927–1972. Karamu Programs. Cleveland Public Library Repository. Accessed May 3, 2018. https://search.clevnet.org/client/en_US/cpl-main/search/detailnonmodal/ent:$002f$002fSD_ILS$002f0$002fSD_ILS:6955396/one.

Kearney, Nicole C. "About the Author." *Time for Bed: Andrew and April's Adventures*, Literary Libations Publications, November 15, 2005. https://www.amazon.com/Time-Bed-Andrew-Aprils-Adventures/dp/0976608677.

Kelly, Grace V. "Gilpin Players' Final Program Highly Praised." *Plain Dealer*, June 10, 1927.

———. "Gilpin Players." *Plain Dealer*, March 4, 1928.

Kelly, Reggie. "Dynamic Musical: Blues in the Night with Reggie Kelly and Michelle Edwards Whitfield." Radio interview with Tina Hobson. *I Am a Superwoman Radio with Tina Hobson*, September 10, 2016. https://www.spreaker.com/user/positivepower21/dynamic-musical-blues-in-the-night-w-reg.

Kenny Leon's True Colors Theatre Company. "About Jane Bishop." Accessed May 2, 2018. https://truecolorstheatre.org/about/staff/jane-bishop/.

———. "Communication Is Key." Accessed September 14, 2018. https://truecolorstheatre.org/events/community-conversations/.

———. "Coping in Corporate Cultures: Being a Minority in Corporate America." Accessed September 14, 2018. https://truecolorstheatre.org/2018/08/16/coping-in-corporate-cultures-community-conversation/.

———. "Education Programs." Accessed September 14, 2018. https://truecolorstheatre.org/education/programs/.

———. "Jamil Jude to Succeed Kenny Leon as True Colors Theatre Company's Artistic Director." Press release, September 24, 2018.

Kernodle, Tammy L. "Arias, Communists, and Conspiracies: The History of Still's *Troubled Island*." *The Musical Quarterly* 83, no. 4 (Winter 1999): 487–508.

King, Daniel J. "Alumnus Takes Helm of Cleveland's Karamu House." Ohio University College of Fine Arts, February 4, 2017. https://www.ohio.edu/finearts/whats-happening/news-story.cfm?newsItem=30ACEE01–5056-A874–1DB1C52F713055DA.

King, Paula. "Black Repertory to Present *Port Chicago 50* Play." *East Bay Times*, February 1, 2018. https://www.eastbaytimes.com/2018/02/01/black-repertory-to-present-port-chicago-50-play/.

King, Woodie, Jr. *The Impact of Race: Theatre and Culture*. New York: Applause 2003.

———. *The National Black Drama Anthology*. New York: Applause Theatre Books, 1995.

Kinzer, Stephen. "From Oblivion to Ovation: An Opera Right out of the Harlem Renaissance." *New York Times*, December 28, 2002. https://www.nytimes.com/2002/12/28/arts/from-oblivion-to-ovation-an-opera-right-out-of-the-harlem-renaissance.html.

Klein, Emily. "The Hill District, a Community Holding On through Displacement and Development." *Public Source*, December 27, 2017. https://www.publicsource.org/hill-district-displacement-development/.

Kolin, Philip C. "An Interview with Whitney J. LeBlanc." "Poetry and Theatre." Special issue, *African American Review* 26, no. 2 (1992): 307–17.

Krigwa Players. "Krigwa Players Little Negro Theatre, ca 1926." W. E. B. Du Bois Papers, MS 312. Special Collections and University Archives, University of Massachusetts Amherst Libraries. https://credo.library.umass.edu/view/pageturn/mums312-b034-i165/#page/1/mode/1up.

Kuntu Repertory Theatre, "About." Accessed September 14, 2018. https://web.archive.org/web/20120422013045/http://www.kuntu.org:80/about/mission.php.

Kuntu Repertory Theatre Archives. Curtis Theatre Collection, Archives and Special Collections, University of Pittsburgh Library System, Pittsburgh.

Kurahashi, Yuko. "Celebrating the 'Historical' Community through Different Voices: Ping Chong and Talvin Wilks's Women of the Hill." Continuum: The Journal of African Diaspora Drama, Theatre, and Performance 3. no. 1 (2016). http://continuumjournal.org/index.php/all-issues/vol-3-no-1-calls-for-social-action/52-volumes/issues/vol-3-no-1/3-1-articles/131-celebrating-the-historical-community-through-different-voices-ping-chong-and-talvin-wilks-s-women-of-the-hill.

Lai, Clement. "The Racial Triangulation of Space: The Case of Urban Renewal in San Francisco's Fillmore District," Annals of the Association of American Geographers 102, no. 1 (2012): 151–70.

Lake, Thomas. "Fixer, Charmer, Builder, Mayor: Fourteen Hours with Kasim Reed, the Man Who Can't Stop Trying to Fix Our City." Atlanta, October 1, 2010. https://www.atlantamagazine.com/great-reads/who-is-kasim-reed/.

Lamb, Yvonne Shinhoster. "Director and Teacher Mike Malone; Nurtured D. C. Black Theater Scene." Washington Post, December 6, 2006. http://www.washingtonpost.com/wp-dyn/content/article/2006/12/05/AR2006120501511.html.

Langford, Lisa. Rastus and Hattie. Dobama Theatre, July 7, 2015. http://www.dobama.org/gym-playwrights-1/2015/7/7/lisa-langford.

Lasch-Quinn, Elisabeth. Black Neighbors: Race and the Limits of Reform in the American Settlement House Movement 1890–1945. Chapel Hill: University of North Carolina Press, 1993.

Lee, Felicia R. "Deferred Dreams That Resonate across Decades." New York Times, February 17, 2008. https://www.nytimes.com/2008/02/17/arts/television/17lee.html.

Leon, Kenny. Curtain speech. Fulton County Southwest Arts Center, August 4, 2018.

Leon, Kenny with John Hassan. Take You Wherever You Go: A Memoir. New York: Grand Central Publishing, 2018.

Lillie, Vernell A. "Dr. Vernell A. Lillie, Social Work and African Studies." University of Pittsburgh, October 4, 2011. https://www.youtube.com/watch?v=eRJAahO1hSA.

Lindfors, Bernth. Ira Aldridge: The African Roscius. Rochester, NY: University of Rochester Press, 2007.

Litt, Steven. "Cleveland Foundation Announces $2M grant to Karamu House, Bolstering Nation's Oldest Black Theatre." Cleveland.com, May 7, 2019. https://www.cleveland.com/arts/2019/05/cleveland-foundation-announces-2m-grant-to-karamu-house-bolstering-nations-oldest-black-theater.html.

———. "Opportunity Corridor Is Back on Track." Cleveland.com, February 15, 2018. https://www.cleveland.com/architecture/index.ssf/2018/02/opportunity _corridor_on_track.html.

Livingstone, B. L. "African Rhythms Prevail in Oberlin Girl's Opera, Given Debut at Cleveland." *Cincinnati Enquirer*, July 1, 1932.

Locke, Alain, ed. *The New Negro: An Interpretation.* New York: Albert and Charles Boni, 1925.

Lorraine Hansberry Theatre. "Our History." Accessed July 20, 2015. http://lhtsf .org/about.html#hist.

———. "Production History." Accessed July 20, 2015. http://www.lhtsf.org/lht -production-history.

———. "2016 Form 990." Guidestar profile. https://pdf.guidestar.org/PDF _Images/2016/942/784/2016–942784213–0d788a00–9.pdf.

———. "2017 Form 990." Guidestar profile. https://pdf.guidestar.org/PDF _Images/2018/942/784/2018–942784213–1012bdc2–9.pdf.

"Lorraine Hansberry Theatre." *San Francisco Examiner*, January 26, 1992.

Madison, D. Soyini. Foreword to *Black Performance Theory*, edited by Thomas F. DeFranz and Anita Gonzalez, vii–ix. Durham, NC: Duke University Press, 2014.

Mahala, Macelle. *Penumbra: The Premier Stage for African American Drama.* Minneapolis: University of Minnesota Press, 2013.

Malovany, Dan. "Karamu Artist's View of Stardom Matures." *Elyria Chronicle Telegram*, June 25, 1982.

"Martin Luther King Jr., Signature Found in Karamu House Guestbook in Cleveland." Cleveland.com, April 4, 2018. https://www.youtube.com/watch?v=8ec _KCBckso.

Mason, Herman "Skip," Jr. *African American Entertainment in Atlanta.* Charleston, SC: Arcadia Publishing, 1998.

Mason, Susan Vanetta, ed. *The San Francisco Mime Troupe Reader.* Ann Arbor: University of Michigan Press, 2005.

Mastroianni, Tony. "Bolder Work from Author of *Fences*, Fine Case in *Joe Turner's Come and Gone* at Karamu." *Akron Beacon Journal*, February 4, 1991.

———. "Drama of Power at Karamu." *Akron Beacon Journal*, February 15, 1992.

———. "Going Back to Basics." *Akron Beacon Journal*, October 23, 1983, 18.

———. "Imagine Macbeth in Haiti." *Akron Beacon Journal*, April 4, 1994.

———. "Karamu's H.M.S. Pinafore Shows Few Sparks." *Akron Beacon Journal*, May 9, 1985.

———. "Karamu's Showdown a Zestful Fable." *Akron Beacon Journal*, October 16, 1987.

———. "Sharper Focus Needed in Play's Two Stories." *Akron Beacon Journal*, October 12, 1984.

———. "Showcase for Playwrights, New Ideas." *Akron Beacon Journal*, September 29, 1985.

———. "Laughs Just Don't Stop in *Monkey.*" *Akron Beacon Journal*, October 26, 1985.

———. "*The Piano Lesson* Resonates at Karamu." *Akron Beacon Journal*, October 9, 1993.

———. "Unfocused *Grapes of Wrath* Is a Good Try, but Falls Short." *Akron Beacon Journal*, October 6, 1992.

———. "Women of Plums Eloquence in Action." *Akron Beacon Journal*, January 21, 1993.

Matier, Phillip, and Andrew Ross. "S.F. Mayor: Homeless 'Have to Leave the Street' for Super Bowl." SF Gate, August 25, 2015. http://www.sfgate.com /bayarea/matier-ross/article/S-F-mayor-Homeless-have-to-leave-the-6465209 .php.

———. "SF Suing Academy of Art over Real Estate Empire." SF Gate, May 6, 2016. http://www.sfgate.com/bayarea/article/SF-suing-Academy-of-Art-over -real-estate-empire-7396553.php.

Mayes, Keith A. *Kwanzaa: Black Power and the Making of the African American Holiday Tradition.* New York: Routledge, 2009.

Mayo, Sandra, and Elvin Holt. *Stages of Struggle and Celebration: A Production History of Black Theatre in Texas.* Austin: University of Texas Press, 2016.

McFadden, Alesia Elaine. "The Artistry and Activism of Shirley Graham Du Bois: A Twentieth Century African American Torchbearer." PhD dissertation, University of Massachusetts Amherst, 2009.

McLaren, Joseph. *Langston Hughes: Folk Dramatist in the Protest Tradition.* Westport, CT: Greenwood Press, 1997.

"Michael Oatman, Playwright: 2011 Emerging Artist Award for Literature." Cleveland Arts Prize. Accessed May 5, 2018. http://clevelandartsprize.org /awardees/michael_oatman.html.

"Mike Malone Named Theatre Director of Karamu House." *Chicago Metro News*, June 25, 1977.

Miller, Hillary. *Drop Dead: Performance in Crisis, 1970s New York.* Evanston, IL: Northwestern University Press, 2016.

"Minnie Gentry, 77, An Actress on Stage and *Cosby Show*." *New York Times*, May 13, 1993. https://www.nytimes.com/1993/05/13/obituaries/minnie-gentry -77-an-actress-on-stage-and-cosby-show.html.

Mishkin, Tracy. *The Harlem and Irish Renaissances: Language, Identity, and Representation.* Gainesville: University Press of Florida, 1998.

Molette, Barbara J. and Carlton W. "About the Authors." Artists' website. Accessed July 5, 2018. http://afrocentrictheatre.com/author/.

———. *Black Theatre: Premise and Presentation.* Bristol, IN: Wyndham Hall Press, 1986.

Moore, Leonard N. *Carl B. Stokes and the Rise of Black Political Power.* Urbana: University of Illinois Press, 2003.

———. "Carl Stokes: Mayor of Cleveland." In *African American Mayors: Race, Politics, and the American City*, edited by David R. Colburn and Jeffrey S. Adler, 80–106. Urbana: University of Illinois Press, 2001.

Morris, Shawn. "Majestic Hotel." Cleveland Historical. Accessed March 5, 2018. https://clevelandhistorical.org/items/show/636.

Morse, Rob. "Is This Police Oppression?" *San Francisco Examiner*, January 4, 1989.

Morton, Marian J. *Cleveland Heights: The Making of an Urban Suburb.* Charleston, SC: Arcadia Publishing, 2002.

National Black Theatre Festival. "The National Black Theatre Festival History."
  July 3, 2007. https://web.archive.org/web/20070703013428/http://www.nbtf
  .org/nbtf_history.html.

"National Endowment for the Arts Funds Organizations throughout Ohio: Search-
  able Database." Cleveland.com, February 11, 2011. https://www.cleveland.com
  /open/index.ssf/2011/02/national_endowment_for_the_art_1.html.

Neal, Larry. "The Black Arts Movement." "Black Theatre," edited by Ed Bullins.
  Special issue, *Tulane Drama Review* 12, no. 4 (Summer 1968): 28–39.

Nelson Jones, Diana. "Obituary: Maisha Baton, Nurturing Poet, Playwright,
  Therapist and Teacher." *Pittsburgh Post-Gazette*, December 31, 2009. http://
  www.post-gazette.com/news/obituaries/2010/01/01/Obituary-Maisha-Baton
  -Nurturing-poet-playwright-therapist-and-teacher/stories/201001010099.

Nelson, Irene. "Home Sweet Home at Lorraine Hansberry Theatre, S.F." *Theatrius*, May 14, 2017. https://www.theatrius.com/2017/05/14/home-sweet-home
  -at-lorraine-hansberry-theatre-s-f/.

"New Teenie Harris Exhibit Opens at Carnegie Museum of Art." *Pittsburgh
  Today Live*, June 26, 2018. https://pittsburgh.cbslocal.com/video/program/750
  /3889119-new-teenie-harrisexhibit-opens-at-carnegie-museum-of-art/.

Newman, Harry. "Holding Back: The Theatre's Resistance to Non-Traditional
  Casting." *Tulane Drama Review* 33, no. 3 (1989): 22–36.

Newman, Shraine L. *Karamu House Inc. 75th Anniversary Souvenir Book*. Cleveland: Karamu House, n.d., ca. 1991.

Nichols, Charles H., ed. *Arna Bontemps-Langston Hughes Letters: 1925–1967*.
  New York: Dodd, Mead, 1980.

"The Night Beat." *Pittsburgh Courier*, December 1, 1973.

94.1 KPFA. "Events: Marvin X in Concert." September 30, 2017. https://kpfa.org
  /event/marvin-x-concert/.

"Nora Vaughn, Founded Black Repertory." *San Francisco Examiner*, April 8, 1994.

"Ntozake Shange, Ishmael Reed Benefit Poetry and Prose Reading." *San Francisco Examiner*, October 24, 1986.

O'Connor, Bill. "Audience Confused by Karamu's *Eyes*." *Akron Beacon Journal*,
  March 19, 1982.

———. "Powerful Play for Karamu's New Company." *Akron Beacon Journal*,
  January 21, 1982.

O'Connor, John, and Lorraine Brown, eds. *The Federal Theatre Project: Free,
  Adult, Uncensored*. London: Eyre Methuen, 1980.

O'Connor, Lydia. "America's Most Expensive City Just Got Even More Expensive." *Huffington Post*, February 4, 2015. http://www.huffingtonpost.com
  /2015/02/03/san-francisco-rent-2015-most-expensive-city_n_6609396.html.

O'Driscoll, Bill. "August Wilson Center Stabilizes, Plans for the Future." 90.5
  WESA FM: Pittsburgh NPR News Station, February 11, 2019. https://www
  .wesa.fm/post/august-wilson-center-stabilizes-plans-future.

———. "A Unique Theatrical Project Blends the Voices of Women from the Hill
  District." *Pittsburgh City Paper*, November 19, 2009. https://www.pghcitypaper
  .com/pittsburgh/a-unique-theatrical-project-blends-thevoices-of-women-from
  -the-hill-district/Content?oid=1342872.

O'Donnell, Patrick. "New Tremont Montessori school, Karamu House Partnership Preferred by Cleveland School Board." Celevland.com, June 19, 2019.

https://www.cleveland.com/news/2019/06/new-tremont-montessori-school
-karamu-house-partnership-preferred-by-cleveland-school-board.html.

Oldenburg, Chuck. "Jack Kerouac." Mill Valley Historical Society, March 2002. https://www.mvhistory.org/history-of/history-of-homestead-valley/jack -kerouac/.

O'Leary, Theodore M. "Co-Existence without Condescension." *Kansas City Times*, August 31, 1966.

Osborne, Bert. "Razor Sharp Dialogue Makes Smart People Terrific." *Atlanta Journal-Constitution*, July 21, 2016.

Pantsios, Anastasia. "Terrence Spivey Shakes Up Our Theater Scene." Cool Cleveland, November 9, 2016. https://coolcleveland.com/2016/11/ex-karamu -artistic-director-terrence-spivey-continues-shake-area-theater-scene/.

———. "Dark Days for the Black Arts: The Theater at Karamu House Has Enjoyed a Resurgence but Can It Weather the Infighting that Threatens to Destroy It?" Cleveland Scene, December 14, 2011. https://www.clevescene .com/cleveland/dark-days-for-the-black-arts/Content?oid=2776400.

Pao, Angela. *No Safe Spaces: Re-casting Race, Ethnicity, and Nationality in American Theater*. Ann Arbor: University of Michigan Press, 2010.

Payton, Brenda. "Black Repertory Theater Has a Dream—Its Own Building." *San Francisco Examiner*, October 16, 1979.

Penny, Rob. *Good Black Don't Crack*. In *The National Black Drama Anthology*, edited by Woodie King Jr., 332–92. New York: Applause, 1995.

———. *Little Willie Armstrong Jones*. Theatre Urge Papers. Curtis Theatre Collection, Archives and Special Collections, University of Pittsburgh Library System, Pittsburgh, PA.

Pepin, Elizabeth, and Lewis Watts. *Harlem of the West: The San Francisco Jazz Era*. San Francisco: Chronicle Books, 2006.

Perkins + Will. "The August Wilson Center for African American Culture." *Arch Daily*, August 28, 2011. http://www.archdaily.com/163047/august-wilson -center-for-african-american-culture-perkinswill.

Perry, Richard. "Karamu House Revives Art, Theater from WPA Era." *Plain Dealer*, May 22, 1992.

———. "Keeping Karamu Legacy Alive." *Plain Dealer*, January 8, 1988.

Perucci, Tony. *Paul Robeson and the Cold War Performance Complex: Race, Madness, Activism*. Ann Arbor: University of Michigan Press, 2012.

Peterson, Bernard L. Jr. *The African American Theatre Directory, 1816–1960: A Comprehensive Guide to Early Black Theatre Organizations, Companies, Theatres, and Performing Groups*. Westport, CT: Greenwood Press, 1997.

Peterson, Jane T., and Suzanne Bennet, eds. *Women Playwrights of Diversity: A Bio-bibliographical Sourcebook*. Westport, CT: Greenwood Press, 1997.

Piepenburg, Erik. "Tupac Shakur, Immortalized Again." *New York Times*, April 7, 2010. https://www.nytimes.com/2010/04/11/theater/11tupac.html.

Ping Chong and Company. "The Women of the Hill, 2009." Production archive. http://www.pingchong.org/undesirable-elements/production-archive/women -of-the-hill/.

Pittsburg Cultural Trust. "Background and History." May 27, 2017. https://www .trustarts.org/about/history.

Pittsburgh Playwrights Theatre. "*Gem of the Ocean.*" https://www.pghplaywrights
.org/gem/.
———. *Seven Guitars.* https://www.pghplaywrights.org/seven-guitars/.
———. "2003 Productions." http://www.pghplaywrights.org/2003-productions/.
Pitz, Marylynne. "Former PSO Keyboardist to Read from Essays." *Pittsburgh
Post-Gazette*, November 2, 2013. http://www.post-gazette.com/ae/books/2013
/11/03/Former-PSO-keyboardist-to-read-from-essays/stories/201311030017.
———. "August Wilson Center Struggles to Reduce $9 Million Debt." *Pitts-
burgh Post-Gazette*, July 27, 2011. http://www.post-gazette.com/local/city
/2011/07/27/August-Wilson-Center-struggles-to-reduce-9-million-debt/stories
/201107270210.
Playwrights Local. *Objectively/Reasonable: A Community Response to the
Shooting of Tamir Rice 11/22/14.* World Premier: http://www.playwrightslocal
.org/objectively-reasonable/. Return Engagement: http://www.playwrightslocal
.org/objectively-reasonable-return/.
Pogrebin, Robin. "Wolfe Is Leaving Public Theater." *New York Times*, February
12, 2004. http://www.nytimes.com/2004/02/12/theater/wolfe-is-leaving-public
-theater.html?_r=0.
Porter Sanford Arts Center. "Our History: Porter Sanford III." Accessed August 7,
2018. http://www.portersanfordartscenter.org/our-history/.
Powell, Diane R. "Jitney Captures Drama behind Hill Substitute Taxi-Cab Service." *Pittsburgh Courier*, November 13, 1982.
Power, Will. "Catching Up with Ntozake Shange: Her Innovations in Stage and
Verse Have Inspired a New Generation." *American Theatre* 24, no. 4 (2007):
30–33.
Prevot, Naima. *Dance for Export: Cultural Diplomacy and the Cold War.* Mid-
dletown, CT: Wesleyan University Press, 1998.
The Progressive Era. Documentary video. Intelecom Learning, 2004. https://www
.kanopy.com/product/progressive-era.
Purdy, Jason. "A Princess and a Drum." *American Theatre*, December 1, 2013.
https://www.americantheatre.org/2013/12/01/djembe-and-the-forest-of
-christmas-forgotten-gets-world-premiere-at-houstons-the-ensemble-theatre/.
"*Purlie* Benefit." *Oakland Tribune*, March 17, 1972, 35.
Rampersad, Arnold. *The Life of Langston Hughes: Volume I: 1902–141, I Too,
Sing America.* New York: Oxford University Press, 1986.
Rawson, Christopher. "August Wilson's Mythic Character Explored in The-
ater Festival." *Pittsburgh Post-Gazette*, November 9, 2009. https://www.post
-gazette.com/ae/theater-dance/2009/11/09/August-Wilson-s-mythic-character
-Aunt-Ester-explored-in-theater-festival/stories/200911090252.
———. "On Stage: Politics Hard on Stage." *Pittsburgh Post-Gazette*, March 26,
2003. http://old.post-gazette.com/ae/20030326rawson7.asp.
———. "Purdy Lends His Energy to Iguana." *Pittsburgh Post-Gazette,* September 28,1990.
Reed, Ishmael. "Black Repertory Theater and the Creation of Opportunity for
Kids." *San Francisco Chronicle*, October 14, 2007. https://www.sfchronicle
.com/performance/article/Black-Repertory-Theater-and-the-creation-of
-3766278.php.

———. "Curtain for Black Rep? African American Theater Fights for Its Life in Berkeley." *San Francisco Chronicle*, September 4, 1999. https://www .sfchronicle.com/opinion/openforum/article/Curtain-for-Black-Rep-African -American-theater-2908539.php?psid=8FN95.

Reiss, Tom. *The Black Count: Glory, Revolution, Betrayal, and the Real Count of Montecristo*. New York: Broadway Books, 2013.

"*The Resurrection of Lady Lester*." *San Francisco Examiner*, May 13, 1988.

"Ricardo Khan Biography." History Makers, August 14, 2007. http://www .thehistorymakers.org/biography/ricardo-khan-41.

Rich, Frank. "Review/Theater; Milner's Checkmates, Story of 2 Households." *New York Times*, August 5, 1988. https://www.nytimes.com/1988/08/05 /theater/review-theater-milner-s-checkmates-story-of-2-households.html.

Ritschel, Nelson O'Ceallaigh. "Synge and the Irish Influence of the Abbey Theatre on Eugene O'Neill." *Eugene O'Neill Review* 29 (2007): 129–50.

Robertson, Campbell. "Lloyd Richards, Theater Director and Cultivator of Playwrights, Is Dead at 87." *New York Times*, July 1, 2006. http://www.nytimes .com/2006/07/01/theater/01richards.html.

Robertson, Michelle. "A Six-Figure Salary Is Considered 'Low Income,' in San Francisco, and the Threshold Is Rising." SF Gate, June 26, 2018. https://www .sfgate.com/expensive-san-francisco/article/low-income-families-sf-bay-area -hud-statistics-13024580.php.

Ronson, Jon. "San Francisco Is Burning." *GQ*, June 22, 2017. https://www.gq .com/story/san-francisco-is-burning.

Rosenberg, Donald. "Karamu House Playwright in Residence Michael Oatman Wins the Cleveland Arts Prize Emerging Artist Award." Cleveland.com, January 2011. https://www.cleveland.com/arts/index.ssf/2011/06/karamu_house _playwright-in-res.html.

Rosenberg, Scott. "Joe Turner's Here to Stay: ACT Turns in Stirring Production of Wilson's Play." *San Francisco Examiner*, January 11, 1989.

Russell and Rowena Jelliffe Papers. Sub Series H: Executive Director Search 1957–1966. Box 9, folders 144–151. Western Reserve Historical Society. http://ead.ohiolink.edu/xtf-ead/view?docId=ead/OCLWHi0297.xml;chunk.id =c02_1DI;brand=default.

Rutheiser, Charles. *Imagineering Atlanta: The Politics of Place in the City of Dreams*. London: Verso, 1996.

Sabir, Wanda. "*Port Chicago 50* at Black Rep This Weekend." *San Francisco Bay View National Black Newspaper*, March 15, 2017. https://sfbayview.com /2017/03/port-chicago-50-at-black-rep-this-weekend/.

———. "*The Urban Retreat*, a Play by A. Zell Williams Directed by Darryl V. Jones at Lorraine Hansberry Theatre through April 6." *Bayview National Black Newspaper*, April 3, 2019. https://sfbayview.com/2019/04/the-urban-retreat -a-play-by-a-zell-williams-directed-by-darryl-v-jones-at-lorraine-hansberry -theatre-through-april-6/.

Sadoff, Dianne F. "Black Matrilineage: The Case of Alice Walker and Zora Neale Hurston." *Signs* 11, no. 1 (Autumn 1985): 4–26.

San Francisco Arts Commission. "San Francisco Arts Commission Strategic Plan: 2014–2019," February 2014. http://www.sfartscommission.org/about/SFAC _FinalFinal_Plan_021414.pdf.

San Francisco Mime Troupe Archives. D-061. Department of Special Collections, Genera Library. University of California, Davis.

San Francisco Playhouse. "2016 990 tax form." Guidestar profile. https://pdf .guidestar.org/PDF_Images/2017/861/089/2017–861089699–0f8b0adc-9.pdf.

Sanchez, Sonia. *I'm Black When I'm Singing, I'm Blue When I Ain't and Other Plays*, edited by Jacqueline Wood. Durham, NC: Duke University Press, 2010.

Saxon, Wolfgang. "Zelma George, 90, Civic Leader, Singer and Black Music Scholar." *New York Times*, July 5, 1994. https://www.nytimes.com/1994/07/05 /obituaries/zelma-george-90-civic-leader-singer-and-black-music-scholar.html.

Saxton, Alexander. "Blackface Minstrelsy and Jacksonian Ideology," *American Quarterly* 27, no. 1 (1975): 3–28.

Schmalenberger, Sarah. "Debuting Her Political Voice: The Lost Opera of Shirley Graham." *Black Music Research Journal* 26, no. 1 (Spring 2006): 39–87.

Scott, M. Alexis. "Yes, Atlanta Is the Black Mecca." *Planning*, January 2014.

Scott, Nancy. "The City's Homeless Ethnic Theatres." *San Francisco Examiner*, October 7, 1984, Scene/Arts 6.

———. "Good News for Black Theater." *San Francisco Examiner*, November 11, 1987.

———. "SEW Threads Jazz, Dance, and Poetry." *San Francisco Examiner*, January 24, 1984.

Scruggs, Afi. "Curtain Stall? Historic Karamu Theater Looks to Regroup after Layoffs and Financial Turmoil." Cleveland Scene, April 13, 2016. https://www .issuu.com/euclidmediagroup/docs/scene_april_13__2016/13.

———. "Karamu House Regains Nonprofit Status, Looks Ahead to New Season." Cleveland Scene, July 1, 2016. https://www.clevescene.com/scene-and -heard/archives/2016/07/01/karamu-house-regains-nonprofit-status-looks -ahead-to-new-season.

Siegel, Robert. "Amahl and the Night Visitors." With Gian Carlo Menotti. National Public Radio. Aired December 24, 2001. https://www.npr.org /templates/story/story.php?storyId=1135273.

Seiler, Andy. "Playwright Evans Not Quite Sure of What He's Got Until He Sees *Sweet* on Stage." *Central New Jersey Home News*, April 11, 1985.

Selby, John. *Beyond Civil Rights: Karamu's 50 Years of Interracial Understanding Achieved through the Pursuit of Excellence in the Arts*. Cleveland: New World Publishing Company, 1966.

Shakespeare, William. *The Arden Edition of the Works of William Shakespeare: Antony and Cleopatra*, edited by M. R. Ridley. London: Methuen, 1981.

———. *As You Like It*. Folger Shakespeare Library, edited by Louis B. Wright and Virginia Lamar. New York: Washington Square Press, 1959.

Shandell, Jonathan. *The American Negro Theatre and the Long Civil Rights Era*. Iowa City: University of Iowa Press, 2019.

Shinoff, Paul. "Cash Crunch Forces Bay Area Arts to the Wall." *San Francisco Examiner*, June 17, 1984.

Shotgun Players. "Shotgun Players, in Association with Lorraine Hansberry Theatre, presents Kill, Move Paradise, by James Ijames, directed by Darryl V. Jones." Press release, May 2019. https://shotgunplayers.org/content/Files/2019 -05-10-kill-move-paradise-press-release-final.pdf.

Shultz, Lance K., dir. *Karamu: 100 Years in the House*. Video documentary. Ideast-ream Special. WVIZ/PBS. Aired February 17, 2017. http://www.ideastream.org/programs/specials/karamu-100-years-in-the-house.

Simakis, Andrea. "Cleveland Schools' Arts Guru Tony Sias to Take the Reins of Karamu House." Cleveland.com, September 2, 2015. https://www.cleveland.com/onstage/index.ssf/2015/09/cleveland_schools_arts_guru_to.html.

———. "Director and Playwright in Residence Michael Oatman Stages *One Monkey Don't Stop No Show* for Karamu House." *Land of Cleve*, November 6, 2014. http://inthelandofcleve.blogspot.com/2014/11/director-and-playwright-in-residence.html.

———. "Historic Karamu House Loses Its Tax-Exempt Status, as Execs Scramble to Figure Out How It Happened." Cleveland.com, May 12, 2016. https://www.cleveland.com/onstage/index.ssf/2016/05/historic_karamu_house_loses_it.html.

———. "Karamu House Axes 15, Including Artistic Director Terrence Spivey in Bid to 'Set the Stage for the Next 100 Years.'" Cleveland.com, March 3, 2016. https://www.cleveland.com/onstage/index.ssf/2016/03/karamu_house_axes_15_including.html.

———. "Pacing Slow in Wilson's Layered *Gem*." Cleveland.com, May 15, 2012. https://www.cleveland.com/onstage/index.ssf/2012/05/pacing_slow_in_wilsons_layered.html.

———. "Planet Silver: The Irresistible Orbit of Cleveland Theater Legend Reuben Silver (an Appreciation)." Cleveland.com, May 29, 2014. https://www.cleveland.com/onstage/index.ssf/2014/05/planet_silver_the_irresistible.html.

Simmons, Sheila. "Hard Times for Karamu: The Black Arts Center Has Struggled to Get Its Act Together, but $100,00 grant, a New Fundraising Campaign, and the Success of *Black Nativity* Offer a Season of Hope." *Plain Dealer*, December 22, 1996.

Silver, Reuben. "A History of the Karamu Theatre of Karamu House, 1915–1960." PhD dissertation, Ohio State University, 1961.

Simonson, Robert. "Mike Malone, Director and Choreographer, Died at 63." *Playbill*, December 11, 2006. http://www.playbill.com/article/mike-malone-director-and-choreographer-died-at-63-com-136958.

Slotnik, Daniel E. "Robert Guillaume, Emmy-Winning Star of *Benson*, Dies at 89." *New York Times*, October 24, 2017. https://www.nytimes.com/2017/10/24/obituaries/robert-guillaume-dead-emmy-winning-star-of-benson.html.

Smeltz, Adam. "Pittsburgh Workers Remove Controversial Stephen Foster Statue from Schenley Plaza." *Pittsburgh Post-Gazette*, April 26, 2018. https://www.post-gazette.com/local/city/2018/04/26/Stephen-Foster-statue-removal-Pittsburgh-Oakland-Schenley-Plaza-Art-Commission-Highland-Park-Bill-Peduto/stories/201804260091.

Smith, Chuck, ed. *Best Black Plays: The Theodore Ward Prize for African American Playwriting*. Evanston, IL: Northwestern University Press, 2007.

Smith, Harry C. "The Rounder on What's Doing." *Cleveland Gazette*, November 9, 1935.

———. "The Rounder on What's Doing." *Cleveland Gazette*, December 11, 1937.

Smith, Jamil. "Why Stacey Abrams Is the Future for Democrats." *Rollingstone*, July 23, 2018. https://www.rollingstone.com/politics/politics-features/stacey -abrams-georgia-democrats-701308/.

Smith, Kelundra. "Black Theatres in the U.S.: Building, Surviving, Thriving." *American Theatre Magazine*, February 26, 2019. https://www.americantheatre .org/2019/02/26/black-theatres-in-the-u-s-building-surviving-thriving/.

———. "A Boom in Filming Gives Atlanta Stage Actors Room to Maneuver." *New York Times*, May 4, 2018. https://www.nytimes.com/2018/05/04/theater /atlanta-film-television-boom-theater-actors.html.

———. "Review: True Colors' Smart People Uses Juicy Dialogue to Evoke Race and Class." *Arts ATL*, July 20, 2016. https://artsatl.com/review-true-colors -smart-people-packed-juicy-dialogue-race-class/.

Smith, Susan H. "Kuntu's *Ma Rainey* Fine Tribute to Wilson." *Pittsburgh Press*, September 28, 1987.

Southers, Mark Clayton. Television interview by Mickey Hood. *Pittsburgh Live Today*, KDKATV, https://pittsburgh.cbslocal.com/video/program/750 /4154570-august-wilson-play/.

"*Spell #7.*" *San Francisco Examiner*, May 3, 1985.

Spivey, Terrence. Artist's biography. *Objectively/Reasonable: A Community Response to the Shooting of Tamir Rice 11/22/14*. Playwrights Local. http:// www.playwrightslocal.org/objectively-reasonable/.

———. "Midwest Theatre Collaboration Rings in The Great White Hope in an Effort to Pardon Jack Johnson (Cleveland/Akron)." *African American Playwrights Exchange*, October 31, 2009. http://africanamericanplaywrightsexcha nge.blogspot.com/2009/10/.

Steidtmann, Nancy. "A Tragic Escape into Drugs and MTV: Local Black Group Stages an Original Rock Musical." *San Francisco Examiner*, July 14, 1985.

"*Stevedore* Becomes 100th Play Offered by Gilpin Players." *Plain Dealer*, February 24, 1935, 12.

Stone, Madeline. "Rent for a 1 Bedroom Apartment Will Cost You More in San Francisco Than Anywhere Else." *Business Insider*, September 17, 2014. http:// www.businessinsider.com/san-francisco-is-more-expensive-than-new-york -city-2014–9.

Suber, Ron. "*Little Willie Armstrong Jones*—a Black Family Affair." *New Pittsburgh Courier*, April 26, 1975

Sullivan, Michael Gene. *The Plays of the San Francisco Mime Troupe: 2000– 2016*. San Francisco: San Francisco Mime Troupe, 2018.

Talbot, Joe, dir. *The Last Black Man in San Francisco*. San Francisco: A24, 2019. https://a24films.com/films/the-last-black-man-in-san-francisco.

"Theater." *San Francisco Examiner*, September 5, 1982.

"Theater." *San Francisco Examiner*, May 27, 1984.

Theodore, Nik, Jamie Peck, and Neil Brenner. "Neoliberal Urbanism: Cities and the Rule of Markets." In *The New Blackwell Companion to the City*, edited by Gary Bridge and Sophie Watson, 15–25. Malden, MA: Blackwell, 2011.

"30th Summer of Love." *San Francisco Examiner*, June 20, 1997.

Tracy, Jon. "Director's Note: The History of Humanity Is the History of Our Quest for Power." *Antony and Cleopatra* playbill. African American Shakespeare Company, May 2016.

Tran, Diep. "The Top 20 Most-Produced Playwrights of the 2017–2018 Season." *American Theatre Magazine*, September 21, 2017. https://www.americantheatre.org/2017/09/21/the-top-20-most-produced-playwrights-of-the-2017–18-season/.

Trotter, Joe. W., and Jared N. Day. *Race and Renaissance: African Americans in Pittsburgh Since World War II*. Pittsburgh: University of Pittsburgh Press, 2010.

"Two One-Act Plays." *San Francisco Examiner*, October 3, 1981.

Ubuntu Theater Project. "Past Productions—How I Learned What I Learned." http://www.ubuntutheaterproject.com/learned.

Ujima Theatre Company. "About the Ujima Theatre Company." Accessed August 5, 2017. http://ujimatheatre.homestead.com/aboutus.html.

United States Census Bureau. "Quick Facts: Atlanta City, Georgia." Population Estimates, July 1, 2021. https://www.census.gov/quickfacts/fact/table/atlantacitygeorgia,GA/PST045219#.

———. "U.S. Census Bureau Projections Show a Slower Growing, Older, and More Diverse Nation a Half Century from Now." December 12, 2012. https://www.census.gov/newroom/releases/archives/population/cb12-243.html.

Vacha, John. *Showtime in Cleveland: The Rise of a Regional Theater Center*. Kent, OH: Kent State University Press, 2001.

Vials, Chris. *Realism for the Masses: Aesthetics, Popular Front Pluralism, and U.S. Culture, 1935–1947*. Jackson: University of Mississippi Press, 2009.

Vine, Hannah. "Look Back at Ntozake Shange's *For Colored Girls Who Have Considered Suicide/When the Rainbow Is Enuf*." *Playbill*, September 15, 2018. http://www.playbill.com/article/look-back-at-ntozake-shanges-for-colored-girls-who-have-considered-suicide-when-the-rainbow-is-enuf.

Wade, James W. "Joe Turner Comes to Karamu House Theater," *Call & Post*, January 21, 2015.

Wadud, Ali. *Companions of the Fire*. New York: Dramatists Play Service, 1980.

Waldron, Travis. "How Super Bowl 50 Became Ground Zero for the Fight over Homelessness." *Huffington Post*, February 6, 2015. http://www.huffingtonpost.com/entry/san-francisco-homeless-protests-super-bowl-50_us_56b625c6e4b01d80b2468235.

"We See You, White American Theater." Accessed June 15, 2020. https://www.weseeyouwat.com.

Weinert-Kendt, Robert. "The Ground on Which He Stood: Revisiting August Wilson's Speech." *American Theatre*, April 21, 2016. http://www.americantheatre.org/2016/04/21/the-ground-on-which-he-stood-revisiting-august-wilsons-speech/.

Wellek, René. "Hippolyte Taine's Literary Theory and Criticism." *Criticism* 1, no. 1 (Winter 1959): 1–18.

Wetmore, Kevin J. Jr. "Big Willie Style: Staging Hip Hop Culture and Being Down with the Bard." In *Shakespeare and Youth Culture*, edited by Jennifer Hulbert, Kevin J. Wetmore Jr., and Robert L. York, 147–70. New York: Palgrave Macmillan, 2006.

Wilmeth, Don B., and Tice L. Miller, eds. *The Cambridge Guide to American Theatre*. Cambridge: Cambridge University Press, 1996.

Whitney LeBlanc Papers. Emory University. Book #3—Directing Designs Reviews, 1983–2001. Stuart A. Rose Manuscript, Archives, and Rare Book Library. https://findingaids.library.emory.edu/documents/leblanc1141/.

Wilkins, John. "Actors' Performances Reveal Fraught Politics of Black Bodies on Stage." KQED Arts, May 18, 2016. https://ww2.kqed.org/arts/2016/05/18 /african-american-actors-performances-reveal-fraught-politics-of-black-bodies -on-stage/.

Wilkinsburg Art Theatre Papers. Curtis Theatre Collection, Archives and Special Collections, University of Pittsburgh Library System, Pittsburgh.

Williams, Carmaletta M., and John Edgar Tidwell, eds. *My Dear Boy: Carrie Hughes's Letters to Langston Hughes, 1926–1938*. Athens: University of Georgia Press, 2013.

Williams, Tennessee. *A Streetcar Named Desire*. New York: Signet, 1947.

Wilson, August, Tony Knox, and Melvyn Bragg. *August Wilson: The American Dream in Black and White*. Princeton, NJ: Films for the Humanities and Sciences, 1990.

Wilson, August. *The Ground on Which I Stand*. New York: Theatre Communications Group, 2001.

———. *Two Trains Running*. New York: Penguin, 1992.

Wilson, Janice Burley. Radio interview in "The Confluence." WESA, September 17, 2018. https://www.wesa.fm/post/realizing-triumphs-and-many-trials -august-wilson-center.

Wilson, Ra'Nesha. "Re: Dark Days for the Black Arts." Cleveland Scene. March 3, 2016. https://www.clevescene.com/cleveland/ranesha-wilson/Profile?oid= 4715213.

Winks, Michael. "Jamaican Culture Meets American in *Two Can Play*." *Pittsburgh Press*, September 28, 1989.

Winn, Steven. "Black Bay Stage: Room to Breathe, Grow." *San Francisco Examiner and Chronicle*, September 12, 1982.

Wulf, Andrew James. *U.S. International Exhibitions during the Cold War: Winning Hearts and Minds Through Cultural Diplomacy*. London: Rowman & Littlefield, 2015.

YBCA Equity Cohort. "What Is the Role of Art in Gentrification and Displacement?" *Street Sheet*, August 15, 2017. https://www.streetsheet.org/?p=3806.

Young, Harvey, and Queen Meccasia Zabriskie. *Black Theater Is Black Life: An Oral History of Chicago Theater and Dance, 1974–2010*. Evanston, IL: Northwestern University Press, 2014.

Zeigler, Joseph Wesley. *Regional Theatre: The Revolutionary Stage*. Minneapolis: University of Minnesota Press, 1973.